Study Guide

ECONOMICS

Fifth Edition

Study Guide
ECONOMICS
Fifth Edition

Edwin G. Dolan
George Mason University

David E. Lindsey
*Deputy Director, Division of Monetary Affairs,
Board of Governors of the Federal Reserve System*

"Careers in Economics"
Keith D. Evans
California State University, Northridge

The Dryden Press
*Chicago New York San Francisco Philadelphia
Montreal Toronto London Sydney Tokyo*

ISBN 0-03-020379-1
Printed in the United States of America
890-066-987654321

Copyright © 1988, 1986, 1983, 1980, 1977 by The Dryden Press, a division of Holt, Rinehart and Winston, Inc.

All rights reserved. No part of this publication may be reproduced or transmitted in any form or by any means, electronic or mechanical, including photocopy, recording, or any information storage and retrieval system, without permission in writing from the publisher.

Requests for permission to make copies of any other part of the work should be mailed to: Permissions, Holt, Rinehart and Winston, Inc., 111 Fifth Avenue, New York, New York 10003.

Address orders:
111 Fifth Avenue
New York, NY 10003

Address editorial correspondence:
One Salt Creek Lane
Hinsdale, IL 60521

The Dryden Press
Holt, Rinehart and Winston, Inc.
Saunders College Publishing

How to Use This Study Guide

This study guide is published for use with the fifth edition of the text by Edwin G. Dolan and David E. Lindsey. The text, your instructor's lectures, and this study guide each cover the same material, but in different, complementary ways. The text is the most comprehensive of the three in coverage, but because of size limitations, it can offer only one or two illustrations of each concept or technique. Your instructor's lectures and class discussions cannot cover the material as extensively as the text, but they offer new points of view, new applications and illustrations, and, most important of all, a chance for you to ask questions. This study guide complements both the text and the lectures. It provides drill, repetition, and hands-on practice. Properly used, it will prepare you for examinations and pinpoint problems and questions for class discussion.

Each chapter contains several elements, some designed to assist initial study and review, others designed to assist exam preparation. Here is how they can be used:

Where You're Going

As each new chapter is assigned, turn first to your text. Read once straight through the chapter to get the big picture. Make marginal notes to identify anything that looks hard. These points will deserve intensive study later—but don't try to master everything the first reading.

When you are done with your first reading of the chapter in the text, before you go to your lecture, turn to the *Where You're Going* section of this study guide. How many of the points have you already mastered? Which are things you need to study again? Which are points that you should particularly listen for in your lecture? Which vocabulary items will require review? If you have asked yourself these questions, you will go to class prepared.

Walking Tour

After you have read the chapter and taken note of the learning objectives, you are ready for the next section of the study guide, the *Walking Tour*. Work your way through this section holding a card over the marginal answers and filling in the blanks as you go along. If you hit any stumbling blocks, go back to your text or lecture notes.

Hands On

Now that you have studied and reviewed, you are ready for serious exam preparation. There are three kinds of exam questions you need to be prepared for: graphical or numerical problems, essay questions, and multiple choice questions. Each of these gets separate attention in this study guide.

Graphical and numerical problems are covered in the *Hands On* section. These are the hardest part of the course for many students, but this study guide is written with that fact in mind. The harder the technical material in each chapter, the more hands-on problems you are given, and the more detailed are the answers. But don't look at the answers until you have really made an effort to work out the problems for yourself.

Suggestion: Always do the graphical problems in pencil and use a straight edge. Work neatly. If you make mistakes—everyone does—go back and carefully correct your own diagram. Your correctly completed diagram will then become an additional resource for exam preparation.

Economics in the News

Just as the *Hands On* section prepares you for numerical or graphical problems, the *Economics in the News* section prepares you for essay questions. Read the item and answer the questions clearly, completely, but not necessarily at agonizing length. Then check the answers. If you can do well on these questions, you have passed one of the biggest hurdles in economics: you have demonstrated an ability not just to solve abstract textbook problems, but to apply what you have learned in real-world situations. That, after all, is what this course is all about.

Suggestion: Read the business section of a good newspaper daily while you are taking this course. Make a clipping file of major stories on economics. Write questions and answers for these stories similar to those that appear in the *Economics in the News* section of the text. *The Wall Street Journal* is the best newspaper to use for this purpose. Ask your professor to call *The Wall Street Journal* Educational Service Bureau at 1-800-257-1200, ext. 802 (In Pennsylvania, 1-800-222-3380, ext. 802) for information on special student subscription rates.

Self Test

The third type of exam question you need to prepare for is multiple choice. Each chapter of this study guide has 15 of these as a final check on what you have learned. Your instructor has a book of 2,000 more questions from which exam questions may be chosen. The questions in this study guide do not exactly duplicate those in your instructor's test bank, but they are representative of the types of questions found there. The *Self Test* is your final check. If you have trouble here, you should be worried. You're supposed to be finished studying by this point.

Suggestion: One of the best techniques for studying for a multiple choice exam is to make variations on the sample questions given in the *Self Test*. For example, if the question requires a numerical calculation, change the numbers, and then change the answer accordingly. If the question asks the effects of an increase in something, change it to a question about the effects of a decrease. Or reverse the question: make one of the answers into the question stem, and base multiple choice answers on the part that was originally the stem. As you do this, work together with another student, and then test each other with your questions.

Don't Make This Common Mistake

Here and there throughout the book, you will find little boxes with the caption *Don't Make This Common Mistake*. Take these seriously. They are based on actual mistakes made year after year by real students taking the same course you are taking. Not one of these mistakes is hard to avoid if you are alert.

Another Valuable Learning Resource

There is now a special magazine, *The Margin*, published for students taking the economics course. It contains news updates, in-depth feature articles, interviews, graduate school profiles, humor, and other material on both micro and macro topics. The articles are written so that they apply and reinforce the concepts you learn in this course. It very well could be the thing that gives you the edge. For information about this magazine, write to

> University of Colorado
> Post Office Box 7150
> Colorado Springs, CO 80933-7150

> or call 1-800-9-MARGIN

The Margin is an independent magazine not connected with The Dryden Press.

We Would Like Your Suggestions

This study guide, and the text itself, incorporates suggestions from hundreds of students. We need suggestions for the next edition. What is still hard to understand after our best efforts at explanation? Are there any errors or misprints? Put your suggestions in the sixth edition! Address your correspondence to

> Prof. Edwin G. Dolan
> Department of Economics
> George Mason University
> Fairfax, VA 22030

Contents

Careers in Economics 1
1. What Economics Is All About 30
2. Exchange and Production 41
3. Supply and Demand 50
4. The Role of Business 65
5. The Role of Government 73
6. The Circular Flow of Income and Product 81
7. Measuring National Income and Product 90
8. Unemployment, Inflation, and the Business Cycle 103
9. Classical and Keynesian Theories of Income Determination .. 112
10. The Income-Expenditure Model 121
11. Fiscal Policy 134
12. Money and the Banking System 145
13. Central Banking and Money Creation 153
14. The Supply of and Demand for Money 164
15. An Integrated View of Monetary and Fiscal Policy 173
16. Inflation in the Aggregate Supply and Demand Model 186
17. Economic Growth and Productivity 197
18. Strategies for Economic Stabilization 207
19. The Accelerationist Model of Inflation 215
20. Foreign Exchange Markets and International Monetary Policy .. 230
21. Applying Supply and Demand 243
22. Rational Choice and Consumer Behavior 258
23. Cost and Production 275
24. Supply under Perfect Competition 290
25. The Theory of Monopoly 304
26. Industrial Organization, Monopolistic Competition, and Oligopoly .. 317
27. Entrepreneurship and the Market Process 328
28. Pricing in Factor Markets 336
29. Labor Unions and Collective Bargaining 351
30. Rent, Interest, and Profit 360
31. The Problem of Poverty 369
32. Antitrust and Regulation 378

33. Externalities and Environmental Policy 387
34. The Theory of Public Choice 396
35. International Trade and Trade Policy 404
36. The Soviet Economy: Central Planning and Reform 418

CAREERS IN ECONOMICS

Keith D. Evans
Chairman, Department of Economics
California State University, Northridge

Prepared with the cooperation of the
National Association of Business Economists and the
Society of Government Economists

I. THE GENERAL VALUE OF AN ECONOMICS DEGREE

In describing the qualities that are essential to a good economist, John Maynard Keynes, himself a master at the profession, remarked:

> He must study the present in the light of the past for the purpose of the future. No part of man's nature or his institutions must lie entirely outside his regard.[1]

As you begin the study of economics, you will quickly become aware of the breadth Keynes refers to. There seem to be no limits to the reaches of economic inquiry. Your first exam may include a question that could apply to today's newspaper headlines. At the same time, economics is very much a part of your everyday life. A discussion with a local merchant concerning the price of an item may lead you to the conclusion that an understanding of economics is a matter of common sense. However, economics is not a subject to be left to common sense alone, since what is "common sense" to one person may well be "nonsense" to another.

The trained economist is a valuable and respected member of many organizations—be they private businesses, public utilities, governments, or colleges and universities—and the career opportunities open to an economist are limited only by the resourcefulness of employers and employees. The following two sections will show you how an economics major can prepare you for a wide variety of careers in economics and will also briefly comment upon the employment outlook for economists between 1987 and 1995. Every effort has been made to provide you, the beginning economics student, with the latest information concerning career opportunities in economics. Major assistance was provided by the National Association of Business Economists (NABE) through its secretary-treasurer, David L. Williams. In addition, the attitudes, opinions, and experiences of successful, currently employed business and government economists were solicited by means of a questionnaire that was sent to a significant number of randomly selected members of the NABE and the Society of Government Economists. (This will be referred to below as the Dryden questionnaire to distinguish it from the NABE publications used.)

Even if your career interests lie in other directions, the analytical training that is emphasized in an economics major can generally make you more *adaptable* to changing employment opportunities after graduation. As one member of the NABE put it, "Some theoretical micro and macro concepts proved useful; however, more often than not my training in analyzing and researching subjects was used." Further, there are definite benefits in having a thorough understanding of how our private enterprise economy works and in having a basis for comparing it with centrally planned economies. Often people have indicated that in their first career job they literally got lost in a maze—they didn't have a sense of where they fit in and how their job related to any larger picture. A background in

---

[1] John Maynard Keynes, *Essays in Biography*, ed. Geoffrey Keynes (New York: W. W. Norton & Company, 1963).

economics can ease that shock. The analytical training, with specific applications to real-life situations, makes it easier to come to grips with the events of the world around us.

One respondent to the Dryden questionnaire put it this way: "My work in economics prepared me well for career advancement and flexibility because of the emphasis my economics study placed on cause and effect relationships, on the link between incentives and resultant actions, all of which have helped me develop a rational and productive way of generating results-oriented thinking." Another replied that the most useful part of his training in economics was "flexibility, perspective, and ability to deal with intangibles and uncertainty." Still another successful career economist reflected on the importance of his economics degree in this way: "It taught me the ability to think and to reason."

You cannot possibly learn all you will need to know in four years of college; but in pursuing a degree in economics you can learn how to think better. With that ability your opportunities are immensely varied and exciting.

II. WHAT KINDS OF CAREER OPPORTUNITIES ARE AVAILABLE TO AN ECONOMICS MAJOR?

It is not enough to say to yourself that you will study economics because in doing so you can learn how to think better, and thinking better is essential to a career as an economist. Choosing a course of study in college is more likely to lead to a successful career if you discover what subjects are of interest to you and what subjects you do well in. So it follows that if you enjoy and do well in courses in economics and business administration, you are very likely to enjoy a career as an economist.

But what are your opportunities as an economics major? What type of work might you actually do as an economist? In general, and depending upon the amount of education you ultimately receive, your future lies in one of three areas—working in one of a wide variety of positions in private business; serving in a local, state, or national government agency; or teaching economics at the college and university level. In fact, many economists combine their primary work in one of these fields with part-time work in another. It is not at all unusual for a business economist to teach part-time, or for a professor also to be a consultant to business or government.

Economics as an academic subject goes back more than a century and a half. In practical terms, economists found their theories influencing federal-government decisions more and more as the Depression of the 1930s occupied worldwide attention. It was not until after World War II, however, that private businesses began to realize the extent to which economic theory might be applied in solving business problems and formulating business policies. Despite this relatively late start, about 23,000 of the people identified as economists by the Bureau of Labor Statistics in 1984 work in private business.[1] They are employed by manufacturing firms,

---

[1] U.S. Department of Labor, Bureau of Labor Statistics. *Occupational Outlook Handbook*, 1986-87 ed. (Washington, D.C.: Government Printing Office, April 1986), p. 102.

banks, insurance companies, securities and investment companies, economic research firms, management consulting firms, and others.

Business organizations that are large enough to warrant their own economists employ them directly. Smaller firms hire the services of economic consultants as needed. Regardless of their size, all businesses are aware that government policies and subsequent actions have economic effect. A major function of the business economist, therefore, is to analyze and interpret government policies in light of their effects on the economy in general and the specific firm in particular.

According to the same 1984 Bureau of Labor Statistics report, another 15,000 economists are employed by government agencies, including a wide range of federal agencies. In addition, approximately 22,000 hold economics and marketing faculty positions at colleges and universities.

Certainly the primary function of the business economist is to apply economic theory to problems faced by the firm. This requires the ability to understand the economic implications of events taking place throughout the world; to project how those events might affect the firm; to prepare guidelines for decision makers in the organization; and to communicate concepts, principles, and conclusions in a clear, effective, and concise manner.

In a booklet entitled *Careers in Business Economics*, the National Association of Business Economists stresses that business economists follow no set patterns. The most successful, established economists have high job mobility because their ability to interpret national and international events in light of their economic impact on a particular sector of business makes them especially adaptable to changing business requirements. The following are descriptions of the activities of several kinds of business economists, as paraphrased from *Careers in Business Economics*.

The Bank Economist

> The primary function of our bank's economics department is to analyze how changes in economic and financial market conditions affect the banking business and to suggest—to the extent possible—appropriate strategies and policies to protect or enhance the bank's earnings. Obviously, this is an assignment of tall order and presents great challenges as well as opportunities.[2]

An essential analytical tool which must be developed by the **bank economist** is the macroeconomic forecast. Such a forecast forms the basis for anticipating changes in the bank's volume of business—primarily its loans and investments. Even more important for the bank economist is a firm grasp of the underlying forces that determine interest rates. Changes in interest rates directly affect the spread between the yields the bank earns on its investments and the cost of acquiring funds to invest. Hence, the profitability of a bank's operations hinges on correctly anticipating changes in interest rates.

A bank also manages and invests money for customers through its trust department. Thus, the bank economist's expertise can be

---

[2]National Association of Business Economists, *Careers in Business Economics*, (Cleveland, Ohio, 1986), p. 10.

highly valuable since sound investment strategies depend on sound judgment of economic and financial trends. In addition, the bank economist represents the bank in interviews with financial reporters and is likely to be quoted in newspapers and magazines. Further, the bank economist may write newsletters for the bank and make numerous presentations both within and outside of the bank. Note the importance of good communication skills!

As you can see, the bank economist's job responsibilities are very important. The bank economist constantly interacts with senior management and is often a member of the senior management team.

The Consulting Economist

The following quote from *Careers in Business Economics* indicates the nature of the duties performed by the **consulting economist**:

> Within our firm, we conduct research and advise clients of developments affecting financial institutions, trends in economic activity, and interest rates in money and capital markets—with special emphasis on the monetary policy of the Federal Reserve. The firm has carried out a number of assignments—including the preparation of estimates of the cost of capital for public utilities, assessments of the impact of alternative tax measures on the volume of investment, the impact of research and development expenditures on technology and innovation in American industry, the economic cost of restrictions on a range of imports, excise taxes and the demand for distilled spirits, monetary policy and the housing sector, and the economic benefits of lease financing.[3]

Like a bank economist, a consulting economist may also do macroeconomic forecasting. The results of research done by consulting economists are usually given to their clients as private reports. Some of the findings of economics consulting firms, however, are made public in the form of reports, congressional testimony, and publications in professional journals.

The Industrial Economist

An **industrial economist** employed by a large, widely diversified manufacturing company writes:

> The most important part of my job is meeting with our management committee every month to discuss economic and political developments in the countries where we have operations, and the likely impact of such developments on our businesses. Preparation for these meetings involves maintaining contacts with a large number of economists, business analysts, and academic experts around the world. This means that I'm usually on an airplane about four out of every five weeks and am physically out of the office about 60 percent of the time.[4]

This economist also does macroeconomic forecasting, but on an international level. It is common for industrial economists to participate in preparing forecasts of their firm's operations for as much as ten years in advance. Some industrial economists also engage in "structural analysis," which involves "the basic econometric

---

[3] NABE, *Careers in Business Economics*, p. 13.
[4] NABE, *Careers in Business Economics*, p. 17.

analysis of the relationships among various businesses with a variety of external series as well as internal data, such as advertising expense, research and development programs, capital expenditures, and so on. The results are used to evaluate strategic plans of individual businesses, to determine the relative impacts of various external policy changes, and to determine strategies for improving profitability."[5]

The industrial economist, like the bank economist, would usually represent his or her firm in interviews requested by the news media, might prepare a newsletter, and would make numerous presentations to groups outside his company.

The Government Economist

The **government economist** may perform essentially the same tasks as economists who work in business as far as forecasting the outcome of economic conditions is concerned. The emphasis, however, may well be on formulating policy rather than reacting to policy changes, since the government agency can be in a position to initiate economic changes. The government economist may be called upon to do research on major policy issues, draft speeches for legislators and government officials, and help determine the purpose and scope of Congressional hearings.

The Academic Economist

Academic economists concentrate on the understanding and improvement of economic theory. In teaching theory, they stress how economies function and how a knowledge of economics applies to business and government decision making and to decisions people have to make as individuals. In addition, academic economists may devote some time to research, writing, and consulting with business firms, government agencies, or private individuals.

Advice from Practicing Economists

The Dryden questionnaire asked members of the National Association of Business Economists and the Society of Government Economists to reflect on the value of their college education and on what advice they might have for people just beginning the study of economics. Of those whose major was economics, more than two-thirds of each group reported that their college study had been very useful to them in their first full-time job; and from the vantage point of their ultimate career, more than half still felt that their college education was useful in carrying out the duties of their present occupation. What courses did they feel were of such lasting value? Both business and government economists most frequently mentioned courses in microeconomic and macroeconomic theory, econometrics (the application of statistical techniques to obtain quantitative estimates of relationships suggested by economic analysis), money and banking, forecasting, international economics,

---
[5] Ibid.

and courses that provided specific applications of economic theory to the decision-making process or had applications to public policy.

Respondents also emphasized the importance of courses involving economic and business applications of statistics and accounting, as well as the study of related business institutions, especially financial ones. Important, too, were courses on how to use computers and how to program them. Mathematics courses were emphasized as having been helpful. Along with the references to applied statistics, there was continual mention of such courses as analytical geometry, calculus, and linear algebra.

One necessary skill for an economist, whether academic, business, or government, cannot be overlooked or overemphasized, and that is the ability to make the results of one's work understandable to a wide range of people. To be useful, economic analyses and forecasts must be understood by those who make the decisions for the business or government agency involved. Therefore, an economist must be able to write and speak clearly and able to state sophisticated economic ideas in a way that can be understood even by people with little economic knowledge. Recognizing this need to make their work clear and usable to other people, both government and business economists placed high value on courses that improved their written and oral communication skills.

The NABE advises potential business economists to strive to be generalists, rather than specialists, and the *Careers in Business Economics* booklet recommends some familiarity with as many as possible of the major fields of economics and business administration. In addition to areas mentioned by the respondents to the Dryden questionnaire, economics and business administration are concerned with economic and business history, national income and public finance, business cycles and government stabilization policies, corporate finance and industrial organization, marketing and consumer behavior, labor and collective bargaining, purchasing and personnel policies, and economic development and comparative economic systems.

Some of the respondents to the Dryden questionnaire had not majored in economics at the undergraduate level. Many of them said that they benefited from the broad-based liberal-arts education they acquired before earning advanced degrees in economics or business. It was generally agreed, however, that any liberal-arts major would be well advised, considering the current job market, to take courses in economics, accounting, statistics, and computer science.

Interestingly, in the last five to seven years, many majors have begun to look increasingly favorably upon candidates who have earned an undergraduate liberal-arts degree. This is especially true if the applicant has done well at a university that is held in high academic regard at least regionally, if not nationally. Such individuals, however, are expected to have taken relevant courses in economics and applied statistics, as well as business courses such as accounting fundamentals and principles of finance. Moreover, business and government recruiters have become increasingly insistent that the student be exposed to a variety of "hands-on" computer applications—ideally including some programming. Any one of the types of economists profiled earlier makes extensive use of computers.

June Hillman, Associate Director of the Office of Career Planning and Placement at California State University, Northridge, summarized this recent change in attitude on the part of the recruiters as follows: "Recruiters are tending to be attracted to the well-educated university graduate with some business-related courses and work experience rather than the specific, vocationally oriented majors. This continues to be a trend in recruiting criteria."[6]

For further support of the recent change in attitude by many recruiters toward liberal arts graduates, please refer to the references at the end of this section.

It should perhaps be added that the guidelines presented here must be taken in the spirit in which they have been given—as suggestions from practicing economists. When you are planning your particular course of study to fulfill the requirements of your college or university and to satisfy your unique interests, these guidelines cannot, and should not, be expected to replace the need for personal faculty advisement.

How important is an advanced degree? For an academic economist it is a must. The master's degree is the minimum qualification for teaching at the community college level, and the Ph.D. is required for most university teaching.

In a 1982 survey of economists employed in commercial and investment banks, Professor George G. Kaufman reported that 96 percent of the commercial bank respondents had advanced degrees and 56 percent of those had Ph.D. degrees.[7] As Professor Kaufman stated at the beginning of his report, the significance of these advanced-degree findings is that "private financial institutions are one of the largest employers of economists outside the academic community, Federal Reserve System, and federal government."[8] This assertion is further supported by reference to the "Number of Respondents" column of Table 6 below.

According to the Dryden questionnaire, 80 percent of the government economists who responded indicated that they consider an advanced degree very important, and 11 percent consider one moderately important. Of that number, 56 percent specified a Ph.D. while an additional 25 percent specified a master's degree.

The business economists surveyed by the Dryden questionnaire placed less importance on an advanced degree. Only 57 percent rated it as very important, and 25 percent considered it moderately important. Those responses were much more evenly distributed regarding which advanced degree is more important. Almost 30 percent favored the M.B.A. (Master of Business Administration), while another group of equal size suggested pursuing either an M.A. or an M.S. degree in economics or business administration. Only 35 percent considered a doctorate essential.

---

[6] Interview given September 30, 1987.

[7] George G. Kaufman, "The Academic Preparation of Economists Employed by Commercial and Investment Banks." *Journal of Money, Credit, and Banking*, August 1984, pp. 351-359.

[8] Kaufman, "The Academic Preparation of Economists," p. 352.

These differences undoubtedly reflect the attitudes of different employers in different businesses and governmental agencies. Again, they are presented here as guidelines that can be one source of help to you as you make your own career decisions.

References

Byrne, John A. "Let's Hear It for Liberal Arts." *Forbes*, July 1, 1985, pp. 112-114.

Cheney, Lynne V. "Students of Success: A liberal-arts training is increasingly valuable in the American corporation." *Newsweek*, September 1, 1986, p. 7.

Garis, Jeff W., Richard Hess, and Deborah J. Marron. "For Liberal Arts Students Seeking Business Careers, Curriculum Counts." *Journal of College Placement*, Winter 1985, pp. 32-36.

Kaufman, George G. "The Academic Preparation of Economists Employed by Commercial and Investment Banks." *Journal of Money, Credit, and Banking*, August 1984, pp. 351-359.

MacKinnon, W. P. Letter: "The View of General Motors on Liberal-Arts Graduates." *Chronicle of Higher Education*, July 3, 1985, p. 27.

National Association of Business Economists. *Careers in Business Economics*. Cleveland, Ohio, April 1986.

Smith, Roger B. "The President's Page: Why Business Needs the Liberal Arts." *Business Week's Guide to Careers*, June 1987, pp. 65-66.

U.S. Department of Labor, Bureau of Labor Statistics. *Occupational Outlook Handbook*, 1986-87 ed. Washington, D.C.: Government Printing Office, April 1986.

III. WHERE ARE ECONOMISTS WORKING AND WHAT ARE THEIR AVERAGE SALARIES?

The 1986 NABE Salary Survey

Probably the best source of information on the current employment and earnings of economists is the latest salary survey (1986) of its membership conducted by the National Association of Business Economists (NABE). This survey consists of 1,327 usable responses from 39 percent of that membership. The median base salary for NABE members in 1986 was $52,500. (This means half the NABE members earned $52,500 or more, and half less than $52,500.) Table 1 indicates the percentage distribution of base salaries by income class.

Table 1
Percentage Distribution of Base Salaries, by Income Class

Base Salary (Thousands of $)	Total (percent)	New York (percent)	Other (percent)
Under 35	14.5	4.7	15.9
35-39.9	8.5	5.8	8.9
40-44.9	10.1	4.1	11.0
45-49.9	8.9	7.6	9.0
50-54.9	10.2	10.5	10.1
55-59.9	5.5	2.3	6.0
60-64.9	8.4	11.1	8.0
65-69.9	6.3	7.6	6.1
70-74.9	4.4	4.1	4.4
75-79.9	4.8	7.0	4.4
80 and over	17.3	35.1	14.7
No response	1.1	0.1	1.5
Median	$52,500	$65,000	$51,000
Mode	50,000	100,000	50,000

(Reprinted or paraphrased by permission of the National Association of Business Economists)

Note that 17.3 percent received base salaries in excess of $80,000. While the median base salary of New York City area respondents significantly exceeded the median for all respondents, the percentage of New York respondents to the continued the decline that has characterized recent NABE surveys. These economists represented 10.6 percent of the total number of respondents in 1986, down from 15.4 percent in 1984, 16.4 percent in 1982, 18.3 percent in 1980, 19.4 percent in 1978, 20.9 percent in 1976, and 22.7 percent in 1974. The difference between the total median salary and the New York median had increased to $14,000 in 1986, up from the $9,000 gap reported in 1984.

In Table 1 and in later tables, "mode" refers to the most frequently given numerical response.

In general, how sensitive was the base salary to geographical location? Tables 2 and 3 provide some answers.

Table 2
Base Salaries, by Major City

City	Number Reporting	Median
Atlanta	21	$51,000
Baltimore	21	45,081
Boston	46	65,000
Chicago	59	62,000
Cleveland	26	40,000
Dallas	23	53,000
Detroit	36	55,190
Houston	18	60,000
Los Angeles	48	56,565
Minneapolis/St. Paul	16	47,650
New York City[1]	171	65,000
Philadelphia	37	55,000
Pittsburgh	25	50,000
St. Louis	29	47,300
San Francisco	37	60,000
Washington, D.C.	111	57,000
Other	622	49,100

[1] Includes Nassau/Suffolk

(Reprinted or paraphrased by permission of the National Association of Business Economists)

Table 3
Base Salaries, by Region

Region	Number Reporting	Median
New England	110	$61,470
Middle Atlantic	319	60,000
East North Central	230	50,000
West North Central	80	46,400
South Atlantic	236	52,000
East South Central	21	52,000
West South Central	81	50,000
Mountain	46	40,030
Pacific	162	52,075
Foreign	40	58,300
No response	2	52,550

(Reprinted or paraphrased by permission of the National Association of Business Economists)

Note that among major cities, median salaries were highest in Boston, New York City, and Chicago. Lowest median salaries were in Cleveland, Detroit, and St. Louis. However, when comparing all of the previous NABE salary surveys, income variation between cities has clearly narrowed.

Table 3 indicates that among geographical regions, the highest median salaries were earned by economists located in the New

England States (Maine, New Hampshire, Vermont, Massachusetts, Rhode Island, and Connecticut) and in the Middle Atlantic States (New York, New Jersey, and Pennsylvania). The lowest reported median salary was received in the Mountain States (Montana, Idaho, Wyoming, Colorado, New Mexico, Arizona, Utah, and Nevada).

How significant was the amount of additional compensation (referred to as additional primary and secondary professional income) received by respondents to the 1986 NABE salary survey? Fifty-two percent of all respondents received additional compensation related to their primary employment (defined as cash bonuses, income from profit-sharing plans, and so on, before deductions). The median amount of additional income was $7,500 or 14.3 percent of the median base salary.

How do the incomes of men and women in the economics profession compare? Tables 4 and 5 provide some answers. While both the median base salary and median additional compensation were significantly greater for men than for women, the percentage of women in the 1986 survey was 12.6 percent of the total, down from 13.9 percent in 1984, and 14.7 percent in 1982, but up from 11.3 percent in 1980, 9.5 percent in 1978, and only 7.2 percent in 1976. The women's median base salary was 80 percent of the men's median base salary compared to 82 percent in 1984, 78 percent in 1982, and 74 percent in 1980.

Table 4
Base Salaries, by Sex

	Number of Respondents	Median Amount
Male—Total	972	$53,650
New York	112	70,500
Other	860	52,000
Female—Total	168	43,060
New York	29	51,000
Other	139	40,000
Not Reported	187	60,000

(Reprinted or paraphrased by permission of the National Association of Business Economists)

Table 5
Additional Compensation, by Sex

	Number of Respondents	Median Amount	Mode
Additional Primary Income	696	$7,500	$5,000
Male	513	8,000	5,000
Female	75	5,000	5,000
Not Specified	108	*	*
Professional Secondary Income	379	5,000	5,000
Male	306	$5,000	$5,000
Female	23	4,000	4,000
Not Specified	50	*	*

* Distribution withheld

(Reprinted or paraphrased by permission of the National Association of Business Economists)

Which industries (or other types of job-location classifications) paid the highest salaries? Please see Tables 6 and 7. Economists employed in securities and investments ranked highest, with a median base salary of $59,000, followed by those working in retail and wholesale trade, with median salaries of $62,700. Consistent with past NABE surveys, the lowest paid economists worked in academic institutions.

Table 7 shows that the *combined* medians for additional primary income and professional secondary income earned in 1985 were again highest in the securities and investments industry. Note that although base salaries for academic economists are low, opportunities for professional secondary income were higher for academics than for any other specific group of economists except those employed by trade associations.

Table 6
Base Salaries by Income Class, by Industry of Employment: Percentage Distribution, Medians and Modes
(Thousands of Dollars)

	Under 35	35-39.9	40-44.9	45-49.9	50-54.9	55-59.9	60-64.9	65-69.9	70-74.9	75-79.9	80 & Over	Median	Mode	Number of Respondents
Durable Manufacturing	5.4	3.8	13.8	7.7	15.4	9.2	6.9	8.5	5.4	4.6	18.5	56.0	40.0	129
Nondurable Manufacturing	7.2	6.0	7.2	12.0	13.3	3.6	6.0	8.4	6.0	3.6	26.5	60.0	45.0	83
Retail and Wholesale Trade	13.6	13.6	4.5	*	9.1	4.5	9.1	4.5	4.5	18.2	18.2	62.7	38.0	22
Banking—All Types	11.9	5.9	6.4	5.9	10.9	6.9	10.9	7.9	5.4	4.0	23.8	60.0	60.0	202
Securities and Investments	6.7	2.2	*	10.1	4.5	*	11.2	6.7	2.2	13.5	40.4	75.0	75.0	88
Insurance	10.3	7.7	10.3	5.1	10.3	5.1	7.7	5.1	7.7	7.7	23.1	62.0	50.0	39
Communications and Utilities	17.0	15.0	15.0	12.2	9.5	6.1	6.1	4.8	2.7	1.4	8.2	45.0	42.0	144
Publishing	14.8	7.4	18.5	11.1	7.4	7.4	11.1	*	*	11.1	7.4	49.0	40.0	27
Transportation	6.9	17.2	17.2	13.8	*	*	13.8	*	6.9	6.9	6.9	46.5	35.0	28
Mining	12.5	*	12.5	8.3	8.3	8.3	8.3	*	*	12.5	20.8	59.3	70.0	24
Construction	*	*	*	*	*	*	*	*	*	*	*	*	*	14
Real Estate	26.7	6.7	23.3	6.7	*	*	13.3	6.7	6.7	6.7	6.7	42.5	42.5	14
Consulting	11.1	6.4	9.9	7.6	8.2	4.7	10.5	1.8	7.0	6.4	22.2	58.1	40.0	164
Nonprofit Research Organization	31.8	13.6	4.5	13.6	4.5	4.5	13.6	*	9.1	*	4.5	40.9	30.0	22
Trade Association	8.6	*	11.4	5.7	20.0	8.6	8.6	8.6	2.9	5.7	20.0	55.0	50.0	35
Government	23.0	10.3	10.3	11.1	15.1	4.8	7.9	13.5	2.4	*	0.8	46.0	30.0	125
Academic	35.5	19.6	12.1	8.4	7.5	5.6	2.8	2.8	*	0.9	3.7	37.8	30.0	106
Other	16.2	8.8	10.3	8.8	5.9	5.9	7.4	7.4	4.4	4.4	20.6	52.1	80.0	68
No Response	*	*	*	*	*	*	*	*	*	*	*	*	*	*

* Distribution withheld

(Reprinted or paraphrased by permission of the National Association of Business economists)

Table 7
Additional Compensation, by Industry of Employment

	Additional Primary Income		Professional Secondary Income	
	Number of Respondents	Median	Number of Respondents	Median
Durable Manufacturing	76	$8,150	28	$4,250
Nondurable Manufacturing	60	7,500	18	3,250
Retail and Wholesale Trade	14	9,900	*	*
Banking	131	8,000	64	2,250
Securities and Investment	70	21,500	26	6,250
Insurance	25	7,000	12	4,250
Communications and Utilities	65	4,500	25	2,700
Publishing	16	7,100	8	5,250
Transportation	11	4,000	8	6,250
Mining	13	5,000	*	*
Construction	*	1,500	*	*
Real Estate	10	15,250	*	*
Consulting	99	10,000	53	7,500
Nonprofit Research	*	2,000	7	4,000
Trade Association	10	3,036	6	8,500
Government	20	2,028	23	3,200
Academic	37	5,000	73	8,000
Other	29	5,000	15	2,450

* Distribution withheld

(Reprinted or paraphrased by permission of the National Association of Business Economists)

What of differences in compensation by areas of responsibility? Respondents to the 1986 NABE salary survey were asked to indicate which of fourteen areas of responsibility best described their jobs. The results are indicated in Table 8 which lists areas of responsibility alphabetically. As in earlier surveys, economists who stated their primary area of responsibility to be general administration economist earned the highest *total* median salaries. Also consistent with previous surveys was the low bottom ranking of respondents describing their job as that of teaching.

Table 8
Compensation, by Area of Responsibility

	Base Salary Number Reporting	Base Salary Median	Additional Primary Income Number Reporting	Additional Primary Income Median	Professional Secondary Income Number Reporting	Professional Secondary Income Median
Consulting Economist	124	$56,100	70	$10,000	43	$10,000
Corporate Planning	171	55,000	104	8,150	34	3,700
Econometrician	37	40,000	19	5,300	7	4,000
Energy Economist	65	50,000	30	6,100	12	4,000
Financial Economist	141	52,000	86	8,150	42	3,550
General Administration	71	59,000	28	10,000	23	3,000
General Administration— Economist	145	64,500	80	10,280	43	5,000
Industrial Economist	72	51,450	33	5,000	16	4,250
International Economist	54	62,250	30	6,100	14	3,250
Macro/Forecaster	103	57,000	61	5,100	29	5,000
Micro/Regional	63	45,911	24	5,000	20	4,250
Marketing Research	75	45,000	38	5,050	18	3,100
Statistician	11	33,600	*	*	*	*
Teaching	76	36,18	30	5,000	47	6,000
Other	119	63,000	59	15,000	29	5,000

* Distribution withheld

(Reprinted or paraphrased by permission of the National Association of Business Economists)

To what extent does the amount of compensation depend upon the size of firm and upon the number of persons supervised by an economist? The 1986 NABE salary survey indicated that economists working at firms employing 10,000 or more employees earned the highest median salary ($60,000). Otherwise, as previous surveys have shown, there appears to be little correlation between the size of firm (measured in terms of number of employees) an economist works for and the amount of salary received.

However, as Table 9 demonstrates, and as would be expected, the number of persons supervised does correlate directly not only with the median base salary of the economist-supervisor, but also with the median amount of additional primary income received. The NABE found this correlation to exist in its previous four salary surveys as well.

Table 9
Primary Compensation, by Number of Persons Supervised

	Base Salary		Additional Primary Income	
Number Supervised	Number Reporting	Median	Number Reporting	Median
None	357	$41,000	134	$4,650
1 to 3	478	51,000	270	6,100
4 to 9	286	60,000	172	10,000
10 to 24	108	70,000	67	15,000
25 and over	85	78,800	49	15,000
No response	13	—	4	—

(Reprinted or paraphrased by permission of the National Association of Business Economists)

How important is the amount of education received with respect to the size of the economist's income? Table 10 provides some rather definite answers.

Table 10
Primary Compensation, by Amount of Education

	Base Salary		Additional Primary Income	
Highest Degree Obtained	Number Reporting	Median	Number Reporting	Median
Bachelor's	140	$45,000	66	$7,000
Master's	557	47,500	275	6,000
Ph.D.	495	61,000	273	10,000
All But Dissertation	125	55,000	77	8,000
No Degree	7	*	*	*
No Response	3	—	1	—

* Distribution withheld

(Reprinted or paraphrased by permission of the National Association of Business Economists)

Eighty-eight percent of the respondents to the 1986 NABE survey reported additional education beyond the bachelor's degree, with 37 percent having completed the Ph.D. Those with Ph.D. degrees had the highest median base salary, 35.8 percent greater than the median base salary of respondents possessing a bachelor's degree. Moreover, those who had completed all requirements for the Ph.D. but the dissertation had a median base salary some 22.2 percent higher than respondents holding a bachelor's. NABE salary surveys continue to indicate that there is little difference in median base salary between holders of bachelor's and master's degrees.

How much is the economist's compensation based upon years of work experience? Not surprisingly, Table 11 suggests that a direct correlation exists between both median base salary and (with one exception) median additional primary income and years of professional experience. Note that respondents with ten or more years' experience surpassed the $52,500 median base salary of all respondents (from Table 1).

Table 11
Primary Compensation, by Years of Professional Experience

	Base Salary			Additional Primary Income		
Years	Number Reporting	Median	Mode	Number Reporting	Median	Mode
0 to 4	191	$34,000	$30,000	65	$ 3,000	$2,000
5 to 9	355	45,000	45,000	177	5,000	2,000
10 to 14	298	60,000	60,000	165	10,000	20,000
15 to 19	198	63,350	100,000	131	7,000	5,000
20 to 24	114	64,225	60,000	64	11,575	20,000
25 and over	156	74,500	100,000	88	17,500	20,000
No response	15	*	*	6	*	*

* Distribution withheld

(Reprinted or paraphrased by permission of the National Association of Business Economists)

Finally, how rapidly have the salaries of NABE survey respondents risen since the inception of such studies? Table 12 provides some interesting results. Note that salary data are in *nominal* terms (that is, they are *not* adjusted for inflation).

Table 12
NABE Salaries: Growth Pattern 1964-1986

Year	Number Reporting	Median Base Salary	Median Additional Primary Income	Approx. percent *Annual* Increase in Median Base Salary
1964	445	$16,800	Not reported	
1968	553	19,600	Not reported	3.9
1972	993	25,000	$3,000*	6.3
1974	1,072	27,000	4,000*	3.9
1976	1,159	30,000	4,000*	5.4
1978	1,402	33,000	4,500*	4.9
1980	1,430	38,000	5,000*	7.3
1982	1,644	43,000	6,723*	6.4
1984	1,503	47,000	6,000*	4.5
1986	1,327	52,500	7,500*	5.7

* For year prior to survey data

(Reprinted or paraphrased by permission of the National Association of Business Economists)

A number of surveys have been done comparing starting salaries of candidates with bachelor's degrees in economics with the salaries of graduates in other fields. Generally, economics degree holders earn more than majors in any other social science discipline, and considerably more than humanities majors. It is especially interesting to compare economics majors with majors in other business-related disciplines. With one exception, Economics majors (whether male or female) now receive *equal or better* average starting-salary offers than do either general business or more specialized business majors. Only women majoring in Management Information

Systems received slightly higher starting salaries than female Economics majors during the period between July 1986 and July 1987.[1]

References

The College Placement Council. *CPC Salary Survey: A Study of 1986-1987 Beginning Offers—Formal Report No. 3*. Bethlehem, Pennsylvania, July 1987.

Endicott, Frank S., and Lindquist, Victor R. *The Northwestern Endicott Report: Trends in the Employment of College and University Graduates in Business and Industry, 1985. Thirty-ninth Annual Report*. Placement Center, Northwestern University, Evanston, Illinois, 1984.

National Association of Business Economists. *Salary Characteristics*. Cleveland, Ohio, 1978, 1980, 1982, 1984, 1986.

National Association of Business Economists. *Salary Survey*. Cleveland, Ohio, 1974, 1976.

IV. WHAT IS THE EMPLOYMENT OUTLOOK FOR ECONOMISTS BETWEEN 1987 AND 1995?

Before launching into some "fearless forecasts" about the employment outlook for economists in the 1990s, it might be well to include a bit of *caveat emptor*. Let the buyer, whether of tangible goods or intangible ideas, beware. Keeping in mind this recognition that all forecasts are fallible, we will indicate the current thought regarding the employment outlook for economists in the decade ahead.

The U.S. Department of Labor offers the following job outlook for economists:

> Employment of economists is expected to grow about as fast as the average for all occupations through the mid-1990's. Most job openings will result from the need to replace experienced economists who transfer to other occupations, retire, or leave the labor force for other reasons.
>
> Overall, economists are likely to have more favorable job prospects than most other social scientists. Opportunities should be best in manufacturing, financial services, advertising agencies, research organizations, and consulting firms, reflecting the complexity of the domestic and international economies and increased reliance on quantitative methods of analyzing business trends, forecasting sales, and planning purchasing and production. The continued need for economic analyses by lawyers, accountants, engineers, health service administrators, urban and regional planners, environmental scientists, and others will also increase the number of jobs for economists".[†1]

The U.S. Department of Labor projects little change in the employment of economists in the Federal Government. "Average growth is expected in the employment of economists in State and local government.[†2]

---

[1]The College Placement Council. *CPC Salary Survey: A Study of 1986-87 Beginning Offers—Formal Report No. 3*. Bethlehem, Pa., July 1987.

[†1]U.S. Department of Labor, Bureau of Labor Statistics. *Occupational Outlook Handbook*, 1986-87 ed. (Washington, D.C.: Government Printing Office, April 1986), p. 103.

[†2]Ibid.

The National Association of Business Economists agrees that job prospects are by far the brightest for various kinds of business economists. Besides the reasons given in the passage just quoted, the NABE points out that more and more firms are becoming aware of the contribution that business economists can make in day-to-day decisions. This greater awareness is due partly to the growing proportion of middle and top management who have a master's degree in business or similar training that equips them to understand and to utilize the professional work of economists.[3]

> Finally, the career of business economics is increasingly recognized as one of the routes to top management. In recent years, business economists have become presidents or senior officers of banks, insurance companies, trade associates, investment houses, and industrial companies. Although not all business economists are capable or even desirous of advancing to a top management position, it is clear that economics is a business function of central importance and thus can be a pathway to the top.[4]

Because of the relative difficulty of obtaining satisfactory employment in an academic setting, many people who might otherwise have directed themselves toward a career in higher education are now accepting nonacademic jobs. That puts graduates with bachelor's degrees in a position of competing not only with others of similar academic background and level, but also with those who have more advanced degrees. However, people who graduate with a bachelor's degree in economics through the mid-1990s should compete well if they have training in applied mathematics, statistics, and use of computers.

These indicators are in harmony with the comments of several respondents to the Dryden questionnaire, who believe that the best preparation for many of today's careers in economics begins with an undergraduate degree in economics and continues through the degree of Master of Business Administration.

References

Hinshew, C.E. "Job Openings for Economists." *American Economic Review*, May 1983, pp. 409-410.

National Association of Business Economists. *Careers in Business Economics*. Cleveland, Ohio, 1986.

U.S. Department of Labor, Bureau of Labor Statistics. *Occupational Outlook Handbook*, 1986-87 ed. Washington, D.C.: Government Printing Office, April 1986.

V. SOME TIPS ON PREPARING A RESUME

While this section will present some ideas on preparing a resume, it should be noted here that the value of a resume, as well as what form it should take, is a controversial subject. Some employers place great importance on the resume; others do not. (Roughly half the respondents to the Dryden questionnaire consider the resume

---

[3] National Association of Business Economists, *Careers in Business Economics*, p. 28.
[4] Ibid.

very important, while the other half consider it only of moderate importance or not important at all.)

A local college placement office should be very useful to you not only in helping you write a resume but in showing you how to tailor your resume to a particular firm. In fact, it is best to visit your college placement office well before your senior year in order to take full advantage of the many services such centers usually offer today. They have many publications available for your use, and you will be better off selecting from their supply rather than buying without direction one of the many guides currently on the market.

The Dryden questionnaire asked those economists who do interviewing for their companies what they would suggest to improve the quality of a potential employee's resume. Perhaps the most prominent comment was that the resume should be suited to the particular job being applied for. You cannot prepare one general resume, send it to fifty different companies, and expect a high percentage of positive responses.

The respondents to the Dryden questionnaire, people who receive resumes in their current work and act upon what they read in them, offer these additional pointers for you to consider when preparing your resume: Be brief and relevant and indicate your career objectives. The person who reads your resume may have as little as forty-five seconds to devote to what you have prepared and to make a decision about asking you to come in for a personal interview. Your resume should be neat, well organized, and clearly and simply written. Career accomplishments should be highlighted. If you have had some work experience while in college that is not directly related to your career goals, some respondents feel that it should still be emphasized, because it shows exposure to the "real world." Even if it is not specifically related to the job being applied for, you have been in a situation where you were trained for the work you did, and every bit of experience helps in your future career. A number of respondents feel that extracurricular college activities should be included.

Negative reaction was given by the Dryden respondents to the use of "canned, prepackaged resumes." The stress seems to be on presenting yourself as a unique individual seeking a specific job. One word of caution was mentioned by several people in exactly the same words: "Don't write a 'cute' resume."

While it still remains an area of some disagreement, the value of a resume might be summarized this way: A good resume may or may not earn you a personal interview, depending upon the importance the particular company's interviewer assigns the resume. But a poorly prepared resume may well close the door to any further contact.

The following sample resume describes the qualifications of a fictitious 1987 college graduate. It is intended to suggest one of the commonly used formats as recommended by the leading books about writing resumes which are listed at the end of this section.

NEILL T. BEARCROFT

Room 119, California Tower California State University Northridge, CA 91330 (213) 555-1919	After May 27, 1987 1327 Welcome Way Salem, Oregon 97302 (239) 555-1987

JOB OBJECTIVE   Desire full-time position in economic research, ultimately leading to a position as an economist for a major banking institution.

EDUCATION   B.A., May 1987, California State University, Northridge
Major: Economics
Minor concentrations: Mathematics, finance, and computer programming

SELECTED COURSES

Money and Banking
Micro- and Macroeconomic Theory (4 courses)
Mathematical Analysis
Econometrics
Linear Algebra
Statistical Theory in Business

Computer Programming and Graphics
Investment Analysis and Management
Management of Financial Institutions
Risk Management

WORK HISTORY

1984-87: Radio Shack, Inc. (Tandy Corporation) Simi Valley, California (45-50 hours/week, summers and holidays).

Duties: Waited on customers, helped replenish inventories, designed product displays, and used the store's terminal to file the daily report of sales and cash flow to Tandy's mainframe computer.

1982-83: John's Bicycles, Sepulveda, California (20-40 hours/week, summers and holidays).

Duties: Waited on customers, assembled and repaired bicycles.

COLLEGE ACTIVITIES

1984-87: Member of cross country track team; also competed in the 880-yard dash.

1985-87: Member of Student Economic Association (president during 1986-87 school year).

1986-87: Member of Omicron Delta Epsilon, International. Honor Society in Economics.

References available upon request.

VI. HOW TO MAKE THE JOB INTERVIEW WORK TO YOUR ADVANTAGE

Unlike the resume, about which a divergence of opinion exists, the job interview was considered extremely important by everyone responding to the Dryden questionnaire. Because of that, you should be in contact with your college placement office well before you are ready to start interviewing for a career job. In addition to providing written information, college placement offices are increasingly making available video-taping equipment as an aid to you in preparing for job interviews. You can participate in a mock interview which will be video recorded, and then watch the tape with a placement counselor who will offer constructive criticism.

June Hillman, a career counselor and presently Supervisor of Career Development Services in the Office of Career Planning and Placement at California State University, Northridge, emphasizes that body language is a key element in any job interview. She stresses that a lasting impression of a candidate is formed within the first five minutes of an interview. Her staff works with students to teach them how to bring out their own positive attributes. Their efforts attempt not to create a stilted image, but rather to show each student how to present his or her own best image.

In offering advice about job interviews, respondents to the Dryden questionnaire had a number of common themes. These items, mentioned by many of the respondents, are listed here as advice from people who actually conduct interviews as part of their jobs.

1. Be honest about your goals and experience. Don't claim to have experience you don't have. Try to have in mind what your goals are.
2. Research the employer before you arrive at the interview. (Some placement offices are extremely helpful here, because often employers send information about themselves.)
3. Emphasize the basic applicability of your economic skills to the firm or organization you hope will hire you. Show you have the ability to apply your knowledge of economics to the particular work that interests you.
4. Show interest in opportunities for personal growth and advancement.
5. Demonstrate an ability to communicate well orally and to get along well with people. In the process, try to be relaxed. Many respondents placed a heavy emphasis on being relaxed during the interview.
6. Don't brag. As one person put it, "Maintain a balance between 'can do' and 'can learn.'"
7. Emphasize your ability to write analytically. Take some evidence of analytical writings in economics, especially for a research-type job.
8. There is a difference of opinion about asking questions. Some respondents feel you should have ready a list of questions to ask. Others indicate it is best to let the interviewer initiate much of the conversation. Your own best judgment in the situation will have to prevail.
9. Avoid a "packaged" appearance. As with the resume, interviewers are looking for a unique individual to fill a specific job.

10. As one respondent put it, "Wear the tribal costume of the company being interviewed."
11. Don't appear uncertain or indecisive.
12. Listen!

In a brochure advising students about the employment interview, Dr. Frank S. Endicott, Director of Placement (emeritus) of Northwestern University, lists fifteen reasons why candidates receive rejection replies after their interviews. These reasons are definitely worth considering as you prepare for your career interviews.

1. Lack of proper career planning—purposes and goals ill defined—needs direction.
2. Lack of knowledge of field of specialization—not well qualified—lacks depth.
3. Inability to express thoughts clearly and concisely—rambles.
4. Insufficient evidence of achievement or capacity to excite action in others.
5. Not prepared for the interview—no research on company—poor presentation.
6. No real interest in the organization or the industry—merely shopping around.
7. Narrow location interest—unwilling to relocate later—inflexible.
8. Little interest and enthusiasm—indifferent—bland personality.
9. Overbearing—overaggressive—conceited—cocky—aloof—assuming.
10. Interested only in the best dollar offer—too money conscious.
11. Asks no or poor questions about the job—little depth and meaning to questions.
12. Unwilling to start at the bottom—expects too much too soon—unrealistic.
13. Makes excuses—evasive—hedges on unfavorable factors in record.
14. No confidence and lack of poise—fails to look interviewer in the eye—immature.
15. Poor personal appearance—sloppy dress—lacks sophistication.

When you near graduation, you will likely wonder how important your college transcript will be to an interviewer. In the Dryden questionnaire, the transcript was considered an "important" part of the evaluation of job candidates by slightly more than half of the economists responding. A little more than one-third considered the transcript to be "moderately important," while the rest paid little or no attention to the transcript.

Those who did find the transcript of at least moderate importance looked at overall GPA first and, to a somewhat lesser extent, the grades in certain key courses second. The "reputation of the college or university" was important to only a small number of the responding economists.

VII. USEFUL PUBLICATIONS FOR ECONOMICS MAJORS

The following is a representative list of publications that you may find useful in the study of economics and in pursuit of a career in economics.

A. General Reference Material

1. *Dictionary of Business and Economics*. Christine Ammer and Dean S. Ammer. New York: Free Press, revised and expanded edition, 1986. A remarkably thorough and complete compilation of definitions of terms and concepts commonly encountered in business and economics courses. Also contains some biographical sketches of famous past and present-day economists.
2. *Encyclopedia of Economics*. Douglas Greenwald, editor-in-chief. New York: McGraw-Hill, 1982. Covers more than 300 subjects written by 178 top authorities on modern economics.
3. *The McGraw-Hill Dictionary of Modern Economics: A Handbook of Terms and Organizations*. Douglas Greenwald, et al. 3rd ed., 1983. Similar in scope to the Ammer's *Dictionary of Business and Economics*, this book places somewhat greater emphasis on the description of some 225 private, public and nonprofit organizations concerned with economics and marketing.

B. Tips on Resume Writing and Interviewing

Many books on these subjects are available. Your college or university placement office or library, as well as your local public library, should contain a representative sample. Here are three that come highly recommended.

1. *Better Resumes for College Graduates*. Adele Lewis. Woodbury, N.Y.: Barron's Educational Series, Inc., 1985. A very thorough discussion of how a college graduate can find a job. Includes sections on what to include in a resume, 78 resume samples (including 23 pertaining to undergraduate business majors), samples of cover letters, job search, the interview, and suggestions for following through and keeping records.
2. *Does Your Resume Wear Blue Jeans?* C. Edward Good. Charlottesville, VA: The Word Store, 1985. A delightfully and humorously written resume writing guide that thoroughly discusses how to write a results-producing resume and its cover letter.
3. *The Perfect Resume*. Tom Jackson. Garden City, New York: Anchor Books, Anchor Press, Doubleday, 1981. A self-help manual that very effectively uses a step-by-step approach on preparing a resume and its cover letter. Includes special resume writing tips for college students and for women re-entering the job market, as well as a lengthy section of sample resumes.

C. Government Publications

The following are published by the U.S. government (or are based upon a federal publication). They contain a wide variety of regularly published statistics pertaining to such areas as national income accounting, money supply data, employment information, population trends, and so on. Most of the following also contain helpful interpretive articles regarding trends and correlations of the various data as well.

1. *Economic Report of the President.* Transmitted to the Congress in February of each year, together with the *Annual Report of the Council of Economics Advisors.* For sale by the Superintendent of Documents, U.S. Government Printing Office, Washington, D.C. 20402.
2. *Federal Reserve Bank of St. Louis Review.* Published monthly by the research department of the Federal Reserve Bank of St. Louis. *No charge* for subscriptions. For information write: Research Department, Federal Reserve Bank of St. Louis, P.O. Box 442, St. Louis, Missouri 63166. This rather independent research department often publishes articles critical of current monetary and fiscal policy.
3. *Federal Reserve Bulletin.* Published monthly under the direction of the Board of Governors of the Federal Reserve System. For information write: Division of Support Services, Board of Governors of the Federal Reserve System, Washington, D.C. 20551.
4. *Monthly Labor Review.* Published monthly by the Bureau of Labor Statistics of the U.S. Department of Labor. For information write: Superintendent of Documents, Government Printing Office, Washington, D.C. 20402.
5. *Survey of Current Business.* Published monthly by the Bureau of Economic Analysis of the U.S. Department of Commerce. For information write: Superintendent of Documents, U.S. Government Printing Office, Washington, D.C. 20402.
6. *The U.S. Fact Book.* The American Almanac for (current year). An unabridged edition of the U.S. Bureau of the Census' *The Statistical Abstract of the United States.* Published annually by Grosset & Dunlap, New York. If the book is not available in your book store, it should be possible for you to order it from that store.

D. Newspapers and Magazines

These selected newspapers and magazines concentrate in whole or in part upon the reporting and interpretation of current business and economic news. All are highly readable.

1. *Barron's National Business and Financial Weekly.* Published every Monday by Dow Jones & Company. For information write: Barron's, 200 Burnett Road, Chicopee, Massachusetts 01012. Student subscription discount available.
2. *Business Week.* Published weekly, except for one issue in January, by McGraw-Hill. Student discount may be available on some campuses. For information write: Business Week, McGraw-Hill Building, 1221 Avenue of the Americas, New York, New York 10020.
3. *Business Week Careers.* Published seven times a year by McGraw-Hill, Inc. For information write: Business Week Careers, 5615 West Cermak Road, Cicero, IL 60650-2290.
4. *Challenge, the Magazine of Economic Affairs.* Published bimonthly by M.E. Sharpe. For information write: Challenge, 80 Business

Park Drive, Armonk, N.Y. 10504. Leading economists write articles aimed at readers with little formal training in economics. These articles primarily contain applications to current problems and policies.
5. *The Economist.* Published weekly. For information write: The Economist Newspaper Limited, P.O. Box 190, 23a St. James's Street, London SW1A 1HF, England. Student subscription discount available. This entertaining British publication frequently contains criticisms of U.S. economic policies.
6. *Forbes.* Published biweekly (and occasionally weekly) by Forbes, Inc., 60 Fifth Avenue, New York, New York 10011. This business-oriented magazine includes a regular "Careers" column.
7. *Fortune.* Published biweekly with three issues in October by Time, Inc., 541 North Fairbanks Court, Chicago, Illinois 60611-3333. Student subscription discount may be available on some campuses.
8. *Managing Your Career: The College Edition of the National Business Employment Weekly.* Fall, 1987. For information write Dow Jones & Company, Inc., 420 Lexington Avenue, New York, N.Y. 10170.
9. *Newsweek.* Published weekly. Student subscription discount may be available on some campuses. For information write: Newsweek, Newsweek Building, Livingston, New Jersey 07039.
10. *Time.* Published weekly. Student subscription discount may be available on some campuses. For information write: Time, Inc., Time-Life Building, Chicago, Illinois 60672-2052.
11. *U.S. News and World Report.* Published weekly except two issues combined into one at year-end. Student subscription discount may be available on some campuses. For information write: U.S. News and World Report, Inc., 2300 N Street, N.W., Washington, D.C. 20037.
12. *The Wall Street Journal.* Published daily except Saturdays, Sundays, and general legal holidays. Student subscription discount available. For information write: The Wall Street Journal, 200 Burnett Road, Chicopee, Massachusetts 01020.

E. Selected Professional Economic and Business Journals

The following is a sample from the rather large number of journals whose intended readership consists primarily of professional economists or professionals in related fields. While many of the articles may be too technical for the beginning economics student, each journal contains writing well within the grasp of the interested student who has completed one year of study of microeconomic and macroeconomic principles.
1. *American Economic Review.* Published quarterly by the American Economic Association, along with its annual *Proceedings* of the annual meetings published in May. Student subscription discount available. For information write: Secretary, C. Elton Hinshaw, 1313 - 21st Avenue South, Nashville, Tennessee 37212. Students should find the *Proceedings* issue especially useful, as it usually contains broad coverage of selected economists' views on current economic issues and government policies.

2. *The American Economist*. Journal of the International Honor Society in Economics, Omicron Delta Epsilon. Published semiannually in Spring and Fall. For information write: Dr. William D. Gunther, Department of Economics, P.O. Drawer AS, University of Alabama, University, Alabama 35486.
3. *Business Economics*. Published quarterly by the National Association of Business Economists. Student subscription discount available. For information write: National Association of Business Economists, 28349 Chagrin Boulevard., Suite 201, Cleveland, Ohio 44122.
4. *Economic Inquiry*. Journal of the Western Economic Association. Published quarterly. Student subscription discount available. For information write: Western Economic Association, Executive Office, Department of Economics, California State University, Long Beach, California 90840.
5. *Harvard Business Review*. "A bimonthly journal for professional managers, is a program in executive education of the Graduate School of Business Administration, Harvard University." For information write: Harvard Business Review, Subscription Service Department, P.O. Box 9730, Greenwich, Connecticut 06835.
6. *Journal of Business*. Published quarterly by the Graduate School of Business of the University of Chicago. Student subscription discount available. For information write: Journal of Business, University of Chicago Press, 5801 Ellis Avenue, Chicago, Illinois 60637.
7. *Journal of Economic Literature*. Published quarterly by the American Economic Association along with the *American Economic Review*. This publication is a must for any economics researcher. It usually contains a survey article of the latest developments in a field of economics and also provides reviews of recently published economics books, an annotated listing of new books, contents of selected current economic and business professional journals, and a classification by economics area of articles and *abstracts* of selected articles in current economic and business journals, among other things. See *American Economic Review*.
8. *Journal of Law and Economics*. Published twice a year by the University of Chicago Law School. Student subscription discount available. For information write: Editor, Journal of Law and Economics, University of Chicago Law School, 1111 East 60th Street, Chicago, Illinois 60637.
9. *Journal of Political Economy*. Published bimonthly by the University of Chicago Press. Student subscription discount available. For information write: The University of Chicago Press, 5801 Ellis Avenue, Chicago, Illinois 60637.
10. *Quarterly Journal of Economics*. Published quarterly by John Wiley & Sons, Inc., and by the President and Fellows of Harvard College. For information write: Journal Department, John Wiley & Sons, 605 Third Avenue, New York, New York 10016.
11. *Southern Economic Journal*. Published quarterly by the Southern Economic Association and the University of North Carolina. For information write: Vincent J. Tarascio, Managing Editor, Southern Economic Journal, Hanes Hall 019-A, Chapel Hill, North Carolina 27514.

Chapter 1

What Economics Is All About

WHERE YOU'RE GOING

When you have mastered this chapter, you will understand

1. What economics is all about.
2. How the need to choose is related to the concept of cost.
3. The roles that households, business firms, and government units play in the economy.
4. What markets are and how they work.
5. Who worries about unemployment, inflation, and economic growth and why.
6. Why economists sometimes disagree.
7. How ethics and value judgments enter into economics.

In addition, you will add the following new terms to your economic vocabulary:

    Scarcity
    Economics
    Goods
    Services
    Factors of production
    Labor
    Capital
    Natural resources
    Production possibility frontier
    Opportunity cost
    Microeconomics
    Market
    Macroeconomics
    Unemployment rate
    Inflation
    Gross national product (GNP)
    Nominal
    Real
    Model
    Conditional forecast
    Positive economics
    Normative economics

	WALKING TOUR *After you have read this chapter at least once, you should work step by step through this walking tour. Fill in the blanks and answer the questions as you go along. After you have answered each question, check yourself by uncovering the answer given in the margin. If you do not understand why the answer given is the correct one, refer back to the proper section of the text.*

Scarcity and Choice

When people do not have enough resources to meet all their wants

scarce — or needs, resources are said to be __scarce__. The study of the choices people make and the actions they take in order to make the best use of scarce resources in meeting their wants is known

economics — as __economics__.

production possibility frontier — The concepts of scarcity and choice can be illustrated using a graph known as a __production possibility frontier__. In drawing this figure, we as-

factors of production — sume given quantities of the basic inputs known as __factors of production__,

labor, capital — which include (1) __labor__, (2) __capital__, and

natural resources — (3) __nat. resources__. The production possibility frontier also assumes a certain state of technology. Points on or inside the frontier

can — represent combinations of goods that [can/cannot] be produced with available factors of production and technology. Points outside the

cannot — frontier represent points that [can/cannot] be produced.

At any point on the frontier, producing more of one good means giving up the opportunity to produce some of the other good. The cost of a good or service measured in terms of what must be given

opportunity — up in order to obtain it is called __opportunity__ cost. This cost

slope — concept is shown by the __slope__ of the production possibility frontier.

What Economists Do

The branch of economics that deals with the choices made by small

microeconomics — economic units is known as __microeconomics__. The units studied by microeconomics include

households —   1. __households__,

firms —   2. __firms__, and

units of government —   3. __units of gov't__.

Any arrangement that people have for trading with one another

market — is known as a __market__. In an economy like that of the

31

United States, markets play a key role in __coordination__ of economic activity. They accomplish this by fulfilling three essential tasks:

1. __transmitting info__,
2. __providing incentives__, and
3. __distributing income__

The branch of economics that deals with large-scale economic phenomena is known as __macroeconomics__. Three of the most important topics covered in macroeconomics are

1. __unemployment__,
2. __inflation__, and
3. __economic growth__.

The percentage of people in the labor force who are not working but are actively looking for work is the __unemployment rate__. People who do not have a job and are not looking for one [are/**are not**] counted as part of the labor force, and [are/**are not**] considered to be unemployed. A "normal" level of unemployment is considered to lie in the range from about __4__ percent to __6.5__ percent of the labor force.

A sustained increase in the average level of prices of all goods and services is known as __inflation__. Price stability means a rate of inflation of __0__ percent per year. However, most economists today would be satisfied with a rate below __3__ percent. The rate of inflation was [**below**/above] 3 percent in most years from World War II until 1967. During the 1970s and early 1980s, the rate of inflation was [**above**/below] 3 percent in most years.

A commonly used measure of the economy's total output is __GNP__. When a quantity such as GNP is adjusted for the effects of inflation, it is known as [**real**/nominal] GNP. If it is stated in the ordinary way, without adjustment for inflation, it is known as [real/**nominal**] GNP. Real GNP [does/**does not**] grow at a steady rate from year to year.

Why Economists Sometimes Disagree

Economists, [**like**/unlike] doctors, physicists, teachers, and so on sometimes disagree with one another. One reason is that economists [try/**do not try**] to make a complete list of everything that influences the economy. Instead, they select certain important features of economic life as the basis for their explanations of how facts are related—their theories, or, in economic terminology, their __models__. Thus, some disagreements arise as a result of differences about which aspects of reality are the most important.

Other disagreements arise from statements about the future, in the form "If A, then B, other things being equal." These are known as __forecasts__. Economic forecasters [**do**/do not] often disagree with one another, and they [**do**/do not] often miss crucial turning points in the economy.

In addition, economists disagree on issues of policy. Typically, a policy decision is based on a three-step chain of reasoning such as the following:

1. __If X then Y, other things being equal__.
2. __Outcome Y is good__.
3. __therefore policy X is good__

The first step, which is limited to a statement of facts or the relationship among facts, is a statement of __positive__ economics. The second step, which makes a judgment about which policies or conditions are good or bad, is part of __normative__ economics. Normative economics must be concerned not only with matters of __efficiency__, but also with matters of __fairness__.

33

HANDS ON

Now that you have reviewed the concepts introduced in this chapter, it is time for some hands-on practice with the analytical tools that have been introduced. Work through each problem in this section carefully, and then check your results against those given at the end of the chapter.

Problem 1

Exhibit 1.1 provides some practice in working with graphs. You may wish to review the appendix to Chapter 1 of the text before answering the questions that follow.

Exhibit 1.1

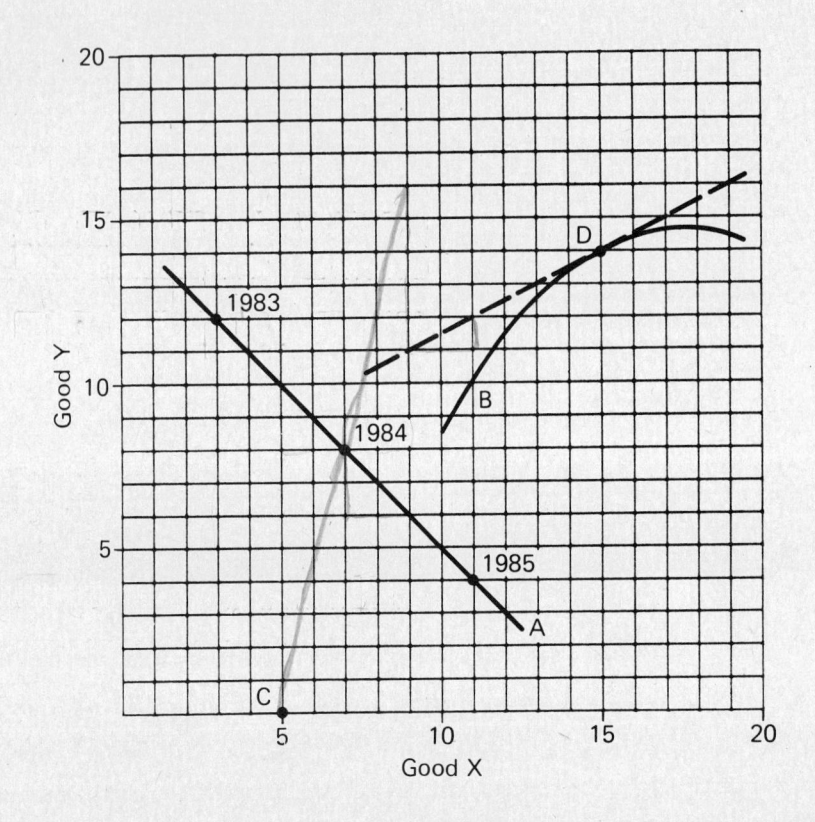

a. Suppose that good X is the average number of microwave ovens sold per day by a large department store, and that good Y is the average number of toaster ovens sold per day by the same store. Use line A in Exhibit 1.1 to complete the following table:

Year	Microwave ovens per day	Toaster ovens per day
1983	3	12
1984	7	8
1985	11	4

As time goes on the # of microwaves sold increases & the # of toaster ovens decreases.

Write a sentence describing in words what the graph tells you about sales of these two products.

b. What is the slope of line A in Exhibit 1.1? What is the slope of line B at point D? Draw a line passing through point C, and having a slope of 4. This line intersects line A at a point having what x value and what y value?

Slope A = −1
Slope B at D = ½
(7, 8)

34

c. Suppose that good X is the quantity of fertilizer used per acre and good Y is the yield of corn per acre. You are asked to draw a graph to represent the following proposition: as the quantity of fertilizer used increases, other things being equal, the yield of corn tends to increase, rapidly at first, then less rapidly, and then the yield begins to decrease. Your graph would look most like which of the curves in Exhibit 1.1?

Problem 2

Exhibit 1.2 shows a production possibility frontier for military goods and civilian goods for a certain economy. Use this graph in answering the questions that follow.

Exhibit 1.2

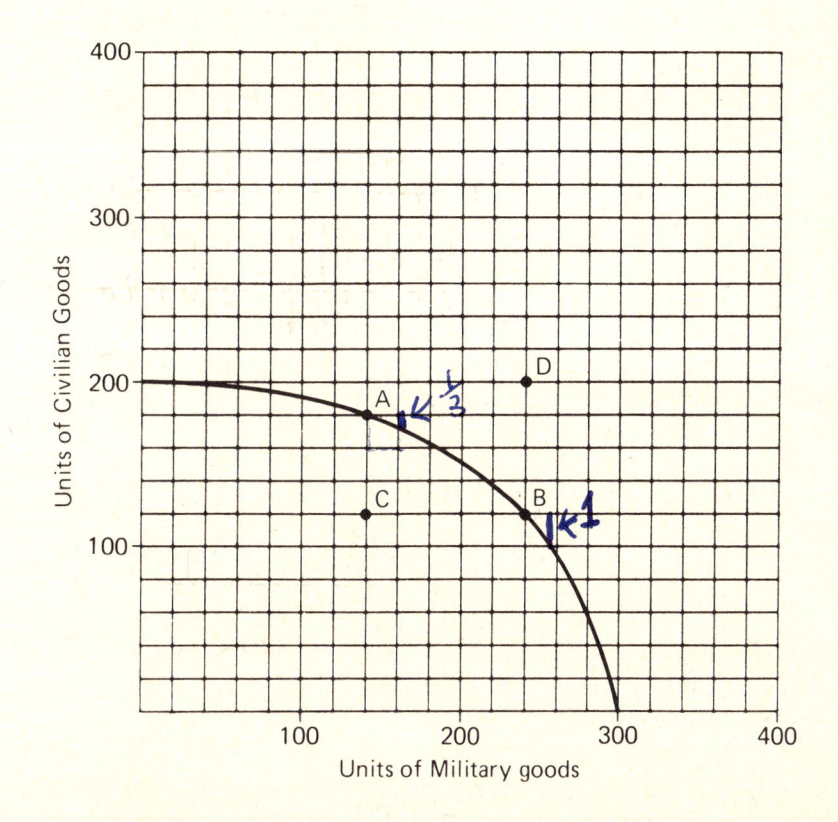

a. Which of the lettered points in Exhibit 1.2 represent possible combinations of civilian goods and military goods for this economy? Which represent impossible combinations? Which point or points represent possible combinations that can be produced without using all of the factors of production available?

b. At point A, what is the approximate opportunity cost of military goods, expressed in terms of civilian goods? What is the opportunity cost of military goods at point B?

ECONOMICS IN THE NEWS

$2 tag-sale candy dish auctioned for $60,000

United Press International

NEW YORK—An 18th-century candy and nut dish was sold at auction Thursday for $60,000—$59,998 more than the seller paid when the dish was bought at a tag sale on Long Island.

A spokeswoman at Sotheby's auction house said the small "sweetmeat stand" was purchased by Manhattan antique dealer J. Garrison Stradling during an auction of American items.

The dish, composed of three porcelain shells at the base with a bowl mounted on a stand in the middle and encrusted with shells and corals, was sold for much more than its estimated value of $20,000 to $30,000, the spokeswoman said.

Only 15 other porcelain items from the factory are known to exist. Fourteen are in museums and one is owned by a private collector.

Source: "$2 tag-sale candy dish auctioned for $60,000," *Dallas Morning News*, January 29, 1982, sec. D, 28. Reprinted by permission of United Press International.

Questions

1. Would both the tag sale and the Sotheby's auction mentioned in the news item be "markets" in the sense the term is used in economics?
2. On the basis of this story, would you say that markets in the U.S. economy do their job of transmitting information perfectly, or less than perfectly? Explain.
3. How does the story illustrate the incentive function of markets?
4. How does the story illustrate the function of markets in distributing income?

SELF TEST

These sample test items will help you check how much you have learned. Answers are found at the end of the chapter. Scoring yourself: One or two wrong—on target. Three or four wrong—passing, but you haven't mastered the chapter yet. Five or more wrong—not good enough; start over and restudy the chapter.

1. Scarcity is
   a. best measured in objective terms such as tons or kilowatt hours.
   b. a problem only in less developed countries.
   c. a matter of the relationship between resources and human wants.
   d. important for microeconomics, but not macroeconomics.

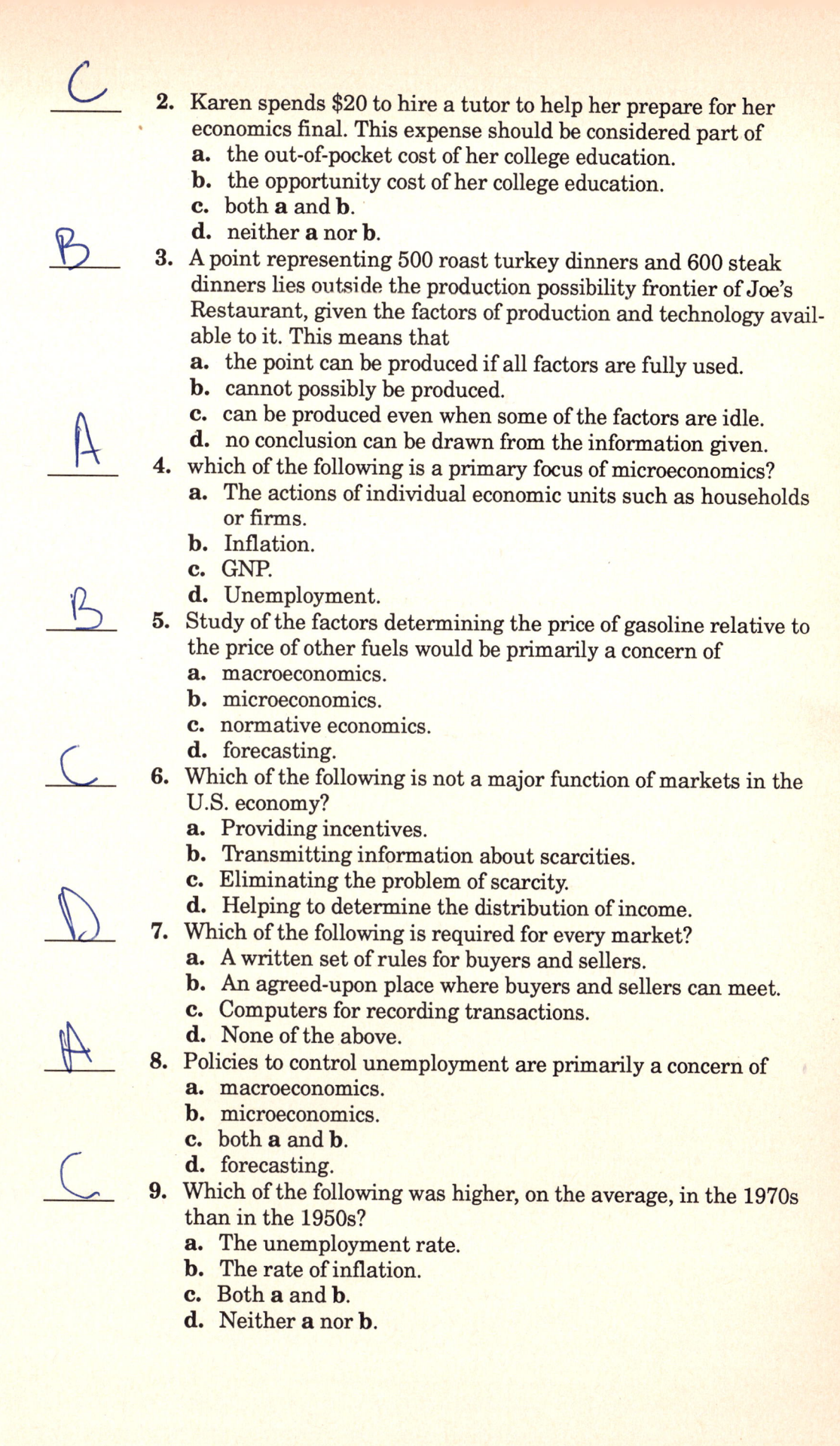

___C___ 2. Karen spends $20 to hire a tutor to help her prepare for her economics final. This expense should be considered part of
   a. the out-of-pocket cost of her college education.
   b. the opportunity cost of her college education.
   c. both **a** and **b**.
   d. neither **a** nor **b**.

___B___ 3. A point representing 500 roast turkey dinners and 600 steak dinners lies outside the production possibility frontier of Joe's Restaurant, given the factors of production and technology available to it. This means that
   a. the point can be produced if all factors are fully used.
   b. cannot possibly be produced.
   c. can be produced even when some of the factors are idle.
   d. no conclusion can be drawn from the information given.

___A___ 4. which of the following is a primary focus of microeconomics?
   a. The actions of individual economic units such as households or firms.
   b. Inflation.
   c. GNP.
   d. Unemployment.

___B___ 5. Study of the factors determining the price of gasoline relative to the price of other fuels would be primarily a concern of
   a. macroeconomics.
   b. microeconomics.
   c. normative economics.
   d. forecasting.

___C___ 6. Which of the following is not a major function of markets in the U.S. economy?
   a. Providing incentives.
   b. Transmitting information about scarcities.
   c. Eliminating the problem of scarcity.
   d. Helping to determine the distribution of income.

___D___ 7. Which of the following is required for every market?
   a. A written set of rules for buyers and sellers.
   b. An agreed-upon place where buyers and sellers can meet.
   c. Computers for recording transactions.
   d. None of the above.

___A___ 8. Policies to control unemployment are primarily a concern of
   a. macroeconomics.
   b. microeconomics.
   c. both **a** and **b**.
   d. forecasting.

___C___ 9. Which of the following was higher, on the average, in the 1970s than in the 1950s?
   a. The unemployment rate.
   b. The rate of inflation.
   c. Both **a** and **b**.
   d. Neither **a** nor **b**.

__A__ 10. A rate of unemployment of 9 percent would be considered by most economists to be
   a. above the acceptable range.
   b. within the acceptable range.
   c. below the acceptable range.
   d. technically impossible, given the way unemployment is defined.

__A__ 11. If the nation's real output rises in a given year, and the price level also rises, then nominal output
   a. must also rise.
   b. must fall.
   c. could either rise or fall.
   d. must remain unchanged.

__A__ 12. Which of the following statements is most nearly true about the ability of forecasters to predict major turning points in the economy?
   a. They sometimes miss major turning points.
   b. They always forecast major turning points accurately.
   c. They never forecast major turning points accurately.
   d. They began forecasting turning points accurately for the first time in the late 1970s.

__D__ 13. Which of the following disciplines relies on theories to explain how facts are related?
   a. Economics.
   b. Physics.
   c. Medicine.
   d. All of the above.

__C__ 14. Which of the following is an example of normative economics?
   a. The rate of inflation was lower in 1985 than in 1980.
   b. The rate of inflation was below 6 percent per year in 1985.
   c. The rate of inflation should be held below 6 percent regardless of what happens to unemployment.
   d. If the budget deficit is reduced, other things being equal, the rate of inflation will fall.

__D__ 15. In positive economic theory, the term "fairness" means
   a. a situation in which everyone has the same income.
   b. a situation in which property rights are protected.
   c. a situation in which the distribution system is efficient.
   d. none of the above; positive economics is not primarily concerned with fairness.

ANSWERS TO CHAPTER 1

Hands On

Problem 1 (a) 1983: 3 microwaves, 12 toasters; 1984: 7 microwaves, 8 toasters; 1985: 11 microwaves, 4 toasters. Between 1983 and 1985, the popularity of microwave ovens grew as that of toaster ovens fell. (b) Slope of line A is -1. Slope of curve B at point D is +1/2 (equal to the slope of the dashed line tangent to the curve at that point). A line through point C with a slope of +4 intersects line A at X = 7, Y = 8. (c) Curve B best represents this proposition.

Problem 2 (a) Points A, B, and C are possible, D is impossible, and C does not use all available factors fully. (b) At point A, the approximate opportunity cost of a unit of military goods is one-third unit of civilian goods, equal to the slope of the production possibility frontier at that point. At point B, the opportunity cost is one.

Economics in the News

(1) Both were markets in the sense that both were arrangements that buyers and sellers used to carry out transactions. (2) It might be said that the tag sale was not a perfectly functioning market, in that the price of $2 conveyed a misleading impression of the dish's true scarcity value. The auction at Sotheby's, attended by more knowledgeable buyers, brought the information out into the open in the form of high bids. (3) The system provided the unidentified man with a strong incentive to search tag sales and other sources for undervalued items and take them to markets where information on their worth was known. (4) In this example, income was distributed in favor of the first person to recognize and take action to overcome the original market imperfection, that is, the undervaluation of the dish at the tag sale.

Self Test

1. **c.** Scarcity is a universal problem, and it is measured in subjective terms, relative to human wants and needs.
2. **c.** Some cost items count as both opportunity costs and out-of-pocket costs; the categories are not mutually exclusive.
3. **b.** Points outside the frontier are impossible, those on the frontier are possible, and those inside the frontier are possible even without full use of available factors.
4. **a.** Inflation, GNP and unemployment are primarily matters of macroeconomics.
5. **b.** Microeconomics is concerned with prices of particular goods, whereas macroeconomics pays more attention to the average level of prices of all goods.
6. **c.** The problem of scarcity can never be eliminated.
7. **d.** Markets are any arrangements by which buyers and sellers trade with one another. No one of these things is necessary.
8. **a.** Unemployment, inflation, and economic growth are the three main concerns of macroeconomics.
9. **c.** The rate of growth of real output was lower.
10. **a.** The acceptable range is roughly 4 to 6.5 percent. Rates of 9 percent or more have been experienced in some recent years.
11. **a.** The rate of growth of nominal output is the sum of the rate of growth of the price level and that of real output.
12. **a.** Forecasters sometimes make major mistakes, but most economists think their efforts are an improvement over uninformed guesswork.

13. **d.** Economics is no different than the others in this regard.
14. **c.** Normative economics is concerned with the way things ought to be.
15. **d.** Fairness is a concern of normative economics.

Chapter 2

Exchange and Production

WHERE YOU'RE GOING

When you have mastered this chapter, you will understand

1. The ways it is decided what goods and services the economy is to produce.
2. The roles of efficiency, investment, and entrepreneurship in the decision on how goods and services will be produced.
3. The impact of positive and normative economics on the decision on for whom goods and services will be produced.
4. The principle that guides the division of labor within an economy and among nations.
5. How capitalist and socialist economies differ in their approach to the questions of what, how, and for whom.

In addition, you will add the following new terms to your economic vocabulary:
- Consumer sovereignty
- Efficiency in production
- Efficiency in distribution
- Economic efficiency
- Investment
- Entrepreneurship
- Comparative advantage
- Capitalism
- Socialism
- Regulation
- Economic planning

	WALKING TOUR — *After you have read this chapter at least once, you should work step by step through this walking tour. Fill in the blanks and answer the questions as you go along. After you have answered each question, check yourself by uncovering the answer given in the margin. If you do not understand why the answer given is the correct one, refer back to the proper section of the text.*

The Economic Problem

Every economy must face three fundamental choices in dealing with the problem of scarcity:

what to produce
how to produce
for whom to produce

1. _what to produce_,
2. _how to produce_, and
3. _for whom to produce_

production possibility frontier

resources, technology

on, inside

outside

The question of what to produce can be represented as the choice of one or another point on a _PPF_. As we saw in Chapter 1, the shape and position of the frontier depend on available _technology_ and _resources_. It is possible to reach any point _on_ the frontier or _inside_ it, but not possible to reach any point _outside_ of it.

substituted

The question of how to produce arises because one factor of production can be _substituted_ for another. For example, building a road using heavy earthmoving equipment instead of large gangs of laborers with shovels is an example of substituting

capital, labor

on

capital for _labor_. If production is carried out in a manner that puts the economy [**on**/inside] the production possibility frontier, so that it is not possible, given technology and factors of production, to produce more of one good without produc-

efficient

ing less of another, then production is said to be _efficient_.

outward

If additional factors of production become available, the production possibility frontier shifts [**outward**/inward]. In particular, the frontier can be shifted outward by increasing the stock of capital, a

investment

process known as _investment_. Another way to shift the frontier outward is through the process of looking for new possibilities—making use of new ways of doing things, being alert to new opportunities, and overcoming old limits. This process is known as

entrepreneurship

entrepreneurship

The question of for whom to produce is partly a matter of achieving a situation in which it is not possible, by redistributing existing goods, to satisfy one person's wants more fully without satisfying

efficiency in distribution	another's less fully. The economy is then said to have __efficiency in distribution__.
production, distribution	Overall economic efficiency is a situation in which there is both efficiency of __production__ and efficiency of __distribution__.

Exchange and Comparative Advantage

comparative advantage	A person who can produce a good or service at a lower opportunity cost than someone else is said to have a __comparitive advantage__. If two
both	people engage in voluntary exchange that is based on comparative advantage, [one/**both**] of them gain(s).
	The concept of comparative advantage can also be applied on an international scale. For example, if the opportunity cost of producing a bottle of wine in Italy is 2 pounds of cheese, whereas the opportunity of producing a bottle of wine in Canada is 4 pounds of cheese,
Italy	then [**Italy**/Canada] is said to have a comparative advantage in producing wine. For the sake of worldwide efficiency, Italy should
export, import	thus [import/**export**] wine and [**import**/export] cheese.

Economic Systems

are	All economies [**are**/are not] alike in the problems they face. They
are not	[are/**are not**] alike in the ways they make decisions.
	One major factor that determines who makes decisions is
ownership	__ownership__. A system in which ownership and control of business firms rests with suppliers of capital is known as __capitalism__.
capitalism	One in which business firms are owned and controlled by the people who work in them, or by the government, acting in the name of the
socialism, is not	workers, is known as __socialism__. The United States [is/**is not**]
is not	a pure capitalist economy. The Soviet Union [**is**/is not] a pure socialist economy.
	Broadly speaking, there are three styles of economic decision making. In a capitalist economy, the most important decisions are
markets, are	made through __markets__. Markets [**are**/are not] used in socialist economies. Government intervention in the economy for the purpose of influencing the production and distribution of par-
regulation	ticular goods and services is called __regulation__. Systematic intervention by government with the goal of improving
planning	coordination, efficiency, and growth is known as __planning__.

43

HANDS ON	*Now that you have reviewed the concepts introduced in this chapter, it is time for some hands-on practice with the analytical tools that have been introduced. Work through this section carefully, and then check your results against those given at the end of the chapter.*

Suppose that an hour's labor in the United States produces 2 tons of wheat or 5 yards of cloth, and that an hour's labor in Taiwan produces 1 ton of wheat or 4 yards of cloth. Given this information, answer the following questions:

a. What is the opportunity cost of a ton of wheat, in yards of cloth, in each country? The opportunity cost of a yard of cloth, in terms of tons of wheat?

b. In which good or goods does the United States have a comparative advantage? Taiwan?

c. The United States will be better off importing cloth than producing it at home provided it can get more than how many yards of cloth in exchange for a ton of wheat? Taiwan is better off importing wheat than growing it at home provided it can get at least how many tons of wheat in exchange for a yard of cloth? Which country or countries would benefit from trade at a ratio of 2 yards of cloth per ton of wheat? Three yards of cloth per ton of wheat? Five yards of cloth per ton of wheat?

d. Suppose the United States takes 1,000 hours out of cloth production and devotes that labor to wheat, while Taiwan takes 1,500 hours out of wheat production and devotes that labor to producing cloth. What will happen to production of each good in each country, and in the world as a whole?

e. Suppose that after the change in production, the United States sends 1,800 tons of wheat to Taiwan in exchange for 5,400 tons of cloth. Compared to the situation before the change in production pattern and before trade, what happens to consumption of each good in each country?

ECONOMICS IN THE NEWS	**Dentist Justified in His Causing Pain to Wallet**

Dear Ann Landers: Recently I overheard my dentist's receptionist tell a patient on the telephone, "The dentist will be able to fit you in at 11 o'clock today. There will be a $25 emergency fee." After a pause, she said, "Well—call us back if you continue to have trouble." Within minutes the phone rang again. That patient was told, "Yes, 11 o'clock is fine. The doctor can see you."

What kind of system lets professionals enrich themselves because people are in trouble? Don't they realize not everyone has health insurance? I am aware how much it costs to become a doctor or a dentist. But are they justified in demanding, "Your money or your life?" —Outraged.

Dear Out: My dentist, Dr. Jordan Block, says he never charges extra for emergencies—but many dentists do.

To my surprise, he added, "It's not a bad idea." When I said I felt this was unethical, he explained, "Some people will have a toothache for several days and ignore it until it becomes severe. They then call a dentist they have never gone to before. If he takes the patient, he must work time in between his regulars. This causes him to run late all day.... When the emergency fee is mentioned, it is easy to discover how genuine the emergency is."

We then checked the Chicago Dental Society and found agreement with what Block had said. So maybe the emergency fee isn't such a bad idea after all.

Source: "Dentist Justified in His Causing Pain to Wallet," *Chicago Sun-Times*, September 10, 1980, p. 60. Reprinted by permission of Ann Landers, Field Newspaper Syndicate and the *Chicago Sun-Times*.

Questions

1. Does an unscheduled emergency visit to a dentist incur a higher opportunity cost than a scheduled visit to have the same service performed? If so, what form does the opportunity cost take, and who bears it?
2. Does the practice of charging an emergency fee improve the efficiency of the economy? Why or why not?
3. At present, the decision of whether to charge an emergency fee is left to individual dentists, and the level of the fee is left to them also. Would you favor a regulation requiring (or forbidding) an emergency fee? Should the regulation set a maximum or a minimum level for the fee? Discuss.
4. Efficiency aside, do you think it is fair to charge an emergency fee? Is it fair not to charge one? Discuss.

SELF TEST

These sample test items will help you check how much you have learned. Answers are found at the end of the chapter. Scoring yourself: One or two wrong—on target. Three or four wrong—passing, but you haven't mastered the chapter yet. Five or more wrong—not good enough; start over and restudy the chapter.

1. The basic decisions that must be made in every economy include
   a. what should be produced.
   b. how things should be produced.
   c. for whom they should be produced.
   d. all of the above.
2. On a production possibility frontier diagram, a point inside the frontier is
   a. inefficient.
   b. possible.
   c. both **a** and **b**.
   d. neither **a** nor **b**.

___C___ 3. Which of the following would be most likely to cause the production possibility frontier for education and other goods to shift outward?
    a. A reduction in average hours per worker per week.
    b. An increase in the price of energy.
    c. An increase in the economy's stock of capital.
    d. None of the above.

___C___ 4. Placing a tariff (that is, a tax) on imported steel causes the price of steel to rise in the United States. This benefits U.S. steel workers by raising wages and creating more jobs, but it hurts U.S. autoworkers, because consumers buy fewer cars when an increase in the price of steel makes cars more costly. From the information given, we can say that the tariff
    a. increases efficiency in production in the United States.
    b. increases efficiency in distribution in the United States.
    c. makes at least one person better off.
    d. all of the above.

___C___ 5. Investment, as the term is used in economics, means
    a. creating money.
    b. putting money in the bank.
    c. increasing the economy's stock of capital.
    d. inventing new ways of doing things.

_C_ ~~D~~ 6. Japan can produce a car in 1,000 hours and a computer in 100 hours. Brazil can produce a car in 2,000 hours and a computer in 300 hours. According to the theory of comparative advantage, both countries can benefit if
    a. Brazil imports both computers and cars.
    b. Japan imports both computers and cars.
    c. Brazil imports computers and exports cars.
    d. Japan imports computers and exports cars.

_B_ ~~~~ 7. Mathew scores 799 on a test of verbal abilities and 650 on a test of math abilities. Andrew scores 600 on verbal abilities and 595 on math. It appears that
    a. Mathew has a comparative advantage in math.
    b. Andrew has a comparative advantage in math.
    c. Mathew has a comparative advantage in both math and verbal abilities.
    d. None of the above.

___D___ 8. In economics, the idea of efficiency applies to
    a. how goods are produced.
    b. whether the division of labor follows the principle of comparative advantage.
    c. whether goods are distributed according to consumer preferences.
    d. all of the above.

___C___ 9. An economic policy is said to improve efficiency if
    a. it makes at least one person better off.
    b. it makes no one worse off.
    c. it makes at least one person better off and makes no one worse off.
    d. it makes a majority of people better off.

___D___ 10. Which of the following is an illustration of entrepreneurship?
  a. Starting a new computer company.
  b. Cutting production costs through an improved method of work in an existing factory.
  c. The weekly job of preparing the payroll in an existing factory.
  d. Both **a** and **b** but not **c**.

___B___ 11. An economic system in which firms are privately owned and controlled by suppliers of capital is
  a. socialism.
  b. capitalism.
  c. communism.
  d. syndicalism.

_C_ ~~B~~ 12. Systematic intervention in the economy by government with the goal of improving coordination, efficiency, and growth is called
  a. capitalism.
  b. regulation.
  c. economic planning.
  d. industrial policy.

___C___ 13. The role of markets in decision making is greatest under which economic system?
  a. Communism.
  b. Regulation.
  c. Capitalism.
  d. Socialism.

A ~~B~~ 14. Karl Marx was
  a. strongly influenced by the British classical school of economics.
  b. a theorist who took no practical interest in revolutionary activities.
  c. called upon to set up a national planning system after the Russian revolution.
  d. all of the above.

___C___ 15. Which of the following systems of decision making is used in the Soviet Union?
  a. Exclusively planning.
  b. Exclusively markets.
  c. Extensive planning, but also some markets.
  d. Mostly markets, with extensive cooperative ownership of factories.

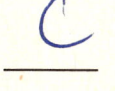

ANSWERS TO CHAPTER 2

Hands On

(a) The opportunity cost of a ton of wheat is 2.5 yards of cloth in the United States and 4 yards of cloth in Taiwan. The cost of a yard of cloth is 0.4 tons of wheat in the United States and 0.25 tons of wheat in Taiwan. Note: When you see this type of problem, pay close attention to whether the costs of production in each country

47

are stated in terms of output per labor hour, or hours of labor per unit. For example, in this case, we could have said that a ton of wheat takes 0.5 hours and a yard of cloth 0.2 hours in the United States, and so on. That is just another way of stating the data. Either way, the opportunity costs are the same. (b) The United States has a comparative advantage in wheat, and Taiwan a comparative advantage in cloth. This is determined by opportunity costs. (c) The United States will be better off if it gets more than 2.5 yards of cloth per ton of wheat, and Taiwan will be better off if it gets more than 0.25 tons of wheat per yard of cloth. Thus, at a ratio of 2 yards per ton (0.5 tons per yard) only Taiwan would benefit from trade. At a ratio of 3 yards per ton, both countries would benefit. At a ratio of 5 yards per ton, only the United States would benefit. (d) This action would increase U.S. wheat output by 2,000 tons while cutting U.S. cloth output by 5,000 yards. At the same time Taiwan's wheat output would fall by 1,500 tons and its cloth output would rise by 6,000 yards. Thus, world output of wheat would rise 500 tons and world output of cloth 1,000 yards. (e) After the production adjustment followed by the suggested trade, U.S. consumers would have 200 more tons of wheat and 400 more yards of cloth than they started with. Taiwanese consumers would have 300 tons more wheat and 600 yards more cloth. Thus consumers in both countries would have more of both goods.

Economics in the News

(1) An unscheduled emergency visit does have a higher opportunity cost. In part, the cost will be borne by other patients, who will show up on time for their appointments, and will have to wait longer to get in to see the doctor. In part, it may also be borne by the dentist, who will have to work through lunch hour or stay late. (2) The emergency fee may increase efficiency, in the sense that emergency patients do not disrupt others' schedules unless they place a higher value on the dentist's time. To make the emergency patient better off without making the regular patients worse off, the fee should perhaps be turned over to the patients who have to wait longer to make room for the emergency patient. This would be similar to the airline system under which passengers "bumped" from an overbooked flight are offered a cash payment. (3) If you are certain that a fee is efficient and fair, you might want to impose it on everyone by regulation. Or, if you think some patients would prefer a dentist with a fee and others a dentist without one, you might leave the matter to be decided by competition. (4) In answering this question, refer to the section on positive and normative economics in Chapter 1.

Self Test

1. **d.** These are all aspects of the problem of dealing with scarcity.
2. **b.** Points on the frontier are efficient, those inside it are possible but inefficient.
3. **c.** The position of the frontier depends on available factors of production and on technology.

4. **c.** It makes some people (steelworkers) better off, but it makes others (autoworkers) worse off, hence it cannot be said to increase efficiency of either production or distribution.
5. **c.** Purely financial transactions are not considered investment in economics; only those that add to physical capital are investment. **d** is an example of entrepreneurship, not investment.
6. **c.** Brazil has the lower opportunity cost for cars. It should import computers and export cars.
7. **b.** Andrew is worse at both skills, but his math skills are better compared to his own verbal skills.
8. **d.** It applies to all the decisions of what, how, and for whom.
9. **c.** Neither **a** nor **b** alone guarantees efficiency.
10. **d.** Entrepreneurship means looking for new ways of doing things, whether in a new firm or an existing one.
11. **b.** The others are various forms of worker control.
12. **c.** Regulation and industrial policy are less general forms of intervention.
13. **c.** The others all limit market decision making to some degree.
14. **a.** Marx was strongly influenced by Ricardo, a follower of Adam Smith. He was an active revolutionary, and died before the Russian revolution.
15. **c.** Markets are used for some consumer goods, and also in many cases for deciding who does a certain job.

Chapter 3

Supply and Demand

WHERE YOU'RE GOING

When you have mastered this chapter, you will understand

1. How the price of a good or service affects the quantity demanded by buyers.
2. Other market conditions that affect demand.
3. How the quantities of goods and services that producers supply are affected by prices and other market conditions.
4. How supply and demand interact to determine the market price of a good or service.
5. Why market prices and quantities change in response to changes in a variety of market conditions.
6. How price supports and price ceilings affect the operations of markets.

In addition, you will add the following new terms to your economic vocabulary:
    Law of demand
    Demand curve
    Change in quantity demanded
    Change in demand
    Substitutes
    Complements
    Normal good
    Inferior good
    Supply curve
    Change in quantity supplied
    Change in supply
    Equilibrium
    Excess quantity demanded (shortage)
    Excess quantity supplied (surplus)
    Inventory

WALKING TOUR

After you have read this chapter at least once, you should work step by step through this walking tour. Fill in the blanks and answer the questions as you go along. After you have answered each question, check yourself by uncovering the answer given in the margin. If you do not understand why the answer given is the correct one, refer back to the proper section of the text.

Demand

According to the law of demand, the quantity of any good demanded tends to increase as the price __decreases__, other things being equal. Demand curves thus normally have a __negative__ slope.

A change in the quantity demanded means a [shift in/**movement along**] the demand curve. Consumer income is one of the "other things" held equal in the statement of the law of demand, so a change in consumer income is said to cause a __change in demand__. If an increase in consumer income causes an increase in demand, the good is said to be a/an __normal__ good. If an increase in consumer income causes a decrease in demand for the good, it is said to be a/an __inferior__ good.

The prices of other goods are also held equal in the statement of the law of demand. If an increase in the price of good X causes a decrease in the demand for good Y, the two goods are said to be __complements__. If an increase in the price of good X causes an increase in the demand for good Y, the two goods are said to be __substitutes__.

Two other conditions that can cause the demand curve to shift are changes in __tastes__ and changes in __expectations__.

Supply

Supply curves normally have __positive__ slopes. This indicates that an increase in the price of a good tends to cause sellers to increase the [supply/**quantity supplied**] of the good in question. Changes in technology, input prices, or the prices of other goods are potential causes of changes in [**supply**/quantity supplied].

Other things being equal, a change in technology that lowers the cost of producing a good tends to [**increase**/decrease] the quantity of the good that suppliers plan to sell at a given price. Such a change thus tends to cause a [**rightward**/leftward]

51

shift in / [shift in/movement along] the supply curve. And other things being equal, an increase in the price of an input used in producing a good

decrease / tends to [increase/decrease] the quantity of the good that suppliers plan to sell at a given price. Such a change thus tends to cause a

leftward, shift in / [rightward/leftward] [shift in/movement along] the supply curve. Finally, a change in expectations regarding future prices can cause

shift in / a [shift in/movement along] a supply curve.

The Interaction of Supply and Demand

When the plans of buyers and sellers of a good exactly mesh, so that the quantity supplied and the quantity demanded at the prevailing

equilibrium / price are equal, the market is said to be in _equilibrium_. At any price higher than the equilibrium price, there will be a

surplus / [shortage/surplus] of the good. Stocks of the good that are finished

inventories / and awaiting sale—that is, _inventories_ of the good—will

grow / tend to [grow/shrink], and the price of the good will tend to

fall / [rise/fall]. At any price below the equilibrium price, there will be a

shortage, shrink / [shortage/surplus] and the inventories will tend to [grow/shrink].

upward / This will put [upward/downward] pressure on the price until equilibrium is restored.

Applications

When market conditions change, equilibrium prices and quantities will also change. For example, suppose that the price of paper

leftward / increases. This will cause a [rightward/leftward] shift in the

supply / [supply/demand/both] curve for books. There will be a temporary

shortage, rise / [shortage/surplus]. The price will tend to [rise/fall] until a new equilibrium is reached.

Or suppose there is an increase in consumer income. In the

demand / market for stereos, a normal good, the [supply/demand/both] curve

right / will shift to the [right/left]. There will be a temporary

shortage, rise / [shortage/surplus] and the price will [rise/fall] until a new equilibrium is reached.

If a price ceiling is imposed on a market, there will tend to be a

shortage / lasting [surplus/shortage]. On the other hand, if a price floor is

surplus / imposed, there will tend to be a lasting [shortage/surplus].

HANDS ON

Now that you have reviewed the concepts introduced in this chapter, it is time for some hands-on practice with the analytical tools that have been introduced. Work through each problem in this section carefully, and then check your results against those given at the end of the chapter.

Problem 1

Supply and demand curves can be used to show the effects of changing market conditions. Exhibit 3.1 shows hypothetical supply and demand curves for oak flooring. Use the diagram to answer the questions that follow.

Exhibit 3.1

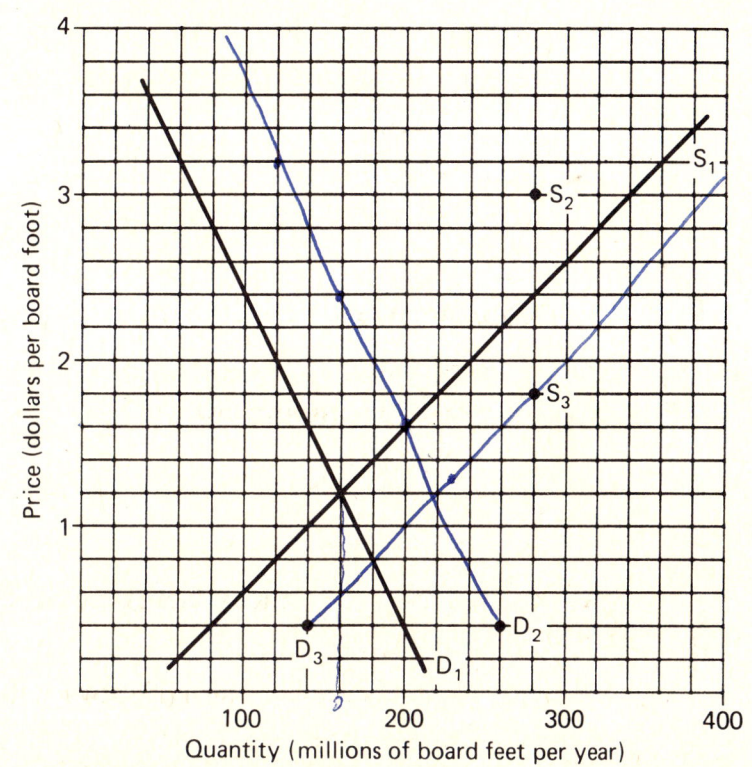

a. What is the equilibrium price as the diagram is drawn? What is the equilibrium quantity?
b. Suppose a boom in home construction occurs, raising the demand for oak flooring. Will this shift the demand curve, or cause a movement along the demand curve D_1? If it shifts the demand curve, draw the new curve parallel to the old one, and passing through point D_2 or D_3, whichever you think better represents the effects of the construction boom. What is the new equilibrium price? The new equilibrium quantity?
c. Next suppose that improvements in sawmill technology cut the cost of producing oak flooring. Will this shift the supply curve, or cause a movement along it? If it shifts the supply curve, draw the new curve parallel to the old one, and passing through either S_2 or S_3, whichever you think is appropriate. Assuming that the demand curve remains where you left it at the end of part b of this problem, what is the new equilibrium price? The new equilibrium quantity?

Problem 2

Exhibit 3.2 shows supply and demand curves for house paint. Use this diagram in answering the questions that follow.

Exhibit 3.2

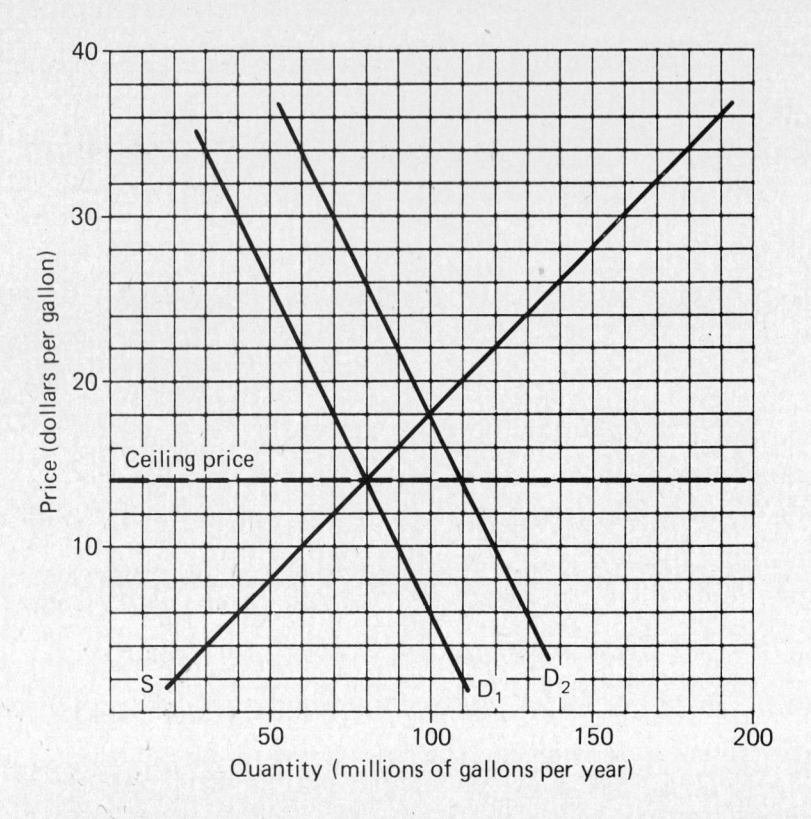

a. Initially the supply and demand curves are in the positions S and D_1. Under these conditions, what is the equilibrium price? The equilibrium quantity?
b. The government now imposes price controls that make it illegal for sellers of housepaint to raise the price above $14 per gallon. Now a boom in housing construction comes along, causing the demand curve to shift to the position D_2. Without the price ceiling, what would happen to the price of house paint and the quantity supplied? What will happen with the price ceiling in effect?
c. The price ceiling combined with the construction boom leads to a black market in house paint. People lucky enough to be able to buy some of the limited supply at the price of $14 per gallon resell it to users of paint at the highest price that demand conditions will allow. As Exhibit 3.2 is drawn, how high would the black market price rise?

Problem 3

Exhibit 3.3 gives supply and demand curves for corn sweetener, a sugar substitute made from corn. Use it in answering the questions that follow. Whenever you need to show a shift in the supply or demand curve, draw the new curve parallel to the original one.

Exhibit 3.3

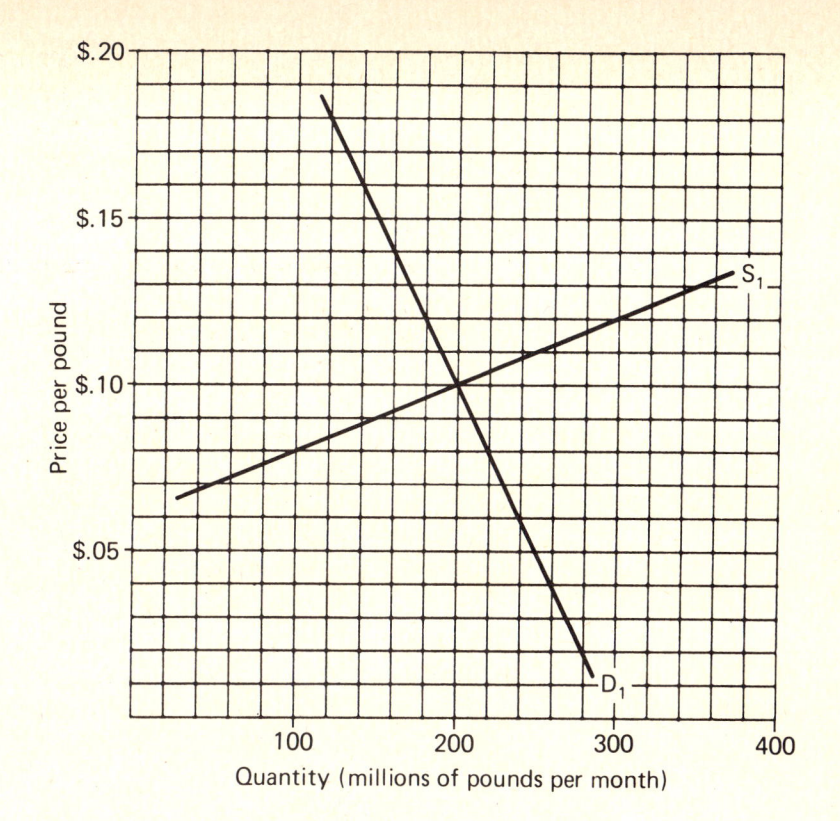

[Graph showing price per pound (y-axis, $.05 to $.20) vs. Quantity (millions of pounds per month, x-axis, 100 to 400), with supply curve S₁ and demand curve D₁ intersecting around $.10 and 200.]

a. Given the supply curve S₁ and the demand curve D₁, what is the equilibrium price of corn sweetener? What is the equilibrium quantity produced? Label the initial equilibrium point E₁.

b. An increase in the price of cane sugar improves market conditions for producers of corn sweetener, raising the equilibrium price to 12 cents per pound. Would this event best be represented by a shift in the supply curve, the demand curve, or both? Draw in the new curve or curves, labeling them with the subscript 2. Label the new equilibrium point E₂.

c. After the market has reached E₂, a crop failure increases the price of corn, pushing up production costs for corn sweetener. The price of corn sweetener rises to 15 cents per pound. Would this event best be represented by a shift in the supply curve, the demand curve, or both? Draw in the new curve or curves, labeling them with the subscript 3. Label the new equilibrium E₃.

Problem 4

Exhibit 3.4 shows supply and demand curves for lettuce. Use it in answering the questions that follow.

a. As the diagram is drawn, the equilibrium quantity of lettuce demanded is _____ crates per day. The equilibrium price is $_____ per crate. Label this equilibrium point E₁.

b. Suppose now that invention of a better mechanical lettuce picker reduces costs. Producers are now willing to supply any given quantity of lettuce for $3 less per crate than previously. What will happen to the equilibrium price of lettuce? Will it fall by the full $3 amount? Explain why or why not by drawing in new supply and/or demand curves as needed. Label the new curve or curves and the new equilibrium with the subscript 2.

Exhibit 3.4

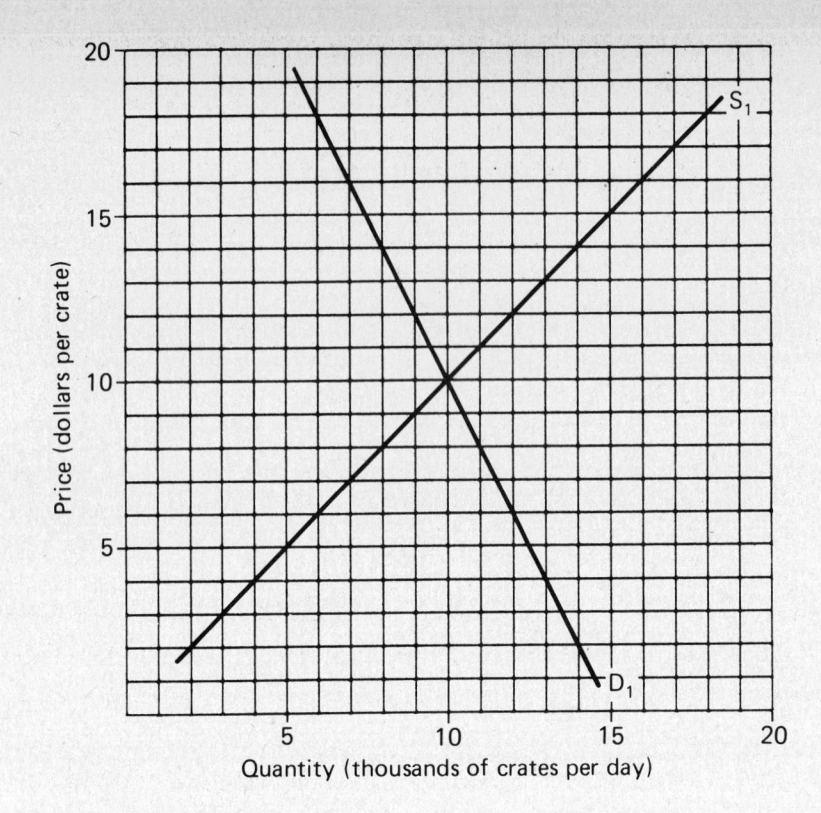

c. Beginning from the point reached in your answer to part b of this problem, suppose a fad for bean sprout salad cuts the demand for lettuce, so that people are now willing to buy only half the lettuce, at any given price, that they would have bought before. What will happen to the equilibrium price and quantity of lettuce? Draw in new supply and/or demand curves, as needed, to illustrate the new situation, labeling the new curve or curves and the new equilibrium with the subscript 3.

d. As the sprout fad cuts lettuce farmers' income, they send a delegation to Washington asking for a bail-out. Congress responds by imposing an $8 per crate minimum price for lettuce, agreeing to buy all surplus lettuce that farmers can't sell for $8 a crate, using it to make salads for the armed forces. How much lettuce will the government have to buy to stabilize the price at $8 per crate? How much will the government have to spend on lettuce? How much more lettuce will be produced than if the price floor had not been imposed?

DON'T MAKE THIS COMMON MISTAKE

The most common mistake on tests covering supply and demand is to mix up shifts in the curves with movements along the curves. Suppose you know, from common sense, that some event will cause people to buy more gasoline. How do you know which curves are shifting and which ones are being moved along? Ask yourself the following key questions:

1. Would the event in question make people buy more *even if the price of gasoline did not change*? If so, the demand curve is *shifting rightward* (that is, there is an *increase in demand*).
2. Does the event in question make people buy more *only because* the price is driven down? If so, there is a *movement downward along* an unchanged demand curve (that is, an increase in quantity demanded).

The same questions can also be asked about the reasons why suppliers decide to sell more. Here are some examples:

Example 1: Airline fares go up, causing many people to drive instead of fly on vacation trips. Analysis: With air fares up, people would use more gas *even if* the price of gasoline did not change. Thus, the demand curve is *shifting rightward*. This shift will, in turn, cause an increase in the price as the market moves along its supply curve. Oil companies will produce and sell more gasoline *only because* the price goes up. There is a movement upward along an unchanged supply curve.

Example 2: A price war among Arab oil producers pushes the price of crude oil down. Analysis: This event will affect gasoline buying habits only because the cut in the crude oil price will be passed through to motorists as a cut in retail gasoline prices. Your diagram should show a downward shift in the supply curve, which then causes a movement along the demand curve.

ECONOMICS IN THE NEWS

U.S. Uranium Mines Are Nearing Extinction

Grants, New Mexico used to be the Pittsburgh of uranium. In 1980, thousands of men working dozens of area mines dug out a third of U.S. production and, on pay of $35,000 to $70,000 a year and sometimes more, spent like kings. They bought Cadillacs, Lincolns, boats and pickups galore. They drank and fought their way from the Pioneer to Pat's Bar, sometimes finishing a raucous night by mowing down a few light stanchions on bustling Santa Fe Avenue.

Today, every mine but one is closed. Pat's is closed. The Lux theater is closed, its marquee blank and broken. Some 200 homes stand vacant. In the Uranium Cafe, dust settles over stacked-up chairs and tables, and a deadly silence has settled over Santa Fe Avenue. Says Mark Lautman, an industrial developer trying to bring new business to a shrinking Grants: "The game is over. Uranium is history."

Much the same thing is happening across the West as the domestic uranium business plunges toward extinction. The industry has been hammered by an enormous glut of uranium that still overhangs non-Communist world markets and probably won't be worked off for 3 to 5 years. The oversupply has already sent spot prices for uranium plummeting from $40 per pound in January 1980 to $15 today—less than half the current cost of producing the metal in the U.S.

Antipathy toward nuclear power after Three Mile Island is only one reason. In the early 1970s, utilities ordered nuclear plants by the fistful to meet electricity demand that they expected to double in 10 years. Even after energy conservation began to short-circuit their forecasts, they were slow to see this.

The uranium glut isn't affecting foreign producers nearly as much. They have the advantages of a strong U.S. dollar, which helps them sell here, and of recently developed deposits so rich—and consequently so cheap to exploit—that domestic mines can't come close to matching them.

Source: William E. Blundell, "Nuclear Reaction: U.S. Uranium Mines, Thriving Five Years Ago, Are Nearing Extinction," *The Wall Street Journal*, June 12, 1985, p. 1. Reprinted by permission of The Wall Street Journal. ©Dow Jones & Company, Inc., 1985. All Rights Reserved.

Questions

1. Would the antipathy to nuclear power and the effects of electric power conservation best be represented by a shift in the demand curve for uranium, or a movement along the curve? If the demand curve would shift, which way would it shift? Would the effects of these changes in public attitudes best be represented by a movement along the supply curve, or by a shift in the curve? If the supply curve would shift, which way would it shift? Taken by themselves, what would these changes have done to the price of uranium and to the quantity used in the United States? Sketch a diagram illustrating your answers.
2. Would the discovery of new low-cost foreign sources of uranium and the effects of the strong U.S. dollar best be represented by a shift in the demand curve for uranium, or a movement along the curve? If the demand curve would shift, which way would it shift? Would the effects of these discoveries best be represented by a movement along the supply curve, or by a shift in the curve? If the supply curve would shift, which way would it shift? Taken by themselves, what would these changes have done to the price of uranium and to the quantity used in the United States? Sketch a diagram illustrating your answers.

SELF TEST

These sample test items will help you check how much you have learned. Answers are found at the end of the chapter. Scoring yourself: One or two wrong—on target. Three or four wrong—passing, but you haven't mastered the chapter yet. Five or more wrong—not good enough; start over and restudy the chapter.

___D___ 1. The "other things being equal" clause in the law of demand covers
   a. consumer incomes.
   b. the prices of other goods.
   c. consumer tastes and preferences.
   d. all of the above.

___D___ 2. A rise in the price of coffee is likely to have which of the following initial effects on the market for tea, a substitute?
   a. A movement up along the tea demand curve.
   b. A downward movement along the tea demand curve.
   c. A leftward shift in the tea demand curve.
   d. A rightward shift in the tea demand curve.

___C___ 3. If consumer incomes go up, which of the following is initially most likely?
   a. An upward movement along the demand curve for cars.
   b. A downward movement along the demand curve for cars.
   c. A rightward shift in the demand curve for cars.
   d. A leftward shift in the demand curve for cars.

___B___ 4. Assuming gasoline and tires to be complementary goods, the initial effect on the tire market of an increase in the price of gasoline (other things being equal) would best be described as
   a. an increase in the demand for tires.
   b. a decrease in the demand for tires.
   c. an increase in the quantity of tires demanded.
   d. a decrease in the quantity of tires demanded.

___A___ 5. If the price of leather rises, other things being equal, which of the following would be the most likely initial effect?
   a. An upward shift of the shoe supply curve.
   b. A downward shift of the shoe supply curve.
   c. An upward movement along the shoe supply curve.
   d. A downward movement along the shoe supply curve.

___D___ 6. Market equilibrium
   a. is represented graphically by the intersection of the supply and demand curves.
   b. is the condition under which the plans of buyers and sellers exactly mesh when tested in the market.
   c. is the condition under which neither buyers nor sellers have an incentive to change their plans.
   d. includes all of the above.

___A___ 7. Using QS to indicate quantity supplied and QD to indicate quantity demanded, which of the following circumstances would be likely to produce an upward movement of the price of a good?
   a. QS = 100, QD = 200.
   b. QS = 100, QD = 100.
   c. QS = 200, QD = 100.
   d. Not enough information given for an answer.

59

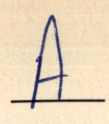

_A_   8. An increase in the cost of raising hogs, other things being equal, would be likely to affect the price of bacon via
   a. an upward shift of the supply curve.
   b. an upward shift of the demand curve.
   c. a downward shift of the supply curve.
   d. a downward shift of the demand curve.

_C_   9. An increase in the price of beef increases the demand for pork. Restoration of equilibrium in the pork market will require
   a. an upward shift of the supply curve.
   b. a downward shift of the supply curve.
   c. a movement up along the supply curve.
   d. a movement down along the supply curve.

_C_   10. Suppose intercity bus travel to be an inferior good. An increase in consumer incomes, other things being equal, is likely to cause which of the following?
   a. A shift in the demand curve and a higher price.
   b. A shift in the supply curve and a higher price.
   c. A shift in the demand curve and a lower price.
   d. A shift in the supply curve and a lower price.

_D_   11. If the steelworkers' union negotiates a new contract with sharply higher wages, we would expect, once a new equilibrium is reached in the steel market,
   a. a shortage of steel.
   b. a decrease in the demand for steel.
   c. a decrease in the price of steel.
   d. a decrease in the quantity of steel demanded.

_D_   12. During a visit to Moscow, you notice long lines outside every butcher shop. The most reasonable conclusion to be drawn from this observation is that
   a. meat is very expensive in the Soviet Union.
   b. citizens of the Soviet Union are insatiable carnivores.
   c. the clerks in Soviet stores work very slowly.
   d. the price of meat is held below the equilibrium price.

_~~B~~ D_   13. If the equilibrium price of natural gas is $2.50 per thousand cubic feet and a price ceiling is imposed of $3 per thousand cubic feet, the likely result will be
   a. a surplus.
   b. a shortage.
   c. a depletion of inventories.
   d. none of the above.

_A ~~B~~_   14. According to supply and demand analysis, the likely effect of a minimum wage law would be
   a. a shortage of jobs for low-skill workers.
   b. a shortage of workers to fill low-skill jobs.
   c. increased incomes for all low-skill workers.
   d. decreased incomes for all low-skill workers.

B 15. If the equilibrium price of sugar is 15 cents per pound and the government imposes a minimum price of 20 cents per pound, the likely result will be
   a. a shortage of sugar.
   b. a surplus of sugar.
   c. a depletion of sugar inventories.
   d. none of the above.

ANSWERS TO CHAPTER 3

Hands On

Problem 1   (a) The equilibrium price is $1.20 and the equilibrium quantity is 160 million board feet per year. (b) The demand curve shifts rightward to D_2. The price rises to $1.60 per board foot and the equilibrium quantity expands to 200 million board feet per year. (c) The cost reduction shifts the supply curve downward to S_3. The equilibrium price is now $1.20 and the equilibrium quantity is 220 million board feet per year. Check your work against the solution graph.

Exhibit 3.1 (ans.)

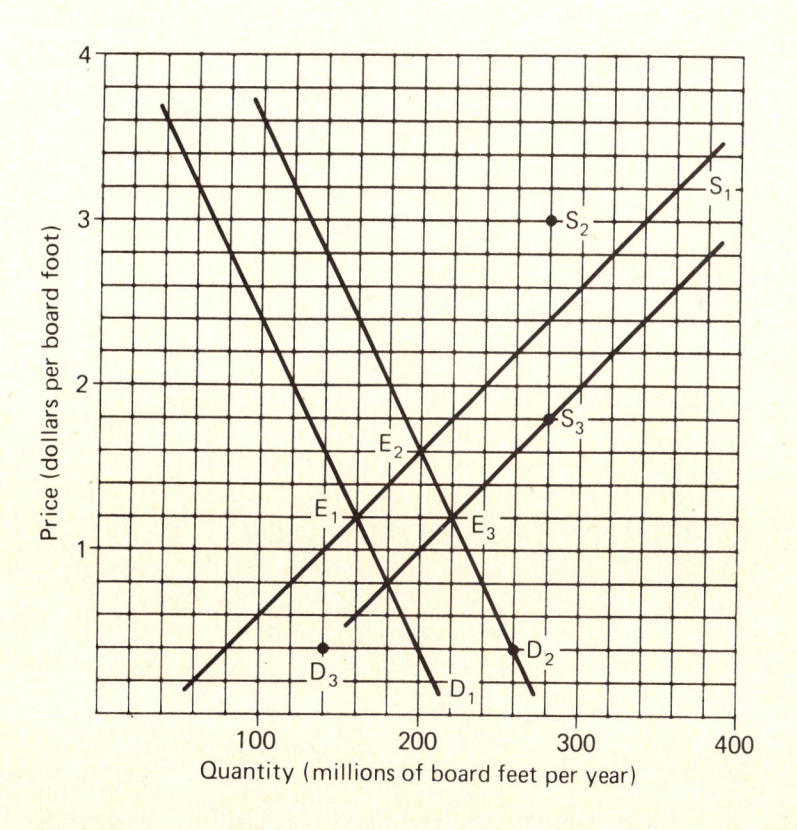

Problem 2   (a) The initial equilibrium price is $14 per gallon and the equilibrium quantity is 80 million gallons per year. (b) Without the price ceiling, the price would rise to $18 per gallon and the equilibrium quantity would rise to 100 million gallons per year. With the ceiling, the price will stay at $14 and there will be a shortage of 30

million gallons per year as the quantity supplied stays at 80 million gallons per year. (c) If the quantity produced remains at 80 million gallons per year, the black market price could rise as high as $26 per gallon. This is the height of the demand curve D2 at the quantity of 80 million gallons per year.

Problem 3 (a) Equilibrium price is 10 cents per pound and equilibrium quantity is 200 million pounds per month. (b) Cane sugar is a substitute for corn sweetener, so an increase in its price shifts the corn sweetener demand curve to the right, as shown by D2 in the solution graph. The supply curve does not shift. The new equilibrium is at E2. (c) An increase in production costs shifts the supply curve upward to the position S3 in the solution graph. This is far enough to raise the equilibrium price to 15 cents a pound, as shown by point E3. The demand curve remains at D2.

Exhibit 3.3 (ans.)

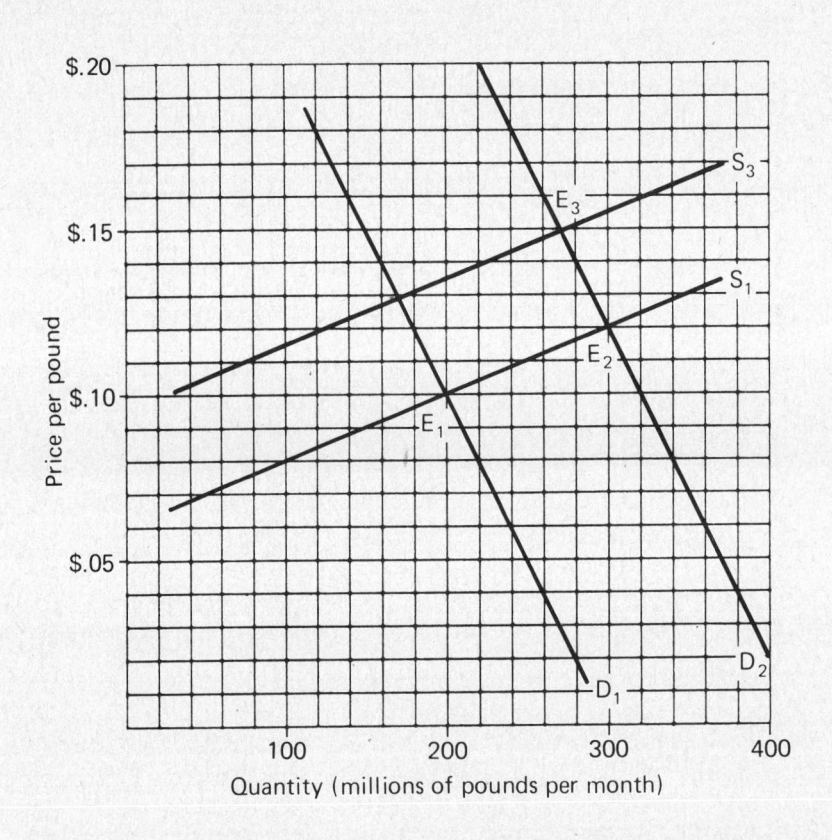

Problem 4 (a) Equilibrium quantity is initially 10,000 crates per day and the equilibrium price is $10 per crate. (b) A $3 per crate decrease in production costs shifts the supply curve straight down by $3, as shown by the supply curve S2 in the solution graph. The new equilibrium is at E2, where the price is $8 per crate. (c) The fad for bean sprout salad (a lettuce substitute) shifts the demand curve to the left, as shown by D3 in the solution graph. D3 lies halfway between D1 and the vertical axis. The supply curve remains at S2. The equilibrium price falls to about $3.50 per crate and the equilibrium quantity falls to about 6,500 crates per day. (d) At the $8 support price, quantity demanded will be 5,500 crates per day, and quantity supplied will be 11,000 crates; the government will thus have to buy 5,500 crates per day at a cost of $44,000 per day.

Exhibit 3.4 (ans.)

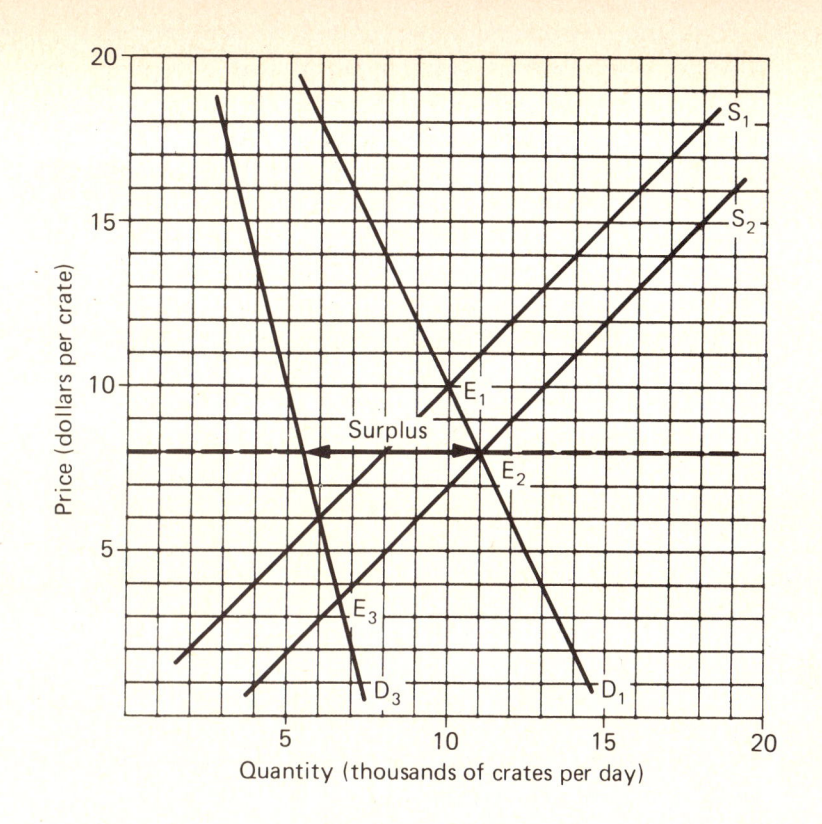

Quantity produced will be 4,500 crates per day above what it would be without the price support. Check your work against the solution graph.

Economics in the News

(1) The effects of the shift in public attitudes would cause the demand curve to shift to the left. There would be a movement along the supply curve with no shift in that curve. Taken by themselves, these changes would have caused the price of uranium to fall.
(2) The discovery of new low-cost sources of uranium would cause the supply curve of uranium, as seen by U.S. buyers, to shift to the right. So would the high value of the dollar, because that also means that U.S. buyers can purchase a given quantity of imported uranium for less. There would be a movement along the demand curve. This factor alone (without the conservation mentioned in part one of the question) would have caused the price to fall and the total quantity demanded to increase. However, the quantity of U.S.-mined uranium would decrease because of stiffer competition from imports.

Self Test

1. **d.** Changes in expectations are also covered.
2. **d.** Because coffee and tea are substitutes.
3. **c.** Assuming that cars are normal goods.
4. **b.** That is, a leftward shift in the demand curve for tires.
5. **a.** Input costs are one of the factors that can shift the supply curve.
6. **d.** These are three ways of expressing the same concept.

7. **a.** An excess quantity demanded (shortage) causes the price to rise.
8. **a.** An increase in costs shifts the supply curve upward.
9. **c.** The demand curve shifts to the right while the supply curve stays in place.
10. **c.** The demand curve will shift to the left.
11. **d.** The supply curve will shift up, resulting in a movement along the demand curve.
12. **d.** Persistent lines are one result of a price ceiling.
13. **d.** A price ceiling above the equilibrium price will have no effect on the market.
14. **a.** A minimum wage is a price floor. There will be an excess quantity of labor offered, which means a job shortage.
15. **b.** A minimum price above the equilibrium price will cause a surplus.

Chapter 4

The Role of Business

WHERE YOU'RE GOING

When you have mastered this chapter, you will understand

1. Why business firms exist in so many different sizes and organizational forms.
2. Why all the business in an economy cannot be handled by one big firm.
3. What can be learned by looking at a firm's balance sheet.
4. The role that financial markets play in the economy.
5. What lies behind headlines dealing with corporate control, takeovers, and insider trading.

In addition, you will add the following terms to your economic vocabulary:
    Sole proprietorship
    Partnership
    Corporation
    Market coordination
    Managerial coordination
    Transaction costs
    Balance sheet
    Assets
    Liabilities
    Net worth
    Owners' equity
    Financial markets
    Direct financing
    Bond
    Common stock
    Financial intermediaries
    Indirect financing
    Primary financial markets
    Secondary financial markets

WALKING TOUR

After you have read this chapter at least once, you should work step by step through this walking tour. Fill in the blanks and answer the questions as you go along. After you have answered each question, check yourself by uncovering the answer given in the margin. If you do not understand why the answer given is the correct one, refer back to the proper section of the text.

Forms of Business Organization

Firms differ in terms of legal form of organization. A firm owned and managed by one person is known as a _____. The owner of such a firm is subject to [limited/unlimited] liability. A firm owned jointly by two or more people, each of whom retains unlimited liability, is known as a _____. A firm having ownership divided into many _____ with each shareholder having [limited/unlimited] liability, is known as a _____. Corporations are the most suitable form of organization for [large/small] business and account for about 85 percent of the receipts of all business firms in the U.S. economy.

Margin answers: sole proprietorship; unlimited; partnership; shares; limited; corporation; large

Coordinating Economic Activity

Two major forms of coordinating economic activity are used in the U.S. economy. Market coordination relies on the market to transmit _____ and to provide the necessary _____. Managerial coordination relies on _____ for communication and relies, for incentives, on the fact that subordinates have pledged obedience, at least within certain limits, as a condition of employment. For each of the following tasks, which form of organization would be more appropriate?

Margin answers: information, incentives; directives

- Deciding which worker sweeps the floors and which washes the windows: _____.   *managerial*
- Deciding whether a clothing firm should specialize in coats or dresses: _____.   *market*
- Deciding how investment funds should be divided between farming and industry: _____.   *market*
- Deciding which plant of a multiplant auto firm should specialize in trucks: _____.   *managerial*

As a general principle, a firm finds it worthwhile to expand its operations only to the point where the managerial costs of organizing one more task within the firm equal the _____ costs of organizing the same task outside the firm through the market.

Financing Private Business

The things that a firm owns, such as cash, inventories, property, plant, and equipment, are known as its _____. They are listed on the [right-hand/left-hand] side of the firm's balance sheet. Claims against the firm by nonowners, such as accounts payable and long-term debt, are known as _____. They are listed on the [right-hand/left-hand] side of the firm's balance sheet. If a firm has assets of, say, $15 million and liabilities of $12 million, it is said to have net worth of $_____ million. Net worth, representing owners' claims against the firm, is listed on the [right-hand/left-hand] side of the balance sheet. Another name for net worth is _____.

In order to purchase additional assets as it grows, a firm must raise new capital funds. It can do this in a number of ways. First, if the firm is earning a profit, it can retain part of the profit to purchase new assets, rather than paying it all out to its owners. If it does this, its [net worth/liabilities] will rise dollar for dollar with its increase in assets. Alternatively, the firm can turn to financial markets. If it raises capital funds by selling stocks, bonds, or short-term obligations to households, it is said to engage in [direct/indirect] financing. Sales of bonds increase the firm's [net worth/liabilities], whereas sales of new shares of stock increase the firm's [net worth/liabilities]. Alternatively, the firm can borrow money from institutions such as banks, savings and loan associations, or insurance companies. These institutions are known as _____. When firms raise funds through such institutions, they are said to engage in [direct/indirect] financing.

Markets in which stocks, bonds, and other securities are traded among investors after they have originally been issued are known as _____ financial markets.

transactions

assets
left-hand

liabilities
right-hand

3

right-hand
owners' equity

net worth

direct
liabilities

net worth

financial intermediaries

indirect

secondary

Corporate Control, Takeovers, and Insider Trading

In a corporation, managers are _____ who are supposed to serve their _____, the stockholders. If they are to do so in fact, they must be given the proper incentives. One way to do this is through some type of profit-sharing plan, such as _____. An even more powerful reason for managers to heed stockholders' interests is the threat of a _____.

Some economists are critical of takeovers. They say that many takeovers burden corporations with excessive [debt/equity]. Some defensive strategies, such as "poison pills," may also injure the firm. Finally, say the critics, the threat of takeover forces managers to pay too much attention to [short-run/long-run] profits. However, many other economists defend takeovers as a necessary tool to ensure that managers do their jobs of serving stockholders.

Takeovers sometimes also raise the issue of illegal _____. The case against insider trading is based on the notion that all traders in secondary markets should have equal access to information. Those who think the practice of insider trading to be not so harmful point to the fact that such trading moves stock prices in the [right/wrong] direction.

Margin terms: agents, principals, stock options, takeover, debt, short-run, insider trading, right

---

ECONOMICS IN THE NEWS

Cable Systems to Merge

Continental Cablevision Inc., the third-largest U.S. cable television company, said it signed a definitive agreement to acquire American Cablesystems Inc. for $46.50 a share, or about $481.7 million.

The acquisition is the latest example of the continuing consolidation in the cable industry.

American Cablesystems shares, which have been trading between $27 and $30 lately, soared to close at $42.50, up $16.125, in American Stock Exchange composite trading yesterday.

Steven Dodge, chairman of Beverly, Massachusetts-based American Cablesystems, said cable companies want to grow because bigger companies get better prices when they buy programming. "Continental has materially better programming contracts," he said, adding "They will be the beneficiary of improved cash flow the day they acquire our company. Dodge added that cable companies benefit by increasing their presence in a given market, spreading overhead costs over more customers.

Continental said it will finance the American Cablesystems acquisition with bank debt.

Source: David Wessel, "Continental Cablevision Signs Accord To Acquire American Cablesystems, Inc.," *The Wall Street Journal*, October 15, 1987, p. 7. Reprinted by permission of The Wall Street Journal. © Dow Jones & Company, Inc., 1987. All Rights Reserved.

Questions

1. What factors propel the growth of cable television firms? What factors limit their growth? For example, why do you think cable television systems usually buy programming from networks, independent studios, and others rather than producing their own programs?
2. How will the acquisition described in this news items affect the balance sheet of Continental Cablevision?
3. Dodge, chairman of American, owns a substantial amount of stock in the company. Do you think his ownership of stock by Dodge beneficial or harmful to American's other stockholders in this case? Discuss.
4. Suppose Jill, a member of Continental's management, mentions the proposed merger to Joe, her boyfriend, a few days before the merger is to be announced. How could Joe profit from this inside information? Who might be harmed by Joe's actions? Who might benefit from them?

SELF TEST

These sample test items will help you check how much you have learned. Answers are found at the end of the chapter. Scoring yourself: One or two wrong—on target. Three or four wrong—passing, but you haven't mastered the chapter yet. Five or more wrong—not good enough; start over and restudy the chapter.

_____ 1. War in the Middle East creates an oil shortage; rising oil prices cause consumers to shift to more abundant natural gas. This is an example of
   a. managerial coordination.
   b. central planning.
   c. consumer exploitation.
   d. market coordination.

_____ 2. Which of the following is not an advantage of the sole proprietorship?
   a. Unlimited life of the firm.
   b. Ownership and control in a single person.
   c. Lower taxes than corporations in many circumstances.
   d. Easy to set up and liquidate.

_____ 3. Which of the following is an advantage of the partnership, compared with the sole proprietorship?
   a. Limited liability.
   b. Can draw on a wider range of skills than a single owner.
   c. Easy for one partner to get in and out.
   d. All of the above.

_____ 4. The fact that corporate stockholders normally cannot lose more than they invested in their firm
   a. is a result of the separation of ownership and control.
   b. is known as limited liability.
   c. puts them on an equal footing with partners in a partnership.
   d. offsets the fact that corporations pay lower taxes than other business forms.

_____ 5. Total liabilities plus net worth must equal
   a. accounts receivable.
   b. liquid assets.
   c. total debt.
   d. total assets.

_____ 6. The XYZ corporation needs to build a new plant. To finance the plant, it sells new common stock to households. The entire set of actions increases
   a. the firm's assets only.
   b. the firm's assets and liabilities.
   c. the firm's assets and net worth.
   d. the firm's liabilities and net worth only.

_____ 7. Mr. Zarnow has enough shares of Z Corp. just barely to give him a majority vote at annual meetings. If he opposes financing a new plant by selling new common stock to the public, his reason might be that the action
   a. would increase the firm's liabilities.
   b. would reduce his voting power below a majority.
   c. would represent indirect financing, which he dislikes.
   d. any of the above might be his reason; we can't tell.

_____ 8. Which of the following is a financial intermediary?
   a. A law firm specializing in corporate takeovers.
   b. A savings and loan association.
   c. A Wall Street speculator.
   d. All of the above.

_____ 9. Financial intermediaries
   a. list debts of net borrowers as their assets.
   b. list assets of net savers as their liabilities.
   c. channel funds from net savers to net borrowers.
   d. All of the above.

_____ 10. Ownership of even one share of a corporation's common stock entitles the stockholder
   a. to attend all meetings of the board of directors.
   b. to have a vote in electing the board of directors.
   c. to receive an annual or semiannual dividend fixed in nominal terms.
   d. None of the above.

_____ 11. Corporations or individuals who specialize in taking over other corporations by buying up their stock on the open market would, in determining their next purchase, look for a firm that is
   a. managed exceptionally well.
   b. managed about average.
   c. managed poorly but has lots of potential.
   d. managed well, but nearly ready for bankruptcy because of circumstances beyond its control.

_____ 12. If you were a manager wanting to insulate yourself from the constant pressure of profit-hungry stockholders, you might be happy to get
  a. part of your salary paid in stock options.
  b. news that a big corporation is planning to buy your firm.
  c. a law passed in your state making takeovers more difficult.
  d. Any of the above would be welcome.

_____ 13. Which of the following is an argument often made by critics of corporate takeovers?
  a. They burden corporations with excessive equity.
  b. Defensive strategies such as "poison pills" can be harmful to stockholders.
  c. They cause managers to neglect their responsibilities to maximize short-run profits.
  d. All of the above are frequently made arguments.

_____ 14. Managers are to stockholders as
  a. tender offers are to proxies.
  b. insider trading is to profits.
  c. debt is to equity.
  d. agents are to principals.

_____ 15. On June 1, Burbank Corp. will announce a takeover of Santa Raymona, Inc., at a price of $40 per share, double Santa Raymona's previous market value of $20. On May 20, Wilfred Spock learns about the deal and starts buying thousands of shares of Santa Raymona stock. Which of the following holders of Santa Raymona stock will be made worse off by Spock's insider trading?
  a. Alice, who sells to Spock on May 22 at $25, and who otherwise would have held her shares until after June 1.
  b. Bill, who sells to Spock on May 24th at $26 per share in order to raise cash for the closing on the purchase of his new house, scheduled to take place May 25.
  c. Chandler, who buys on May 19 at $20 and holds his shares until after June 1.
  d. All of the above will be made worse off.

ANSWERS TO CHAPTER 4

Economics in the News

(1) As in Coase's theory, firms grow so long as they can coordinate tasks by managerial means more effectively than by market means. For example, a larger firm is evidently able to coordinate bargaining with sellers of programming more effectively, and is able to serve subscribers at lower cost by spreading overhead. However, trying to run a good cable operation and at the same time to manage studios producing original programming would apparently strain the capabilities of management coordination. The transactions costs of negotiating for programming with outsiders are less

than the management costs of doing the same work in house. (2) Immediately, it will add American's assets to Continental's balance sheets, and at the same time, add a corresponding amount of bank debt to its liabilities. If the merger increases profit in the long run and the profits are retained by the firm, equity will then also grow. (3) The prospect of selling his own stock at an advantageous price will make Dodge bargain hard for the best possible deal from Continental. If Dodge held no American stock, he might prefer to keep the company independent, if he thought being chairman of an independent company was more prestigious than taking a job offered to him by Continental. (4) Joe could profit if he bought American stock at its market price, so long as the market price was below about $46.50 a share. People who would have held their stock instead of selling to Joe might suffer. However, if Joe's buying bids the price up before the merger is announced (as insider trading tends to do), then people who would have sold just before the merger will be better off selling to Joe than selling at the previous market price.

Self Test

1. **d.** No one issues a directive to make the switch from one fuel to the other.
2. **a.** The proprietorship's life is limited to that of the owner.
3. **b.** Answers **a** and **c** are not true of a partnership.
4. **b.** Proprietorships and partnerships do not have limited liability.
5. **d.** Net worth is defined as assets minus liabilities.
6. **c.** The plant is an asset, and the stock reflects an increase in net worth.
7. **b.** The sale of stock would not increase liabilities, and it is a form of direct financing.
8. **b.** A financial intermediary channels funds from savers to borrowers; **a** and **c** do not do this.
9. **d.** Answers **a** and **b** are a reflection of the activity **c**.
10. **b.** Of course, in a large corporation it would require many shares to have an effective voice in choosing the directors.
11. **c.** The new owner would hope to replace the old management with new management that would raise profits, and hence the firm's stock price.
12. **c.** Answers **a** and **b** are measures to increase management's attention to profit.
13. **b.** Critics say that takeovers may burden the corporation with excessive *debt*, and cause managers to pay *too much* attention to short-run profits.
14. **d.** Managers are supposed to act as servants hired by stockholders to serve stockholders' interests.
15. **a.** Bill would be made better off by the insider trading, and Chandler would not be affected one way or the other.

Chapter 5

The Role of Government

WHERE YOU'RE GOING

When you have mastered this chapter, you will understand

1. How large the government sector of the U.S. economy is.
2. Why government action is needed to control pollution.
3. Why the Army, Navy, and Air Force are not private firms.
4. Why the government does not leave the questions of what, how, and for whom entirely to the market.
5. Why some government programs seem designed to enrich private firms and individuals rather than promote the goals of efficiency and fairness.
6. Which government roles might be turned over to the private sector.

In addition, you will add the following terms to your economic vocabulary:
  Government purchases of goods and services (government purchases)
  Transfer payments
  Market failure
  Externality
  Common property
  Public good
  Merit good
  Economic rent
  Rent seeking
  Privatization

WALKING TOUR

After you have read this chapter at least once, you should work step by step through this walking tour. Fill in the blanks and answer the questions as you go along. After you have answered each question, check yourself by uncovering the answer given in the margin. If you do not understand why the answer given is the correct one, refer back to the proper section of the text.

Government in the U.S. Economy

The total of all goods bought by governments plus the costs of hiring services of government employees and contractors is known as

government purchases of goods and services	_____, for short. The level of government purchases, expressed as a percentage of GNP, has
remained constant	[grown/remained constant] over the past 25 years. As of 1986,
20	government purchases accounted for about _____ percent of GNP.
	Payments made by government to individuals, not in return for current services, are known as _____. The level of trans-
transfer payments	
grown	fer payments, measured as a percentage of GNP has [grown/ remained constant] over the past 25 years. In 1960, transfer pay-
5	ments accounted for about _____ percent of GNP. By
15	1986, they accounted for about _____ percent.
income security	The largest item of federal expenditure is _____, fol-
national defense	lowed by _____. For state and local governments, the
education	largest expenditure item is _____. The largest source of
personal income tax	revenue for the federal government is _____, followed
social security, sales	by the _____ tax. For state governments, _____ taxes are the largest source of revenue, and for local governments,
property taxes	_____.

The Economic Role of Government

According to one theory, the role of government is to compensate for instances in which the market does not meet accepted standards of

market failures	efficiency or fairness—that is, for _____. For example, in order to do their job properly, market prices should reflect
opportunity	_____ costs. They do not do this in cases where the actions of producers or consumers have effects on third parties that
externalities	are not reflected in prices. These effects are called _____. For example, when a firm's production process causes pollution, the
below	price of its product will tend to be [below/above] opportunity cost. Another example of an externality can occur when all members of a
common	community have open access to _____ property.

A second category of market failure concerns goods that cannot be provided for one person without also being provided to others, and also can be provided to others at zero cost once they have been

public	provided to one person. These are known as _____
difficult	goods. It is [difficult/impossible] for private firms to make a profit providing goods having the characteristics of public goods.

74

insufficient	A third example of market failure is [excessive/insufficient] competition. If competition is insufficient, market prices may [exceed/fall short of] opportunity costs.
exceed	
	Some people consider unfairness in the distribution of income a type of market failure. Finally, [macro-/micro-] economic problems such as excessive inflation and unemployment are sometimes considered examples of market failure.
macro-	
	The market failure theory of government, which asks what government ought to do, is a [normative/positive] theory. An alternative theory is based on the notion of _____. A rent means a payment to a factor of production than [exceeds/falls short of] its opportunity cost. Firms may seek rents by way of [entrepreneurship/government/both]. Rent seeking often results in [government/market] failure.
normative	
rent seeking	
exceeds	
both	
government	

Privatization

government	Privatization means turning over _____ functions to private firms, either through a change of _____ or through _____. The United States [is/is not] one of the world leaders in privatization. The perceived benefits of privatization include
ownership	
contracting, is not	
political advantages	1. _____,
improved administration	2. _____,
cost saving	3. _____,
suppression of rent seeking	4. _____, and
improved service quality	5. _____.

ECONOMICS IN THE NEWS

Doubled Cigarette Tax Would Aid Health, Economy

The good news about cigarette smoking is that 30 million smokers have quit and millions have not started.

In 1964, when medical evidence of the physical damage caused by smoking surfaced, 42 percent of Americans smoked. The current figure is 24 percent.

The bad news is that an estimated 350,000 Americans die each year of diseases caused or aggravated by smoking.

President Reagan and Congress are wrestling with tax ideas. One is to double the federal tax on cigarettes, which has been

8 cents a pack since 1952. In addition to raising revenue, the tax hike would bring an estimated 5 percent drop in cigarette consumption.

The National Bureau of Economic Research makes this estimate. It is more significant than it first appears because young people are more sensitive to price than adults. Fifteen percent fewer young males would start smoking in the long run, the study estimates.

Robert Rodale, editor of Prevention magazine and a tireless voice for common sense in health matters, wants a charge of 88 cents added to each pack.

He calculates that smoking costs the American economy $26.9 billion a year, and that 88 cents a pack would cover that cost.

Rodale has written for years about the human toll in cancer, emphysema, and heart disease caused by smoking. Now he is taking a pragmatic approach. Like all of us, he is concerned about the relentless march of hospital rooms toward $1,000 a day. (One Chicago hospital is at $775 a day for a bed in the intensive care unit.)

"Because of that economic problem, we need to give ourselves more weapons against smoking than the standard approach of pointing a finger and saying 'You are killing yourself!'" says Rodale.

"Many smokers *know* they are shortening their lives by continuing the habit.... Nine out of 10 adult cigarette smokers would like to quit if they could.

"A steep rise in the cost of cigarettes would be welcomed by some as a further inducement to stop, and would be accepted by some others as a way to put an economic burden where it belongs."

These are Rodale's calculations: Each adult American is paying $174.65 a year in added insurance payments, doctors' fees and related costs because of smokers.

In 1980, Americans smoked 611 billion cigarettes—more than 30 billion packs—which cost their buyers about $19.3 billion.

No price tag can be put on the human suffering caused by fires started by smokers, but the property destruction attributed to cigarette misuse is at least $293 million a year.

Business and industry pay $12.8 billion a year as the cost of employees missing work because of smoking-related illnesses and the extra money life insurance companies pay out when smokers die or become prematurely disabled.

The hospital and doctors' charges for patients with smoker-related diseases is $20.3 billion a year. With our system of third-party payment for health problems, all of us pick up this bill through our monthly payroll deductions for health insurance, through taxes, or through direct payments to Blue Cross and private insurers.

There are a few more odd millions added to the tab. The administrative structure operating the U.S. government's loan program to tobacco growers costs taxpayers $14 million a year.

And Washington spends $2 million a year trying to persuade people not to smoke.

Most of us have learned by now, says Rodale, that some things about the way this world operates simply aren't fair, and one of those things is the way non-smokers have to help pay for the harm that smokers do to themselves and to property.

"Medical costs are rising at 10.7 percent, and no one has much hope they can be brought into line," says Rodale.

"There is also in our population a big group of still-healthy middle-aged smokers who soon will be taking their cancerous lungs to operating rooms. In a few years they will then be signing receipts for hospital rooms costing one or two thousand dollars a day, and all of us will be paying insurance premiums as big as today's rental cost of a luxury apartment.

"Let's not let that happen."

Source: "Doubled Cigarette Tax Would Aid Health, Economy," *Chicago Tribune*, February 17, 1982, sec. 1, p. 9. © *Chicago Tribune*, 1982. Used with permission.

Questions

1. Which of the costs of cigarette smoking that are cited in the article can be considered externalities? Can you think of any externalities of cigarette smoking that are not mentioned in the article?
2. Would the imposition of an $.88-per-pack cigarette tax best be viewed in terms of the market failure theory of government, in terms of the rent seeking theory, or partly in terms of both? Discuss.
3. A tax is one means that could be used to internalize the externalities of cigarette smoking. Can you think of other ways that some or all of the externalities could be internalized?

SELF TEST

These sample test items will help you check how much you have learned. Answers are found at the end of the chapter. Scoring yourself: One or two wrong—on target. Three or four wrong—passing, but you haven't mastered the chapter yet. Five or more wrong—not good enough; start over and restudy the chapter.

_____ 1. As of 1986, government purchases were about what percent of GNP in the United States?
   a. 10 percent.
   b. 20 percent.
   c. 30 percent.
   d. 40 percent.

_____ 2. Government transfer payments in the United States
   a. equal more than half of government purchases.
   b. are about the same as government purchases.
   c. are about twice as large as government purchases.
   d. are well over twice as large as government purchases.

_____ 3. Public housing
   a. is a public good because taxes pay for it.
   b. is a public good because everyone deserves a fair minimum standard of housing.
   c. is not a public good because people can easily be excluded from living in it.
   d. is not a public good because more can be added at zero cost.

_____ 4. Which of the following was the second largest category of federal expenditure as of 1986?
   a. Income security.
   b. National defense.
   c. Education.
   d. Interest on the national debt.

_____ 5. Which of the following was the largest source of federal revenue as of 1986?
   a. The personal income tax.
   b. The corporate income tax.
   c. Social security contributions.
   d. Federal sales and excise taxes.

_____ 6. Which of the following would not be considered an example of market failure?
   a. Pollution from a paper mill ruins a recreational fishing area.
   b. A public beach becomes so crowded that one can't find room to sit down.
   c. The price of building lots in a growing city rises because a great many developers compete for space to build new houses.
   d. All of the above are market failures.

_____ 7. Before the 1987 football strike, Henry Williams was earning $1,000 a week as a stockbroker. During the strike, he earned $3,000 a week as a replacement linesman for the Washington Redskins. How much of the $3,000 could be considered economic rent?
   a. All of it.
   b. $2,000.
   c. $1,000.
   d. None of it.

_____ 8. Pollution from a steel mill causes health problems to people who live downwind. Which of the following are the "third parties" referred to in the definition of externality?
   a. The people who live downwind.
   b. Owners of the mill.
   c. Buyers of steel.
   d. All three of the above are the third parties.

_____ 9. Which of the following types of market failure is thought to keep the market price of some goods higher than opportunity cost?
   a. Pollution.
   b. Insufficient competition.
   c. Both of the above.
   d. Neither of the above.

_____ 10. A "merit good" is one that
   a. has a market price higher than its opportunity cost.
   b. has a market price below its opportunity cost.
   c. all citizens deserve to have regardless of ability to pay.
   d. has a price so high that only people of exceptional merit can afford it.

_____ 11. The fact that less than one dollar in three spent on farm programs goes to a farmer in need suggests that the programs can best be explained in terms of
   a. externalities
   b. insufficient competition
   c. public goods
   d. rent seeking

_____ 12. Which of the following could be considered to be an example of rent-seeking?
   a. Import quotas on shoes.
   b. Farm subsidies.
   c. A state law limiting entry into the profession of dentistry.
   d. All of the above.

_____ 13. Which of the following is an example of privatization?
   a. The U.S. government sells the railroad Conrail to private investors.
   b. The town of Bethel, Vermont hires a private contractor to spread salt on town roads during the winter.
   c. Both **a** and **b**.
   d. Neither **a** nor **b**.

_____ 14. Which of the following countries have experimented with privatization in one form or another?
   a. Jamaica.
   b. The United States.
   c. Hungary.
   d. All of the above.

_____ 15. The perceived benefits of privatization include
   a. improved administration.
   b. greater opportunities for rent seeking.
   c. an increase in externalities.
   d. all of the above.

ANSWERS TO CHAPTER 5

Economics in the News

(1) Some of the costs mentioned in the article are borne by smokers themselves, and hence, are not externalities. The $19.3 billion that smokers pay for cigarettes is the clearest example. Other costs are spread partly to others. For example, health problems of smokers are spread to others, in part, through increased government and employer payments for health benefits. Not mentioned in the article

are externalities of "passive smoking"—health damage and discomfort to people in an area where others are smoking. (2) The tax could be viewed as correcting a market failure in the form of externalities. (3) Another way to internalize many of the externalities of smoking is through life and health insurance premiums that recognize the risk of smoking. However, many group life and health policies, especially those paid for by employers, do not make smokers pay their own hospital costs via higher insurance premiums. As smoking becomes less socially accepted, some employers may become reluctant to hire smokers at all. That is another way to impose the cost of smoking on smokers.

Self Test

1. **b.** Transfer payments added nearly 15 percent.
2. **a.** The total was about 35 percent of GNP.
3. **c.** A public good must have the property that people cannot be excluded, and also that more beneficiaries can be added at zero cost.
4. **b.** National defense was the largest category 20 years ago.
5. **a.** Social security taxes were a close second as of 1986, and may move into first place in the next few years.
6. **c.** This is normal operation of supply and demand; it is not competition, but insufficient competition that can cause market failure.
7. **b.** The $1,000 a week as a stockbroker can be considered his opportunity cost of playing football.
8. **a.** Owners and buyers are direct parties to the transaction and are affected by the price of steel.
9. **b.** Pollution keeps prices below opportunity costs.
10. **c.** These are sometimes provided by government because of the fairness issue.
11. **d.** Well-to-do farmers have enough political influence to make sure they get a piece of the pie.
12. **d.** All are attempts to raise prices above opportunity costs.
13. **c.** Selling public property and hiring private contractors are the two most common forms of privatization.
14. **d.** Privatization is in use around the world.
15. **a.** Suppression of rent seeking is another advantage; externalities are usually not a major consideration in privatization.

Chapter 6

The Circular Flow of Income and Product

WHERE YOU'RE GOING

When you have mastered this chapter, you will understand

1. How households and firms are linked by incomes and expenditures.
2. How income is related to money.
3. How the concepts of supply and demand can be applied to the economy as a whole.
4. How the various pieces of the economy—households, firms, government, and financial markets—fit together.
5. How the U.S. economy is linked to the rest of the world.

In addition, you will add the following terms to your economic vocabulary:

Circular flow of income and product
Flow — *measured in units & time*
Stock — *" " units only*
National income — *total income earned by households*
National product — *total $$ value of all goods & services produced*
Saving
Fixed investment — *purchases of capital goods*
Inventory investment — *changes in stocks of finished goods & raw materials*
Investment — *portion of income not spent on goods/services kept on hand / taxes*
Aggregate supply — *the value of all goods & services produced in econ*
Aggregate demand — *the value of all planned expenditures*
Realized expenditure
Realized investment
Net taxes — *taxes paid by households — transfer payments*
Closed economy — *economy that has no imports/exports*
Open economy — *economy linked to outside world through imports/exports*
Net exports
Capital inflow — *foreign investment into our financial markets*
Capital outflow

WALKING TOUR

After you have read this chapter at least once, you should work step by step through this walking tour. Fill in the blanks and answer the questions as you go along. After you have answered each question, check yourself by uncovering the answer given in the margin. If you do not understand why the answer given is the correct one, refer back to the proper section of the text.

The Structure of the Circular Flow

In economics, it is important to distinguish carefully between stocks and flows. For example, the number of radios that a factory produces per month would be a __flow__, while the number of radios in the warehouse awaiting shipment on any given date would be a __stock__. The distinction between stocks and flows applies to quantities measured in dollars as well as to those measured in physical units. For example, your consumption expenditures measured in dollars per month would be a __flow__, while the funds you have accumulated in your bank account as of a certain date would be a __stock__.

The fluid that keeps the economy's circular flow working is __money__. The most commonly used forms of money are __coins__, __paper money__, and __checking accts__ balances. The quantity of money is a [(stock)/flow]. National income is [(several times)/a small fraction of] the stock of money.

Two of the most important components of the circular flow of income and product are the total current dollar value of all wages, rents, interest, and profits earned by households, known as __national income__, and the total current dollar value of all goods and services produced by the economy, known as __national product__. National product is alternatively known as __Aggregate Supply__.

The sum of consumption, planned investment, government purchases, and net exports—that is, total planned expenditure—is known as __Aggregate Demand__. When aggregate supply and aggregate demand are equal, the economy is said to be in __equilibrium__. If aggregate demand is not equal to aggregate supply, the difference must be made up by [planned/(unplanned)] inventory investment. For example, if total planned expenditure exceeds national product, there will be unplanned inventory [accumulation/(depletion)]. If aggregate supply exceeds aggregate demand, there will be unplanned inventory __accumulation__.

82

Unplanned inventory changes act as a signal to producers that the production plans they have formulated are not meshing with the expenditure plans of households, firms, government, and the foreign sector. If unplanned inventory accumulation takes place, producers are likely to react by [**cutting**/raising] prices and/or output until inventories fall to the desired level. Similarly, producers will tend to raise prices and/or output when inventory depletion indicates an excess aggregate nominal [supply/**demand**].

The part of household income that is not used to buy goods and services or pay taxes is known as **savings**. Saving flows to financial markets, where it can be used by firms for the purpose of **investment**.

Adding Government to the Circular Flow

Government is linked to the circular flow in three ways. First, it is connected to households via **taxes**. Second, it is connected to product markets via **govt. purchases**. Third, it is connected to **financial** markets. If the government budget is in deficit, the flow of funds runs [**from**/to] financial markets [from/**to**] the government. If the budget is in surplus, the flow runs [from/**to**] financial markets [**from**/to] the government.

Adding the Foreign Sector to the Circular Flow

The foreign sector, like the government, is connected to the circular flow in three ways. The first connection is imports, which is shown as an arrow [into/**out of**] the domestic economy. The second connection is exports, which is shown as an arrow [**into**/out of] the domestic economy. The third connection runs from the foreign sector to **financial** markets. If imports exceed exports, there is a flow [**into**/out of] domestic financial markets, which is known as a **capital inflow**. If exports exceed imports, there is a flow [into/**out of**] domestic financial markets, which is known as a **capital outflow**.

DON'T MAKE THIS COMMON MISTAKE

Many mistakes are made in macroeconomics because of confusion between statements that are *identities* and statements that are *conditional equalities*. Both types of statements occur in this chapter.

For example, the statement,

$$\text{Aggregate Supply} = \text{Aggregate Demand} + \text{Unplanned Inventory Investment}$$

is an example of an *identity*. That means the two sides of the equation are *equal by definition*, or *identical*. Whether the economy is in equilibrium or not, whether the plans people make work out or not, that relationship will always hold. It holds because, by definition, any part of aggregate supply (that is, national product) that is not used up for consumption, *planned* investment, government purchases, or net exports goes into unplanned inventory investment. (After all, unclaimed goods can't just disappear into thin air.) Similarly, by definition, if the sum of consumption, planned investment, government purchases, and net exports exceeds aggregate supply, demands for those uses can be satisfied only by running down inventories accumulated from production of previous periods—negative unplanned inventory investment. (Goods can't appear out of thin air either.)

But consider, by contrast, the following seemingly similar statement:

$$\text{National Product} = \text{Consumption} + \text{Planned Investment} + \text{Government Purchases} + \text{Net Exports}$$

This one is a *conditional equality*. It holds only when the economy is in equilibrium, that is, only when the plans of producers of goods just mesh with the plans of users when tested in the market place. When plans mesh, nothing unplanned takes place—no unplanned inventory accumulation, no unplanned inventory rundown. Planned investment and total investment are then equal.

HANDS ON

Now that you have reviewed the concepts introduced in this chapter, it is time for some hands-on practice with the analytical tools that have been introduced. Work through each problem in this section carefully, and then check your results against those given at the end of the chapter.

Problem 1

Fill in the blanks in the following table, then answer the questions below.

Output resulting from producers' plans: 200,000 [1]
  Shirts $70,000
  Tennis rackets   80,000
  Drill presses   50,000
Expenditures resulting from buyers' plans:
  Total consumption expenditure   160,000 [2]
    Shirts   70,000
    Tennis rackets   90,000

  Total planned investment expenditure   50000 [3]
    Fixed investment   50,000
    Planned inventory investment   0
  Total planned expenditure   210000 [4]
  Total unplanned inventory investment   -10000 [5]

Summary
National product   200000 [6]
Total expenditure   200000 [7]
  Planned   210000 [8]
  Unplanned   -10000 [9]

a. What is the value of aggregate supply? Of aggregate demand?
b. As the table is constructed, is the economy in equilibrium? How can you tell? If it is not in equilibrium, how would you expect producers to react, and why?

Problem 2

Each of the questions below can be answered by using one or more of the following equations:

$$AD = C + I_p + G + X - M$$
$$AS = AD + I_u$$
$$I + G + X = S + T + M$$

In these equations, AD = aggregate demand, AS = aggregate supply, C = consumption, I_p = planned investment, I_u = unplanned inventory investment, I = total investment, G = government purchases, X = exports, S = saving, T = net taxes, and M = imports.

a. Aggregate supply = 1,200, consumption = 800, planned investment = 200, government purchases = 200, exports = 50, and imports = 100. Is the economy in equilibrium? What is unplanned inventory investment?
b. Aggregate supply = 800, planned investment = 100, consumption = 500, and exports exceed imports by 75. How much must government purchases be in order for the economy to be in equilibrium at an aggregate supply of $800?
c. If the government budget is in deficit by 100 and exports exceed imports by 50, by how much must total investment exceed or fall short of saving? Can the economy be in equilibrium under these conditions?

d. Is the following statement true or false? Explain. "If planned investment exceeds saving and government purchases exceed net taxes, then the economy cannot be in equilibrium unless there is a foreign trade deficit (that is, unless imports exceed exports)."

SELF TEST

These sample test items will help you check how much you have learned. Answers are found at the end of the chapter. Scoring yourself: One or two wrong—on target. Three or four wrong—passing, but you haven't mastered the chapter yet. Five or more wrong—not good enough; start over and restudy the chapter.

1. Which of the following is not a flow?
   a. National income.
   b. Exports.
   c. Aggregate nominal supply.
   d. All of the above are flows.
2. Which of the following is a true statement about the role of money in the circular flow?
   a. Money is the most important example of a quantity measured as a flow.
   b. Currency and checking deposits are common forms of money.
   c. The measured stock of money is several times the nation's annual national income.
   d. All of the above are true.
3. A firm that produced $10 million worth of shoes in a year, sold $11 million worth of shoes in the year, and purchased $5 million in new shoemaking equipment during the year would have made a total realized investment of
   a. $4 million.
   b. $5 million.
   c. $6 million.
   d. $17 million.
4. Aggregate supply is another term for
   a. national income.
   b. national product.
   c. total expenditure.
   d. total planned expenditure.
5. Aggregate supply minus aggregate demand is equal to
   a. saving.
   b. total investment.
   c. total inventory investment.
   d. unplanned inventory investment.
6. A flow of funds from financial markets to the government indicates that
   a. the government budget is in surplus.
   b. the government budget is in deficit.
   c. there is unplanned inventory investment.
   d. there is unplanned inventory depletion.

__B__ 7. In an economy with no foreign sector, if planned investment equals saving and government purchases equal net taxes, then
   a. aggregate demand exceeds aggregate supply.
   b. the economy is in equilibrium.
   c. planned inventory investment must be zero.
   d. none of the above.

__A__ 8. If national product = 1,000, consumption = 800, planned investment = 100, government purchases = 150, exports = 50, and imports = 75, then unplanned inventory investment must be
   a. -25.
   b. 0.
   c. 25.
   d. none of the above.

__B__ 9. If exports from the United States exceed imports into the United States,
   a. there must be a capital inflow into the U.S. economy.
   b. there must be a capital outflow from the U.S. economy.
   c. the government budget must be in deficit.
   d. saving must exceed investment.

__A__ 10. Which of the following is an example of a capital inflow into the U.S. economy?
   a. A U.S. firm borrows from a London bank to finance a purchase of imported stilton cheese.
   b. The pension fund of a U.S. labor union buys bonds issued by the Canadian government.
   c. The Bank of America loans $100 million to the government of Mexico.
   d. None of the above is a capital inflow.

__B__ 11. Let C stand for consumption, I for total investment, G for government purchases, X for exports, M for imports, S for saving, and T for net taxes. Which of the following equations always holds?
   a. C + I + G + X = C + S + T - M.
   b. C + I + G + X - M = C + S + T.
   c. G - T = I + X - S - M.
   d. None of the above always holds.

__C__ 12. If the government budget is in surplus by $100 and exports exceed imports by $60, then
   a. saving must exceed investment by $40.
   b. saving must exceed investment by $160.
   c. investment must exceed saving by $40.
   d. investment must exceed saving by $160.

__B__ 13. If total investment exceeds saving,
   a. the economy cannot be in equilibrium.
   b. there must be either a government budget surplus or a foreign trade deficit.
   c. prices and/or output must increase.
   d. None of the above.

___C___ 14. National product equals
   a. consumption plus investment plus government purchases.
   b. consumption plus investment plus government purchases plus exports.
   c. consumption plus investment plus government purchases plus net exports.
   d. investment plus government purchases plus net exports.

___B___ 15. If aggregate supply exceeds aggregate demand
   a. prices and/or output will tend to rise.
   b. prices and/or output will tend to fall.
   c. prices will tend to rise and output to fall.
   d. output will tend to rise and prices to fall.

ANSWERS TO CHAPTER 6

Hands On

Problem 1   (Blanks in table): [1] $200,000; [2] $160,000; [3] $50,000; [4] $210,000; [5] -$10,000; [6] $200,000; [7] $200,000; [8] $210,000; [9] -$10,000. (a) Aggregate supply is $200,000 and aggregate demand is $210,000. (b) The economy is not in equilibrium because aggregate demand exceeds aggregate supply. Producers would react to the unplanned inventory drawdown by raising output, or prices, or both, causing the circular flow to expand.

Problem 2   (a) Applying the first equation gives AD = 1,150. The second equation tells us that I_u = AS - AD, so unplanned inventory investment is 50. (b) For equilibrium, AD must equal AS. C + I_p + X - M = 675. 800 - 675 = 125 gives the required value of G, the missing component of AD. (c) In the government sector, G exceeds T by 100. In the foreign sector, X exceeds M by 50. For I + X + G to equal S + T + M, investment must fall short of saving by 150. If *planned* investment falls short of saving by 150, then the economy will be in equilibrium, since then aggregate demand will equal aggregate supply. (d) This must be true in order for I + X + G to equal S + T + M. If the economy is in equilibrium, with no unplanned investment, then to balance, imports must exceed exports, i.e., a trade deficit. If there is no trade deficit, the only way to make the equation balance is by unplanned inventory depletion, which would mean disequilibrium.

Self Test

1. **d.** Because all are measured in terms of dollars per year.
2. **b.** Money is a stock, and annual national income is several times the stock of money.
3. **a.** Total realized investment is $5 million fixed minus $1 million depletion of inventories.

4. **b.** National income and product are, however, equal in a simple economy.
5. **d.** Unplanned inventory change is equal to the difference between what is produced and what buyers purchase in the course of carrying out their plans.
6. **b.** The flow represents borrowing by government.
7. **b.** With no foreign sector, $I_p + G = S + T$, an alternative way of expressing AS = AD, is the condition for equilibrium.
8. **a.** The sum of consumption, planned investment, unplanned investment, government purchases, and net exports must equal national product.
9. **b.** Foreign buyers must pay for U.S. exports either by selling imports to the United States or by means of capital outflows, that is, by borrowing from the United States or sales of assets to the United States.
10. **a.** In both **b** and **c**, dollars flow out of the U.S. economy.
11. **b.** This equation says, roughly, that total expenditure equals total uses of national income.
12. **c.** To get the answer, apply the formula $I + G + X = S + T + M$.
13. **b.** This question is based on the same formula as question 12.
14. **c.** Imports must be subtracted from exports to get net exports in order to arrive at national product.
15. **b.** This will happen as a response to unplanned inventory accumulation.

Chapter 7

Measuring National Income and Product

WHERE YOU'RE GOING

When you have mastered this chapter, you will understand

1. How gross national product is officially defined and measured.
2. How national income differs from gross national product.
3. What the major types of international transactions are.
4. How changes in the price level are measured.
5. What the limitations of official economic statistics are.

In addition, you will add the following terms to your economic vocabulary:
   Gross national product (GNP)
   Final goods and services
   Value added
   Net national product
   Personal income
   Disposable personal income (disposable income)
   Current account
   Merchandise balance
   Current account balance
   Capital account
   Official reserve account
   Base year
   Price level
   Price index
   GNP deflator
   Consumer price index (CPI)
   Producer price index (PPI)
   Indexing

WALKING TOUR

After you have read this chapter at least once, you should work step by step through this walking tour. Fill in the blanks and answer the questions as you go along. After you have answered each question, check yourself by uncovering the answer given in the margin. If you do not understand why the answer given is the correct one, refer back to the proper section of the text.

Measuring Nominal Income and Product

The dollar value at current market prices of all final goods and services produced by a nation's factors of production is known as _____ _____GNP_____. This measure of economic activity [includes/excludes] goods such as sheet metal sold to General Motors for use in making cars, flour sold to a baker for use in making bread, and so on. These are known as [intermediate/final] goods. At each level of production, the value of output minus the value of intermediate goods used is known as __value added__. Thus, GNP is a measure of the total __value added__ for the economy.

GNP is measured by adding together data on __expenditures__. The four categories of expenditures included in GNP are

1. __consumption__,
2. __investment__,
3. __govt purchases__, and
4. __net exports__.

When an allowance for depreciation and obsolescence (the __capital consumption allowance__) is subtracted from GNP, the result is __net national product__.

National income [is/is not] measured using the same set of data as is used for measuring GNP. National income is measured using the __income__ approach, which means adding together the following:

1. __compensation of employees__,
2. __net interest income__,
3. __corporate profits__,
4. __rental income__, and
5. __proprietor's income__.

These categories [do/do not] correspond closely to the theoretical classification of factor income according to labor, capital, and natural resources.

Margin answers:
- gross national product
- excludes
- intermediate
- value added
- value added
- expenditures
- consumption
- investment
- government purchases
- net exports
- capital consumption allowance, net national product
- is not
- income
- compensation of employees
- rental income of persons
- net interest income
- corporate profits
- proprietor's income
- do not

In order to reconcile GNP with national income, one first obtains net national product by subtracting the __capital consumption allowance__ from GNP. Next an adjustment is made for revenue received by firms from sales of products but taken directly by government before it is received by suppliers of factor services. These are __indirect business__ taxes, such as __sales__ taxes and __business property__ taxes. In theory, this [**should**/should not] give national income. The remaining difference, if any, reflects the fact that national income and product are estimated from different sets of data. This difference is called the __statistical discrepancy__.

The total income actually received by households is called __personal income__. It excludes three items earned by households but not received by them:

1. __contributions for social insurance__,
2. __corporate profits taxes__, and
3. __undistributed corporate profits__

It includes payments received by households but not earned by them, that is, __transfer__ payments. When personal taxes are subtracted from personal income, the result is __disposable personal income__.

Measuring the Balance of Payments

From 1960 to 1986, as the value of U.S. imports rose as a share of GNP, the value of U.S. exports [**rose, but less rapidly**/rose more rapidly/fell]. The value of imports and exports is recorded in a section of the international accounts that is called the __current__ account. In addition to imports and exports of merchandise, this section of the accounts records trade in __services__ and international __transfer payments__. In 1986, the current account showed a [surplus/**deficit**/exact balance].

International financial transactions are recorded in a section of the accounts known as the __capital__ account. Categorize each of the following capital account items as either a capital inflow or a capital outflow:

1. Sales of U.S. assets to foreign buyers. __inflow__
2. Purchases of foreign assets by U.S. buyers. __outflow__
3. Loans by U.S. banks to foreign borrowers. __outflow__
4. Borrowing by U.S. firms from foreign banks. __inflow__

inflow — In 1986, the U.S. capital account showed a net capital [inflow/outflow].

A third section of the accounts records transactions by the central banks of various nations. This section is known as the

official reserve — official reserve account. Except that they are made by central banks rather than private individuals, these transactions closely

capital — resemble those in the [current/capital] account.

In principle, the sum of the current, capital, and official reserve

zero — accounts should be [positive/negative/zero]. However, in practice there is a statistical discrepancy. In recent years, the discrepancy in

much larger — the international accounts has been [much larger/much smaller] than that in the domestic GNP accounts.

Setting aside the statistical discrepancy, and assuming a zero official reserve balance, a nation that runs a current account deficit

inflow — will have a net capital [inflow/outflow], and one that runs a current

outflow — account surplus will have a net capital [inflow/outflow].

Measuring Real Income and the Price Level

The most broadly based measure of the price level is the one known

GNP deflator — as the GNP deflator. This shows the price level relative to a

base — chosen year known as the base year. The deflator can be stated relative to a base-year value of 1.0, in which case we refer

price level — to it as the price level, or in terms of a base-year value of

price index — 100, in which case we call it a price index.

The GNP deflator can be used to calculate the value of current year real GNP, given the value of current year nominal GNP. For example, in 1986, nominal GNP was $4,208 billion, and the GNP

3,659 — deflator was 1.15. That means that real GNP in 1986 was $3,659 billion.

The GNP deflator is not the only commonly used price index. A widely used index of goods and services purchased by a typical

consumer price index — urban household is the CPI. An index of goods traded

producer price index — among business firms is the producer price index.

How Good Are the National Income Accounts?

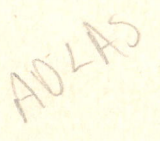

The U.S. national income accounts are considered to be among the best in the world, yet they have some definite limitations. One limitation is that of timeliness. For example, the preliminary estimates of GNP growth released just after the end of each quarter are revised, on the average, by [**more**/less] than a percentage point. Also, many kinds of economic activity are not officially measured. These activities, ranging from babysitting to organized crime, constitute the __underground__ economy.

There is also a problem of systematic inaccuracies, or __biases__, in the price indexes. One is the bias associated with the changing composition of output. This is called the __substitution__ bias. This bias is believed to cause the consumer price index to [**overstate**/understate] the true rate of inflation. There is also a bias associated with changes in the quality of goods and services. This is believed to cause the consumer price index to [**overstate**/understate] the true rate of inflation. Finally, a shortcoming of the official national income accounts is their failure to account for __nonmaterial__ sources of welfare, such as health and environmental quality.

HANDS ON

Now that you have reviewed the concepts in this chapter, it is time for some hands-on practice with the analytical tools that have been introduced. Work through each problem in this section carefully, and then check your results against those given at the end of the chapter.

Problem 1

Exhibit 7.1 presents national income accounting data for a hypothetical economy. Use this data to answer the questions that follow.

Exhibit 7.1

Capital consumption allowance	$180
Change in business inventories	-20
Compensation of employees	930
Contributions to social insurance	110
Corporate profit taxes	50
Dividends	30
Exports	150
Fixed investment	220
Government purchases	380
Imports	125
Indirect business taxes	140
Net interest	75
Personal consumption expenditures	975
Personal taxes	170
Proprietors' income	90
Rental income	25
Transfer payments	210
Undistributed corporate profits	10

a. Using the expenditure approach, compute gross and net national product for this economy.
b. Using the income approach, compute national income. How large is the statistical discrepancy between the expenditure and income approaches?
c. Compute personal income and disposable personal income. What items are included in personal income that do not appear in national income? What items are included in national income but not in personal income?

Problem 2

Exhibit 7.2 presents price and quantity data for two years for a hypothetical economy in which only three goods are produced. Use this data to answer the questions that follow.

Exhibit 7.2

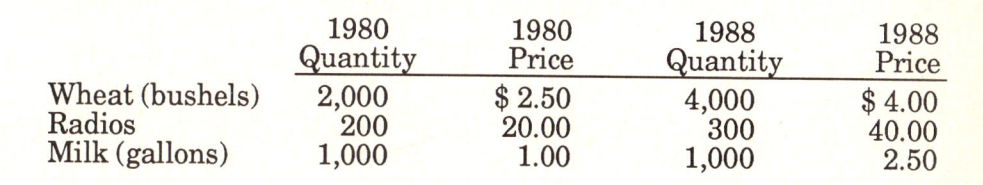

	1980 Quantity	1980 Price	1988 Quantity	1988 Price
Wheat (bushels)	2,000	$ 2.50	4,000	$ 4.00
Radios	200	20.00	300	40.00
Milk (gallons)	1,000	1.00	1,000	2.50

a. Calculate real GNP for 1988, using 1980 as a base year. Explain your procedure in detail.
b. What is the GNP deflator for this economy for 1988?
c. Calculate the consumer price index for this economy for 1988, using 1980 as a base year? Explain your procedure in detail.
d. Compare the consumer price index and the GNP deflator. Are they the same? If so, why? If not, why not?

ECONOMICS IN THE NEWS

Allowances Stay Flat, Candy Rises

Lauren Krzywkowski is fed up with inflation. She's working as hard as ever, she says, but has less to show for her efforts. To supplement her meager wages, Miss Krzywkowski has begun to seek out odd jobs. "They need it, I do it," she says.

Kelly Collings is feeling the pressure, too. She has been on a fixed income for three years. When asked about inflation, she shakes her head and says glumly, "It's depressing."

Common enough sentiments, these. Except for one thing: The ages of the beleaguered citizens are, respectively, 12 and 14. If schoolyard chatter is any indication, inflation has joined thunderstorms, low grades, and neighborhood bullies among kids' most dreaded adversaries.

Although the government doesn't keep such statistics and private research is very limited, there are indications that the buying power of children has shrunk significantly over the past 5 years. Because even dime and quarter increases in the cost of childrens' items often mean huge leaps in terms of percentages (and weekly allowances), "kidflation" in some cases has outpaced the adult variety.

Based on conversation with over 50 children, this newspaper compiled a "market basket" of 15 items frequently purchased by children, then determined from manufacturers approximately what has happened to the retail prices of those items. [The data are presented in Exhibit 7.3.] While the resulting "Kiddie Consumer Price Index" isn't scientific, and prices may vary from city to city, it offers some insight into what the younger generation is up against.

Exhibit 7.3

Kiddie Consumer Market Basket

	1975	1979	1980
1. Chicago White Sox General Admission Ticket	$2.00	$2.00	$3.00
2. Jack & Jill Soap Bubbles	.29	.45	.45
3. Wham-O Regular Frisbees	.97	1.26	1.29
4. MAD Magazine	.50	.75	.75
5. Vending Machine 12-Oz. Canned Soft Drink	.20	.30	.40
6. Wrigley's Chewing Gum (7-Stick Pack)	.15	.20	.25
7. Hershey's Milk Chocolate Candy (Per 1.05 Oz.)	.15	.22	.25
8. Marvel Comic Book (Per 18 editorial pages)	.25	.40	.41
9. McDonald's Hamburger, Small Fries, and 12-Oz. Soft Drink	.80	1.18	1.39
10. Arista Record Album	6.98	7.98	8.98
11. Crayola Crayons (8 Crayons)	.25	.35	.45
12. Duncan Imperial Yo-Yo	1.29	1.49	1.79
13. Milky Way Candy Bar (Per ounce)	.083	.137	.122
14. Drumstick (Ice Cream with Chocolate and Nuts)	.20	.30	.35
15. Topps Chewing Gum Football Trading Cards (Cost per Dozen)	.18	.20	.25
Kiddie Consumer Price Index	14.29	17.27	20.13
Consumer Price Index	166.3	229.9	258.4

The kiddie market basket includes, among other items, gum, ice cream, candy, records, toys, fast food, and a ticket to a major-league baseball game. The total would have cost $14.29 on December 31, 1975. But that same day in 1979, the price for the basket had risen 21 percent to $17.27, and by the end of 1980 it was up a further 17 percent to $20.13. The Consumer Price Index, meanwhile, rose 38 percent from 1975 to 1979, and then an additional 12 percent from 1979 to 1980.

While the numbers indicate that until 1979, kids had fared pretty well compared with adults, a look at children's incomes in the period suggests otherwise. Unfortunately for kids, income from allowances, paper routes, baby-sitting, and mowing lawns isn't tied to the Kiddie Consumer Price Index.

For example, in 1975, a paper boy or girl for the Cleveland Press was paid 24 cents per customer per week. By December 31, 1979, that amount had risen only 8.3 percent to 26 cents and the paper was still paying deliverers that on December 31, 1980.

Baby-sitters apparently fared somewhat a better, according to the child-research division of New York-based Hyatt Esserman Research Associates. It says the top hourly wage most common among baby-sitters in 1980 was $2.50, compared with $1.50 in 1973. Figures for the interim weren't available.

Source: Dean Rotbart, "Penny Wise, Allowances Stay Flat, Candy Rises—and Kids Lose Their Innocence," *The Wall Street Journal*," March 2, 1981, p. 1. Reprinted by permission of The Wall Street Journal. ©Dow Jones & Company, Inc., 1981. All Rights Reserved.

Questions

1. Restate both the Kiddie Consumer Price Index (KCPI) and the regular CPI using a 1975 base year, i.e., 1975 = 100. They can now be compared directly. Who fared better over each period, kids or grownups?
2. Note that the market basket for the KCPI consists of one of each item listed. That makes the KCPI a simple average of prices, whereas the regular CPI is a weighted average. This means that items with a small unit price get low weights in the KCPI even though they might be purchased very often and might represent a large part of total expenditures. Take food for example. In the 1975 base year, the seven food items on the list accounted for only $1.76 of the $14.29 total. Do you think kids spend more (or less) than 12 percent of their incomes on food? Calculate a separate index (1975 = 100) for kid food. Did it rise faster or slower than the whole index? What would a greater weight for food in the index do to the whole picture of kids and inflation?
3. The KCPI, like the regular CPI, can be used to deflate nominal quantities to any desired base year. Earnings provide an example. According to the article, nominal earnings per customer for a Cleveland paper boy or girl rose from 24 cents per customer per week in 1975 to 26 cents in 1980. What happened to real earnings, stated in constant 1975 dollars, deflated by the KCPI? What happened to real hourly earnings of baby-sitters, using nominal wages as reported by Hyatt Esserman Research Associates? What if the baby-sitter spent all his or her earnings on food? Deflate by the kid food index to find out how such a baby-sitter would have fared in real terms.

SELF TEST

These sample test items will help you check how much you have learned. Answers are found at the end of the chapter. Scoring yourself: One or two wrong—on target. Three or four wrong—passing, but you haven't mastered the chapter yet. Five or more wrong—not good enough; start over and restudy the chapter.

_B_ 1. Gross national product is officially measured by
   a. multiplying the quantity of each final good and service produced by the price at which it is sold and adding the totals.
   b. adding together the totals of all expenditures on newly produced final goods and services.
   c. adding together the totals of all incomes received by households from the sale of productive services.
   d. multiplying the quantity of all factor services by factor prices actually paid and adding the totals.

_D_ 2. Which of the following would be counted as a final good or service in calculating GNP?
   a. An automotive brake unit sold by Bendix Corporation to General Motors for use in a new Buick.
   b. A truckload of fertilizer sold to an Iowa farmer.
   c. A used typewriter purchased by a real estate agent.
   d. A haircut purchased by a retired bank teller.

_D_ 3. Which of the following would not be counted as an investment for purposes of computing GNP?
   a. Construction of a new movie theater.
   b. Purchase by an appliance dealer of a newly produced refrigerator, which the dealer subsequently fails to sell to a consumer during the year in question.
   c. Construction of a new, single family house.
   d. Purchase of 1,000 shares of IBM stock by a union pension fund.

_A_ 4. Which of the following would not be counted as part of government purchases of goods and services as recorded in the GNP accounts?
   a. Unemployment compensation payments.
   b. The salary of a worker in a state employment commission office.
   c. Purchase of furniture by the U.S. Department of Labor.
   d. Purchase of a new radar gun for the local sheriff's office.

_C_ 5. The word "gross" in gross national product indicates that GNP includes
   a. intermediate as well as final goods.
   b. imported goods as well as domestically produced goods.
   c. investment that goes to replace worn out capital as well as investment for expansion of productive capacity.
   d. farm products consumed on the farm as well as those sold.

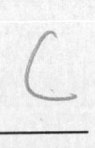

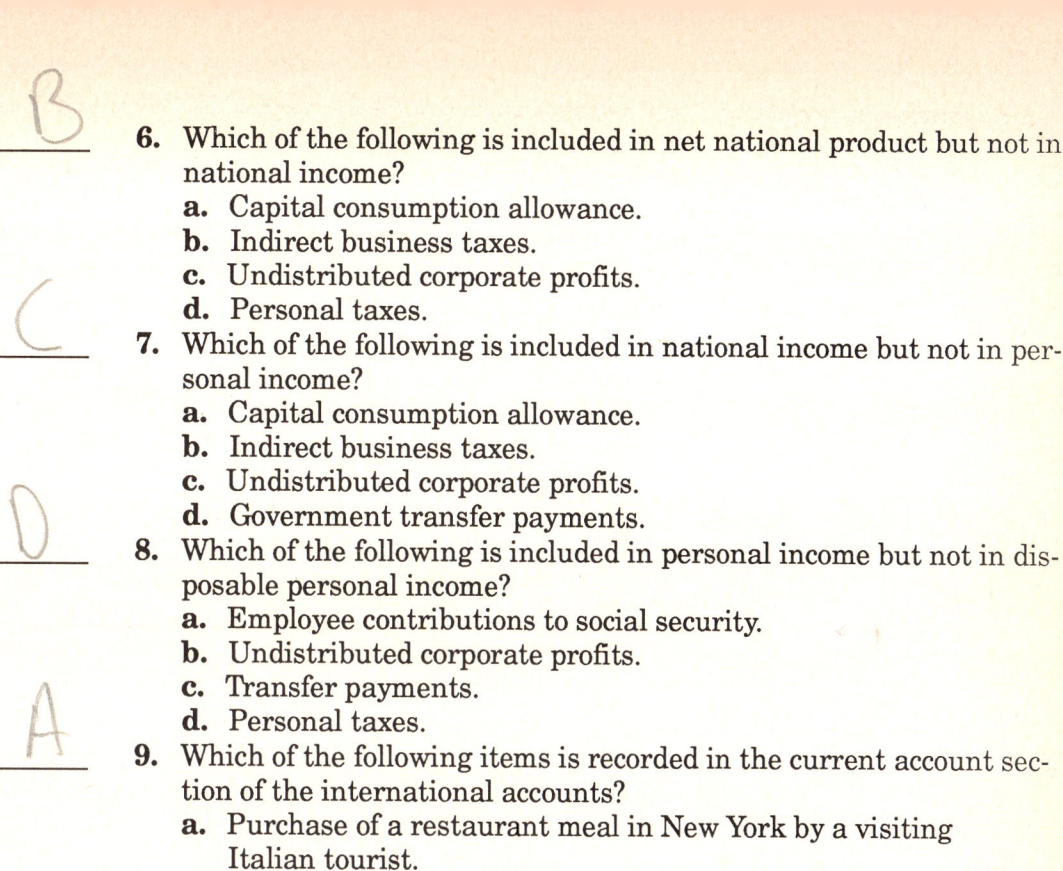

__B__ 6. Which of the following is included in net national product but not in national income?
   a. Capital consumption allowance.
   b. Indirect business taxes.
   c. Undistributed corporate profits.
   d. Personal taxes.

__C__ 7. Which of the following is included in national income but not in personal income?
   a. Capital consumption allowance.
   b. Indirect business taxes.
   c. Undistributed corporate profits.
   d. Government transfer payments.

__D__ 8. Which of the following is included in personal income but not in disposable personal income?
   a. Employee contributions to social security.
   b. Undistributed corporate profits.
   c. Transfer payments.
   d. Personal taxes.

__A__ 9. Which of the following items is recorded in the current account section of the international accounts?
   a. Purchase of a restaurant meal in New York by a visiting Italian tourist.
   b. Purchase of a condominium on the French Riviera by a rich U.S. lawyer.
   c. Sale of $100 million in British government securities by the U.S. Federal Reserve.
   d. None of the above.

__A__ 10. Suppose that the United States has a current account deficit of $100 billion, that the U.S. Federal Reserve increases its holdings of foreign official reserve assets by $5 billion while foreign central banks make no net change in their holdings of U.S. reserve assets, and that there is no statistical discrepancy. Then the U.S. must experience
   a. a net capital inflow of $105 billion.
   b. a net capital outflow of $105 billion.
   c. a net capital inflow of $95 billion.
   d. a net capital outflow of $95 billion.

__C__ 11. Let P_c stand for current year prices, P_b for base year prices, Q_c for the current year market basket of goods, and Q_b for the base year market basket. Then the correct formula for the consumer price index is
   a. (Q_c valued at P_c / Q_b valued at P_b) x 100.
   b. (Q_c valued at P_b / Q_b valued at P_b) x 100.
   c. (Q_b valued at P_c / Q_b valued at P_b) x 100.
   d. (Q_c valued at P_c / Q_c valued at P_b) x 100.

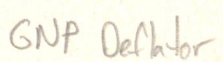

GNP Deflator

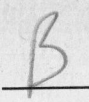

__B__ 12. If 1982 quantities valued at 1982 prices are 150; 1982 quantities valued at 1990 prices are 300; 1990 quantities valued at 1982 prices are 200; and 1990 quantities valued at 1990 prices are 600; the price level for 1990, measured by the GNP deflator for 1990, using 1982 as the base year, is
   a. 2.0.
   b. 3.0.
   c. 4.0.
   d. impossible to calculate with the information given.

__C__ 13. One way the consumer price index differs from the GNP deflator is that it
   a. uses current year quantities.
   b. includes all final goods and services.
   c. includes only goods bought by typical urban consumers.
   d. includes services as well as physical goods.

__A__ 14. If there is a tendency for the consumption of goods whose prices increase relatively slowly to grow more rapidly than the consumption of goods whose prices increase relatively rapidly, then
   a. the CPI will increase more rapidly than the GNP deflator.
   b. the GNP deflator will increase more rapidly than the CPI.
   c. only the CPI will give a true measure of inflation.
   d. only the GNP deflator will give a true measure of inflation.

__A__ 15. Suppose a typical automobile tire cost $20 in 1935 and $40 in 1988 and that the 1935 tire had a useful life of 10,000 miles, whereas the 1988 tire has a useful life of 40,000 miles. If no adjustment is made for mileage,
   a. the CPI would overestimate inflation between the 2 years.
   b. the CPI would underestimate inflation between the 2 years.
   c. the CPI would accurately measure inflation between the 2 years.
   d. It is not possible to judge how well the CPI would measure inflation between the 2 years without knowing how the quantity sold changed.

ANSWERS TO CHAPTER 7

Hands On

Problem 1 (a) GNP = $1,580, the sum of personal consumption, private investment, government purchases, and net exports. Subtracting the capital consumption allowance gives NNP = $1,400. (b) National income is the sum of compensation of employees, rental income, net interest, corporate profits, and proprietor's income, which comes to $1,210. The difference between national income and net national product is partly accounted for by indirect business taxes of $140. The remaining difference of $50 is the statistical discrepancy. (c) To compute personal income, subtract contributions for social insurance, corporate profits taxes, and undistributed corporate profits from national income, and then add transfer payments. The result is $1,250. Subtracting personal taxes of $170 gives disposable personal income of $1,080.

Problem 2 (a) Real GNP is defined as current year output evaluated at base year prices. The evaluation is made one product at a time, and the resulting figures are summed. For example, for wheat, the current year quantity of 4,000 bushels is multiplied by the base year price of $2.50 per bushel to give $10,000 as the current year quantity of wheat evaluated at base year prices. Proceeding in this way, a real GNP of $17,000 is obtained for 1988. (b) The GNP deflator (in index form) is defined as 100 times the ratio of current year nominal GNP to current year real GNP. To find current year nominal GNP, evaluate current year quantities at current year prices. The result is a 1988 nominal GNP of $30,500. The ratio $30,500/$17,000 x 100 gives the GNP deflator of 179.4. (c) The consumer price index is defined as 100 times the ratio of the base year market basket valued at current prices ($18,500) to the base year market basket valued at base year prices ($10,000). The CPI for 1988 is thus 185. (d) The CPI exceeds the GNP deflator because of the substitution bias. Consumers bought no more of the good with the largest price increase (milk) and a lot more of the good with the smallest price increase (wheat).

Economics in the News

(1) To convert to a 1975 base, set 1975 = 100, and for other years, divide the current year number given by the 1975 number given and multiply by 100. For example, the KCPI for 1979 would be (17.27/14.29) x 100 = 121. The complete figures are as follows:

KCPI 1975 = 100; 1979 = 121; 1980 = 141
CPI 1975 = 100; 1979 = 138; 1980 = 155

Although kids fared better than grownups over the whole period shown, they were hit harder between 1979 and 1980. The KPCI rose by 17 percent that year, compared with just 12 percent for the CPI. (2) To calculate a kid food index based on the 8-item unweighted food market basket alone, divide each year's food total by the 1975 total and multiply by 100. The results are

Kid Food Index: 1975 = 100; 1979 = 144; 1980 = 171

This index rose faster than the KCPI as a whole. Probably kids do spend more than 12 percent of their incomes on food. If so, the 141 value for the KCPI understates the true impact of inflation on kids. (3) To deflate nominal earnings for any year, divide that year's nominal earnings figure by the ratio of that year's price index to the base year price index. For example, to find the 1980 real earnings of the paper boy or girl, divide 26 cents by the ratio (141/100). The results are as follows: Real earnings of paper boys and girls fell from 24 cents per customer per week to 18 cents per customer per week. Real earnings of baby-sitters, deflated by the KCPI, rose from $1.50 to $1.77. But if the figure for baby-sitter earnings were deflated by the kid food index, the heavy-eating baby-sitter would have found real earnings to fall from $1.50 in 1975 to $1.46 in 1980.

Self Test

1. **b.** In principal, any of the methods would work, but **b** is the one used for GNP. National income is measured by method **c**.
2. **d.** The others are intermediate goods.
3. **d.** This is a financial transaction. Items **a** and **c** are purchases of newly produced capital goods, and **b** is inventory investment.
4. **a.** This is a transfer payment.
5. **c.** This part of investment, as estimated by the capital consumption allowance, is subtracted from GNP to get net national product.
6. **b.** These are considered not to be "earned" by the firm's owners.
7. **c.** The others are not part of national income.
8. **d.** Personal income taxes are the principal item in this category.
9. **a.** Item **b** goes in the capital account and **c** goes in the official reserve account.
10. **a.** The $5 billion increase in U.S. official reserve assets is similar to a private capital outflow, and appears in the accounts with a negative sign. Capital inflows must be large enough to balance this plus the $100 billion current account deficit.
11. **c.** Answer **d** is the formula for the GNP deflator.
12. **b.** This is the ratio of current year quantities at current year prices to current year quantities at base year prices.
13. **c.** The CPI uses base year quantities. Both include services.
14. **a.** This is called the substitution bias; the bias is positive for the CPI and negative for the GNP deflator, so neither gives a true measure of inflation.
15. **a.** This is the quality bias.

Chapter 8

Unemployment, Inflation, and the Business Cycle

WHERE YOU'RE GOING

When you have mastered this chapter, you will understand

1. What unemployment means and how it is measured.
2. The pattern that the business cycle follows.
3. How changes in real output are linked to changes in unemployment.
4. How supply and demand curves can be drawn for the macroeconomy.
5. How changes in real output are linked over time to changes in the price level.

In addition, you will add the following terms to your economic vocabulary:
  Employed
  Unemployed
  Civilian labor force
  Civilian unemployment rate
  Discouraged worker
  Employment rate
  Frictional unemployment
  Structural unemployment
  Cyclical unemployment
  Natural rate of unemployment
  Business cycle
  Recession
  Natural level of real output
  Okun's law

WALKING TOUR

After you have read this chapter at least once, you should work step by step through this walking tour. Fill in the blanks and answer the questions as you go along. After you have answered each question, check yourself by uncovering the answer given in the margin. If you do not understand why the answer given is the correct one, refer back to the proper section of the text.

Measuring Unemployment

All people aged 16 years or older who are not in institutions or the armed services constitute the _____. Of these, those who are working or actively looking for work make up the _____ _____. Those who work at least 1 hour a week for pay or at least 15 hours a week not for pay in a family business are counted as _____. Those who are actively looking for work but are not employed are counted as _____. The civilian unemployment rate is the number of unemployed stated as a percentage of the _____. The employment rate, on the other hand, is the number of employed stated as a percentage of the _____. It [is/is not] possible for the employment rate and the unemployment rate to rise or fall at the same time.

Some people who can't find a job are not counted among the unemployed. For example, those who would work if a job were available, but who have given up looking for work, are known as _____. In other cases, people are counted as employed even though they are not working. For example, workers on strike [are/are not] counted as employed.

The portion of unemployment that is accounted for by short periods of unemployment needed for matching jobs with job seekers within the mainstream of the economy is known as _____ unemployment. That accounted for by people out of work for long periods because their skills do not match available jobs is _____ unemployment. The sum of frictional and structural unemployment when the rate of inflation is [steady/accelerating/decelerating] is called the _____ of unemployment. The difference between the actual rate of unemployment and the natural rate at any given time is called _____ unemployment.

Margin answers:
- adult civilian population
- civilian labor force
- employed
- unemployed
- civilian labor force
- adult civilian population, is
- discouraged workers
- are
- frictional
- structural
- steady
- natural rate
- cyclical

104

The Business Cycle

The business cycle is a pattern of alternating economic growth and contraction. It can be divided into four phases. The point where output reaches a maximum is known as the _____ of the cycle. The point of minimum output is the _____. The part of the cycle when output is growing is an _____. The part when output is shrinking is a _____. When a contraction lasts 6 months or more, it is known as a _____.

The trend around which the economy grows over the course of the business cycle is called the _____ level of real output. This level of real output is associated with the _____ of unemployment. When real output is above its natural level, unemployment is [above/below] its natural rate, and when real output is below its natural level, unemployment is [above/below] its natural rate.

According to Okun's law, for each _____ percent by which real output rises above (or falls below) its natural level, the unemployment rate falls below (or rises above) its natural rate by _____ percentage point. For example, suppose the natural level of real output is $2 trillion and the natural unemployment rate is 6 percent. If the actual level of real output is $2.18 trillion, or _____ percent above its natural level, we would then expect the unemployment rate to be about _____ percent. If the actual level of real output were $1.94 trillion, or _____ percent below its natural level, we would expect the unemployment rate to be about _____ percent.

The Aggregate Supply and Demand Model

The concepts of supply and demand can be applied in a macroeconomic context to link real output and the price level. The relationship between the price level and the total level of real planned expenditures is shown by the aggregate _____ curve. This curve has a [positive/negative] slope, because each of the components of planned expenditure tends to decrease as the price level increases.

Real consumption tends to decrease as the price level increases because the [nominal/real] value of money balances declines. Real planned investment tends to decrease as the price level increases

Margin answers:
peak
trough
expansion
contraction
recession

natural
natural rate

below
above

3

one

9
3

3
7

demand
negative

real

105

interest rates	because _____ tend to rise. Real government purchases tend to decrease as the price level increases because some government purchases are fixed in _____ terms. And real net exports tend to decrease as the domestic price level increases provided the _____ in other countries and the exchange rate remains constant. Changes in economic conditions other than the price level will cause the aggregate demand curve to shift. Among the sources of shifts are changes in _____, _____, and _____.
nominal	
price level	
expectations, government policy, world economy	
supply	A graph showing the relationship between the price level and real output is known as the aggregate _____ curve. The slope of the aggregate supply curve depends on assumptions made about the prices of _____. If input prices are fully flexible, so that firms expect them to change in step with every change in output prices, the aggregate supply curve will be _____. On the other hand, if firms expect input prices to remain fixed as the prices of outputs change, the aggregate supply curve will be _____.
inputs	
vertical	
positively sloped	
vertical, positively sloped	In the long run, the aggregate supply curve tends to be _____. In the short run, it tends to be _____. Among the reasons for the gradual adjustment of input prices that gives the short-run aggregate supply curve its positive slope are _____, _____, and _____.
long-term contracts, inventories, incomplete knowledge	
increase	When the aggregate demand curve shifts to the right, starting from the natural level of real output, the initial short-run reaction of the economy includes [an increase/no change] in real output and [an increase/no change] in the price level. As a result, there is [an increase/a decrease/no change] in the unemployment rate in the short run. The economy [can/cannot] remain in the new short-run equilibrium indefinitely. As input prices adjust fully to the new situation, real output will return to its _____ level and unemployment will return to its _____ rate. As this happens, there will be a [further increase/no change] in the price level.
increase	
a decrease	
cannot	
natural	
natural	
further increase	

HANDS ON

Now that you have reviewed the concepts introduced in this chapter, it is time for some hands-on practice with the analytical tools that have been introduced. Work through each problem in this section carefully, and then check your results against those given at the end of the chapter.

Exhibit 8.1 shows a short-run aggregate supply curve SRAS and an aggregate demand curve AD_0 for a hypothetical economy. Use this exhibit in answering the following questions.

Exhibit 8.1

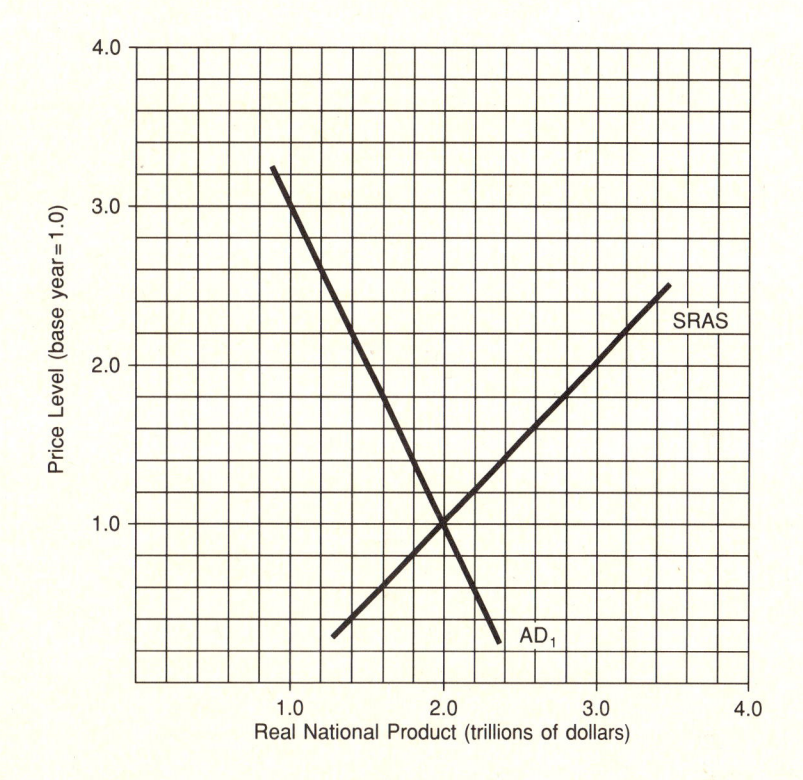

a. What is the initial equilibrium level of real output (real national product) as the exhibit is drawn? What is the initial equilibrium price level? Label this point E_0.

b. A change in government policy causes various components of aggregate demand to increase, so that total planned expenditures at any given price level are now $1 trillion greater than before. Is this change best represented by a movement along the aggregate demand curve or a shift in the curve? If the curve shifts, draw the new curve and label it AD_1.

c. Firms initially expect input prices not to change. Given this expectation, how will the economy react, in the short run, to the change in aggregate demand? What will be the new price level? The new level of real output? Label the new short-run equilibrium point E_1.

d. Assume that the natural level of real output for this economy is $2 trillion. Draw the economy's long-run aggregate supply curve given this level of real output. Label it LRAS.

e. In the long run, input prices will adjust fully to the changed conditions. How will real output and the price level behave as this adjustment takes place? What will be the new long-run equilibrium level of real output? The new long-run equilibrium price level? Label the new long-run equilibrium point E₂.

SELF TEST

These sample test items will help you check how much you have learned. Answers are found at the end of the chapter. Scoring yourself: One or two wrong—on target. Three or four wrong—passing, but you haven't mastered the chapter yet. Five or more wrong—not good enough; start over and restudy the chapter.

_____ 1. Which of the following would be officially classified as unemployed?
   a. A girl, aged 15, working 10 hours per week on her family's farm, without being paid.
   b. A construction worker off the job because of a winter storm.
   c. A person just entering the labor force for the first time who is looking for a job, but who has never lost one.
   d. None of the above would be officially unemployed.

_____ 2. If "discouraged workers" were classified as part of the labor force and unemployed,
   a. the unemployment rate would rise.
   b. the employment rate would fall.
   c. both **a** and **b**.
   d. neither **a** nor **b**.

_____ 3. To be officially counted as part of the labor force, a person must be
   a. over 18.
   b. 65 or under.
   c. both **a** and **b**.
   d. aged 16 or over and working or looking for work.

_____ 4. The term *frictional unemployment* refers to
   a. workers in low paid, dead-end jobs.
   b. workers whose skills are obsolete because technology has changed before they have reached retirement age.
   c. the same thing as the natural rate of unemployment.
   d. workers spending relatively short periods between jobs.

_____ 5. Which of the following types of unemployment is sometimes less than zero at the peak of the business cycle?
   a. Frictional unemployment.
   b. Structural unemployment.
   c. Natural unemployment.
   d. Cyclical unemployment.

_____ 6. According to Okun's law, other things being equal, if real output is 6 percent above its natural level, the unemployment rate will be
   a. six percentage points above its natural rate.
   b. two percentage points above its natural rate.
   c. two percentage points below its natural rate.
   d. six percentage points below its natural rate.

_____ 7. A *recession* is
   a. a business cycle trough at least 6 percent below the previous peak.
   b. a contraction lasting 6 months or more.
   c. a contraction in which real output drops at a 6 percent annual rate.
   d. a contraction that raises the unemployment rate to at least 6 percent.

_____ 8. During the Great Depression of the 1930s
   a. the unemployment rate reached 24 percent.
   b. the economy experienced terrible inflation.
   c. real national product fell to one-tenth of its previous level.
   d. all of the above.

_____ 9. The economy's aggregate demand curve relates
   a. real planned expenditures to the unemployment rate.
   b. real planned expenditures to the price level.
   c. planned real output to the price level of output.
   d. planned real output to the expected input price level.

_____ 10. Which of the following components of planned expenditures tends to decrease, in real terms, when the price level rises?
   a. Consumption.
   b. Planned investment.
   c. Net exports.
   d. All of the above.

_____ 11. Which of the following tends to happen as the price level rises?
   a. Interest rates tend to fall.
   b. The real value of currency and bank deposits tends to fall.
   c. Real government purchases tend to increase.
   d. All of the above.

_____ 12. Which of the following would tend to cause the aggregate demand curve to shift to the left?
   a. An increase in government purchases.
   b. An increase in consumer optimism about the future.
   c. An increase in taxes.
   d. An increase in real income in foreign countries.

_____ 13. If input prices are expected to adjust fully to any change in the level of final goods prices, the economy's aggregate supply curve will be
   a. horizontal.
   b. positively sloped.
   c. vertical.
   d. negatively sloped.

_____ 14. In the short run, a rightward shift in the aggregate demand curve will tend to cause
   a. real output to rise.
   b. the level of final goods prices to rise.
   c. both **a** and **b**.
   d. neither **a** nor **b**.

15. After a rightward shift in the aggregate demand curve, real output will tend to
    a. increase in the short run and return to its natural level in the long run.
    b. increase in the short run and remain permanently above its natural level.
    c. fall in the short run but return to its natural level in the long run.
    d. fall in the short run and remain permanently below its natural level.

ANSWERS TO CHAPTER 8

Hands On

(a) The initial equilibrium real output is $2 trillion and the price level is 1.0. See point E₀ in the solution graph. (b) The aggregate demand curve shifts to the right by $1 trillion. The new curve AD₁ is parallel to the initial aggregate demand curve, as shown in the solution graph. (c) In the short run, real output increases to $2.66 trillion and the price level rises to 1.66 trillion as the economy moves to point E₁ in the solution graph. (d) The long-run aggregate supply curve is a vertical line at the natural level of real output, as shown in the solution graph. (e) In the long run, real output returns to its natural level of $2 trillion and the price level rises to 3.0. This is shown by point E₂ in the solution graph, where the long-run aggregate supply curve intersects AD₂.

Exhibit 8.1 (ans.)

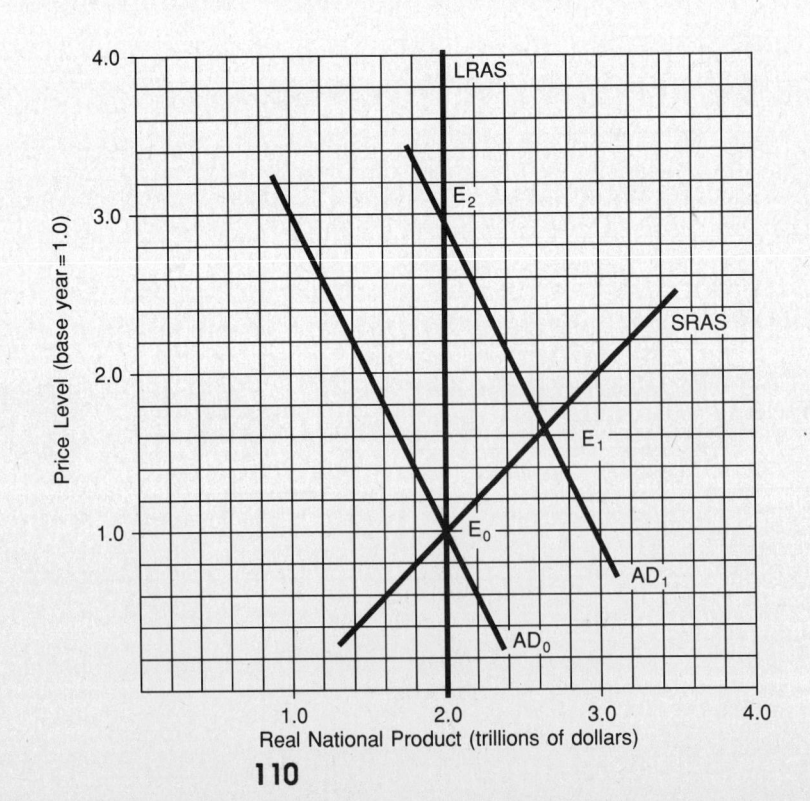

Self Test

1. **c.** Person a is not in the labor force, and person b is counted as employed even though not working.
2. **a.** This would happen because the labor force and the number of unemployment would increase by an equal amount. The employment rate would not change because neither the size of the adult civilian population nor the number of employed would change.
3. **d.** There is no maximum age.
4. **d.** Answer **c** is frictional plus structural unemployment.
5. **d.** Cyclical unemployment is zero when real output is at its natural rate.
6. **c.** Okun's law says unemployment will be one percentage point below its natural rate for each 3 percent by which real output exceeds its natural level.
7. **b.** Shorter contractions are not counted as recessions.
8. **a.** Prices fell and real output fell by about a third.
9. **b.** This curve has a negative slope.
10. **d.** Real government purchases also tend to decrease.
11. **b.** Interest rates tend to rise and real government purchases tend to fall.
12. **c.** Because it depresses disposable income. The others would tend to shift the aggregate demand curve to the right.
13. **c.** This is the long-run case. Answer **b** applies in the short run when firms tend to expect uncharged input prices.
14. **c.** In the long run, only **b**.
15. **a.** Answer **c** applies in response to a leftward shift in the aggregate demand curve.

Chapter 9

Classical and Keynesian Theories of Income Determination

WHERE YOU'RE GOING

When you have mastered this chapter, you will understand

1. Why the classical economists thought flexible prices would prevent lasting depressions.
2. How planned investment and saving respond to changes in the interest rate.
3. Why the theories of John Maynard Keynes were so favorably received by economists of the 1930s.
4. Why Keynes thought that small changes in planned expenditures could cause large disturbances in the economy.
5. The implications of Keynes's theories for economic policy.

In addition, you will add the following terms to your economic vocabulary:
   Planned-investment schedule
   Saving schedule
   Say's law
   Multiplier effect
   Marginal propensity to consume
   Expenditure multiplier

WALKING TOUR

After you have read this chapter at least once, you should work step by step through this walking tour. Fill in the blanks and answer the questions as you go along. After you have answered each question, check yourself by uncovering the answer given in the margin. If you do not understand why the answer given is the correct one, refer back to the proper section of the text.

The Classical Self-Regulating Economy

classical

natural

flexibility

A fundamental tenet of pre-Keynesian, or _____ economics was the notion that the economy would gravitate toward the _____ level of real output. One mechanism that would help accomplish this was thought to be [flexibility/rigidity] of prices.

left	Suppose that a decrease in aggregate demand causes the aggregate demand curve to shift to the [right/left]. In the classical view, the short-run result would be [an increase/a decrease/no change] in the price level and [an increase/a decrease/no change] in the level of real output. The result would be a [permanent/temporary] equilibrium with real output [above/below/at] its natural level.
decrease	
decrease	
temporary	
below	
fall, increase	In the long run, there would be a tendency for expected input prices to [rise/fall]. As this happened, real output would [increase/decrease/remain unchanged]. In the long-run equilibrium, real output would be [above/below/at] its natural level and the price level would be [above/below/at] the level that prevailed before the shift in aggregate demand.
at	
below	
saving, investment	A second shock-absorbing mechanism, in the classical view, involved the interaction of _____ and _____. Both of these were seen as depending on _____. As interest rates fell, in the classical view, real planned investment would tend to [increase/decrease] and real saving would tend to [increase/decrease]. This meant that it would always be possible to achieve equilibrium at the natural level of real output with real saving equal to real planned investment. If a decline in business confidence shifted the planned investment schedule to the left, then the interest rate would tend to [rise/fall]. If consumers decided to save less at any given interest rate, shifting the saving schedule to the left, the interest rate would tend to [rise/fall].
interest rates	
decrease	
increase	
fall	
rise	
Say's	The classical proposition that aggregate demand will automatically be great enough to absorb all of national product at the natural level of national product is known as _____ law.

Keynes's Challenge to the Classics

British	John Maynard Keynes, a [British/American] economist, challenged the classical notion of a self-regulating economy. For one thing, he believed that [saving/investment/both] tended to be unresponsive to changes in interest rates. This meant that there might be no interest rate [high/low] enough to bring real saving and real planned investment into equality at the natural level of real output.
both	
low	
wage rates	In addition, Keynes thought that [final goods prices/wage rates/both] would be unresponsive to changes in aggregate demand.

113

Taking the two together, the Keynesian version of the aggregate supply and demand model implies, for recession conditions, a [positively sloped/horizontal] aggregate supply curve and a [negatively sloped/vertical] aggregate demand curve. Given a leftward shift in the aggregate demand curve, the economy, in the short run, would experience [a decrease/no change] in the price level and [a decrease/no change] in real output. In the long run, assuming rigid wages, the price level would [decrease further/stay the same] and real output would [stay the same/return to the natural level]. On the other hand, if wages were flexible but aggregate demand did not respond to changes in the price level, the long run would see [no change/a further drop] in the price level while real output would [stay the same/return to the natural level].

positively sloped
vertical

decrease
decrease
stay the same
stay the same

a further drop
stay the same

The Multiplier Effect

According to Keynes, a $100 billion initial change in real planned investment (or another component of aggregate demand) will shift the aggregate demand curve by [more than/less than/exactly] $100 billion. This is known as the _____ effect.

more than
multiplier

The origin of the multiplier effect lies in the fact that for each $1 change in disposable income, households change their consumption expenditure by [more than/less than/exactly] $1. The proportion of each added dollar of real disposable income that households tend to consume is known as the _____. For example, suppose that households tend to consume 60 cents out of each dollar of added disposable income. In this case, the marginal propensity to consume is _____. Give this marginal propensity to consume, a $100 million addition to real disposable income will cause real consumption to increase by $_____.

less than

marginal propensity to consume

0.6

60 million

Given a marginal propensity to consume of 0.6, suppose there is a $10 million decrease in planned investment, say, in the form of a decrease in purchases of oil-drilling rigs. This is considered a "first round" decrease in aggregate demand of $_____. As a result, the income of workers who make the rigs and owners of the companies they work for will fall by $_____. These workers and others, in turn, will cut their own consumption by $_____. This is the "second round" decrease in aggregate demand. The "third round" decrease will be $_____,

10 million

10 million

6 million
3.6 million

2.16 million	the "fourth round" decrease $_____, and so on. Thus, the total decrease in aggregate demand, adding together an infinite
25 million	number of rounds, will be $ _____. The ratio of the induced shift in aggregate demand to the initial shift in real
expenditure multiplier	planned investment is known as the _____. In the simple Keynesian model, the value of the expenditure multiplier
1/(1 - mpc)	can be given by the formula _____. Thus, with a marginal propensity to consume of 0.6, the value of the expenditure mul-
2.5	tiplier would be _____.

Keynes and his followers drew the conclusion from the multiplier effect that the economy, left to its own devices, would be

unstable	[stable/unstable]. However, since the expenditure multiplier
also applies	[does not apply/also applies] to changes in real government pur-
would	chases, the government [would/would not] be able to counteract the effects of changes in planned investment.

HANDS ON

Now that you have reviewed the concepts introduced in this chapter, it is time for some hands-on practice with the analytical tools that have been introduced. Work through each problem in this section carefully, and then check your results against those given at the end of the chapter.

Problem 1

Exhibit 9.1 represents a hypothetical economy in which natural real output is $2,000 billion per year. Initially this economy is in equilibrium at a price level of 1.0, as shown by point E_1. Use this exhibit to answer the following questions:

a. Beginning from the initial equilibrium, suppose a decrease in real planned investment causes the aggregate demand curve to shift, so that at any given price level, aggregate demand is $500 billion less than previously. Draw the new aggregate demand curve and label it AD_2.
b. According to classical theory, how would the economy respond to the shift in aggregate demand in the short run? Label the new classical short-run equilibrium E_2. Compare E_2 to the short-run equilibrium that would be predicted by Keynesian theory.
c. According to classical theory, where will the economy's long-run equilibrium be, assuming no further shift in aggregate demand? Label the long-run equilibrium point E_3.
d. According to the views expressed by Keynes in his *General Theory*, where would the economy's long-run equilibrium be,

Exhibit 9.1

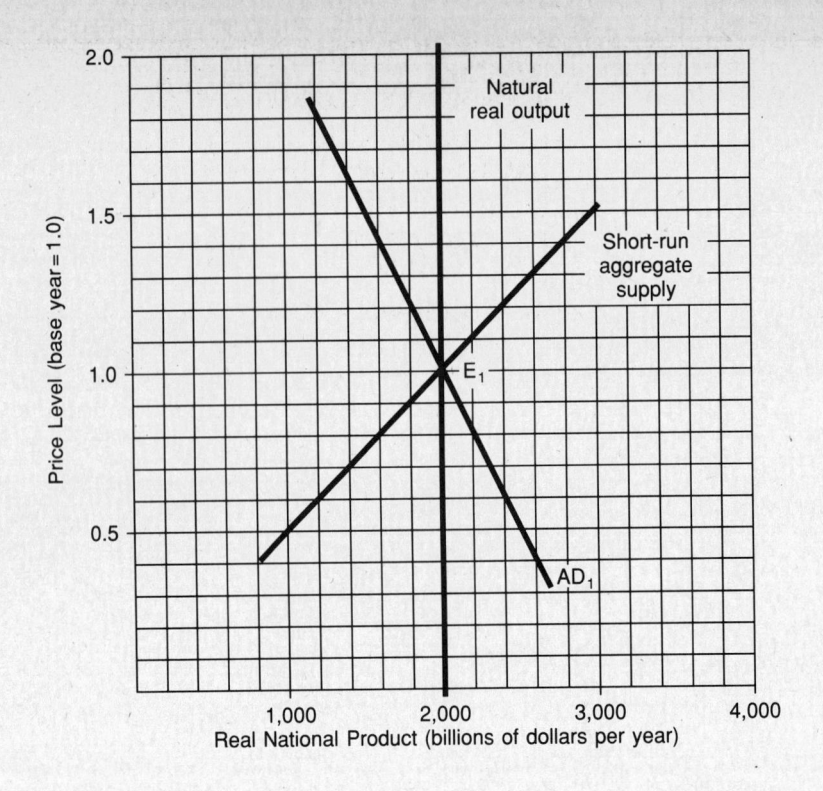

[Graph: Price Level (base year = 1.0) vs. Real National Product (billions of dollars per year), showing Natural real output (vertical line at ~2,000), Short-run aggregate supply (upward sloping), and AD₁ (downward sloping), intersecting at E₁ at price level 1.0]

assuming no further change in aggregate demand and also assuming rigid nominal wages? If wages were flexible but other Keynesian assumptions held, where would the economy go from E₂? Indicate its path by drawing a "Keynesian" aggregate demand curve through point E₂. Label this curve AD₃.

Problem 2

Complete the following table, assuming a marginal propensity to consume of 0.8.

Round	Change in Income	Change in Expenditure
1		$100,000
2	$100,000	_____
3	_____	_____
4	_____	_____
5	_____	_____

If the process continues without limit, what will the total change in expenditure be for all rounds? What is the expenditure multiplier, given the marginal propensity to consume of 0.8?

SELF TEST

These sample test items will help you check how much you have learned. Answers are found at the end of the chapter. Scoring yourself: One or two wrong—on target. Three or four wrong—passing, but you haven't mastered the chapter yet. Five or more wrong—not good enough; start over and restudy the chapter.

_____ 1. According to the classical economists, the economy's tendency, following a drop in aggregate demand, would be
   a. to fall permanently below the natural level of real output.
   b. experience a constantly falling price level along a vertical aggregate demand curve.
   c. experience permanent inflation.
   d. return, after a time, to the natural level of real output.

_____ 2. Which of the following statements reflects the classical view?
   a. Prices and wages tend to be flexible in response to changes in aggregate demand.
   b. Real planned investment expenditure is not much affected by interest rates.
   c. Saving tends to fall when interest rates rise.
   d. All of the above.

_____ 3. The classical saving-investment model is best represented by
   a. a saving schedule with a positive slope and an investment schedule with a negative slope.
   b. a saving schedule with a negative slope and a vertical investment schedule.
   c. an investment schedule with a negative slope and a vertical saving schedule.
   d. saving and investment schedules that do not intersect.

_____ 4. The market rate of interest is an approximate measure of the opportunity cost of investment funds
   a. for a firm that borrows to finance investment.
   b. for a firm that sells common stock to finance investment.
   c. for a firm that sells bonds to finance investment.
   d. all of the above.

_____ 5. An increase of business optimism will best be shown as
   a. a leftward shift of the planned investment schedule.
   b. a rightward shift of the planned investment schedule.
   c. a movement up along the planned investment schedule without a shift.
   d. a movement down along the planned investment schedule without a shift.

_____ 6. The proposition that aggregate demand will automatically be sufficient to absorb all of the output that firms and workers are willing to produce with given technology and resources is known as
   a. Smith's law.
   b. Keynes's law.
   c. Say's law.
   d. Ricardo's law.

7. Compared with the classical theorists, Keynes thought
   a. saving would be less responsive to changes in interest rates.
   b. planned investment would be less responsive to changes in interest rates.
   c. both **a** and **b**.
   d. neither **a** nor **b**.
8. According to Keynes, the economy's short-run aggregate supply curve, in an economy where the price level was flexible but nominal wages were rigid, would
   a. be vertical
   b. have a positive slope.
   c. have a negative slope.
   d. be horizontal.
9. Keynes's views, as expressed in his *General Theory*, imply that the economy's aggregate demand curve is
   a. vertical, or nearly so.
   b. horizontal, or nearly so.
   c. negatively sloped.
   d. positively sloped.
10. In Keynes's view, a decrease in planned investment could lead to a continuous fall in the price level over an extended period, without a return of real output to its natural level, if
    a. wages were rigid and the aggregate supply curve were horizontal.
    b. wages were flexible and the aggregate demand curve were vertical.
    c. wages were flexible and the aggregate demand curve were negatively sloped.
    d. wages were rigid and the aggregate demand curve were positively sloped.
11. To economists in the 1930s, the fact that real output and the price level declined for nearly 4 years, beginning in 1929, followed by only a partial recovery in the next few years, appeared consistent with
    a. Say's law.
    b. Classical economic theory.
    c. Keynes's views as expressed in his *General Theory*.
    d. Alfred Marshall's version of aggregate supply and demand.
12. According to Keynes, a $100 million initial decrease in planned investment spending will tend to shift the aggregate demand curve
    a. to the left by exactly $100 million.
    b. to the left by more than $100 million.
    c. to the right by exactly $100 million.
    d. to the right by more than $100 million.
13. If people tend to spend 80 cents of each added dollar of disposable income on consumer goods, the marginal propensity to consume is
    a. 80.
    b. 20.
    c. 0.8.
    d. 0.08.

14. If the value of the marginal propensity to consume is 0.6, the value of the expenditure multiplier will be
    a. 4.
    b. 6.
    c. 2.5.
    d. 25.
15. Keynes concluded that because of the multiplier effect,
    a. small shifts in planned investment would produce large disturbances in real output and the price level.
    b. changes in government purchases and taxes could be used to offset disturbances to private real planned investment.
    c. both **a** and **b**.
    d. neither **a** nor **b**.

ANSWERS TO CHAPTER 9

Hands On

Problem 1 (a) The new aggregate demand curve is shifted to the left by $500 million and is parallel to AD$_1$. See AD$_2$ in the solution graph for Exhibit 9.1. (b) Classical theory predicts a movement down and to the left along the aggregate supply curve. See E$_2$ in the solution graph. This is the same short-run result predicted by Keynesian theory. (c) Under classical assumptions, flexibility of

Exhibit 9.1 (ans.)

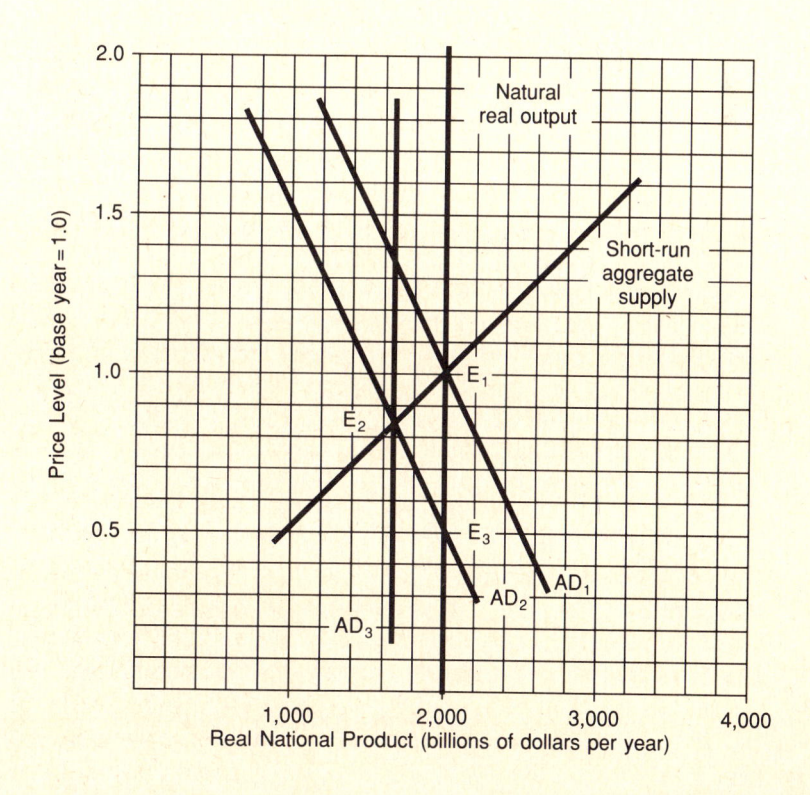

prices and wages will result in a return to the natural level of real output at E₃, as shown in the solution graph. (d) In the Keynesian view, assuming rigid wages, the economy would remain indefinitely at E₂. If wages were flexible, the economy would move downward along the vertical aggregate demand curve AD₃ without ever returning to the natural level of real output.

Problem 2 The completed table should appear as follows:

Round	Change in Income	Change in Expenditure
1		$100,000
2	$100,000	80,000
3	80,000	64,000
4	64,000	51,200
5	51,200	40,960

The process would continue for an infinite number of rounds. The total addition to expenditure after all rounds would be $500,000. The expenditure multiplier, as given by the formula $1/(1 - mpc)$ would be 5.

Self Test

1. **d.** Keynesian theory would predict **a**, and **b** if wages were flexible.
2. **a.** Answer **b** is a Keynesian assumption.
3. **a.** The classical saving-investment diagram resembles an ordinary supply and demand diagram.
4. **d.** There is no free source of investment funds.
5. **b.** Changes in the interest rate produce movements along the schedule.
6. **c.** After Jean Baptiste Say, an early follower of Adam Smith.
7. **c.** He thought there might be no interest rate that would allow real saving to equal real planned investment at the natural level of real output.
8. **b.** Keynes agreed with classical economists about the shape of the short-run aggregate supply curve.
9. **a.** Because none of the components of aggregate demand is responsive to changes in the price level, in the Keynesian view.
10. **b.** Keynes thought wages would be rigid, but he maintained that the economy would not return to natural real output even if they were flexible.
11. **c.** There appeared to be no sign of quick, automatic return to equilibrium.
12. **b.** Because of the multiplier effect.
13. **c.** The marginal propensity to consume is the quantity of added real consumption that results from a dollar's increase in real disposable income.
14. **c.** The formula is $1/(1 - mpc)$, or, in this case, $1/0.4 = 2.5$.
15. **c.** It was his view that the private economy was unstable because of the multiplier, but that the multiplier also made fiscal policy a powerful remedial tool of government policy.

Chapter 10

The Income-Expenditure Model

| **WHERE YOU'RE GOING** | *When you have mastered this chapter, you will understand*

1. More about the relationship between consumption and disposable income.
2. How consumption is affected by various kinds of taxes.
3. How the equilibrium level of national income is determined in the income-expenditure model.
4. How the income-expenditure model can be used to demonstrate the multiplier effect.
5. How the income-expenditure model can be reconciled with the aggregate supply and demand model.

In addition, you will add the following terms to your economic vocabulary:
    Consumption schedule (consumption function)
    Autonomous consumption
    Autonomous
    Average propensity to consume
    Autonomous net taxes
    Marginal tax rate
    Income-expenditure model
    Planned-expenditure schedule
    Marginal propensity to import
    Income-product line

| **WALKING TOUR** | *After you have read this chapter at least once, you should work step by step through this walking tour. Fill in the blanks and answer the questions as you go along. After you have answered each question, check yourself by uncovering the answer given in the margin. If you do not understand why the answer given is the correct one, refer back to the proper section of the text.*

The Consumption Schedule

not all   Each year consumers spend [all/not all] of their income. The relationship between real consumption spending and real disposable income can be represented in the form of a graph known as a _____ (consumption schedule). This graph intercepts the vertical axis at a level [above/below/equal to] (above) zero and has a slope [greater than/less than/equal to] (less than) 1. The level of real consumption associated with zero real disposable income is known as _____ (autonomous) consumption. The slope of the consumption schedule is equal to the _____ (marginal propensity to consume). At any level of disposable income, total consumption divided by total disposable income is known as the _____ (average propensity to consume). This is always [greater than/less than/equal to] (greater than) the marginal propensity to consume, given a positive level of an autonomous consumption.

The value of the marginal propensity to consume depends on the time horizon. Over a long period of time, consumption has tended to increase by about _____ (90 cents) for each $1 increase in disposable income. In the short run, however, the marginal propensity to consume tends to be [greater than/less than] (less than) in the long run. One reason is thought to be that year-to-year changes in income are not always _____ (permanent). The share of temporary changes in income that is consumed is thought to be [greater than/less than] (less than) the share consumed of permanent changes.

Shifts in the Consumption Schedule

A change in real consumption spending caused by a change in real disposable income, other things being equal, is shown as a [shift in/movement along] (movement along) the consumption schedule. Changes in other economic conditions can cause [shifts in/movements along] (shifts in) the schedule. For example, for any given level of real income, households with greater wealth tend to consume [more/less] (more) than those with less wealth. Thus any event that affects wealth—say a change in the average level of stock prices—can potentially cause a [shift in/movement along] (shift in) the consumption schedule.

If the consumption schedule is drawn with real national income on the horizontal axis, rather than real disposable income, changes in net taxes can also cause shifts in the consumption schedule. Taxes and transfers that do not vary as the taxpayer's income varies are known as _____ (autonomous) net taxes. An increase in autonomous net taxes will cause the consumption schedule to shift [upward/downward], and [will/will not] change the slope of the schedule.

In an economy with a proportional income tax, a change in the marginal tax rate will cause a change in the _____ of the consumption schedule. In such an economy, using mpc to stand for the marginal propensity to consume and t to stand for the marginal tax rate, the formula for the slope of the consumption schedule can be written as _____.

Graphing the Income-Expenditure Model

The circular flow can be in equilibrium only when aggregate demand is _____ aggregate supply. If aggregate demand exceeds aggregate supply, then national income will tend to [rise/fall]. If aggregate supply exceeds aggregate demand, the level of national income will tend to [rise/fall].

The relationships can be shown more clearly by drawing a graph that shows the level of total planned expenditure associated with each level of nominal national income, that is, a _____ schedule. The starting point for such a schedule is the _____ schedule. Then three items are added:

1. _____,
2. _____, and
3. _____.

When planned investment and government purchases are added, the slope of the planned expenditure is still the same as the slope of the _____ schedule. However, adding the net export component changes the slope of the planned expenditure schedule. The reason is that exports are autonomous with regard to domestic national income, but imports tend to [increase/decrease] as national income increases. The percentage of each added dollar of real disposable income that is devoted to purchases of imported goods and services is known as the _____. With the net exports component added, then, the slope of the planned expenditure schedule [increases/decreases].

It is also possible to construct a graph that shows the level of national product associated with each level of national income, that is, a/an _____ line. Such a line always has a slope of _____, because national income is equal to national product (at least in the case of a simplified economy with no capital consumption allowance, indirect business taxes, undistributed corporate profits, or statistical discrepancy).

The point at which the planned expenditure schedule and income-product line intersect represents the _____ level of real national income. If income is higher than the equilibrium level, there will be unplanned inventory [accumulation/depletion]. This will cause the level of national income to [rise/fall]. If income is lower than the equilibrium level, there will be unplanned inventory [accumulation/depletion], and the level of national income will tend to [rise/fall].

An upward shift in the planned expenditure schedule of, say, $100 billion will cause the equilibrium level of national income to [rise/fall] by [more than/less than/exactly] $100 billion. This phenomenon is known as the _____. The ratio of the induced increase in national income to the initial increase in planned expenditure is known as the _____.

In an economy where there is no income tax, the formula for the expenditure multiplier is _____. If there is an income tax with a marginal tax rate t, the formula for the expenditure multiplier becomes _____.

If there is also a marginal propensity to import of mpm, then the formula for the expenditure multiplier is _____.

Relationship of the Income Determination Models

If the assumption of a fixed price level is dropped, the income-expenditure model can be reconciled with the aggregate supply and demand model. In the short run, an increase in autonomous expenditure will shift the aggregate demand curve to the [right/left] by an amount approximately equal to the _____ times the change in autonomous expenditure. This will cause the price level to [increase/decrease] and the level of real output to [increase/decrease] as the economy moves up and to the right along the short-run aggregate supply curve. As the price level rises, other things being equal, there will be a tendency for the planned expenditure schedule to shift up by [less/more] than it would have in the fixed-price case. Thus, the short-run increase in the equilibrium value of

---

Margin notes (left column):

equilibrium

accumulation
fall

depletion
rise

rise, more than
multiplier effect

expenditure multiplier

$1/(1 - mpc)$

$1/[1 - mpc(1 - t)]$

$1/[(mpc - mpm)(1 - t)]$

right
expenditure multiplier

increase, increase

less

less than	real national product is [more than/less than] the expenditure multiplier times the original change in autonomous expenditure.
	In the long run, expected input prices will increase and the
short-run	economy will move off the original [short-run/long-run] aggregate
natural	supply curve. As the economy returns to the _____ level
further increase	of real output, there is a [decrease/further increase] in the price level. This causes the planned expenditure schedule to shift further
downward	[upward/downward]. In the new long-run equilibrium, the planned
at	expenditure will be [above/below/at] its original position, and real
at	output will be [above/below/at] its natural level.
	The conclusion, for a flexible price world, is that an increase in
temporary	autonomous expenditure will cause a [permanent/temporary]
permanent	increase in real output and a [permanent/temporary] increase in the price level.

DON'T MAKE THIS COMMON MISTAKE

It is amazing how often students lose points on an exam by neglecting to study something that is very simple and very obvious. For example, a question that is almost certain to crop up on every professor's exam involves calculation of the value of the expenditure multiplier. The general rule is that the expenditure multiplier equals 1 divided by 1 minus the slope of the planned expenditure schedule. The exact formula depends on the variables included in the model.

In the simplest case, there are no taxes and no imports. Then the formula for the expenditure multiplier is $1/(1 - mpc)$, where mpc is the marginal propensity to consume. For example, with an mpc of 0.8, the multiplier will be 5 in the simple case.

If an income tax is added with a marginal tax rate t, the slope of the planned expenditure schedule is reduced to $1 - mpc(1 - t)$. Thus, the formula for the expenditure multiplier in this case becomes $1/[1 - mpc(1 - t)]$. If mpc = 0.8 and t = 0.25, then the slope of the planned expenditure schedule is $0.8(1 - .25) = 0.6$, and the expenditure multiplier is $1/(1 - 0.6) = 1/0.4 = 2.5$.

If the model is made still more complex by adding a marginal propensity to import of mpm, while retaining the income tax at a marginal tax rate of t, then the formula for the expenditure multiplier becomes $1/[(mpc - mpm)(1 - t)]$. Suppose that mpc = 0.8, mpm = 0.05 and t = 0.33. Then the term in the denominator of the multiplier formula (that is, 1 minus the slope of the planned expenditure schedule) is $1 - (0.8 - 0.05)(1 - 0.33) = 1 - (0.75)(0.67) = 0.5$. Thus, the multiplier is 2.

HANDS ON

Now that you have reviewed the concepts introduced in this chapter, it is time for some hands-on practice with the analytical tools that have been introduced. Work through each problem in this section carefully, and then check your results against those given at the end of the chapter.

Problem 1

The following table gives data on disposable income and consumption, and saving for a hypothetical economy. Use these data to answer the questions that follow.

Disposable income	Consumption
$1,000	$1,400
2,000	2,200
3,000	3,000
4,000	3,800
5,000	4,600

a. What is the marginal propensity to consume implied by the data in this table? The level of autonomous consumption?
b. If disposable income is $4,000, what is the average propensity to consume?
c. Plot the consumption schedule for this economy in Exhibit 10.1.

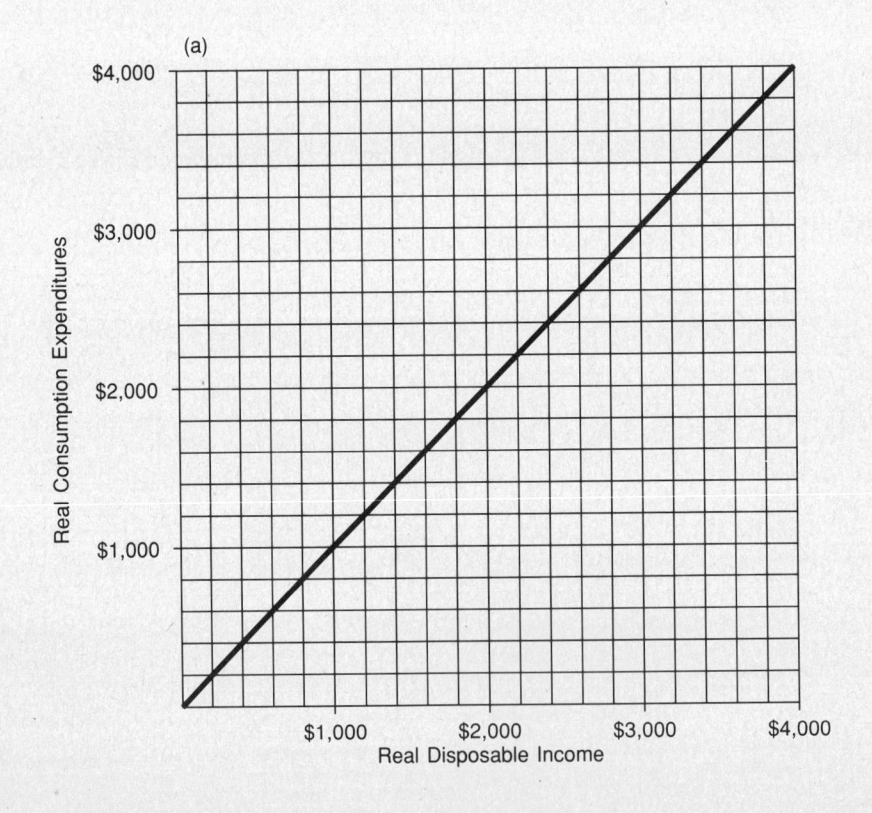

Exhibit 10.1

Problem 2

Assume autonomous consumption of $160, autonomous net taxes of $100, government purchases of $200, planned investment of $200, and a marginal propensity to consume of 0.6 in a closed economy with no imports or exports. In the space provided in Exhibit 10.2, construct an income-expenditure diagram and use it to answer the questions that follow.

Exhibit 10.2

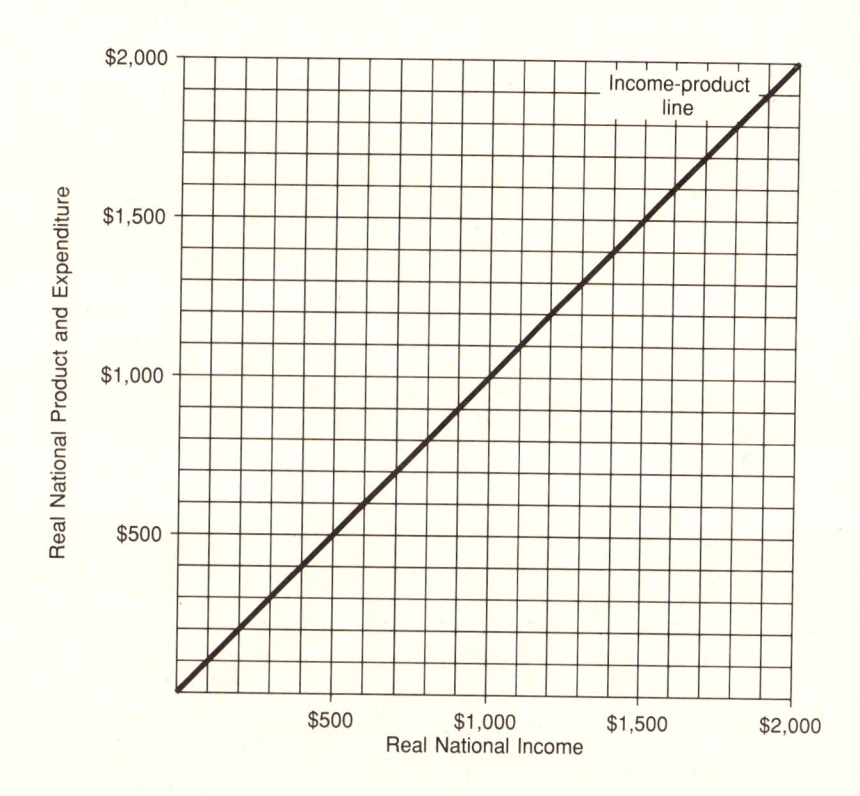

a. What is the value of consumption when disposable income is zero? When national income is zero? At what level does the consumption schedule intersect the vertical axis? What is the slope of the consumption schedule? At what point does the planned expenditure schedule intersect the vertical axis? What is the slope of the planned expenditure schedule?

b. What is the equilibrium level of real national income as you have drawn your diagram? At a real national income of $1,500, what would be the rate of unplanned inventory accumulation or decrease? What would it be at a real national income of $1,000?

c. Suppose autonomous planned expenditure were to increase by $200, shifting the planned expenditure schedule upward by that amount. Draw the new schedule and label it PE$_2$. What would be the new equilibrium level of real national income? What is the value of the expenditure multiplier for this economy?

ECONOMICS IN THE NEWS

Market Crash Cuts Consumer Spending

The following item appeared in *The Wall Street Journal* on October 21, 1987, two days after the stock market fell a record 508 points as measured by the Dow Jones Industrial Average.

> Wall Street is now Main Street U.S.A.
>
> In barber shops and boutiques from Maine to California, the gyrations of the stock market are local gossip. What's more, the news from New York is causing American consumers to reassess how, when, why, and what they consume—and for many that means cutting back.
>
> A typical tale is told by Scotty Addison, a salesman at the Erhard BMW dealership in Southfield, Michigan. Yesterday morning, he says, a customer who was "almost in tears" told him that she didn't have enough money left in her stock account to make the $5,000 down payment on the $24,000 car she had selected. Now "the deal's on hold," Addison says.
>
> In Atlanta, Mary Smith, a secretary at an engineering firm, says she and her husband put off buying a new car for another reason: "We figured that people may be so desperate to sell cars, furniture, houses and things like that that if we waited awhile maybe we could get a better price."
>
> Whatever the motives, purchases are being deferred in areas ranging from real estate to fine art. In New York City—where people, until recently, have thought nothing of plunking down $500,000 or even $1 million for a cramped apartment—the long-booming luxury housing market is taking it on the chin.
>
> On the day the market crashed, as a New York attorney was getting a root canal, he turned to his dentist, Philip Terman, and said, "Doctor, nothing you could do to me could hurt as much as the market."

Source: "Market Jitters Cause Consumers to Reassess Their Spending Plans," *The Wall Street Journal*, October 21, 1987, p. 1. Reprinted by permission of The Wall Street Journal. ©Dow Jones & Company, Inc., 1987. All Rights Reserved.

Questions

1. Economists have estimated that each $1 decrease in real wealth cuts real consumption spending by 5 cents. It has also been estimated that each one-point drop in the Dow Jones Industrial Average is equivalent to a $1 billion drop in wealth. Given these estimates, what effect would a 500-point drop in the Dow have on the planned expenditure schedule? Assuming an expenditure multiplier of 2, and fixed prices, what would be the impact on equilibrium national income?
2. Wealth and expectations are both factors that can affect the consumption schedule. Do you see any evidence in this news item that a market crash might shift the consumption schedule by more than the loss in wealth alone would imply? Discuss.
3. Assuming a flexible price model, discuss the short- and long-run effects of a stock market crash in terms of the income-expenditure model and the aggregate supply and demand model.

SELF TEST

These sample test items will help you check how much you have learned. Answers are found at the end of the chapter. Scoring yourself: One or two wrong—on target. Three or four wrong—passing, but you haven't mastered the chapter yet. Five or more wrong—not good enough; start over and restudy the chapter.

_____ 1. If autonomous consumption were zero,
   a. the marginal propensity to consume would have to be 1.
   b. the marginal propensity to consume would have to be zero.
   c. the consumption schedule would lie entirely below the income-product line.
   d. saving would be less than zero for all income levels.

_____ 2. If the consumption schedule is drawn on a diagram having real national income on the horizontal axis, an increased autonomous net tax
   a. will increase the slope of the consumption schedule.
   b. will decrease the slope of the consumption schedule.
   c. will cause an upward parallel shift in the consumption schedule.
   d. will cause a downward parallel shift in the consumption schedule.

_____ 3. In an economy with only a proportional income tax, the marginal tax rate is cut from 0.5 to 0.35. What happens to the consumption schedule, as graphed using real national income on the horizontal axis?
   a. It shifts upward without changing slope.
   b. The slope increases.
   c. The slope decreases.
   d. It shifts downward without changing slope.

_____ 4. An increase in exports, other things being equal,
   a. adds to aggregate demand.
   b. reduces aggregate demand.
   c. increases the slope of the consumption schedule.
   d. does none of the above unless imports also change.

_____ 5. Which of the following would produce an upward shift in the income-product line?
   a. An increase in nominal GNP.
   b. An increase in real GNP.
   c. An increase in the marginal propensity to consume.
   d. None of the above.

_____ 6. If the marginal propensity to consume is 0.75 and the planned expenditure schedule intersects the vertical axis at $500, where must it intersect the income-product line?
   a. $500.
   b. $2,000.
   c. $2,500.
   d. Insufficient information is given for an answer to be reached.

7. When real national income exceeds its equilibrium value, there will be
   a. unplanned inventory depletion.
   b. unplanned inventory accumulation.
   c. a government budget deficit.
   d. a government budget surplus.
8. In a fixed-price model with no income tax or imports, where the marginal propensity to consume is 0.9, a $100 increase in planned investment expenditure, other things being equal, will cause an increase in equilibrium real national income of
   a. $90.
   b. $100.
   c. $900.
   d. $1,000.
9. If the marginal propensity to consume is 0.75 and there is no income tax or imports, the value of the expenditure multiplier will be
   a. 0.75.
   b. 2.5.
   c. 4.
   d. 8.
10. If the marginal propensity to consume is 0.8 and if there is a proportional income tax with a marginal rate of 25 percent, then the value of the expenditure multiplier is
    a. 8.
    b. 5.
    c. 2.5.
    d. 0.25.
11. If the expenditure multiplier is equal to 8 and if the planned expenditure schedule intersects the vertical axis at $1,000, equilibrium real national income must be
    a. $800.
    b. $2,000.
    c. $8,000.
    d. none of the above.
12. If the equilibrium value of real national income is $2,000 and if unplanned inventory accumulation is $200 when real national income is $3,000, the value of the expenditure multiplier must be
    a. 2.
    b. 5.
    c. 8.
    d. Impossible to compute from the information given.
13. Other things being equal, as real domestic national income increases, net exports tend to
    a. decrease because exports decrease.
    b. increase because exports increase.
    c. decrease because imports increase.
    d. increase because imports decrease.

____ 14. In the short run, given an expenditure multiplier of 3, a $100 billion increase in autonomous planned expenditure will tend to shift the aggregate demand curve
   a. to the right by $100 billion.
   b. to the left by $100 billion.
   c. to the right by $300 billion.
   d. to the left by $300 billion.

____ 15. In the long run, an increase in autonomous planned investment will, other things being equal, tend to
   a. cause the equilibrium price level to rise.
   b. cause equilibrium real output to rise.
   c. both a and b.
   d. neither a nor b.

ANSWERS TO CHAPTER 10

Hands On

Problem 1 (a) For each $1,000 increase in disposable income, consumption increases by $800, thus, the mpc is 0.8. Autonomous consumption is $600. (b) The average propensity to consume at $4,000 is $3,800/$4,000 = 0.95. (c) See solution graph for Exhibit 10.1

Exhibit 10.1 (ans.)

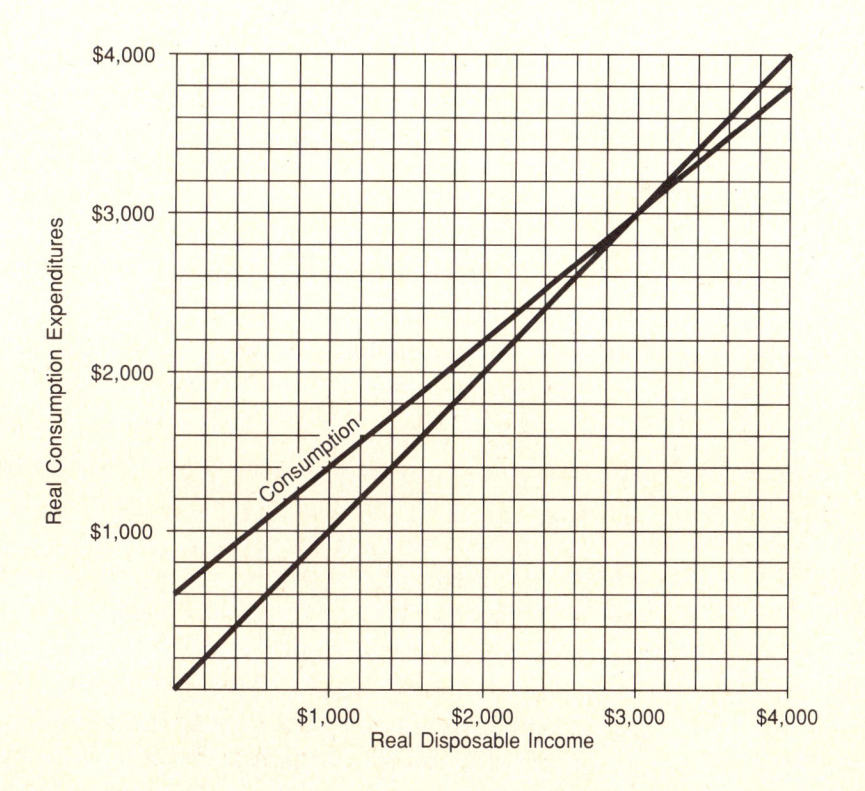

131

Problem 2 (a) Autonomous consumption of $160 means that consumption is $160 when disposable income is zero. However, when national income is zero, disposable income is -$100 because of the $100 in autonomous net taxes. With a marginal propensity to consume of 0.6, this means just $100 in consumption expenditure when national income is zero. The consumption schedule thus intersects the vertical axis at $100 and has a slope of 0.6, equal to the mpc. The planned expenditure schedule PE_1 is parallel to the consumption schedule and has a vertical intercept of $500 (add I = 200 and G = 200 to the $100 consumption intercept). See Exhibit 10.2 (answer). (b) Equilibrium real national income is $1,250. At $1,500, there would be unplanned inventory accumulation of $100; at $1,000, there would be unplanned inventory depletion of $100. (c) The new equilibrium is $1,750. The multiplier is 2.5. You can find this by looking at the ratio of the change in equilibrium national income to the initial change in autonomous planned expenditure ($500/$200 = 2.5) or by applying the formula: Expenditure Multiplier = 1/(1 - mpc).

Exhibit 10.2 (ans.)

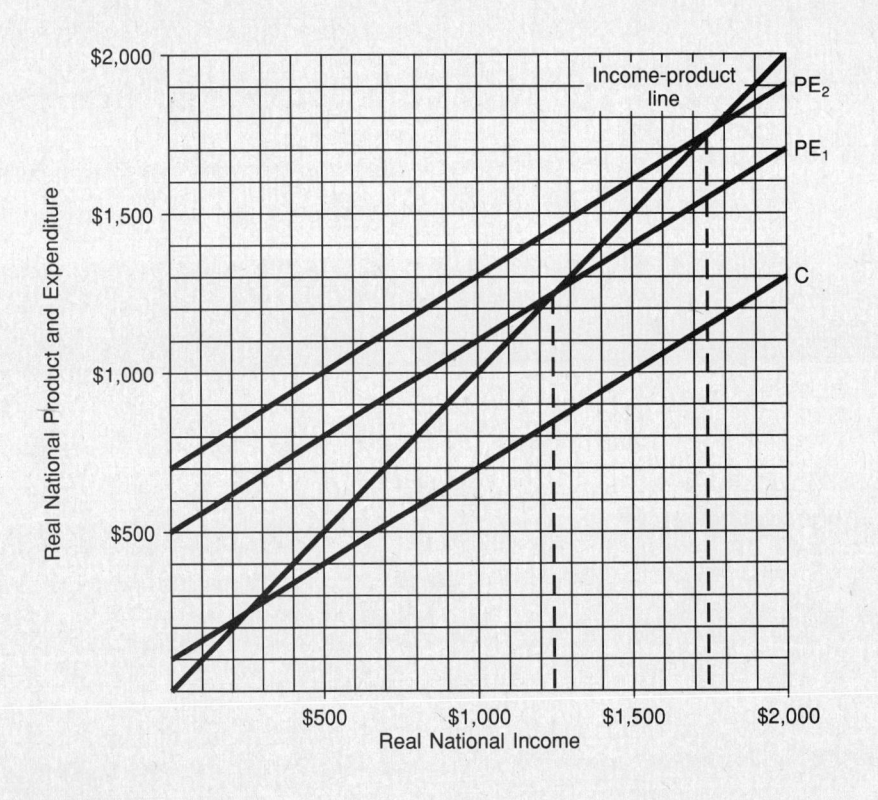

Economics in the News

(1) Given the reported estimates, a 500-point drop in the Dow would cut $500 billion from wealth, and would thus cut $25 billion from consumption expenditure. With an expenditure multiplier of 2, this would mean a $50 billion drop in equilibrium national income. (2) Addison's customer cancelled a purchase because of a loss of wealth. However, the Smiths cut back on their consumption spending because of a change in expectations. Also, although not mentioned here, the expectations of business managers responsible for investment decisions might also be adversely affected by stock

prices. When both the change in wealth and the adverse change in expectations are considered, the wealth effect alone may underestimate the impact of a stock market crash on the economy. (3) In the short run, the planned expenditure curve would shift down and the aggregate demand curve would shift to the left. Real output and the price level would fall. The fall in the price level would limit the downward shift in the planned expenditure schedule. In the long run, real output would return to its natural level and the price level would fall further. As this happened, the planned expenditure schedule would shift back to its original position. In long-run equilibrium, real output would return to its natural rate and the price level would be lower than it was to begin with.

Self Test

1. **c.** The consumption schedule would pass through the origin and have a slope less than 1.
2. **d.** Consumption is reduced, and the shift is parallel because the tax is the same at all levels of real income.
3. **b.** The slope of the schedule is equal to mpc(1 - t).
4. **a.** An increase in exports with no change in imports means an increase in net exports, one of the components of aggregate demand.
5. **d.** The income-product line passes through the origin and has a slope of 1 by definition, regardless of the particular conditions mentioned.
6. **b.** A short-cut way to calculate the intersection (the equilibrium real income level) is to multiply the vertical intercept by the expenditure multiplier.
7. **b.** Which will tend to cause a decrease in income.
8. **d.** The multiplier in this case is 1/(1 - 0.9) = 10.
9. **c.** The formula is 1/(1 - mpc).
10. **c.** Here the formula that applies is 1/[1 - mpc(1 - t)], which works out to 1/0.4, or 2.5, in this case.
11. **c.** The same short-cut method applies as in question 6.
12. **b.** First figure what the slope of the planned expenditure schedule must be. A $1,000 increase in income raises planned expenditure by $800, leaving $200 unplanned inventory accumulation. Thus the slope of the planned expenditure schedule is 0.8. This, in turn, implies an expenditure multiplier of 5.
13. **c.** Net exports decrease because imports increase; the level of exports depends on the level of income abroad (other things being equal).
14. **c.** The (approximate) shift in the aggregate demand curve is equal to the expenditure multiplier times the change in autonomous expenditure.
15. **a.** In the long run, real output returns to its natural level and the planned expenditure schedule returns to its original position.

Chapter 11

Fiscal Policy

WHERE YOU'RE GOING

When you have mastered this chapter, you will understand

1. How fiscal policy—changes in government purchases and net taxes—can be used to fight recession and inflation.
2. How government receipts and expenditures are affected by changing economic conditions.
3. How the federal budgetary system works and what its limitations are.
4. The priorities that have guided federal tax and spending decisions in the 1980s.
5. How the deficit is measured and why it has grown.
6. Whether large federal deficits are a threat to economic stability.

In addition, you will add the following terms to your economic vocabulary:
- Fiscal policy
- Net tax multiplier
- Discretionary fiscal policy
- Automatic fiscal policy
- Automatic stabilizers
- Fiscal year
- Entitlements
- Structural deficit
- Cyclical deficit

WALKING TOUR

After you have read this chapter at least once, you should work step by step through this walking tour. Fill in the blanks and answer the questions as you go along. After you have answered each question, check yourself by uncovering the answer given in the margin. If you do not understand why the answer given is the correct one, refer back to the proper section of the text.

The Theory of Fiscal Policy

Policy concerning government purchases, taxes, and transfer payments is known as ____fiscal____ policy. The use of fiscal policy as a tool of economic stabilization is especially associated with the ____Keynesian____ school of economics.

fiscal

Keynesian

134

Suppose, for example, that the aggregate demand curve has shifted to the left by $100 billion, and that as a result, real output is below its natural level. In order to restore real output to its natural level, government purchases could be [**increased**/decreased]. Assuming an expenditure multiplier of 4, the increase in government purchases required to shift the aggregate demand curve back to the right by $100 billion would be **$25 billion**. Such a shift in the aggregate demand curve would result in an increase in real output from the initial short-run equilibrium of [more than/**less than**/exactly] $100 billion.

Instead of an increase in government purchases, an [increase/**decrease**] in taxes or an [**increase**/decrease] in transfer payments could be used to shift the aggregate demand curve to the right by $100 billion. Assuming a marginal propensity to consume of 0.75 and no complications arising from income taxes or net exports, a tax cut of **$33 billion** would be required. The ratio of the shift in aggregate demand to a given change in net taxes is known as the **net tax** multiplier. The formula for this multiplier is **mpc/(1 − mpc)**. Recent experience in the United States indicates that in practice, the actual impact of changes in net taxes on aggregate demand, at least in the short run, tends to be [more/**less**] than predicted by the net tax multiplier.

Changes in laws setting government purchases and net taxes that are made for the purpose of affecting aggregate demand or for other reasons are known as **discretionary** fiscal policy. Government purchases and net taxes [**can**/cannot] change even if there are no discretionary changes in laws. Changes in fiscal variables that result from changes in economic conditions without changes in laws are known as **automatic** fiscal policy.

Among the most important conditions that affect government purchases and net taxes are changes in **real output**, **inflation**, and **interest rates**. Other things being equal, when the economy enters a recession, the federal budget tends to move toward [surplus/**deficit**]. When the economy expands, the federal budget tends to move toward [**surplus**/deficit].

135

Fiscal Policy in the Income-Expenditure Model

Note: Skip this section unless you have read Chapter 10.

The income-expenditure model developed in Chapter 10 provides an alternative framework for looking at fiscal policy. In the fixed-price version of the income-expenditure model, an increase in government purchases causes the <u>planned expenditure</u> schedule to shift [upward/downward]. For example, assuming a marginal propensity to consume of 0.8, no income tax, and a closed economy, a $20 billion increase in government purchases will cause the planned expenditure schedule to shift up by <u>$20</u> billion. As a result of this shift, the equilibrium level of real national income will shift up by <u>$100</u> billion. Under the same assumptions, a $10 billion increase in net taxes would cause the planned expenditure schedule to shift [up/down] by <u>$8</u> billion and would cause the equilibrium level of real national income to [rise/fall] by <u>$40</u> billion.

In a flexible price world, the impact of changes in government purchases or net taxes on equilibrium real national income is [greater than/less than] predicted by the fixed-price income-expenditure model. In the short run, the flexible price model predicts that an increase in government purchases will have [some/no] effect on real output and [some/no] effect on the price level. In the long run, the flexible price model predicts that an increase in government purchases will have [some/no] effect on real output and a [greater/smaller] effect on the price level than in the short run.

U.S. Fiscal Policy in the 1980s

In the actual fiscal policy process of the U.S. government, macroeconomic goals play a [decisive/relatively minor] role in decisions regarding government purchases, taxes, and transfer payments. Part of the problem is that Congress often [ignores/follows too closely] its own rules for fiscal decision making. There is also a problem with expenditures governed by long-term laws not subject to the annual budget process. These are known as <u>entitlements</u>. Entitlements are sometimes called "uncontrollable" expenses. Another expense that is uncontrollable is <u>interest payments</u>.

Margin answers:
- planned expenditure
- upward
- $20
- $100
- down, $8
- fall, $40
- less than
- some, some
- no
- greater
- relatively minor
- ignores
- entitlements
- interest payments

In 1985, a law was passed that attempted to reform the budget process by limiting federal deficits. This was the <u>Gramm-Rudman-Hollings</u> law. Federal deficits in the next 2 years [**did**/did not] decline from their peaks. Thus, the law can be judged to have been at least a partial success.

Budget priorities can be judged by looking at actual budget patterns as well as at what government officials say priorities are. If fiscal priorities in the 1980 to 1986 period are viewed this way, it appears that key priorities included

1. [raising/lowering/**holding the line on**] the share of federal taxes in GNP.
2. [**increasing**/decreasing] entitlements.
3. [**increasing**/decreasing] defense expenditures.
4. [**reducing**/increasing] discretionary nondefense spending.
5. shifting GNP share toward increased [**consumption**/investment].

The Debate over the Deficit and the National Debt

The budget surplus or deficit that the federal government would incur given current tax and spending laws and a 6 percent unemployment rate is known as the <u>structural</u> deficit. The difference between the actual deficit and the structural deficit is known as the <u>cyclical</u> deficit. In the period 1983 to 1986, a dramatic feature of U.S. fiscal policy was a sharp growth in the [cyclical/**structural**] deficit.

Some economists think that the federal deficit is not as big a problem as has sometimes been maintained. They point to several factors. First, at least through 1986, [**some**/none] of the deficit was cyclical. Second, they point out that in most recent years, state and local governments have run a [deficit/**surplus**]. Third, they think that federal [current/**capital**] spending should be deducted from the deficit. Finally, they think an adjustment should be made for <u>inflation</u>.

Other economists continue to be concerned about the deficit. They fear that the deficit tends to [**raise**/lower] interest rates, and hence to [raise/**lower**] investment. Second, they are concerned about the [**increase**/decrease] in borrowing from abroad. Finally, they are concerned that rising <u>interest</u> payments could cause the

137

inflation | budget deficit to "explode." The result of an exploding deficit, they fear, would be runaway _inflation_.

HANDS ON

Now that you have reviewed the concepts introduced in this chapter, it is time for some hands-on practice with the analytical tools that have been introduced. Work through this section carefully, and then check your results against those given at the end of the chapter.

You are a federal official engaged in the early stages of fiscal policy planning for the fiscal year 1990. According to your forecasts, based on current tax and spending laws and current trends in the economy, the economy's short-run aggregate supply curve will be in the position AS₁ in 1990 (as shown in Exhibit 11.1) and the aggregate demand curve will be in the position AD₁, if no policy changes are made. You estimate the economy's natural level of real output to be $2,000 billion per year. Use Exhibit 11.1 to answer the following questions:

Exhibit 11.1

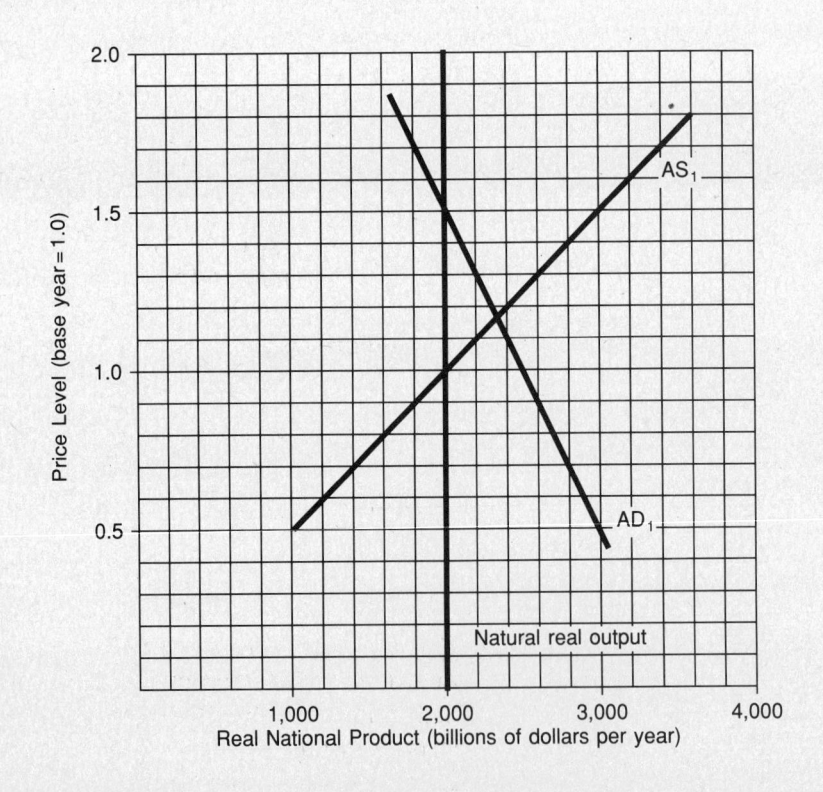

a. Given no change in policy, what will be the equilibrium price level in 1992? The equilibrium level of real output? Label the short-run equilibrium point for 1992 as E₁.
b. Fearing that inflationary pressure may develop, you would prefer to see real output at its natural level in 1992 and to see

138

the price level at 1.0. How much would the aggregate demand curve have to be shifted to achieve this result? Sketch the needed aggregate demand curve, and label it AD$_2$. Label the short-run equilibrium point, given the new aggregate demand curve, as E$_2$.

c. Assuming a marginal propensity to consume of 0.8, and no complications arising from income taxes or the foreign sector, what change in government purchases could be used to bring about the desired shift in the aggregate demand curve?

d. Still assuming a marginal propensity to consume of 0.8, what change in net taxes would be needed to bring about the desired shift in the aggregate demand curve?

ECONOMICS IN THE NEWS

WASHINGTON, NOVEMBER 3, 1987—Congressional Democrats came up with a new offer in yesterday's budget talks, but it was rejected by the Reagan administration as containing too much in taxes and too little in domestic spending cuts.

The plan, put forward by the chairmen of the House and Senate budget committees, would reduce the projected deficit by about $31 billion in fiscal 1988, which began October 1.

Administration negotiators complained that the plan contained only $6 billion in domestic spending cuts, but had more than $10 billion in new taxes, according to congressional and administration sources. The White House is seeking a plan that would match tax increases dollar-for-dollar with domestic spending cuts.

"Most of what that package says is that if we raise taxes, they'll agree to cut defense," said one administration official. "If we are going to have real taxes, we need real domestic spending cuts."

The talks between the White House and Congress were begun last week in response to the precipitous drop in the stock market, which President Reagan yesterday said was "one warning we can't afford to ignore" if the 5-year economic expansion is to continue.

Source: Jeffrey H. Birnbaum and Alan Murray, "Reagan Rejects Deficit Proposal By Democrats," *The Wall Street Journal*, November 4, 1987, p. 3. Reprinted by permission of The Wall Street Journal. ©Dow Jones & Company, Inc., 1987. All Rights Reserved.

Questions

1. Comment on the budget priorities reflected in this article. How do congressional and administration priorities differ, if at all? Do you see any sign of a shift in priorities compared with earlier years of the Reagan administration? What role, if any, do macroeconomic considerations appear to play in the budget negotiations reported here?

2. The deficit reduction package under discussion consists partly of tax increases and partly of spending cuts. What difference does the division between spending cuts and tax increases make for aggregate demand? Does it matter whether the "spending" cuts discussed here mean cuts in transfer payments or cuts in government purchases? Explain.

3. President Reagan expresses the concern that the October 1987 stock market crash could bring on a recession, thus ending the 5-year economic expansion then in progress. Other things being equal, do you think raising taxes and cutting government spending would help reduce the danger of a recession? Why or why not? In answering this part of the question, first consider the simple analytics of the aggregate supply and demand model, and then also take into account the concerns about the deficit expressed by some economists.

SELF TEST

These sample test items will help you check how much you have learned. Answers are found at the end of the chapter. Scoring yourself: One or two wrong—on target. Three or four wrong—passing, but you haven't mastered the chapter yet. Five or more wrong—not good enough; start over and restudy the chapter.

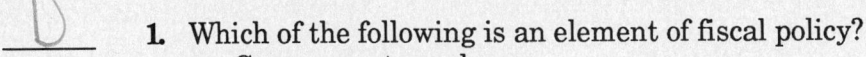

_D_ 1. Which of the following is an element of fiscal policy?
   a. Government purchases.
   b. Transfer payments.
   c. Taxes.
   d. All of the above.

_B_ 2. Suppose equilibrium real output is $100 billion below the natural level. According to the aggregate supply and demand model, what shift in the aggregate demand curve will be needed to bring equilibrium real output to the natural level?
   a. A $100 billion rightward shift.
   b. A rightward shift of more than $100 billion.
   c. A $100 billion leftward shift.
   d. A leftward shift of more than $100 billion.

_D_ 3. Fiscal policymakers decide that they would like to shift the aggregate demand curve to the left by $10 billion. They estimate that the marginal propensity to consume is 0.6. Ignoring income taxes and net exports, what change in government purchases will be required to bring about the desired shift?
   a. A $10 billion cut.
   b. A $10 billion increase.
   c. A $6 billion cut.
   d. A $4 billion cut.

_C_ 4. Policymakers desire to shift the aggregate demand curve to the right by $20 billion. They estimate that the expenditure multiplier is 5. Ignoring income taxes and net exports, which of the following policy changes will bring about the desired shift?
   a. A $20 billion cut in transfer payments.
   b. A $4 billion tax cut.
   c. A $5 billion dollar tax cut.
   d. A $4 billion increase in transfer payments.

__B__ 5. Assuming a net tax multiplier of 3, a $100 billion tax cut will, according to the aggregate supply and demand model, tend in the short run to cause equilibrium real output to
   a. rise by $300 billion.
   b. rise, but by less than $300 billion.
   c. fall by $300 billion.
   d. fall, but by less than $300 billion.

__D__ 6. Economists estimate that the marginal propensity to consume is 0.75. As a practical matter, it is likely that a one-time temporary $100 billion tax cut will increase consumption purchases by
   a. exactly $100 billion.
   b. exactly $75 billion.
   c. between $75 and $100 billion.
   d. less than $75 billion.

__B__ 7. Given a marginal propensity to consume of 0.9, the value of the net tax multiplier will be
   a. 10.
   b. 9.
   c. 8.
   d. 1.

__A__ 8. Changes in government purchases and net taxes that result from changes in economic conditions, with no changes in laws, are called
   a. automatic fiscal policy.
   b. autonomous fiscal policy.
   c. discretionary fiscal policy.
   d. cyclical fiscal policy.

__B__ 9. Other things being equal, when the economy enters a recession, the federal budget tends to
   a. move toward surplus.
   b. move toward deficit.
   c. remain unchanged.
   d. no reason to think one rather than another of the above will happen.

__C__ 10. The federal government's fiscal year 1990 runs from
   a. January 1, 1990, to December 31, 1990.
   b. October 1, 1990, to September 30, 1991.
   c. October 1, 1989, to September 30, 1990.
   d. September 1, 1989, to August 31, 1990.

__C__ 11. Compared with the 1970s, which of the following fell as a share of GNP in the 1980s?
   a. Total federal government outlays.
   b. Federal government revenues.
   c. Discretionary nondefense spending.
   d. Both b and c, but not a.

__C__ 12. Compared with the 1960s, federal defense spending in the period 1980 to 1986, considered as a share of GNP, was
   a. much higher.
   b. almost exactly the same.
   c. somewhat lower.
   d. less than half as high.

___A___ 13. Which of the following appears not to have been a strong government priority in the period 1980 to 1986, judging from results, rather than from what was said?
   a. Cutting entitlement spending.
   b. Raising defense spending above the levels of the late 1970s.
   c. Holding the line on taxes as a share of GNP.
   d. Cutting discretionary nondefense spending.

___C___ 14. In the period 1983 to 1986, which of the following increased rapidly?
   a. The actual deficit.
   b. The cyclical deficit.
   c. The structural deficit.
   d. All increased at about the same rate.

___C___ 15. In the period 1983 to 1986, state and local government budgets, on the whole, showed
   a. a deficit.
   b. exact balance, or close to it.
   c. a moderate surplus.
   d. a surplus that was larger than the federal deficit.

ANSWERS TO CHAPTER 11

Hands On

(a) Given no change in policy, the equilibrium price level will be about 1.16, as shown by the intersection of AS$_1$ and AD$_1$. The equilibrium level of real output will be about $2,333 billion. See solution

Exhibit 11.1 (ans.)

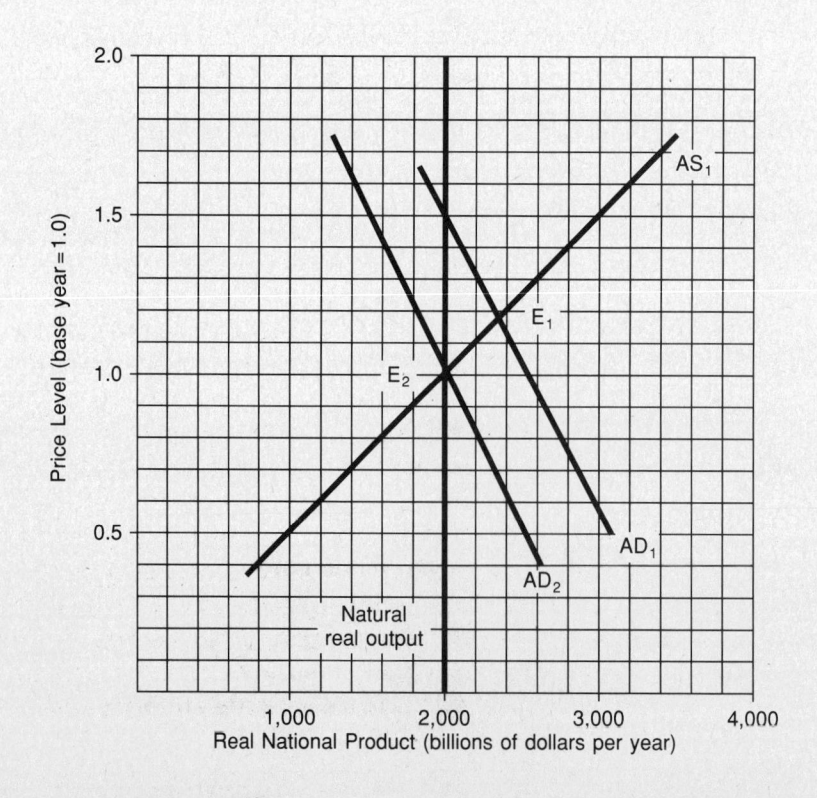

142

graph, point E$_1$. (b) The aggregate demand curve needs to shift to the left by $500 billion, as shown by AD$_2$ in the solution graph. (c) An mpc of 0.8 implies a multiplier of 5. Other things being equal, the shift in the aggregate demand curve approximately equals the change in government purchases times the multiplier. Thus a $100 billion cut in government purchases would be needed to accomplish the needed shift. (d) The net tax multiplier is 4, thus a $125 billion tax increase would be needed to accomplish the required shift.

Economics in the News

(1) Compared with Congress, the administration gives a greater priority to spending cuts and resists tax increases. Of spending cuts, it prefers more domestic spending cuts. These are the priorities that prevailed throughout the Reagan administration, except that by late 1987, the administration was no longer resisting all tax increases, but merely insisting that they be matched by spending cuts. The reason for the administration shift on tax cuts was macroeconomic in nature. White House officials came to think that without action on the deficit, there might be a recession. (2) According to standard theory, changes in government purchases have a stronger effect on aggregate demand, dollar for dollar, than do changes in net taxes. It does matter what the "spending" cuts are. Cuts in transfers, which are subject to the net tax multiplier, will have less of an effect on aggregate demand than cuts in government purchases, which are subject to the full expenditure multiplier. (3) The simple analytics of the AS/AD model suggest that a cut in the deficit, other things being equal, will shift the AD curve to the left and will thus help bring on a recession, not prevent it. The argument that a cut in the deficit could help prevent a recession hinges in part on the tendency of a deficit to "crowd out" investment. More will be said about this in later chapters. In part, it was also hoped that a showing of government will to act on the politically difficult deficit problem would boost consumer and investor confidence, thereby offsetting the direct negative impact on aggregate demand.

Self Test

1. **d.** Another way to put it is that fiscal policy is concerned with government purchases and net taxes.
2. **b.** In the AS/AD model, the short-run change in equilibrium real output is always less than the shift in the aggregate demand curve because some of the impact of the shift in the demand curve is felt on the price level.
3. **d.** With an mpc of 0.6, the expenditure multiplier is 2.5. The shift in the aggregate demand curve is equal to the expenditure multiplier times the change in government purchases.
4. **c.** If the expenditure multiplier is 5, the net tax multiplier is 4.
5. **b.** The aggregate demand curve shifts to the right by $300 billion but real output increases by less than that because the price level rises as the economy moves up and to the right along its short-run aggregate supply curve.

6. **d.** In practice the change in consumption resulting from a temporary tax cut tends to be less than the mpc would indicate, and the change in saving tends to be more, at least in the short run.
7. **b.** The formula is mpc/(1 - mpc).
8. **a.** Discretionary changes require a change in laws.
9. **b.** In part because taxes tend to decrease and in part because transfers tend to rise.
10. **c.** Each fiscal year starts on October 1 of the preceding calendar year.
11. **c.** **a** rose substantially and **b** did not change much.
12. **c.** Defense spending rose in the 1980s compared with the late 1970s, but that was an unusually low base.
13. **a.** Entitlements rose; the other three objectives were accomplished.
14. **c.** The cyclical component of the deficit fell sharply, becoming zero by mid-1987.
15. **c.** The state and local surplus partially offset the impact of federal deficits.

Chapter 12

Money and the Banking System

WHERE YOU'RE GOING

When you have mastered this chapter, you will understand

1. What money is and what it does.
2. How the stock of money in the economy is measured.
3. The structure of the U.S. banking system.
4. How the safety and stability of the banking system are maintained.

In addition, you will add the following terms to your economic vocabulary:
    Money
    Liquidity
    Currency
    Transaction deposits
    Commercial banks
    Thrift institutions (thrifts)
    M1
    Savings deposits
    Time deposits
    Repurchase agreements
    M2
    Depository institutions
    Reserves

WALKING TOUR

After you have read this chapter at least once, you should work step by step through this walking tour. Fill in the blanks and answer the questions as you go along. After you have answered each question, check yourself by uncovering the answer given in the margin. If you do not understand why the answer given is the correct one, refer back to the proper section of the text.

Money and What it Does

Money is any asset that functions as a

means of payment   1. _means of payment_,
store of value   2. _store of value_, and
unit of account   3. _unit of account_.

Because money has a constant nominal value and can be used directly as or readily converted to a means of payment, it is known as a __liquid__ asset.

Deposits from which funds can be withdrawn without notice, by check, for the purpose of making payments to third parties are known as __transaction deposits__. Traditionally, only commercial banks were able to offer such deposits, which were known as __demand__ deposits. Today savings and loan institutions as well as banks also offer transactions deposits known as __NOW__ accounts, and credit unions offer __share draft__ accounts. Transactions deposits at depository institutions of all types, together with currency, constitute the narrowly defined money supply known as __M1__.

In addition to the components of M1, there are many other highly liquid assets available to businesses and consumers in the U.S. economy. One important example is the shares of __money market mutual funds__ which are financial intermediaries that sell shares to the public, using the proceeds to buy short-term securities and passing most of the interest income through to shareholders. Many money market mutual funds allow funds to be withdrawn by check. Large corporations often make use of another type of highly liquid asset, consisting of an agreement to buy securities from a financial institution for resale the next day at a specified price. These are called __overnight purchases__. Finally, depository institutions offer some types of deposits that are not fully checkable, but are still considered fairly liquid. These are __MMDA's__, __savings__, and __small denomination time__ deposits. All of these and other liquid assets, plus M1, constitute the broad measure of the money supply known as __M2__. Altogether, M2 is more than __five__ times as large as M1.

The Banking System

The two main types of financial intermediaries that constitute the banking system are __commercial banks__ and __thrift institutions__. All banks and thrifts include among their assets vault cash and non-interest-bearing deposits with the Federal Reserve. These are known as __reserves__. The main income earning assets of banks and thrifts are __loans__ and __securities__.

deposits	The main categories of liabilities are __deposits__ and __borrowing__.
borrowing	
central	The Federal Reserve serves as the __central__ banking system of the United States. Its major duties include
providing services	1. __providing services__
regulating banks	2. __regulating banks__, and
conducting monetary policy, 1913, is not	3. __conducting monetary policy__.
	The Fed was established in __1913__. It [is/~~is not~~] subor-
is not	dinate to the executive branch, and [is/~~is not~~] directed by Congress
12	in its day-to-day operations. The system consists of __12__ Federal Reserve Banks. Its highest policy making body is the
Board of Governors	__BOG__. Authority over purchases and sales of securities
Federal Open Market Committee, Not all	rests with the __Federal Open Market Committee__.
	[All/~~Not all~~] banks are members of the Federal Reserve System. The Depository Institutions Deregulation and Monetary Control Act
1980, abolished	of __1980__ [abolished/strengthened] many of the distinctions between member and nonmember banks and thrifts.
only a fraction	Banks are able to earn a profit because they keep [all/~~only a fraction~~] of the deposits they receive as reserves. This approach to banking entails certain risks. Two possible sources of bank failure are
loan losses, illiquidity	__loan losses__ and __illiquidity__. The main tools used by government to ensure safety and soundness of the banking system include
supervision and regulation, loans to troubled banks, deposit insurance, have not	1. __loans to troubled banks__,
	2. __supervision & regulation__, and
	3. __deposit insurance__
	These tools [have/~~have not~~] prevented failures of individual banks.
have	Since the 1930s, they [~~have~~/have not] prevented widespread failure of the country's banking system as a whole.

DON'T MAKE THIS COMMON MISTAKE

Many student mistakes in macroeconomics arise from careless use of the word *money*. As you have learned in this chapter, *money* has a single, specialized meaning in the language of economics—an asset serving as a means of payment, a store of value, and a unit of account. Unfortunately, in everyday life, the word *money* is used very loosely. Try to break the habit of these loose usages when talking the language of economics. Here are some examples:

Everyday language: "After Joan got the promotion, she earned a lot more money than before." *Economics language:* "After Joan got the promotion, she earned a *higher income* than before." Income is a flow, a measure of the value of what Joan is paid per unit of time. Maybe she decides, after her promotion, to save part of her income by adding to the stock of money she has in her checking account; maybe she spends it all, adding to her stock of durable consumer goods; we don't know without more information.

Everyday language: "President Reagan's defense spending plans will pump so much money into the economy that inflation will become a real danger." *Economics language:* "The defense plans will add so much to *planned expenditure* that inflation will become a real danger." What starts as a slip of terminology here could grow into a confusion between fiscal and monetary policy. Defense spending adds to the flow of aggregate demand; it is a fiscal policy action. Such spending does not add directly to the stock of money which is under control of the Federal Reserve (more on this in Chapters 13 and 14). Think of an electric mixer beating a bowl of cake mix. Fiscal policy is like turning up the speed on the mixer—the stuff in the bowl flows around faster than before, but there is still the same amount of it. Monetary policy adds to the stock of money in the economy just as a cook might add to the quantity of batter in the bowl by breaking in another egg.

In short: Whenever you are tempted to use the word *money*, do you really mean to refer to the stock of one of those special kinds of assets that go into M1 and M2? Or do you really mean income, demand, investment, spending, saving, or some other specialized word referring to an economic flow? *Be precise!*

ECONOMICS IN THE NEWS

WASHINGTON, D.C., MAY 1987—Falling profits and bad loans are squeezing many of the nation's commercial banks and about 200 of them will fail this year, L. William Seidman, chairman of the Federal Deposit Insurance Corp. said yesterday.

The bad loans primarily are in agriculture, energy or real estate, and to Third World countries, but efforts to keep loan volume and profits up in the face of new competitive pressures have led banks generally to accept greater loan risks, Seidman told the Senate Banking committee.

"It seems clear that the risk in the system has been increased by deteriorating loan portfolio quality," said Seidman, whose agency insures deposits at commercial banks.

In 1986, a record 144 banks went under, and earlier this year, Seidman had estimated this year's total at about 150. However, in the first 4-1/2 months of this year, 78 banks failed and 3 stayed in business only as a result of FDIC aid. "If the current pace continues, we can anticipate at least 200 failures and assistance transactions this year," Seidman said.

The FDIC chairman nevertheless said the banking system remains basically sound. "The system remains viable despite the record numbers of problem and failed banks," he said.

Foreign problem loans are concentrated among the nation's biggest banks. "Nine large money-center banks recently accounted for 60 percent of the U.S. banking system's exposure to foreign debt and 65 percent of the exposure to Latin American debt," he continued.

Source: John M. Berry, "200 Banks Facing Failure This Year," *The Washington Post*, May 22, 1987, sec. F, 1. ©*The Washington Post*, 1987. Reprinted with permission.

Questions

1. Explain, with reference to a balance sheet, why loan losses (non-repayment of loans) can cause a bank to fail.
2. Seidman believes that some banks are taking greater risks in making loans than formerly because of competitive pressures. How does federal deposit insurance encourage banks to make risky loans? Why would they tend to be more conservative in their loan practices if there were no deposit insurance?
3. According to Seidman, the banking system as a whole is fundamentally sound despite record bank failures. How can he be so confident that failures of individual banks will not spread into a panic that brings the whole system down?

SELF TEST

These sample test items will help you check how much you have learned. Answers are found at the end of the chapter. Scoring yourself: One or two wrong—on target. Three or four wrong—passing, but you haven't mastered the chapter yet. Five or more wrong—not good enough; start over and restudy the chapter.

1. Funds on deposit in a passbook savings account at a savings and loan association are not counted as part of M1 because they do not serve as
   a. a means of payment.
   b. a store of value.
   c. a unit of account.
   d. they do not serve as any of the above.

2. The statement that profits of General Motors in 1982 totaled $500 million represents the use of money as
   a. a means of payment.
   b. a store of value.
   c. a unit of account.
   d. a liquid asset.

3. Which of the following is counted as part of M1?
   a. Checkable money market mutual funds.
   b. Small-denomination time deposits.
   c. NOW accounts at savings and loan associations.
   d. None of the above.

_C_ 4. Which of the following assets is most liquid?
   a. A long-term bond.
   b. A credit card balance.
   c. A NOW account.
   d. A small-denomination time deposit.

_A_ 5. Which of the following would appear on the asset side of a commercial bank balance sheet?
   a. Loans.
   b. Demand deposits.
   c. Savings deposits.
   d. Net worth.

_B_ 6. If a commercial bank has assets of $100 million and liabilities of $80 million, its net worth is
   a. -$20 million.
   b. $20 million.
   c. $180 million.
   d. Insufficient information given for an answer.

_C_ 7. Which of the following is a liability of the Federal Reserve System?
   a. Securities.
   b. Loans to banks and thrifts.
   c. Federal Reserve Notes.
   d. All of the above.

_B_ 8. The Federal Deposit Insurance Corporation
   a. has managed to prevent even a single bank failure since it was founded.
   b. has helped prevent rumors of bank failure from causing runs and actual bank failures.
   c. has not been very effective one way or the other in preventing bank failures.
   d. has probably increased the rate of bank failures.

_D_ 9. The Federal Reserve System
   a. provides many services to banks and thrifts.
   b. provides direct banking services for the U.S. government.
   c. regulates many aspects of commercial banking activity.
   d. all of the above.

_C_ 10. A bank whose liabilities exceed its assets is said to be
   a. in default.
   b. illiquid.
   c. insolvent.
   d. in dissolution.

_C_ 11. Which of the following tools for ensuring the safety and stability of the banking system was most recently made law?
   a. Bank inspections.
   b. The Fed's function as lender of last resort.
   c. Federal deposit insurance.
   d. All were made law at the same time, in 1913.

_C_ 12. Runs on banks or thrifts
   a. have been common throughout the twentieth century.
   b. have been unknown since 1933.
   c. have taken place in some states with private deposit insurance in recent years.
   d. are an unfortunate by-product of federal deposit insurance.

150

___B___ 13. The Monetary Control Act of 1980
   a. established the distinction between banks and thrifts.
   b. was intended to improve the Fed's conduct of monetary policy.
   c. barred savings and loan associations from Fed services such as check clearing and wire transfers.
   d. all of the above.

___A___ 14. Which of the following policies was used to prevent a total collapse of Continental Illinois in 1984?
   a. The loan of large sums to the bank by the Fed.
   b. Cancellation of the bank's federal deposit insurance.
   c. A forced merger of the bank with Chase Manhattan Bank of New York.
   d. Conversion of the institution from a commercial bank to a savings and loan association.

___C___ 15. In the world of banking, a "zombie" is
   a. a person who refuses to repay a loan.
   b. a bank that converts itself into a savings and loan association.
   c. a bank or thrift that stays in business despite negative net worth.
   d. a bank that operates without the protection of federal deposit insurance.

ANSWERS TO CHAPTER 12

Economics in the News

(1) When a loan is not repaid, that loan, until then listed on the bank's balance sheet as an asset, becomes worthless. That reduces the bank's total assets. Its net worth is equal to its assets minus its liabilities. Since nonrepayment of the loan does not affect the bank's liabilities, the bank's net worth falls. If enough loans go bad, net worth falls to or below zero, and the bank becomes insolvent; in short, it fails. (2) Without deposit insurance, depositors in a bank that failed because of loan losses might lose all or part of the funds that they deposited in the bank. Thus, without deposit insurance, depositors would be unwilling to put their money in a bank known to make risky loans—or they would do so only if the bank paid correspondingly high interest on its deposits. This would give the bank a strong incentive to avoid risky loans. With deposit insurance, the bank can promise depositors high interest based on high rates charged for its risky loans. If enough of the risky loans are repaid, everyone wins. If the loans are not repaid and the bank fails, depositors at least are shielded by insurance. Some economists and federal officials have advocated changes in federal deposit insurance to remove these incentives to risk taking. (3) The major factor that keeps failure of one bank from spreading to a general

banking panic is federal deposit insurance. The willingness of the Fed to act as a lender of last resort also helps.

Self Test

1. **a.** Savings deposits do serve as a store of value and unit of account.
2. **c.** Here, dollars are used to measure the size of the flow of the firm's net income.
3. **c.** Answers **a** and **b** count as part of M2.
4. **c.** It is liquid because checks can be written on it. Answer **b** is a liability, not an asset, from the consumer point of view.
5. **a.** Answers **b** and **c** are commercial bank liabilities.
6. **b.** Net worth equals assets minus liabilities.
7. **c.** Answers **a** and **b** are assets of the Fed.
8. **b.** Many small and a few large banks have failed.
9. **d.** It also provides banking services to foreign governments.
10. **c.** It is illiquid if it does not have cash to pay depositors who want to withdraw their money.
11. **c.** It dates from 1934. Bank inspections date from the nineteenth century, and the Fed from 1913.
12. **c.** For example, in Ohio and Maryland in 1985, but these systems of privately insured thrifts were fairly small.
13. **b.** It lessened distinctions between banks and thrifts, and gave thrifts access to many Fed services.
14. **a.** Also, deposit insurance was extended even to very large deposits. A merger partner was sought, but could not be found.
15. **c.** The number of zombie thrifts has been fairly high in the 1980s.

Chapter 13

Central Banking and Money Creation

WHERE YOU'RE GOING

When you have mastered this chapter, you will understand

1. How banks create money.
2. Why the size of the money stock is limited by the quantity of bank reserves.
3. The instruments available to the Fed for controlling the money stock.
4. How well the money stock can be controlled.
5. The activities that the Fed undertakes in the international sphere.

In addition, you will add the following terms to your economic vocabulary:
Required reserves
Required-reserve ratio
Excess reserves
Open market operation
Money multiplier
Federal funds market
Federal funds rate
Discount window
Discount rate
Foreign exchange market
Sterilization

WALKING TOUR

After you have read this chapter at least once, you should work step by step through this walking tour. Fill in the blanks and answer the questions as you go along. After you have answered each question, check yourself by uncovering the answer given in the margin. If you do not understand why the answer given is the correct one, refer back to the proper section of the text.

Creation of Money by Banks

One way to understand better how the banking system works and how the Fed controls the supply of money is to look at a simplified banking system in which demand deposits are the only form of money and the only commercial bank liability. Suppose that demand deposits are subject to a uniform 20 percent required reserve ratio and that initially all banks in the system have balance sheets that look like this:

	Assets		Liabilities	
Reserves		$20,000	Demand deposits	$100,000
Required	$20,000			
Excess	0			
Loans		80,000		
Total assets		$100,000	Total liabilities	$100,000

increasing

Suppose now that the Fed makes an open market purchase of $1,000 in government securities for the purpose of [increasing/ decreasing] reserves available to the banking system. The seller of the securities is paid by wire transfer to the Littletown National Bank. The effect will be to make its balance sheet, which initially looked like the one above, look like this:

[1] 21,000, [2] 101,000
[3] 20,200
[4] 800

	Assets		Liabilities	
Reserves		[1]$ 21000	Demand deposits	[2]$ 101000
Required	[3] 20200			
Excess	[4] 800			
Loans		80,000		
Total assets		[5]$ 101000	Total liabilities	[6]$ 101000

[5] 101,000, [6] 101,000

800

The Littletown National Bank could now increase its earnings by using its excess reserves to finance $ __800__ in new loans. Suppose that it chooses to make the loan and that the borrower writes a check for the amount of the proceeds, which is subsequently deposited in the Norrisville National Bank. After all of these transactions have taken place, total reserves at the Littletown National Bank will be $ __20200__ , __all__ of which will be required reserves, given its $ __101000__ in demand deposits. Assuming that the Norrisville bank starts with the same initial balance sheet, its deposits will now be $ __100800__. Its total reserves will be $ __20800__, of which $ __20160__

20,200, all
101,000

100,800
20,800, 20,160

154

640	will be required and $_____640_____ excess. That means that it
640	can add earning assets of $_____640_____ in the form of loans. As the process continues, more and more of the initial $1,000 in reserves injected into the banking system by the Fed will be converted into required reserves. When the money expansion process is complete, total demand deposits of all banks (and hence the total
5,000	money stock) will have increased by $_____5000_____. The value of the money multiplier for this simplified economy is thus seen to
5	be _____5_____.

The Tools of Monetary Policy

Fed	The supply of money is subject to control by the _____FED_____. The most common means used by the Fed to control the money
open market operations	supply, discussed in the previous section, is that of open market operations.
buys	If the Fed wants to expand the money supply, it [**buys**/sells] government
increases	ment securities. This action [**increases**/decreases] commercial bank reserves, and causes the money supply to expand by an amount
greater than	[equal to/**greater than**] the amount of the change in reserves. If the Fed wants to cause the money supply to contract, it undertakes an
sale, decreases	open market [purchase/**sale**], which [increases/**decreases**] the quantity of bank reserves.
	The Fed can also control the money supply through changing the attractiveness of loans of reserves to banks. These loans are
discount window	made via a facility known as the discount window, and the rate of
discount rate	interest charged for loans of reserves is known as the discount rate. Banks wanting to borrow reserves can also borrow from one another
federal funds	in the federal funds market, paying an interest rate known as
federal funds	the federal funds rate. If the Fed wants to encourage banks to borrow through the discount window, thus expanding reserves, it
lowers	[raises/**lowers**] the discount rate relative to the federal funds rate. If
raises	it wants to discourage borrowing, it [**raises**/lowers] the discount rate relative to the federal funds rate.
	In the past, the Fed sometimes used a third tool to control the
required reserve ratios	money supply, namely, changes in required reserve ratios. An increase in the required reserve ratio on transactions deposits would cause the
contract	money supply to [expand/**contract**], while a decrease in the required
expand	reserve ratio would cause the money supply to [**expand**/contract].
has not	Since the Monetary Control Act of 1980, the Fed [has/**has not**] used

changes in required reserve ratios as an active instrument of control.

In practice, the Fed [does/does not] have complete control over the money supply. One source of imprecision in the Fed's control is unpredicted variations in the _money multiplier_. For example, a shift in deposits from demand deposits to large time deposits subject to reserve requirement would cause the ratio of M1 to total reserves to [rise/fall]. A shift in demand deposits from large banks subject to a 12 percent reserve requirement to small banks subject to a lower reserve requirement would cause the money multiplier to [rise/fall]. Also, reserves can be subject to unexpected variations. For example, a deposit of currency will [increase/decrease] bank reserves and cause the money stock to [rise/fall].

The Federal Reserve in the International Economy

Markets in which the currency of one country is traded for other currencies are known as _foreign exchange_ markets. Aside from small currency transactions for tourist purposes, most foreign exchange transactions involve money in the form of deposits in _trading_ banks. The quantity of any currency—say Swiss francs—that one can buy for $1 is determined by _supply/demand_. The price of one country's currency in terms of another is known as the _exchange rate_.

Exchange rates [do/do not] have an impact on the economy. For example, suppose the exchange rate of the dollar rises from 160 Japanese yen to 200 yen. That will tend to [help/hurt] U.S. firms that export goods to Japan and [help/hurt] U.S. firms that compete with imports from Japan. It will, at the same time, tend to [help/hurt] U.S. consumers who buy Japanese products.

If the Fed wants to resist upward pressure on the exchange rate of the dollar relative to the yen, it needs to increase the quantity of dollars [supplied/demanded] in foreign exchange markets. It can do this by [buying/selling] Japanese securities. In order to do this, the Fed must first [buy/sell] a yen-denominated deposit at a trading bank, paying for that deposit by supplying _dollars_. This transaction will tend to [increase/decrease] reserves of the U.S. banking system. If the Fed wants to resist downward pressure on the dollar relative to the yen, it [buys/sells] Japanese securities and

buy	uses the proceeds to [buy/sell] dollars. This transaction has the
decreasing	indirect effect of [increasing/decreasing] reserves of the U.S. banking system.
	If the Fed wants to avoid any impact on the domestic banking
open market operations	system, it can use _open market operations_ to offset the impact of its
sterilization	foreign transactions on reserves. This is known as _sterilization_.
	For example, in order to sterilize a sale of foreign currencies, which
reduce	tends to [increase/reduce] domestic bank reserves, the Fed can
purchase, does not	engage in an open market [sale/purchase]. Sterilization [does/does not] achieve a complete separation of domestic and international monetary policy.

HANDS ON

Now that you have reviewed the concepts introduced in this chapter, it is time for some hands-on practice with the analytical tools that have been introduced. Work through each problem in this section carefully, and then check your results against those given at the end of the chapter.

Problem 1

The following questions refer to Exhibit 13.1, which shows the balance sheet of a typical bank in a simplified banking system.

Exhibit 13.1

Balance Sheet of Sycombeville National Bank

Assets		Liabilities	
Reserves	$ 25,000	Demand Deposits	$250,000
Required $25,000			
Excess 0			
Loans	225,000		
Total Assets	$250,000	Total Liabilities	250,000

a. What is the required reserve ratio for the bank shown? If all banks have the same required reserve ratio, what is the money multiplier for this banking system?

b. If this bank received a new deposit of $50,000, what would it do with the funds in order to maximize profit?

c. The Fed makes an open market sale of $10,000. The buyer pays for the sale with funds previously on deposit at the Sycombeville National Bank. What is the immediate impact on Sycombeville's reserve position? What would this bank do in response to the change in its reserve position? What would be the effect of the open market sale on the money supply as a whole once the banking system had returned to equilibrium?

Problem 2

The following questions refer to Exhibit 13.2, which shows the balance sheet of a typical bank in a different simplified banking system.

Exhibit 13.2

Balance Sheet of Random National Bank

Assets		Liabilities	
Reserves	$ 20,000	Demand Deposits	$100,000
Required $25,000			
Excess −5,000			
Loans	80,000		
Total Assets	$100,000	Total Liabilities	$100,000

a. What is the required reserve ratio for this bank? What is the money multiplier for this banking system?
b. Is the bank in a position of equilibrium as the balance sheet is shown? If not, what would it do to achieve equilibrium in the simplified banking system? In the real world, what other options would a similarly situated bank have in trying to achieve equilibrium?
c. Assume that this bank makes the necessary adjustment to return to balance sheet equilibrium. Then the Fed makes a $10,000 open market purchase. The funds are credited to the seller's account at the Random National Bank. What is the immediate impact on Random's reserve position? What actions would random take to attain equilibrium? What would be the effect on the money supply once the banking system as a whole had attained equilibrium?

Problem 3

The following questions are based on Exhibit 13.3, which shows an incomplete balance sheet for a typical bank in a third simplified banking system.

Exhibit 13.3

Balance Sheet of Tylertown National Bank

Assets		Liabilities	
Reserves	$_____	Demand Deposits	$500,000
Required $_____			
Excess 5,000			
Loans	370,000		
Total Assets	$_____		$500,000

a. Begin by filling in the blanks in the balance sheet. What is Tylertown's required reserve ratio? Assuming other banks in the system to have the same required reserve ratio, what is the money multiplier for the system?
b. Is Tylertown in balance sheet equilibrium as shown? If not, what would it do to attain balance sheet equilibrium? In the real world, what other options to attain equilibrium would a similarly situated bank have?
c. Beginning from just the position shown, suppose the Fed cuts the required reserve ratio to 20 percent. What would be the immediate impact on Tylertown's reserve position? What would it do to attain equilibrium? If the complete banking system consists of ten banks just like Tylertown, with exactly the beginning balance sheet shown, what will the total money supply be after the reserve requirement is cut and all banks have achieved equilibrium?

DON'T MAKE THIS COMMON MISTAKE

One of the most common and least necessary mistakes on exams covering monetary policy is to confuse the effects of *open market sales* and *open market purchases*.

An open market *sale* is a sale of securities (government bonds, short-term Treasury securities, and so on) by the Fed to the public. The sellers—private securities dealers—*pay* for these securities with funds that would otherwise stay in the private banking system and be available as bank reserves.

Remember: An open market SALE of securities by the Fed moves funds OUT OF the banking system INTO the Fed, thus LOWERING reserves and LOWERING the money supply.

Similarly, in an open market purchase, the Fed buys securities from private dealers. How does it pay for them? With funds that then become available to the banking system as new reserves.

Remember: An open market PURCHASE of securities by the Fed injects funds INTO the banking system, thus INCREASING reserves and INCREASING the money supply.

In short, when the Fed sells securities to the public in the open market, reserves come out of the banking system; when it buys securities from the public on the open market, reserves go into the banking system. It is the quantity of reserves in the banking system, not the quantity of securities in the hands of the public, that determines the level of the money supply.

SELF TEST

These sample test items will help you check how much you have learned. Answers are found at the end of the chapter. Scoring yourself: One or two wrong—on target. Three or four wrong—passing, but you haven't mastered the chapter yet. Five or more wrong—not good enough; start over and restudy the chapter.

___C___ 1. The required-reserve ratio is the minimum reserves that the Fed requires a bank or thrift to hold stated as a percentage of
   a. its liquid assets.
   b. its total assets.
   c. the deposits to which the reserve requirement applies.
   d. its net worth.

___B___ 2. A bank's balance sheet is said to be in equilibrium when
   a. net worth is zero.
   b. excess reserves are zero.
   c. total reserves are zero.
   d. required reserves are zero.

___A___ 3. Which of the following adds reserves to the banking system?
   a. An open market purchase of securities by the Fed.
   b. Making of a loan by a commercial bank.
   c. Writing of a check by a commercial bank customer.
   d. All of the above.

___C___ 4. When the Fed makes an open market purchase of securities,
   a. its assets increase.
   b. its liabilities increase.
   c. both **a** and **b**.
   d. neither **a** nor **b**.

___C___ 5. A bank is subject to a 20 percent required-reserve ratio. When this bank receives a deposit of $1,000, its
   a. total reserves rise by $200.
   b. excess reserves rise by $200.
   c. required reserves rise by $200.
   d. all of the above.

___B___ 6. A bank is subject to a 10 percent required-reserve ratio. When this bank has excess reserves of $1,000, it can safely extend new loans of
   a. $10,000.
   b. $1,000.
   c. $900.
   d. $100.

___A___ 7. A check for $450 written on an account in the First National Bank is deposited in the Second National Bank. When the check is cleared by the Fed,
   a. First's total reserves fall by $450.
   b. First's total reserves fall by $45.
   c. Second's total reserves fall by $450.
   d. Second's total reserves fall by $4,500.

___C___ 8. All banks in a banking system are subject to a 12.5 percent required-reserve ratio and demand deposits are the only form of money. The value of the money multiplier for this simplified banking system is
   a. 125.
   b. 12.5.
   c. 8.
   d. 2.5.

___B___ 9. In a simplified banking system where all banks are subject to a 20 percent required-reserve ratio and demand deposits are the only form of money, a $100,000 open market purchase by the Fed will
   a. cause the money stock to increase by $100,000.
   b. cause the money stock to increase by $500,000.
   c. cause the money stock to decrease by $100,000.
   d. cause the money stock to decrease by $500,000.

___C___ 10. A certain bank is initially in balance sheet equilibrium. Then a customer writes a $1,000 check on an account subject to a required-reserve ratio of 5 percent. As a result, the bank will experience
   a. a $50 decrease in total reserves.
   b. a $50 deficiency of required reserves.
   c. a $950 deficiency of required reserves.
   d. a $20,000 deficiency of required reserves.

___C___ 11. The interest rate charged by the Fed on loans of reserves to banks and thrifts is known as the
   a. federal funds rate.
   b. prime rate.
   c. discount rate.
   d. window rate.

___B___ 12. Which of the following actions will increase total reserves of the banking system?
   a. Bank One borrows from Bank Two via the federal funds market.
   b. Bank One borrows from the Fed via the discount window.
   c. Both a and b.
   d. Neither a nor b.

___D___ 13. Which of the following actions by the Fed will tend to cause the money stock to expand?
   a. An open market sale of securities.
   b. An increase in the discount rate.
   c. An increase in the required reserve ratio.
   d. None of the above.

___B___ 14. If I withdraw $500 in currency that I previously held in a demand deposit at a commercial bank,
   a. total M1 increases.
   b. total bank reserves decrease.
   c. both a and b.
   d. neither a nor b.

___C___ **15.** If the Fed sells French francs and buys dollar-denominated demand deposits from a trading bank, the effects will include
   a. support for the exchange rate of the dollar relative to the franc.
   b. a decrease in the U.S. money stock, unless the transaction is sterilized.
   c. both **a** and **b**.
   d. neither **a** nor **b**.

ANSWERS TO CHAPTER 13

Hands On

Problem 1 (a) The required reserve ratio is 10 percent, and the money multiplier is 10. (b) The bank would retain $5,000 of the funds as new required reserves and would extend $45,000 in new loans. (c) Sycombeville would lose $10,000 in deposits and reserves. That would give it $15,000 in total reserves. It would have required reserves of $24,000, so it would have a $9,000 reserve deficiency (negative excess reserves). It would have to call in, or allow to be repaid, $9,000 in loans before it could achieve balance sheet equilibrium. In the banking system as a whole, the $10,000 open market sale ultimately would cause a $100,000 drop in the money supply.

Problem 2 (a) The required reserve ratio is 25 percent, and the money multiplier is 4. (b) The bank is not in equilibrium; it has a $5,000 reserve deficiency. Given the balance sheet as shown, its only recourse would be to call in or allow to be repaid $5,000 in loans. In the real world, it would have other ways to make up the deficiency. It could borrow from another bank in the federal funds market, or borrow from the Fed. It could also sell other assets it might own, such as securities. (c) Reserves and deposits increase by $10,000. Required reserves increase by $2,500, so excess reserves rise by $7,500. The bank would make $7,500 in new loans to achieve equilibrium. The money supply as a whole would grow by $40,000 once all banks reached a new equilibrium.

Problem 3 (a) Assets must equal liabilities, so assets are $500,000. Loans plus reserves must equal total assets, so total reserves are $130,000. Of these, $5,000 are excess, so required reserves are $125,000. The required reserve ratio is thus 25 percent, and the money multiplier for the system is 4. (b) It is not in equilibrium. In the simplified system, Tylertown would make $5,000 in new loans to businesses or consumers. In the real world, it might also buy securities, lend the reserves to other banks via the federal funds market, or use the funds to pay back previous reserve borrowings from the Fed's discount window. (c) Tylertown would now have the same $130,000 total reserves, but now only $100,000 would be required. It could make up to $30,000 in new loans, etc. The new money multiplier will be 5. With ten banks, total system reserves are $1.3 million, so the money supply will rise from $5.2 million to $6.5 million as a result of the cut in required reserve ratios.

Self Test

1. **c.** Reserve requirements vary from one bank to another and one type of deposit to another.
2. **b.** If the bank has excess reserves, it can increase profit by converting them to earning assets such as loans or securities. In practice, some banks purposely maintain a small quantity of excess reserves in connection with the process of check clearing.
3. **a.** The others only pass reserves from one bank to another.
4. **c.** The securities it buys are added to its assets, and the increase in reserves are a liability.
5. **c.** Its total reserves rise by $1,000 and its excess reserves by $800.
6. **b.** New loans can safely equal excess reserves.
7. **a.** Second's reserves rise by $450.
8. **c.** For a simplified banking system, the money multiplier is equal to 1/rr.
9. **b.** The money stock increases because an open market *purchase* causes reserves to increase; the increase is $500,000 because the money multiplier is 5 when the required reserve ratio is 0.20.
10. **c.** Total reserves will fall by $1,000 when the check clears, but since deposits fall by $1,000, required reserves also fall, by $50. Thus, the reserve deficiency is just $950.
11. **c.** The federal funds rate applies to loans between banks.
12. **b.** Answer a only moves reserves from one bank to the other.
13. **d.** All will cause the money stock to contract.
14. **b.** At first one form of M1 is just exchanged for another, but as the banking system reacts to the loss of reserves, M1 will eventually contract.
15. **c.** Result a happens because the action adds to the demand for the dollar on foreign exchange markets; result b occurs because reserves of U.S. banks fall.

Chapter 14

The Supply of and Demand For Money

WHERE YOU'RE GOING

When you have mastered this chapter, you will understand

1. How classical economists viewed the demand for money.
2. How income and interest rates affect money demand according to current theory.
3. How money demand has behaved in the U.S. economy in recent years.
4. How supply and demand determine interest rates in the money market.
5. What targets the Fed has used as guides to its open market operations.

In addition, you will add the following terms to your economic vocabulary:
  Equation of exchange
  Velocity
  Portfolio
  Operating target

WALKING TOUR

After you have read this chapter at least once, you should work step by step through this walking tour. Fill in the blanks and answer the questions as you go along. After you have answered each question, check yourself by uncovering the answer given in the margin. If you do not understand why the answer given is the correct one, refer back to the proper section of the text.

The Demand for Money

stock

The demand for money is a demand for a [stock/flow]. Thus the quantity of money demanded means the size of the stock that people want to hold at any time.

MV = Py

One early view of the demand for money arose from the equation of exchange, which can be written ____MV = Py____. The letters in this equation represent the following quantities:

164

M = money
V = velocity
P = price level
y = real income

1. _M = money_,
2. _V = velocity_,
3. _P = price level_, and
4. _y = real income_.

velocity

The equation of exchange itself is not a theory, but it forms the basis of a theory in which equilibrium _velocity_ is assumed to be determined independently of monetary policy. In that case, money demand is proportional to nominal income.

Keynes developed a more complex theory of the demand for money based on three motives for holding money. These are the

transactions
precautionary
speculative

1. _transactions_,
2. _precautionary_, and
3. _speculative_.

both

In the Keynesian theory, money demand depends on [income/interest rates/**both**].

portfolio
transaction

Today, the demand for money is often explained in terms of the importance of liquidity in one's _portfolio_ of assets. Liquidity allows one to reduce _transaction_ costs, and also avoids the risk of a loss in nominal value associated with some less liquid assets. However, liquid assets usually bear less interest than less liquid ones. Thus, the interest rate that could be earned on non-

opportunity

monetary assets represents the _opportunity_ cost of holding non-interest-bearing money. For interest-bearing forms of money such as NOW accounts, the opportunity cost is the difference between the interest rate and that available on nonmonetary assets and that paid on the monetary asset.

falls
increases

According to the portfolio balance theory of money demand, other things being equal, the quantity of money demanded increases as the interest rate [rises/**falls**], and increases as nominal national income [**increases**/decreases]. If a money demand curve is drawn on a diagram with the quantity of money demanded on the horizontal axis and the interest rate on the vertical axis, an

movement along

increase in the interest rate produces a [shift in/**movement along**] the curve, and an increase in nominal national income produces a

shift in

[**shift in**/movement along] the curve.

shifts in

Other factors too, such as changes in payments practices of businesses and the introduction of new deposits can also cause [**shifts in**/movements along] the money demand curve. Over time, an income-adjusted money demand curve for the U.S. economy appears to have shifted to the [right/**left**].

Supply, Demand, and Interest Rates and the Money Market

Interest rates can be viewed as being determined by the interaction of supply and demand in the money market. The money demand curve has a [positive/**negative**] slope. The slope of the money supply curve depends on __Fed Policy__. If the Fed sets a target for the money stock and sticks to that target regardless of what happens to interest rates, the money supply curve will be __vertical__.

The money market can be used to trace the effects of a change in the money supply. For example, the Fed can expand the money supply by means of an open market [**purchase**/sale] of securities. This causes banks' reserves to [**rise**/fall]. The banks convert their new reserves into earning assets by __making loans__ and __buying securities__. Both of these actions tend to [**increase**/decrease] the money supply and to [raise/**lower**] interest rates. As interest rates [rise/**fall**], there is a [leftward/**rightward**] [shift in/**movement along**] the money demand curve. The money market moves to a new equilibrium in which the money stock is [**larger than**/smaller than/the same as] before, and the interest rate is [higher/**lower**] than before.

The effects of an increase in nominal national income can also be traced in the money market. An increase in nominal national income causes a rightward shift in the money [supply/**demand**] curve. As a result of the higher level of income, people will want to hold [**more**/less] money in their portfolios at any given rate of interest. The increase in income [does/**does not**] cause the stock of money to increase. Thus, to bring the market into equilibrium, the interest rate must [**rise**/fall], so that people will be willing to hold the existing quantity of money, no more and no less.

Changes in domestic interest rates brought about by Federal Reserve policy [**do**/do not] have effects on foreign exchange markets. These effects arise because of transactions made on [current/**capital**] account.

For example, suppose an open market [purchase/**sale**] by the Fed raises the domestic interest rate. Other things being equal, this will make people [**more**/less] willing to buy U.S. assets. That will

166

increase tend to [increase/decrease] in net capital inflows. Also, it will make
less people [more/less] likely to borrow from U.S. banks. That will tend
decrease to [increase/decrease] in net capital outflows. Taking these effects
together, the result will be a tendency for the exchange value of the
rise dollar to [rise/fall].

Similarly, a reduction in U.S. interest rates as the result of an
purchase, decrease open market [sale/purchase] by the Fed will tend to [increase/
increase decrease] net capital inflows and to [increase/decrease] net capital
downward outflows. Taken together, these effects will put [upward/downward]
pressure on the exchange value of the dollar.

does The practical result is that the Fed [does/does not] need to take
international repercussions into account when conducting domestic
monetary policy.

Monetary Control Strategies

The money supply curve is vertical only if the Fed is determined to
hold the money stock constant regardless of what happens to interest rates. Other monetary control strategies are also possible. For
example, the Fed may adopt a strategy of targeting an interest rate,
such as the federal funds rate. In this case, the money supply curve
horizontal will be _horizontal_. Or it can allow the money supply to
expand whenever the interest rate rises, but not by enough to fully
offset the upward movement of the interest rate. In this case the
positive money supply curve will have a _positive_ slope.

The response of the money market to an increase in money
demand depends on the shape of the money supply curve. Under a
interest rates strict money stock target, an increase in money demand causes [the
money stock/interest rates/both] to increase. Under an interest rate
money stock target, an increase in money demand causes [the money stock/
interest rates/both] to increase. And under an intermediate policy,
both an increase in money demand causes [the money stock/interest
rates/both] to increase. The Fed's monetary control strategy in
positively sloped recent years is best characterized by a/an [vertical/horizontal/
positively sloped] money supply curve.

HANDS ON

Now that you have reviewed the concepts introduced in this chapter, it is time for some hands-on practice with the analytical tools that have been introduced. Work through each problem in this section carefully, and then check your results against those given at the end of the chapter.

Problem 1

The questions that follow refer to Exhibit 14.1, which shows money supply and demand curves for a hypothetical economy.

Exhibit 14.1

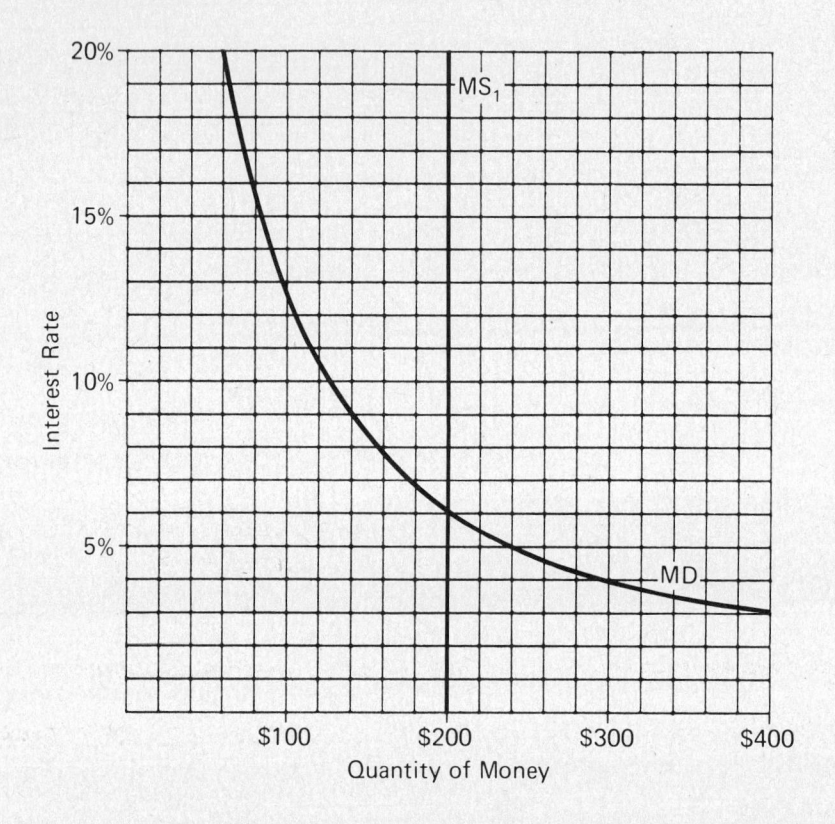

a. As the diagram is drawn, what is the equilibrium interest rate?
b. Beginning from the equilibrium position shown, suppose the Federal Reserve uses open market operations to reduce the money supply by half. Draw in the new money supply curve and label it MS_2.
c. Will the supply curve shift produce an excess supply or demand for money? How will banks and others react to the Fed's actions? What will happen to bond prices and interest rates?

Problem 2

The questions that follow refer to Exhibit 14.2, which shows a money supply curve and two possible money demand curves for a hypothetical economy.
a. With the money supply as shown and with money demand curve MD_1 in effect, what would be the equilibrium rate of interest?
b. Beginning from equilibrium at the intersection of MS and MD_1, suppose a decrease in nominal national income shifted the

Exhibit 14.2

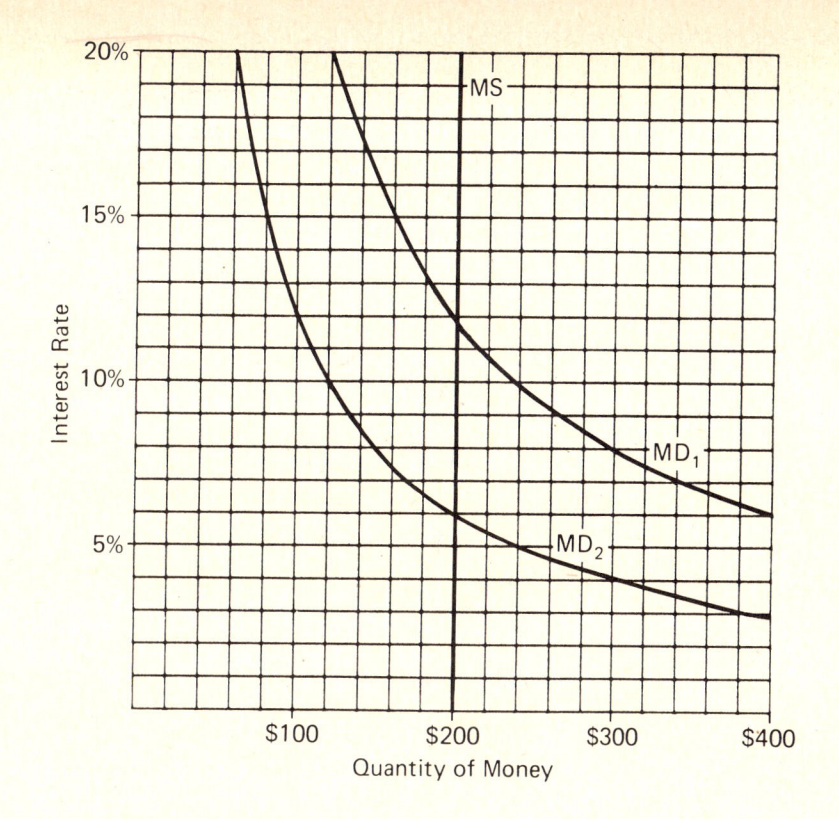

money demand curve to the new position MD₂. How will banks and others react to the change in money market conditions?

c. Assume that the money supply does not change. As the economy moves to a new equilibrium, what will happen to the price of bonds? To the interest rate?

SELF TEST

These sample test items will help you check how much you have learned. Answers are found at the end of the chapter. Scoring yourself: One or two wrong—on target. Three or four wrong—passing, but you haven't mastered the chapter yet. Five or more wrong—not good enough; start over and restudy the chapter.

1. According to the equation of exchange, nominal national income is equal to
   a. the money stock divided by the price level.
   b. the money stock times velocity.
   c. the money stock divided by velocity.
   d. real income divided by velocity.

2. John Maynard Keynes considered which of the following to be an important part of the demand for money?
   a. the speculative motive.
   b. the precautionary motive.
   c. the transactions motive.
   d. all of the above.

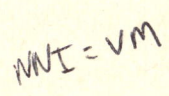

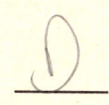

___C___ 3. A person's collection of assets is often called
   a. net worth.
   b. a liability.
   c. a portfolio.
   d. an opportunity cost.

___A___ 4. The opportunity cost of holding a non-interest-bearing form of money is
   a. the rate of interest available on nonmonetary assets.
   b. the rate of real economic growth.
   c. the unemployment rate.
   d. zero.

___B___ 5. According to the modern theory of the demand for money, the quantity of money that people want to hold in their portfolios tends to increase, other things being equal, as
   a. the rate of interest increases.
   b. nominal national income increases.
   c. real output decreases.
   d. the price level falls.

___B___ 6. If a money demand schedule is drawn with the interest rate on the vertical axis and the quantity of money on the horizontal axis, the effects of an increase in nominal national income are properly represented by
   a. a leftward shift in the schedule.
   b. a rightward shift in the schedule.
   c. a downward movement along the schedule.
   d. an upward movement along the schedule.

___A___ 7. Which of the following would tend to cause a leftward shift in an income-adjusted money demand curve?
   a. A change in business payments practices that allowed firms to carry on a given level of operations using lower transactions balances.
   b. A decrease in the level of nominal national income.
   c. An increase in the interest rate.
   d. All of the above.

___B___ 8. Over the past 25 years, the ratio of M1 to nominal national income in the United States has
   a. remained roughly constant.
   b. fallen substantially.
   c. risen substantially.
   d. risen and fallen with the business cycle, but remaining roughly constant on average.

___A___ 9. Compared with the 1970s and 1960s, the income adjusted money demand curve for the U.S. economy in the 1980s appears to <u>have</u> become
   a. more stable, but flatter.
   b. more subject to sharp leftward shifts.
   c. more subject to sharp rightward shifts.
   d. positively sloped

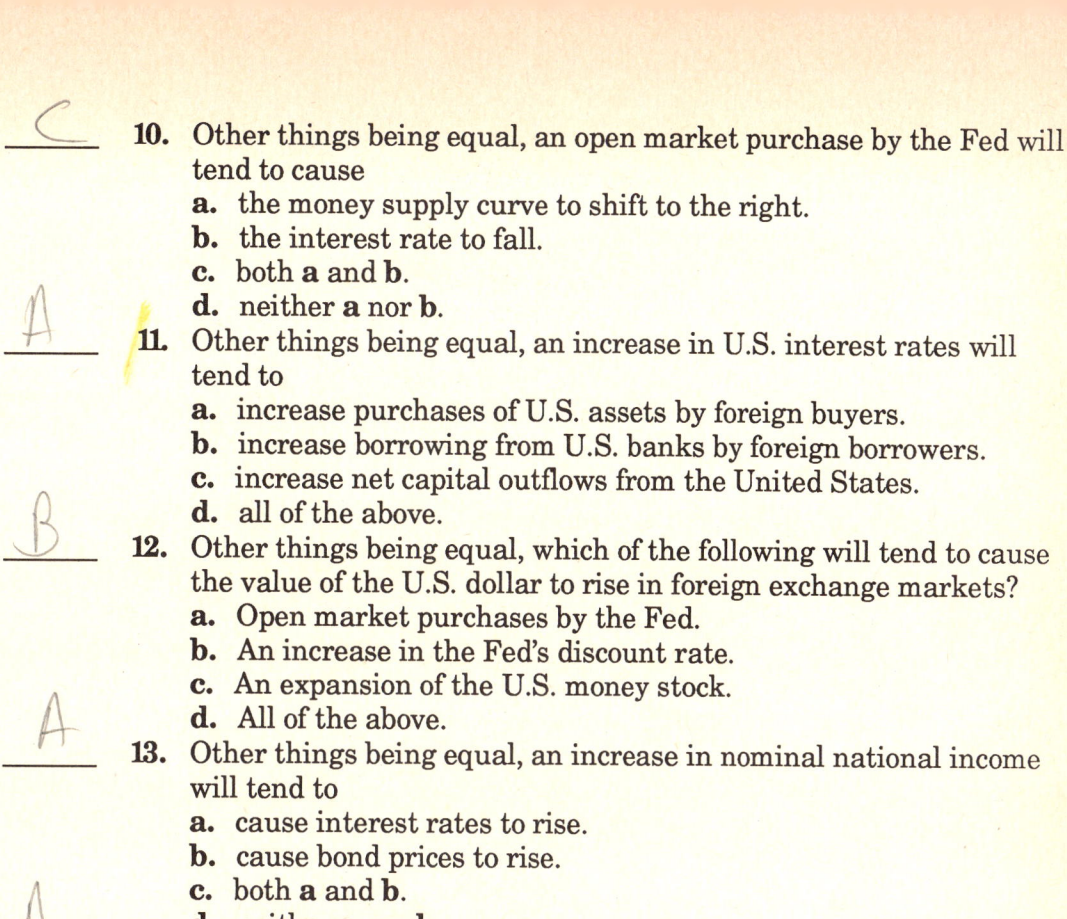

___C___ 10. Other things being equal, an open market purchase by the Fed will tend to cause
   a. the money supply curve to shift to the right.
   b. the interest rate to fall.
   c. both **a** and **b**.
   d. neither **a** nor **b**.

___A___ 11. Other things being equal, an increase in U.S. interest rates will tend to
   a. increase purchases of U.S. assets by foreign buyers.
   b. increase borrowing from U.S. banks by foreign borrowers.
   c. increase net capital outflows from the United States.
   d. all of the above.

___B___ 12. Other things being equal, which of the following will tend to cause the value of the U.S. dollar to rise in foreign exchange markets?
   a. Open market purchases by the Fed.
   b. An increase in the Fed's discount rate.
   c. An expansion of the U.S. money stock.
   d. All of the above.

___A___ 13. Other things being equal, an increase in nominal national income will tend to
   a. cause interest rates to rise.
   b. cause bond prices to rise.
   c. both **a** and **b**.
   d. neither **a** nor **b**.

___A___ 14. A monetary control strategy under which the Fed sets a target interest rate, and takes whatever actions are necessary to achieve the target, gives rise to
   a. a horizontal money supply curve.
   b. a positively sloped money supply curve.
   c. a vertical money supply curve.
   d. a negatively sloped money supply curve.

___A___ 15. If the Fed's monetary control strategy gives rise to a positively sloped money supply curve, then, other things being equal, a rightward shift in the money demand curve will
   a. cause both the interest rate and the money stock to rise.
   b. cause both the interest rate and the money stock to fall.
   c. cause the interest rate to rise and the money stock to fall.
   d. cause the interest rate to fall and the money stock to rise.

ANSWERS TO CHAPTER 14

Hands On

Problem 1 (a) The equilibrium interest rate is initially 6 percent. (b) The new money supply curve will be a vertical line drawn at a money supply of $100 billion. (c) The Fed's actions drain reserves from the banking system. There will be an excess demand for money at the initial 6 percent interest rate. Banks will have to reduce their holdings of loans and securities. Sales of securities and reduced willingness to make loans will drive up the interest rate to 12 percent, as Exhibit 14.1 is drawn. At the higher interest rate, people will become content to hold the new, lower quantity of money. In the new equilibrium, bond prices will be lower and the interest rate on bonds will be higher.

Problem 2 (a) The initial nominal interest rate is 12 percent. (b) The new, lower level of nominal national income means a reduced demand for money. People will react to the excess supply of money by using the money to buy bonds and other assets. (c) Individual purchases of bonds for money do not reduce the money supply in the economy as a whole—they just drive up the price of bonds. As bond prices rise, interest rates fall, moving the economy down and to the right along MD_2. A new equilibrium is eventually reached at a 6 percent interest rate, where people are content to hold $200 of money in their portfolios even given the reduced nominal income.

Self Test

1. **b.** To put it another way, velocity can be defined as the ratio of nominal national income to the money stock.
2. **d.** He considered the speculative motive to be responsive to changes in interest rates while the others were responsive to changes in nominal national income.
3. **c.** The original meaning is a case for carrying papers.
4. **a.** The opportunity cost of holding interest bearing forms of money is the difference between the interest rate on nonmonetary assets and the rate on the form of money in question.
5. **b.** The others would cause the quantity of money demanded to fall.
6. **b.** Changes in the interest rate are shown as movements along the schedule.
7. **a.** Item **b** would have no effect on the income-adjusted curve, and **c** would result in a movement along it.
8. **b.** This is reflected in a leftward shift of the income-adjusted demand curve has shifted to the left.
9. **a.** The saw-toothed pattern of earlier years has not held for the 1980s.
10. **c.** This is because an open market purchase injects reserves into the banking system.
11. **a.** It will tend to discourage borrowing from U.S. banks and increase net capital inflows.
12. **b.** Anything that tends to raise U.S. interest rates will, other things being equal, also tend to raise the value of the dollar.
13. **a.** *Important*: Remember that when interest rates rise, bond prices fall.
14. **a.** Such a policy was pursued during and just after World War II.
15. **a.** This represents a movement up and to the right along a positively sloped money supply curve.

Chapter 15

An Integrated View of Monetary and Fiscal Policy

WHERE YOU'RE GOING

When you have mastered this chapter, you will understand

1. How changes in the money stock affect real output, the price level, and unemployment.
2. What is meant by the *neutrality* of money.
3. How fiscal policy affects interest rates and planned investment.
4. The role that Keynes understood money to have played during the Great Depression.
5. How the *monetarists* have influenced economic thought.

In addition, you will add the following terms to your economic vocabulary:
  Transmission mechanism
  Neutrality of money
  Nominal interest rate
  Real interest rate
  Crowding-out effect
  Monetarism

WALKING TOUR

After you have read this chapter at least once, you should work step by step through this walking tour. Fill in the blanks and answer the questions as you go along. After you have answered each question, check yourself by uncovering the answer given in the margin. If you do not understand why the answer given is the correct one, refer back to the proper section of the text.

Money and Aggregate Demand

The set of channels through which money affects the economy is

transmission mechanism   known as the ___transmission mechanism___. The most important aspect of the

transmission mechanism, in the Keynesian view, runs from money

interest rates, planned   to ___interest rates___ to the ___planned investment___ component of
  investment   aggregate demand.

173

Suppose, for example, that the Fed uses an open market [purchase/sale] to bring about a one-time increase in the money stock. In the money market, this can be illustrated by a [rightward/leftward] [shift in/movement along] the money supply curve. As a result, the interest rate will begin to [rise/fall]. As this happens, planned investment will begin to [rise/fall]. This, in turn, will cause a [rightward/leftward] shift in the aggregate [demand/supply] curve. The short-run result will be a/an [increase/decrease/no change] in real output an a/an [increase/decrease/no change] in the price level.

The combination of increasing real output and a rising price level means that nominal national income will begin to [rise/fall]. As it does so, there will be a [leftward/rightward] shift in the money [supply/demand] curve. This will limit the decline in the interest rate. When the economy reaches a short-run equilibrium, the interest rate will be [a little higher/a little lower/the same] compared with its value before the Fed caused the money stock to increase.

To summarize, the short-run effects of a one-time expansion of the money stock include

1. A [higher/lower] interest rate.
2. A [higher/lower] level of real output.
3. A [higher/lower] price level.

In the case of a one-time contraction of the money stock, the short-run effects will include

1. A [higher/lower] interest rate.
2. A [higher/lower] level of real output.
3. A [higher/lower] price level.

In the long run, the economy [will/will not] remain at the short-run equilibrium described. Following a one-time expansion of the money stock, both prices and real output will rise in the short run. Soon, however, firms will begin to [raise/lower] the level of input prices that they expect. As this happens, the economy will move [along/off] the initial short-run aggregate supply curve. Real output will [rise/fall] and the price level will [rise/fall] until real output reaches a new equilibrium at its _____natural_____ level. In the new equilibrium, prices will have risen _in proportion to_ the change in the money stock. Nominal national income in the new long-run equilibrium will be [above/below/the same as] the initial equilibrium. The money demand curve will shift to the [right/left] to a point where the interest rate in long-run equilibrium will be [higher than/lower than/the same as] initially.

In sum, the long-run effects of a one-time increase in the money stock include

1. __a higher__ price level.
2. __the same__ level of real output.
3. __the same__ equilibrium interest rate.

Money is said to be __neutral__ in the long run, because a one-time change in the money stock does not affect any [real/nominal] variables.

If there is a lasting increase in money growth, rather than a one-time change in the money stock, these results must be somewhat modified. In this case, it becomes necessary to distinguish between nominal and real interest rates. Using r to represent the real interest rate, R the nominal rate, and P^* the rate of inflation, the formula for calculating the real rate of interest is r = __$R - P^*$__. For example, if the nominal interest rate is 8 percent and the rate of inflation is 5 percent, the real interest rate is __3__ percent.

A lasting increase in the rate of money growth, to a rate exceeding the growth of natural real output, will cause __inflation__. The expectation of inflation will cause lenders and bondholders to demand an "inflation premium" in the form of a higher [nominal/real] interest rate. Thus, a lasting increase in the rate of money growth will tend to cause [an increase/a decrease/no change] in the nominal interest rate.

The effect on real interest rates is not certain. In the short run, it is possible that real interest rates will fall. However, some economists believe that the real interest rates will remain unaffected in the long run. That doctrine is known as the __superneutrality__ of money.

Money and Fiscal Policy

Knowledge of the monetary transmission mechanism is also important for understanding the effects of fiscal policy. Suppose that the economy is initially in equilibrium at the natural level of real output. The government then undertakes expansionary fiscal policy by *expansionary fiscal policy ↑ GVT*

raising, lowering	[raising/lowering] real government purchases or [raising/lowering] real net taxes.
rightward	The initial effect will be a [rightward/leftward] shift in the
demand	aggregate [supply/demand] curve. In response, real output will
rise, rise	[rise/fall] and the price level will [rise/fall]. Together, the effect will
increase	be to [increase/decrease] nominal national income. That, in turn,
rightward, demand	will cause a [rightward/leftward] shift in the money [supply/
rise	demand] curve. The interest rate will begin to [rise/fall]. The change
reduce	in the interest rate will [increase/reduce] the rate of planned investment expenditure, which will [limit/intensify] the shift of the
limit	aggregate demand curve. The tendency of expansionary fiscal policy
crowding-out	to reduce planned investment is known as the _crowding-out_ effect.

In sum, the short-run effects of expansionary fiscal policy include

higher	1. A [higher/lower] level of real output.
higher	2. A [higher/lower] price level.
higher	3. A [higher/lower] interest rate.
lower	4. A [higher/lower] level of real planned investment.

fall	In the long run, firms adjust the input price expectations to the change in circumstances. As they do so, real output will tend to [fall/
natural, rise further	rise] to its _natural_ level, and the price level will [fall/rise
further increase	further]. As this happens, there will be [no change/a further increase] in nominal national income. The money demand curve will
further to the right	shift [back to the left/further to the right] and the interest rate will
rise, fall further	[rise/fall]. As a result, planned investment will [rise/fall further]. Compared with the initial equilibrium, before expansionary fiscal policy was undertaken, the new long-run equilibrium will include

unchanged	1. A [higher/lower/unchanged] level of real output.
higher	2. A [higher/lower/unchanged] price level.
higher	3. A [higher/lower/unchanged] interest rate.
lower	4. A [higher/lower/unchanged] level of real planned investment.
is not	In the long run, then, fiscal policy [is/is not] neutral.

Fiscal Policy and the Dollar

Fiscal policy, like monetary policy, has international implications. One way to view these implications is in terms of the circular flow. Financial markets occupy a central place in the circular flow. There are two flows of funds into financial markets: __net capital inflows__ and __domestic saving__. There are also two flows of funds out of financial markets: __gov't budget deficit__ and __domestic invest__. The first two must always balance the second two.

It must also be kept in mind that in the country's balance of payments accounts, the __current acct__ account is the mirror image of the __capital acct__ account assuming no official reserve transactions. If there is a current account deficit, then, there must be a net capital [**inflow**/outflow], and if there is a current account surplus, there must be a net capital [inflow/**outflow**].

Suppose, then, that the economy begins from a long-run equilibrium in which the government budget and the current account are both in balance. This means that domestic saving must equal domestic __investment__. Now the government increases purchases without increasing taxes. This action will tend to cause interest rates to [**rise**/fall]. This will cause some [increase/**decrease**] in planned investment—the __crowding-out__ effect. However, when the economy's international linkages are taken into account, the crowding-out effect is not the whole story. Higher interest rates will also stimulate a net capital [**inflow**/outflow]. This means that domestic planned investment will need to fall by [more/**less**] than otherwise in order to bring the financial sector back into balance—or more precisely, to ensure that domestic planned investment plus the government deficit remain equal to __domestic saving__ plus the __net capital inflow__.

Fiscal policy also has implications for the dollar's exchange rate. When expansionary fiscal policy [**raises**/lowers] domestic interest rates and swings the international accounts toward a net capital [**inflow**/outflow], the exchange rate of the dollar, relative to foreign currencies, will tend to [**rise**/fall]. Similarly, if fiscal policy becomes less expansionary and the deficit falls, domestic interest rates will tend to [rise/**fall**], there will be a swing toward net capital [inflow/**outflow**], and the dollar's exchange rate will tend to [rise/**fall**].

The Keynesian-Monetarist Debate over the Role of Money

Keynes and his early followers thought that under depression conditions, changes in the money stock would have a relatively [strong/**weak**] effect on the economy. They reasoned, first, that

would not	planned investment [would/~~would not~~] respond strongly to a decrease in interest rates. Further, they thought that there would
liquidity trap	be a limit to how low interest rates could fall, because of _liquidity trap_.
	After World War II, some economists came to think that money had a strong influence on the economy after all. These economists,
Milton Friedman, monetarists	led by _Milton Friedman_, came to be known as the _monetarists_. As they interpreted the Great Depression, the problem was not that monetary policy was powerless, but that the Fed failed to take
decline	action to prevent a sharp [increase/~~decline~~] in the money stock.
	Keynesians and monetarists also debated the nature of the transmission mechanism. The original Keynesian conception of the
narrow	transmission mechanism was relatively [broad/~~narrow~~]. It empha-
money, interest rates	sized a channel leading from _money_ to _interest rates_
planned investment, broader	to _planned investment_. The monetarist view is [~~broader~~/narrower]. In the monetarist view, a change in the money stock will affect the explicit and implicit returns on a variety of assets, including
bonds, stocks, real estate, commodities, consumer durables, increased	_bonds_, _stocks_, _real estate_, _commodities_, and _consumer durables_. Thus, an increase in the money stock is likely to spill over into [~~increased~~/decreased] spending on a wide variety of assets, both financial and nonfinancial.

HANDS ON

Now that you have reviewed the concepts introduced in this chapter, it is time for some hands-on practice with the analytical tools that have been introduced. Work through each problem in this section carefully, and then check your results against those given at the end of the chapter.

Problem 1

Exhibit 15.1 shows the money market for a certain economy. Initially the economy is in long-run equilibrium with the money market being in equilibrium at point C, where MD_1 and MS_1 intersect. Beginning from this point, the government initiates an expansionary fiscal policy taking the form of extensive tax cuts. Use the exhibit to trace the consequences of the fiscal policy action for the money market.

a. In the short run, how will the tax cut affect real output? The price level? Nominal national income?
b. What effect will these short-run changes have on the money market? If the money demand curve shifts, will the position of

Exhibit 15.1

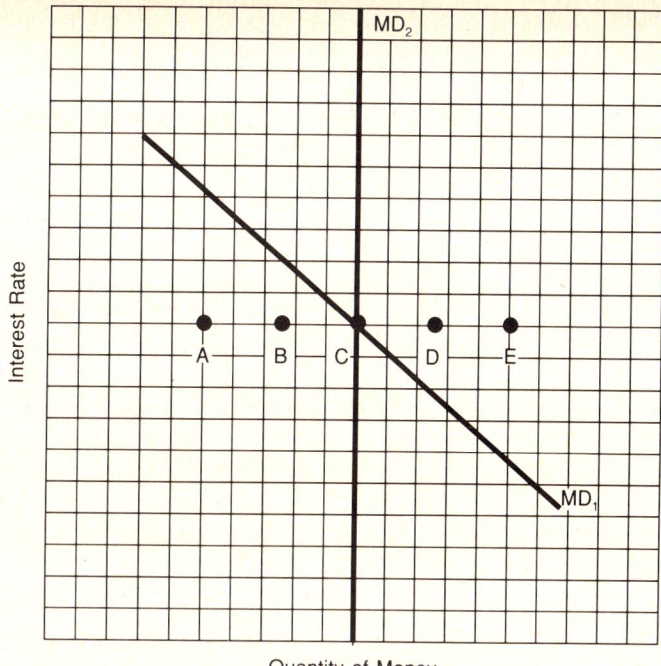

the money demand curve in the new short-run equilibrium best be represented by a curve drawn parallel to MD₁ through point A, B, D, or E? If the curve shifts, sketch in the appropriate money demand curve and label it MD₂.

c. If these developments cause a shift in the money supply, will the position of the money supply curve in the new short-run equilibrium best be represented by a curve drawn parallel to MS₁ through A, B, D, or E? If the curve shifts, sketch in the appropriate curve, and label it MS₂. In the new short-run equilibrium, will the interest rate be higher than, lower than, or the same as in the initial equilibrium?

d. Assuming that there is no further change in fiscal policy, the economy will undergo a process of long-run adjustment to the new conditions. In the course of this long-run adjustment, what will happen to real output? To the price level? To nominal national income?

e. Compared to the short-run position, how will the process of long-run adjustment affect the money market? If the money demand curve shifts, will the position of the money demand curve in the new long-run equilibrium best be represented by a curve drawn parallel to MD₁ through point A, B, C, D, or E? If the curve shifts, sketch in the appropriate money demand curve and label it MD₃.

f. If these further developments cause a shift in the money supply, will the position of the money supply curve in the new long-run equilibrium best be represented by a curve drawn parallel to MS₁ through A, B, C, D, or E? If the curve shifts, sketch in the appropriate curve, and label it MS₃. In the new long-run equilibrium, will the interest rate be higher than, lower than, or the same as in the initial equilibrium? Higher than, lower than, or the same as in the preceding short-run equilibrium?

g. What will happen to the level of planned investment as the economy moves from the initial equilibrium to the new short-run equilibrium? To the final long-run equilibrium?

Problem 2

Exhibit 15.2 shows the economy in the same initial position of long-run equilibrium as in Problem 1. This time contractionary monetary policy is undertaken that cuts the money stock to half of its previous level. Use the figure to trace the effects.

Exhibit 15.2

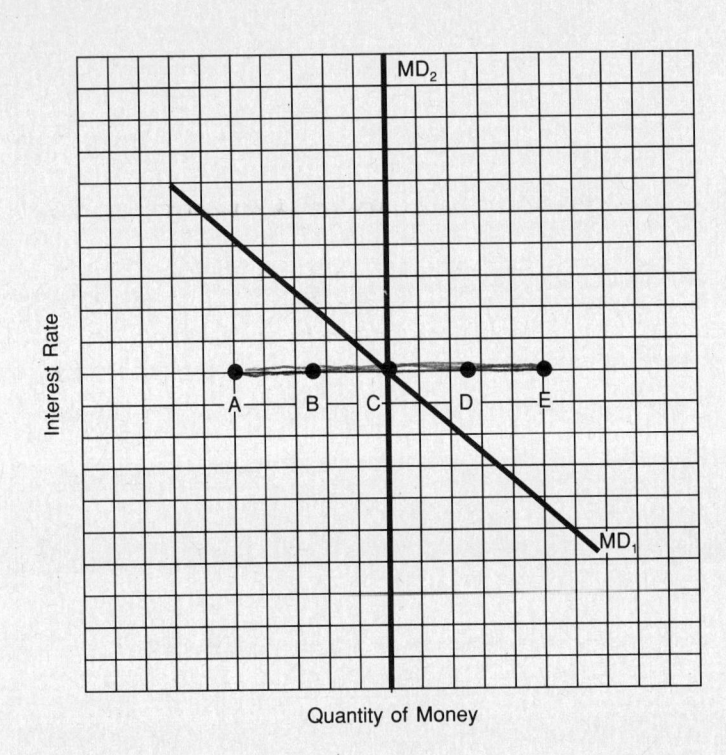

a. What short-run effect, if any, will the contractionary monetary policy have on the money supply curve? If the money supply curve shifts, will its new position best be represented by a curve parallel to MS_1 through point A, B, D, or E? Sketch in the new curve, if there is one, and label in MS_2.

b. As the money market begins to adjust to the contractionary policy, how will the interest rate be affected? What will happen to planned investment? Aggregate demand? Real output? The price level? Nominal national income?

c. Turn back now to the money market. As real output and the price level begin to respond to the contractionary monetary policy, what, if anything, will happen to the money demand curve? If it shifts, will the position of the curve in the new short-run equilibrium best be represented by a curve parallel to MD_1 drawn through A, B, D, or E? Sketch in the new curve, if there is one, and label it MD_2. In the new short-run equilibrium, is the interest rate higher than, lower than, or the same as it was before the contractionary monetary policy was undertaken?

d. If the money stock remains at its new value, firms and households will adjust their expectations fully to the new circumstances. As they do so, what will happen to real output? The price level? Nominal national income?

e. As real output and the price level move to their new long-run equilibrium values, what will happen in the money market? Will the money supply curve shift? If so, sketch in the new money supply curve through the appropriate lettered point and label it MS3. Will the money demand curve shift? If so, sketch in the new money demand curve through the appropriate lettered point and label it MD3.

f. In the new long-run equilibrium, how does each of the following compare to its value before the contractionary policy was undertaken: the interest rate, planned investment, real output, the price level, nominal national income?

SELF TEST

These sample test items will help you check how much you have learned. Answers are found at the end of the chapter. Scoring yourself: One or two wrong—on target. Three or four wrong—passing, but you haven't mastered the chapter yet. Five or more wrong—not good enough; start over and restudy the chapter.

1. The set of channels through which money affects the economy is known as the
    a. discount mechanism.
    b. multiplier mechanism.
    c. transmission mechanism.
    d. monetarist mechanism.

2. As the economy moves to a new short-run equilibrium following an increase in the money stock, which of the following will be observed?
    a. a rightward shift in the money supply curve.
    b. a rightward shift in the money demand curve.
    c. both a and b.
    d. neither a nor b.

3. The short-run effects of a one-time reduction in the money stock include which of the following?
    a. An increase in the interest rate.
    b. A decrease in the level of real output.
    c. A decrease in the price level.
    d. All of the above.

4. Expansionary monetary policy tends to do which of the following in the short run?
    a. Cause planned expenditure to increase.
    b. Cause bond prices to fall.
    c. Cause the unemployment rate to rise.
    d. All of the above.

___B___ 5. The long-run effects of a one-time increase in the money stock include which of the following?
   a. An increase in real output.
   b. An increase in the price level.
   c. An increase in the unemployment rate.
   d. All of the above.

___C___ 6. The idea that money is "neutral" in the long run refers to the fact that
   a. a one-time increase in the money stock will not affect the price level.
   b. a lasting increase in the rate of money growth will not affect the rate of inflation.
   c. a one-time increase in the money stock will not affect real output, real investment, or the real interest rate.
   d. the real interest rate always equals the rate of money growth in the long run.

___D___ 7. If the nominal interest rate is 12 percent and the rate of inflation is 7 percent, then the real interest rate will be
   a. 19 percent.
   b. 12 percent.
   c. 7 percent.
   d. 5 percent.

___C___ 8. A lasting increase in the rate of money growth, unlike a one-time increase in the money stock, will include among its long-run effects
   a. a higher long-run equilibrium level of real output.
   b. a lower long-run equilibrium level of real planned investment.
   c. a higher nominal interest rate.
   d. none of the above.

___B___ 9. The short-run effects of expansionary fiscal policy include which of the following?
   a. A higher level of planned investment.
   b. A higher interest rate.
   c. A higher level of unemployment.
   d. All of the above.

___C___ 10. The crowding out effect refers to the tendency of
   a. tax increases to cause higher interest rates.
   b. increases in government purchases to cause lower real interest rates.
   c. any kind of expansionary fiscal policy to cause lower planned investment.
   d. an increase in the real interest rate to cause an increase in real planned investment.

___B___ 11. Which of the following is thought to be a long-run effect of expansionary fiscal policy, but not expansionary monetary policy?
   a. An increase in the equilibrium level of real output.
   b. A decrease in the equilibrium level of planned investment.
   c. An increase in the long-run equilibrium price level.
   d. An increase in the unemployment rate.

___A___ 12. Compared with what would happen in a closed economy, in an open economy, an increase in government purchases will tend to
   a. cause less of a decrease in planned investment.
   b. cause less of an increase in planned investment.
   c. cause more of an increase in planned investment.
   d. cause more of a decrease in planned investment.

___C___ 13. Net capital inflows plus domestic saving must be equal to
   a. domestic investment.
   b. the government deficit.
   c. **a** plus **b**.
   d. **a** minus **b**.

___A___ 14. Other things being equal, an increase in the government budget deficit will tend to have which of the following effects on the international accounts?
   a. A swing toward deficit on current account.
   b. A swing toward surplus on current account.
   c. A reduction in net capital inflows.
   d. No reason to think one rather than another of the above.

___C___ 15. The monetarist view of the transmission mechanism differs from the Keynesian view in which of the following respects?
   a. Monetarists think there is a great likelihood of a liquidity trap.
   b. Keynesians emphasize the role of stock prices and stock yields.
   c. Monetarists think a change in the money stock will affect explicit and implicit yields on a broad spectrum of financial and nonfinancial assets.
   d. Monetarists think money will have no long-run effect on the price level.

ANSWERS TO CHAPTER 15

Hands On

Problem 1 (a) The expansionary policy will stimulate aggregate demand. Real output, the price level, and nominal national income will all rise as the economy moves up and to the right along its short-run aggregate supply curve. (b) The increase in nominal national income will cause the money demand curve to shift to the right. Indicate the new short-run situation with a money demand curve by MD_2 drawn through point D. (c) The money supply curve does not shift. In the new short-run equilibrium, the interest rate will be higher, as shown by the intersection of MD_2 and MS_1. (d) In the long run, as firms adjust input price expectations, the economy will move off its original short-run aggregate supply curve. As it moves up and to the left along the aggregate demand curve, real output will fall, the price level will rise, and nominal national income will rise. (e) As the economy moves to its new long-run equilibrium, the money demand curve shifts further to the right. This should be shown as a curve MD₃ through point E. (f) The money supply curve still does not shift. In the new long-run equilibrium, the interest rate will be higher than before, as shown by the intersection of MD₃ and MS₁. (g) Investment falls initially as interest rates rise in the new short-run equilibrium, and then falls still more in long-run equilibrium.

Problem 2 (a) A reduction of the money stock to half its previous level is shown as a leftward shift in the money supply curve. The new curve, MS₂, will pass through point A. (b) The interest rate will rise. Planned investment will fall as the economy moves up and to the left along its planned investment curve. The aggregate demand curve will shift to the left. As it does so, real output, the price level, and nominal national income will all fall. (c) Falling nominal national income will cause the money demand curve to shift to the left, but not by enough to prevent some increase in the interest rate. The new short-run position for the money demand curve should be shown by MD₂ drawn through point B. (d) As expectations fully adjust to the new situation, the economy will leave its original short-run aggregate supply curve and move down and to the right along its aggregate demand curve. As it does so, real output will rise while the price level and nominal national income fall. (e) In the money market, the supply curve will not shift but there will be a further leftward shift in the money demand curve to a position MD₃ running through point A. (f) At that point, the interest rate, planned investment, and real output will all return to their original values. The price level and nominal national income will both be lower than they were to begin with.

Self Test

1. **c.** The Keynesian version of the transmission mechanism focuses on interest rates and planned investment.
2. **c.** But the money demand curve will not, in the short run, shift by enough to prevent some reduction in the interest rate.
3. **d.** Result a causes planned investment to fall, shifting the aggregate demand curve to the left, which causes results **b** and **c**.
4. **a.** It causes interest rates to fall, which means an increase in bond prices. The unemployment rate falls as real output rises.
5. **b.** Real output returns to its natural level in the long run and unemployment to its natural rate.
6. **c.** Answer **c** is both consistent with the neutrality of money because it does not involve changes in real variables.
7. **d.** The real interest rate is the nominal rate minus the rate of inflation.
8. **c.** This result comes about as an "inflation premium" is added to the initial nominal interest rate.
9. **b.** Planned investment and the unemployment rate both fall in the short run.
10. **c.** The lower level of planned investment is a result of a higher interest rate.

11. **b.** Neither monetary nor fiscal policy cause **a** or **d** in the long run; both cause **c** in the long run.
12. **a.** This is true because higher interest rates attract a capital inflow which can be used partly to finance private investment.
13. **c.** When this equality holds, inflows into financial markets will balance outflows from financial markets.
14. **a.** This is the mirror image of the increase in net capital inflow that the expansionary policy causes.
15. **c.** Among other things, this means that there can be no liquidity trap.

Chapter 16

Inflation in the Aggregate Supply and Demand Model

WHERE YOU'RE GOING

When you have mastered this chapter, you will understand

1. What are the sources of shifts in aggregate supply curves.
2. What are the characteristics of inflation that arises from excessive growth in aggregate demand.
3. How inflation can arise from shifts in aggregate supply curves.
4. What contributions the new classical economists have made.
5. What types of policy can be used to combat inflation.

In addition, you will add the following terms to your economic vocabulary:
   Demand-pull inflation
   Cost-push inflation
   Supply shock
   Inflationary recession
   Adaptive-expectations hypothesis
   Rational-expectations hypothesis
   New classical economics
   Hyperinflation

WALKING TOUR

After you have read this chapter at least once, you should work step by step through this walking tour. Fill in the blanks and answer the questions as you go along. After you have answered each question, check yourself by uncovering the answer given in the margin. If you do not understand why the answer given is the correct one, refer back to the proper section of the text.

Price Expectations, Inflation, and the Aggregate Supply Curve

The economy's short-run aggregate supply curve shows firms' reactions to an increase in demand assuming no change in the expected

input   level of _____input_____ prices. In graphical terms, the expected level of input prices corresponds to the intersection of the

186

short-run aggregate supply curve with the __natural__ level of real output.

If there is an increase in aggregate demand while the expected level of input prices remains the same, there will be an [**upward**/downward] [shift in/**movement along**] the short-run aggregate supply curve. In the new short-run equilibrium, the level of final-goods prices will be [**above**/below] the expected level of input prices (measured relative to the same base year), and the level of real output will be [**above**/below] the natural level. The economy [will/**will not**] remain in this position indefinitely. Soon, the increase in output prices will cause expected input prices to [**rise**/fall]. As this happens, there will be an [**upward**/downward] [**shift in**/movement along] the short-run aggregate supply curve. Eventually, if there is no further shift in the aggregate demand curve, the economy will reach a new long-run equilibrium where real output has returned to its __natural__ level.

An episode such as that just described, in which the price level is driven up by an increase in aggregate demand, is known as __demand-pull__ inflation. The short-run effect of demand-pull inflation, beginning from a situation of price-stability, is an [**increase**/decrease] in real output and an [increase/**decrease**] in the unemployment rate. In order to hold real output above the natural level for a prolonged period, however, __continued__ inflation will be required.

Inflation that is caused by an upward shift in the aggregate supply curve is called __cost-push__ inflation. One source of cost-push inflation is an event, such as an increase in world oil prices, that increases input costs for all firms and pushes up workers' cost of living. Such an event is known as a __supply shock__.

Suppose that a supply shock causes the aggregate supply curve to shift upward, beginning from a position of price stability. The short-run effect, assuming no change in aggregate demand, will be a/an [**increase**/decrease] in the price level, a/an [increase/**decrease**] in the level of real output, and a/an [**increase**/decrease] in the unemployment rate. If policymakers want to avoid the drop in real output and the rise in unemployment, they can allow aggregate demand to [**increase**/decrease]. Doing so will cause [**more**/less] inflation than would otherwise take place.

A second source of upward shift in the aggregate supply curve is

inflationary expectations   _inflationary expectations_ fueled by past experience with inflation. For example, suppose that aggregate demand stops growing after a prolonged period of demand-pull inflation. If firms expect input prices to continue to rise in the coming year at the same rate they

supply   rose in the previous year, the aggregate [**supply**/demand] curve will
inflationary recession   continue to shift upward. The result will be a/an _inflationary recession_
falling, rising   characterized by [rising/**falling**] real output, [**rising**/falling] unemployment, and a [**rising**/falling] price level.
rising

Rational Expectations and the New Classical Economics

Because the position of the aggregate supply curve depends on firms' expectations regarding input prices, it is important to understand how expectations are formed. According to one view, people form their expectations about future economic events mainly on the basis of past economic events. This is known as the

adaptive   _adaptive_-expectations hypothesis. An alternative view is that people form their expectations on the basis not only of past events, but also on their expectations about economic policies and

rational   their likely effects. This is known as the _rational_-expectations hypothesis. Economists who think that the rational-expectations hypothesis provides a superior explanation of the

new classical   behavior of the economy are referred to as the _new classical_ school.

According to the new classical school, the economy will move up and to the right along a positively sloped aggregate supply curve in response to an increase in aggregate demand only if the shift in

unexpected   aggregate demand is [expected/**unexpected**]. If the increase in aggregate demand is expected, it will not cause an increase in [the price
real output   level/**real output**], but only an increase in [**the price level**/real
the price level   output].

As far as policy is concerned, the implication of the rational expectations hypothesis is that policy changes announced in

will not   advance [will/**will not**] have an effect on real output or unemployment. Policy changes can affect these variables only when they
surprise   come as a _surprise_.

188

Strategies for Ending Inflation

According to the aggregate supply and demand model, stopping entrenched inflation by stopping or slowing the growth of aggregate demand will cause an _inflationary recession_. This means that in the short run, real output will [rise/**fall**], the unemployment rate will [**rise**/fall], and the price level will [**rise**/fall]. Because stopping inflation solely by restricting aggregate demand is costly in terms of real output and employment, economists have looked for ways to reduce the cost.

One approach features the use of wage and price controls. The purpose of wage and price controls is to slow the upward shift of the aggregate [**supply**/demand] curve. They are thought to work best if imposed at a time when the growth of aggregate demand is [rapid/**slowing down**]. If wage and price controls are imposed during a period of rapid growth of aggregate demand, they are likely to be [effective/**ineffective**]. Under such conditions, controls will probably cause _shortages_.

Another way of dealing with inflation is to make wages, taxes, debts, and other quantities inflation-proof by adjusting their nominal values in step with changes in the _price level_. This is called _indexing_. It has sometimes been argued that indexing can reduce the cost of stopping [cost-push/**demand-pull**] inflation. However, indexing can make things worse rather than better when inflation is caused by a _supply shock_.

Many new classical economists say that what is needed to end entrenched inflation is a change in _policy regime_. By this, they mean not just a single shift in monetary or fiscal policy, but a change in the government's whole approach to conducting policy. According to the new classicists, if there were a credible change to an anti-inflationary policy regime at the time the growth of aggregate demand is slowed, inflation can be stopped without an _inflationary recession_. In support of this view, they cite the experience of countries such as Germany and Bolivia, which have experienced very rapid inflation, or _hyperinflation_. In these countries, the end of the hyperinflation was very [**rapid**/gradual], and was accompanied by [huge/**moderate**] reductions in real output.

HANDS ON

Now that you have reviewed the concepts introduced in this chapter, it is time for some hands-on practice with the analytical tools that have been introduced. Work through each problem in this section carefully, and then check your results against those given at the end of the chapter.

Problem 1

Exhibit 16.1 can be used to trace the effects of a one-time increase in aggregate demand for a certain economy. Add the appropriate curves and equilibrium points to the exhibit as requested.

Exhibit 16.1

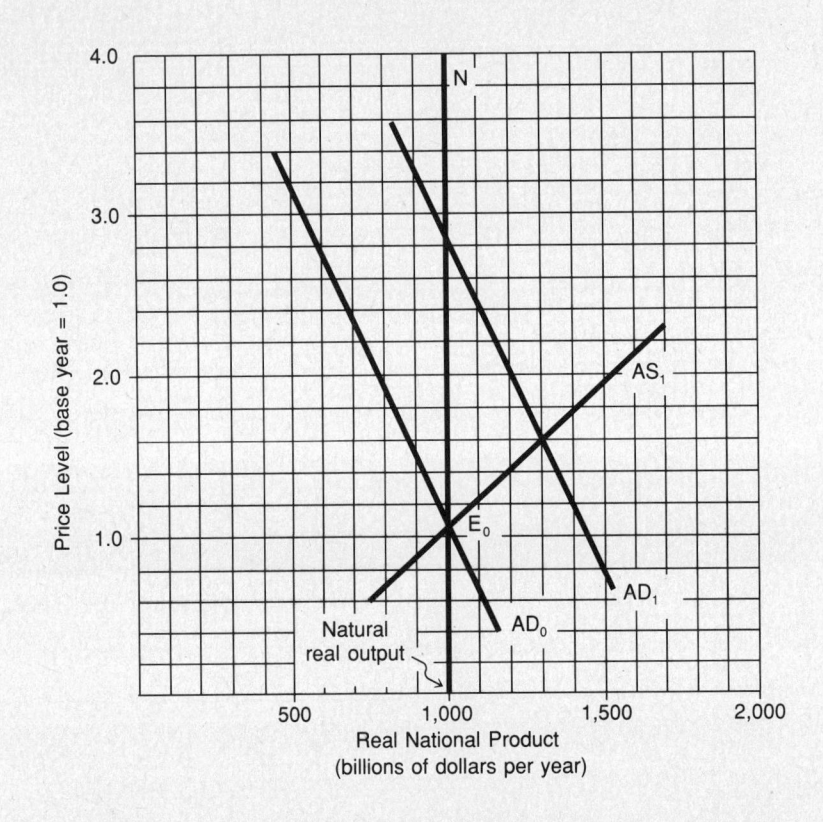

a. Assume that the economy is initially in long-run equilibrium at E₀, with prices stable and with real output at its natural level of $1,000 billion. The position of the short-run aggregate supply curve AS₁ indicates that the expected level of input prices is what in this equilibrium?
b. Assume now that the aggregate demand curve shifts from AD₀ to AD₁. If there is no change in the expected level of input prices, what will happen, in the short run, to real output, the price level, and unemployment? Identify the new short-run equilibrium point as E₁.
c. Suppose that in the next period, firms expect the level of input prices to catch up with the level of final goods prices reached at E₁. What will happen to the aggregate supply curve? Draw in a new aggregate supply curve parallel to the old one, and label it AS₂. Where does AS₂ intersect the natural level of real output? What is the new short-run equilibrium price level for final goods

and the new level of real output, assuming that the aggregate demand curve remains at AD₁? Label this new short-run equilibrium point E₂.
d. If, in the next period, firms expect the level of input prices to catch up with the level of final goods prices at E₂, what will happen to the short-run aggregate supply curve? Sketch in the new curve and label it AS₃. Label the corresponding short-run equilibrium E₃.
e. As the process described continues, the economy will continue to move up and to the right along AD₁ until it reaches the natural level of real output. Label this long-run equilibrium position E₄. Sketch in the short-run aggregate supply curve corresponding to E₄ and label it AD₄. What is the level of final goods prices at E₄? The expected level of input prices?

Problem 2

Exhibit 16.2 shows a certain economy initially in long-run equilibrium at E₀. Use the diagram to trace the effects of a supply shock.

Exhibit 16.2

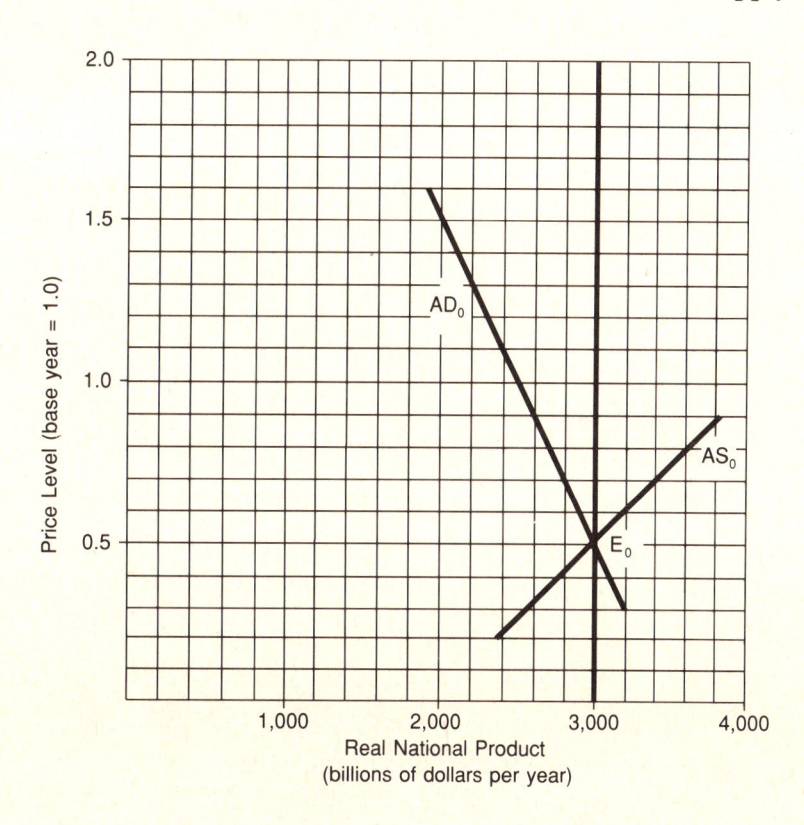

a. What is the expected level of input prices at E₀? How can you tell?
b. Suppose that a depreciation of the value of the dollar relative to foreign currencies makes all imported goods and services more expensive. As a result, firms expect the level of input prices to rise to 1.1 in the coming year. Will this cause the short-run aggregate supply curve to shift? If so, sketch in the new aggregate supply curve, parallel to the old one, and label it AS₁. What will be the new short-run equilibrium? Label the new short-run

191

equilibrium E_1. What has happened to real output, the unemployment rate, and the price level as the economy has moved from E_0 to E_1?

c. What, if anything, can policy makers do to prevent the supply shock from decreasing real output? Show how the demand curve can be shifted in order to keep the short-run level of real output at the natural level. Label the new aggregate demand curve AD_1, and the corresponding equilibrium E_2. What might be the disadvantages of this way of reacting to the supply shock?

SELF TEST

These sample test items will help you check how much you have learned. Answers are found at the end of the chapter. Scoring yourself: One or two wrong—on target. Three or four wrong—passing, but you haven't mastered the chapter yet. Five or more wrong—not good enough; start over and restudy the chapter.

__C__ 1. During which of the following periods was the "misery index"—the sum of the inflation rate and the unemployment rate—the highest?
   a. 1960-1964.
   b. 1971-1972.
   c. 1979-1981.
   d. 1983-1986.

__A__ 2. On an aggregate supply and demand diagram, the expected level of input prices corresponds to the intersection of the short-run aggregate supply curve with
   a. the natural level of real output (the long-run aggregate supply curve).
   b. the aggregate demand curve, even when the economy is not in long-run equilibrium.
   c. the horizontal axis.
   d. the vertical axis.

__b__ 3. Other things being equal, a decrease in the expected level of input prices will cause
   a. an upward shift in the short-run aggregate supply curve.
   b. a downward shift in the short-run aggregate supply curve.
   c. a movement up along the short-run aggregate supply curve.
   d. a movement down along the short-run aggregate supply curve.

__C__ 4. If the economy is in a short-run equilibrium where real output is above its natural level, then the actual level of final goods prices must be
   a. equal to the expected level of input prices.
   b. less than the expected level of input prices.
   c. greater than the expected level of input prices.
   d. no way to tell without additional information.

5. If, in a given year, the level of final goods prices is higher than the expected level of input prices, which of these results would be expected in the following year?
   a. An increase in the expected level of input prices.
   b. A decrease in the expected level of input prices.
   c. An increase in the natural level of real output.
   d. A decrease in the natural level of real output.
6. Which of the following would be likely, other things equal, to cause demand-pull inflation?
   a. An increase in the money stock.
   b. An increase in autonomous net taxes.
   c. A reduction in the federal budget deficit.
   d. An increase in the price of imported oil.
7. If expansionary policy is used to keep real output above its natural level for a period of several years, which of the following will be a likely result?
   a. Brief inflation, followed by a return to price stability.
   b. Sustained inflation, very likely growing more severe each year.
   c. A recession accompanied by a falling price level.
   d. An unemployment rate well above the natural rate.
8. Inflation caused by an increase in expected input prices while the aggregate demand curve remains fixed would be called
   a. demand-pull inflation.
   b. recessionary inflation.
   c. cost-push inflation.
   d. hyperinflation.
9. If the economy undergoes a supply shock as the result of a widespread crop failure, and no change is made in policy governing aggregate demand, we would expect the results to include which of the following?
   a. An increase in the price level.
   b. A decrease in the level of real output.
   c. An increase in the unemployment rate.
   d. All of the above.
10. If policy makers stop the growth of aggregate demand following a sustained period of inflation, the result is likely to be
    a. a runaway increase of real output.
    b. an inflationary recession.
    c. a recession with a falling price level.
    d. a quick return to the natural level of real output.
11. The notion that people, when forming expectations, consider not just past events, but also expected future policy actions and their likely effects, is known as
    a. the adaptive-expectations hypothesis.
    b. the hyperinflation hypothesis.
    c. the inflationary recession hypothesis.
    d. the rational-expectations hypothesis.

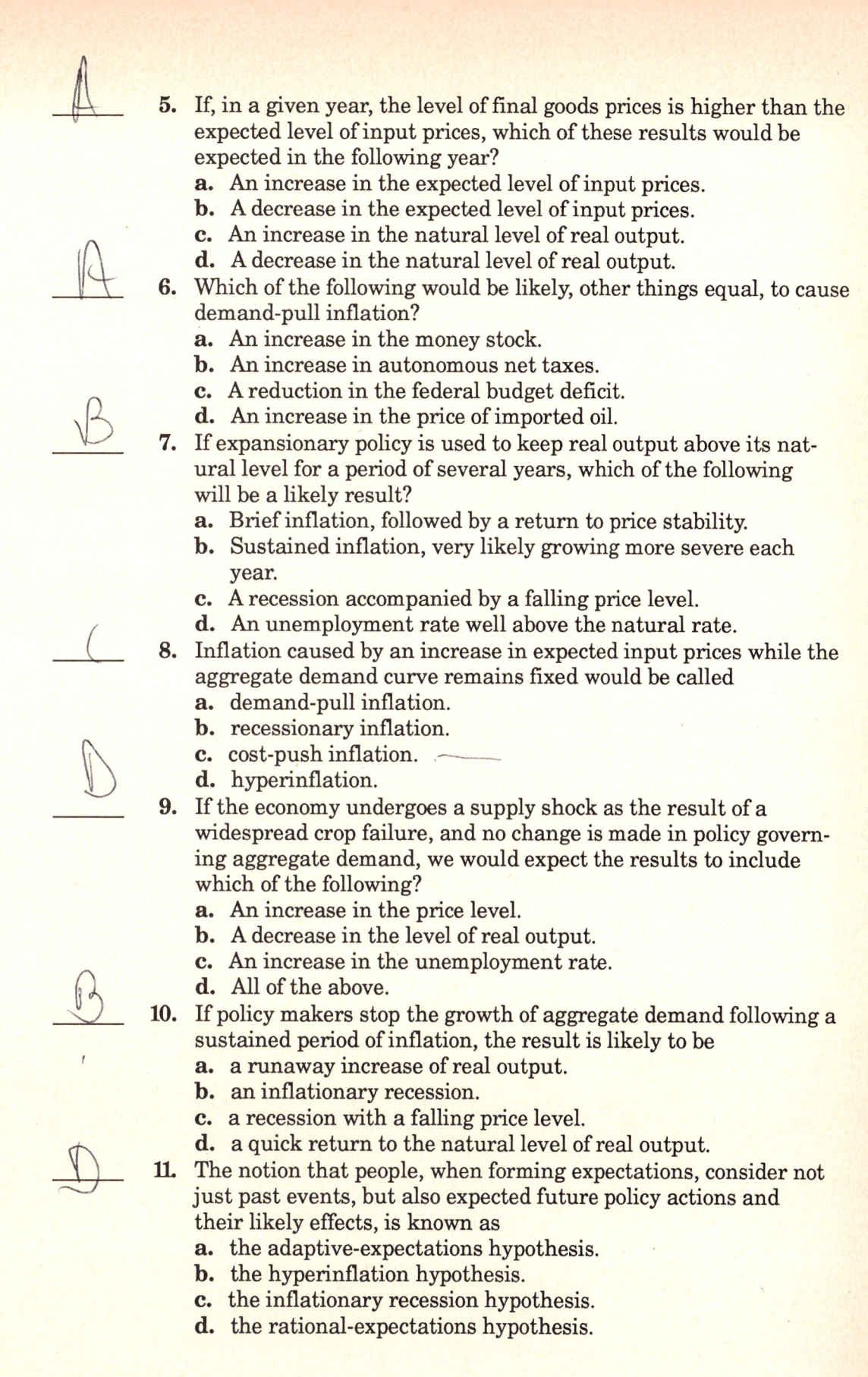

_C_ 12. According to the views of the new classical school of economics, an increase in the rate of money growth that was announced in advance would, in the short run, by comparison with a surprise increase in money growth,
   a. cause a greater increase in real output.
   b. cause a greater increase in the unemployment rate.
   c. cause a greater increase in the price level.
   d. all of the above.

_D_ 13. Which of the following is thought to be a good substitute for restraint of aggregate demand as a means of stopping inflation?
   a. Indexing.
   b. Wage and price controls.
   c. Both a and b.
   d. Neither a nor b.

_D_ 14. Which of the following best describes U.S. experience with wage and price controls?
   a. They have never been tried.
   b. They were tried in World War II, but never since.
   c. President Nixon tried them in the 1970s, and they brought a quick and lasting end to inflation.
   d. President Nixon tried them in the 1970s with at best mixed results.

_B_ 15. A rate of inflation of 1,000 percent or more per year would be classified as
   a. recessionary inflation.
   b. hyperinflation.
   c. cost-push inflation.
   d. indexation inflation.

ANSWERS TO CHAPTER 16

Hands On

Problem 1 (a) The expected level of input prices is shown by the intersection of the aggregate supply curve with the natural level of real output. Thus, the expected level of input prices is 1.0 at E_0. (b) Real output will rise to $1,300 billion and the price level will rise to 1.6, as shown by E_1 in the solution graph. The unemployment rate will fall as this happens. (c) If the expected level of input prices rises to 1.6, the aggregate supply curve will shift up to the position AS_2 shown in the solution graph. This curve intersects N at the expected input price level 1.6. The new short-run equilibrium will be at E_2, where the level of final goods prices will be 2.0. (d) As the expected input price level rises to 2.0, the aggregate supply curve shifts up to AS_3. The new short-run equilibrium is E_3. (e) The final long-run equilibrium will occur at a price level of 2.8, shown by E_4 in the solution graph. In this equilibrium, the expected input price level will also be 2.8.

Exhibit 16.1 (ans.)

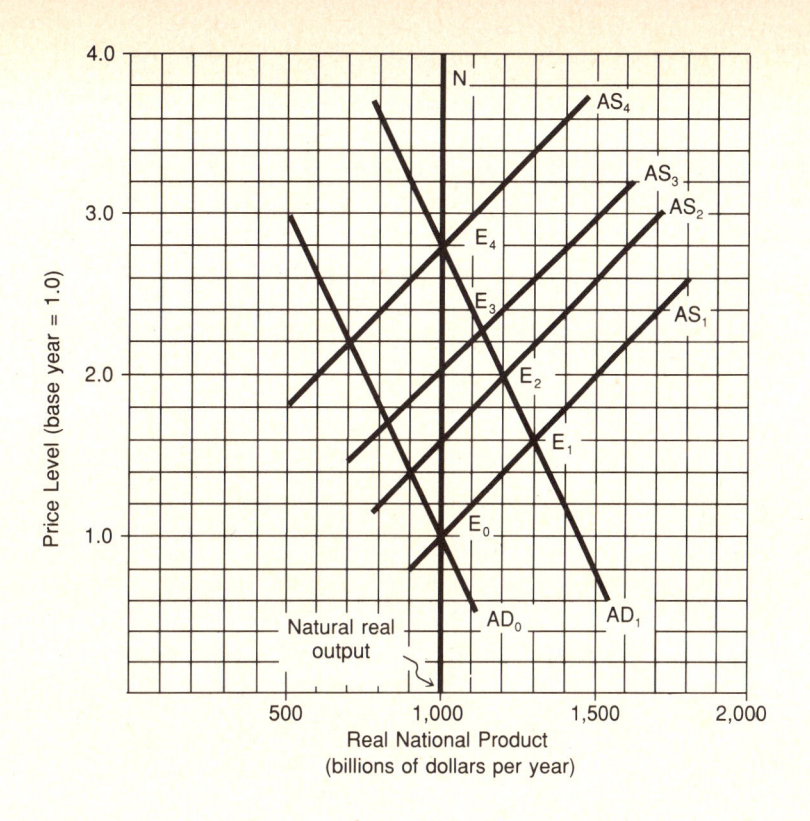

Problem 2 (a) The expected level of input prices is 0.5, as shown by the intersection of AS₀ and N. (b) If the expected level of input prices rises to 1.1, the short-run aggregate supply curve will shift up to AS₁, as shown in the solution graph. This curve intersects N at the new expected input price level. The new short-run equilibrium will be E₁, where the level of final goods prices has risen to 0.9 and real output has fallen to $2,600 billion. The unemployment

Exhibit 16.2 (ans.)

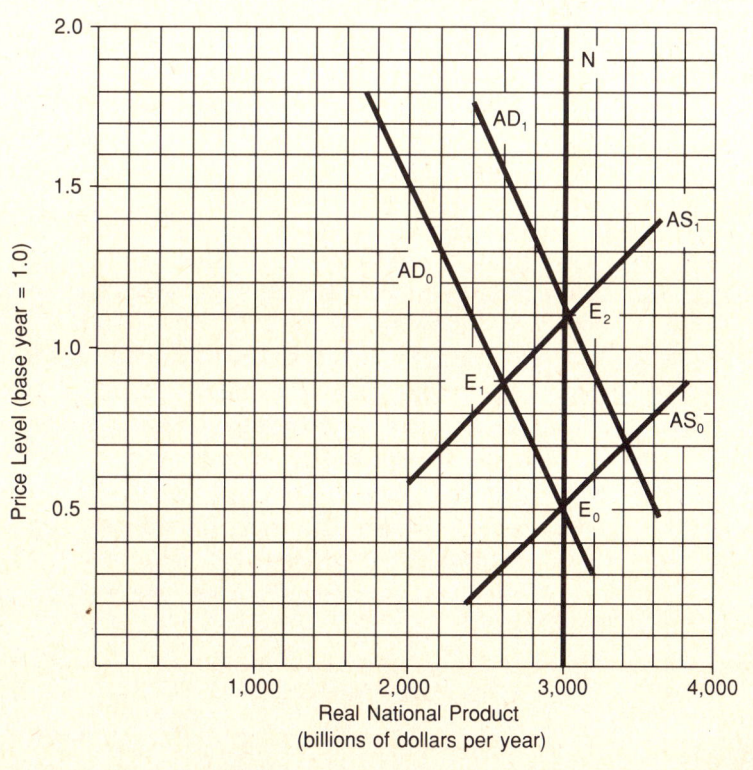

rate at E_1 will be above the natural rate. (c) To hold real output at its natural level, expansionary fiscal or monetary policy could be used to shift the aggregate demand curve up to AD_1. This would, however, cause a greater increase in the price level. Under the adaptive expectations hypothesis, the upward shift in the price level might touch off inflationary expectations. This would cause a further upward shift of the aggregate supply curve, and the economy might not end up at E_2 after all.

Self Test

1. **c.** The "misery index" reached a level of 20 at one point, a peak for the past 50 years, before dropping again in the mid-1980s.
2. **a.** The aggregate supply curve also intersects the aggregate demand curve at this point only when the economy is in long-run equilibrium.
3. **b.** Any change in the expected level of input prices will move the intersection of the aggregate supply curve with the natural level of real output.
4. **c.** Because the economy is then at a point above and to the right of the intersection of the aggregate supply curve with the natural level of real output.
5. **a.** This will happen because an increase in final goods prices eventually affects input prices via its effect on wages and the cost of living, and also on the prices of nonlabor inputs.
6. **a.** This would shift the aggregate demand curve to the right. Answers **b** and **c** would shift the demand curve to the left, and **d** would shift the aggregate supply curve.
7. **b.** If the aggregate demand curve does not continually shift upward to match the shift in the aggregate supply curve, real output will return to its natural level.
8. **c.** Inflation caused by a shift in the aggregate demand curve is called demand-pull inflation.
9. **d.** All of these happen as the economy moves up and to the left along its aggregate demand curve.
10. **b.** During such an episode, the aggregate supply curve continues to be pushed up by the momentum of inflationary expectations while the aggregate demand curve remains fixed or shifts up more slowly.
11. **d.** Answer **a** assumes that people look only at past events.
12. **c.** According to the new classical view, expected policy changes have no effect on real output or unemployment, only the price level.
13. **d.** Neither policy will be effective unless used in conjunction with restraint of aggregate demand.
14. **d.** They were also tried in World War II, at which time they slowed inflation but at the cost of widespread shortages and rationing.
15. **b.** Hyperinflation simply means very rapid inflation.

Chapter 17

Economic Growth and Productivity

WHERE YOU'RE GOING

When you have mastered this chapter, you will understand

1. How the economy can grow while maintaining price stability.
2. How insufficient growth of aggregate demand can cause a growth recession.
3. How expansion of aggregate demand beyond the rate of growth of natural real output can cause inflation.
4. What may have caused the slowdown in productivity growth in the U.S. economy beginning in the 1970's.
5. What are the traditional Keynesian recommendations for promoting growth of real output.
6. What policies are recommended by the supply-side school of economics.

In addition, you will add the following terms to your economic vocabulary:
   Growth recession
   Supply-side economics
   Laffer curve

WALKING TOUR

After you have read this chapter at least once, you should work step by step through this walking tour. Fill in the blanks and answer the questions as you go along. After you have answered each question, check yourself by uncovering the answer given in the margin. If you do not understand why the answer given is the correct one, refer back to the proper section of the text.

Economic Growth with Price Stability

can

natural real output
labor force
productivity

In the short run, real output [can/cannot] rise above or fall below its natural level. Long-run growth, on the other hand, has to do with growth in __natural real output__ ~~itself~~. The main sources of long-run growth are increases in the __labor force__ and increases in __productivity__.

197

On an aggregate real supply and demand diagram, long-run growth is shown as a [leftward/**rightward**] [**shift in**/movement along] the long-run aggregate supply curve, which represents the level of natural real output. As the level of natural real output increases, the short-run aggregate [**supply**/demand] curve automatically shifts to the right at the same rate, assuming that expected input prices do not change. In order to achieve steady economic growth with price stability, fiscal and monetary policy must be managed in such a way that *aggregate demand* also grows at the same rate. If this happens, the *AD* curve will shift to the right at the same speed as natural real output is growing, and the price level [will/**will not**] change over time.

If the growth rate of aggregate demand fails to keep up with the growth of natural real output, the economy may experience a situation in which real output grows [**less**/more] rapidly than its natural level. In this case, the unemployment rate will tend to [**rise**/fall], and the economy will experience a/an *growth recession*. On the other hand, if aggregate demand grows more rapidly than natural real output, the economy will experience *growth with inflation*. Real output will, at least for a time, [**rise above**/fall below] its natural level. If this situation persists, the rate of inflation can be expected to [**increase**/decrease] each year.

Recent Trends in U.S. Economic Growth

In the period 1954 to 1973, productivity in the United States grew at a rate of about __2.2__ percent per year. Then, in the period 1974 to 1981, productivity growth [**slowed**/speeded up] to about __0.6__ percent per year.

A number of proposed explanations for the productivity slowdown have been advanced, including

1. changes in labor force,
2. supply shocks,
3. inflation,
4. falling research, and
5. increasing regulation.

No one of these has been conclusively shown to be the major source of the slowdown. Since 1981, productivity growth in the later 1980s appears somewhat [**better**/worse] than in the 1974 to 1981 period. Gains in productivity in the [manufacturing/service] sector have been especially strong, although productivity in the [manufacturing/service] sector has lagged.

Policies for Promoting Economic Growth

In the 1960s, economic growth [was/was not] a strong priority for the Keynesian economists working in the Kennedy and Johnson administrations. In part, they aimed to promote growth by fine-tuning the economy to avoid _recessions_. In part also, they sought to promote growth through the proper mix of fiscal and monetary policy. In the Keynesian model, a lower real interest rate and, hence, higher real investment and real growth, can be achieved with relatively [tight/easy] monetary policy combined with relatively [tight/easy] fiscal policy. Even under this theory, a deficit in the federal budget [was/was not] considered acceptable during a recession. However, the _structural_ deficit should be kept near zero. From the Keynesian perspective, the policy mix of the Reagan administration, which included a relatively [large/small] structural deficit was seen as [helpful/harmful] to economic growth.

However, policies of the Reagan administration find their defenders among the _supply side_ school of economics, which focuses on efforts to speed up the growth of natural real output through the incentive effects of _marginal tax rate cuts_. According to the supply-siders, such tax cuts would promote growth in part by boosting _saving_. Supply-siders also think that properly designed changes in marginal tax rates will, as a result of incentive effects, cause the tax base to [grow/shrink], and that as a result, the revenue loss to the government will be [more/less] than static estimates indicate. In fact, experience indicates that in the highest tax brackets, cuts in marginal tax rates can [increase/decrease] total revenue.

HANDS ON

Now that you have reviewed the concepts introduced in this chapter, it is time for some hands-on practice with the analytical tools that have been introduced. Work through each problem in this section carefully, and then check your results against those given at the end of the chapter.

Problem 1

The questions that follow are based on Exhibit 17.1. Initially, the economy is shown in long-run equilibrium at E_1, where the natural level of real output is $800 billion per year.

Exhibit 17.1

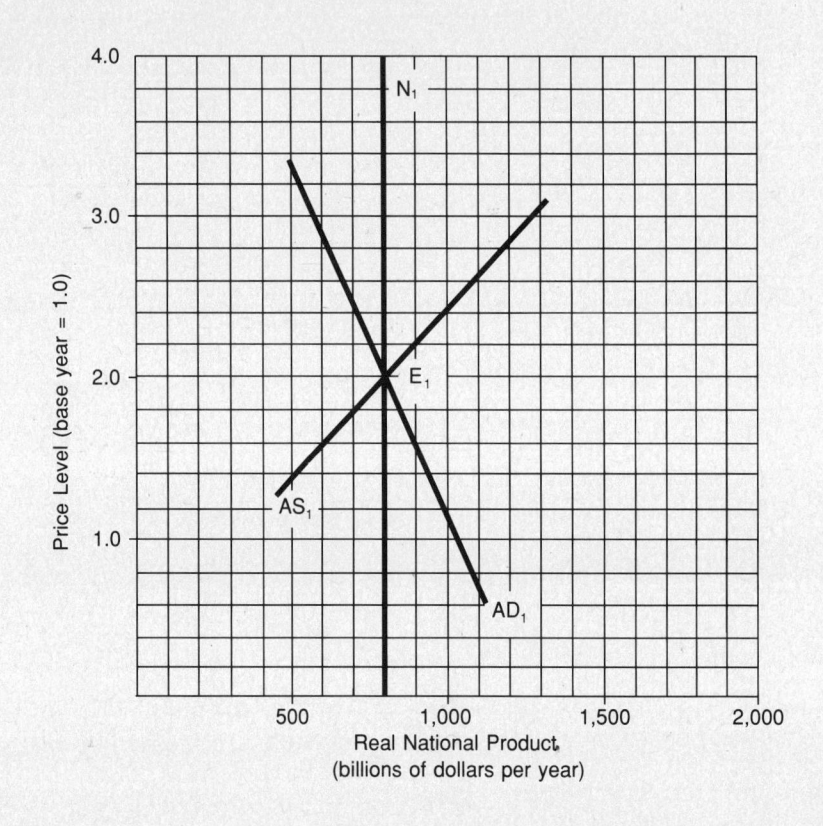

a. Suppose that the natural level of real output increases from $800 billion to $1,500 billion. Sketch the economy's new long-run aggregate supply curve, and label the new curve N_2.
b. Assuming that there is no change in the expected level of input prices as natural real output increases, what will happen to the economy's short-run aggregate supply curve? Sketch in the new position of the curve, and label it AS_2.
c. In order to maintain price stability and keep unemployment at its natural rate as the economy grows, what must happen to the aggregate demand curve? Sketch in the required new position of the aggregate demand curve, and label it AD_2. Label the new position of long-run equilibrium E_2.

Problem 2

The questions that follow are based on Exhibit 17.2. That exhibit shows the economy initially in equilibrium at a natural level of real output of $2,000 billion.

Exhibit 17.2

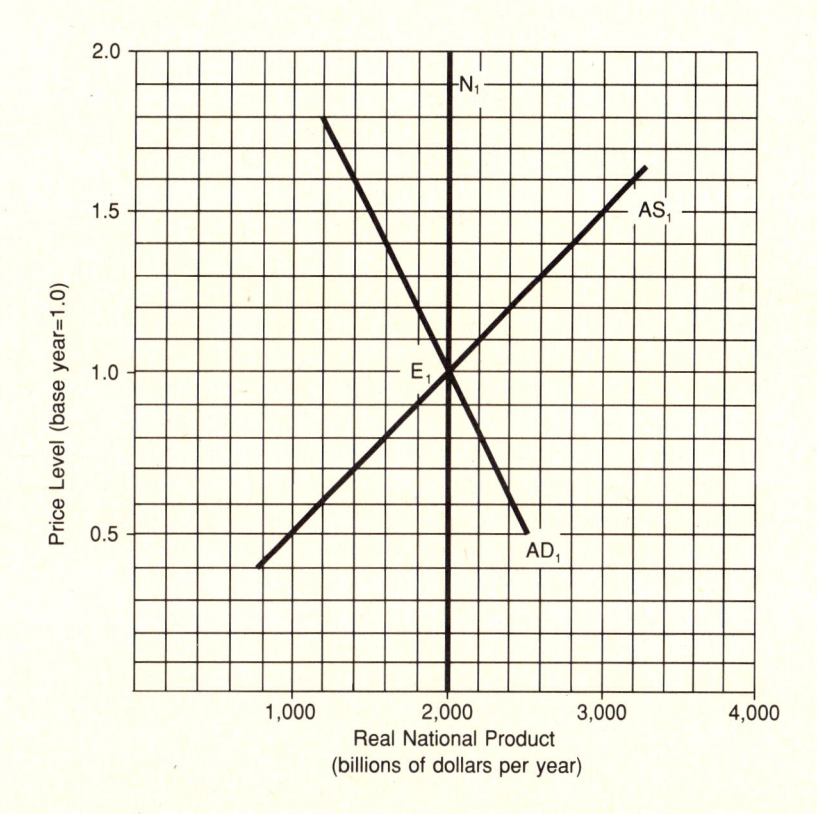

a. If the natural level of real output increases from $2,000 billion to $3,200 billion, what will happen to the long-run aggregate supply curve? Sketch the new curve and label it N_2. Assuming no change in the expected level of input prices, what will happen to the short-run aggregate supply curve? Sketch this new curve also, and label in AS_2.

b. Suppose now that as the supply curves shift, restrictive monetary and fiscal policy prevent any growth of aggregate demand, so that the aggregate demand curve remains in the position AD_1. What will then happen to real output, the unemployment rate, and the price level? Locate the new short-run equilibrium on the graph, and label it E_2. How would this situation be described?

SELF TEST

These sample test items will help you check how much you have learned. Answers are found at the end of the chapter. Scoring yourself: One or two wrong—on target. Three or four wrong—passing, but you haven't mastered the chapter yet. Five or more wrong—not good enough; start over and restudy the chapter.

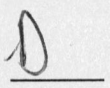

1. Economic growth is possible without inflation, and with unemployment remaining at its natural rate, if
   a. the level of natural real output increases.
   b. the expected level of input prices remains unchanged.
   c. aggregate demand grows at the same rate as natural real output.
   d. all of the above.
2. In a growth recession,
   a. real output increases and the unemployment rate falls.
   b. the unemployment rate increases and real output falls.
   c. real output and the unemployment rate both increase.
   d. real output and the unemployment rate both decrease.
3. The economy can recover from a growth recession
   a. via an increase in the rate of growth of aggregate demand.
   b. via a decrease in the expected level of input prices.
   c. either a or b.
   d. neither a nor b.
4. If aggregate demand is allowed to grow faster than natural real output for a sustained period, the likely result is
   a. an inflationary recession.
   b. growth with inflation.
   c. a growth recession.
   d. a classic recession.
5. In order to keep unemployment below its natural rate for a sustained period in a growing economy, it will be necessary for policy makers to accept
   a. a rate of inflation that increases from year to year.
   b. a steady rate of inflation, which firms and workers come to expect.
   c. a falling price level.
   d. a falling level of real output.
6. During which of the following periods did the United States experience the slowest rate of productivity growth?
   a. 1954 to 1973.
   b. 1974 to 1981.
   c. 1982 to 1986.
   d. Productivity growth was about the same in all of the above periods.
7. During the past 30 years in the United States, rapid inflation has
   a. been associated with relatively high rates of productivity growth.
   b. been associated with lagging productivity growth.
   c. shown no systematic relationship to productivity growth.
   d. explained nearly 100 percent of changes in the rate of productivity growth.

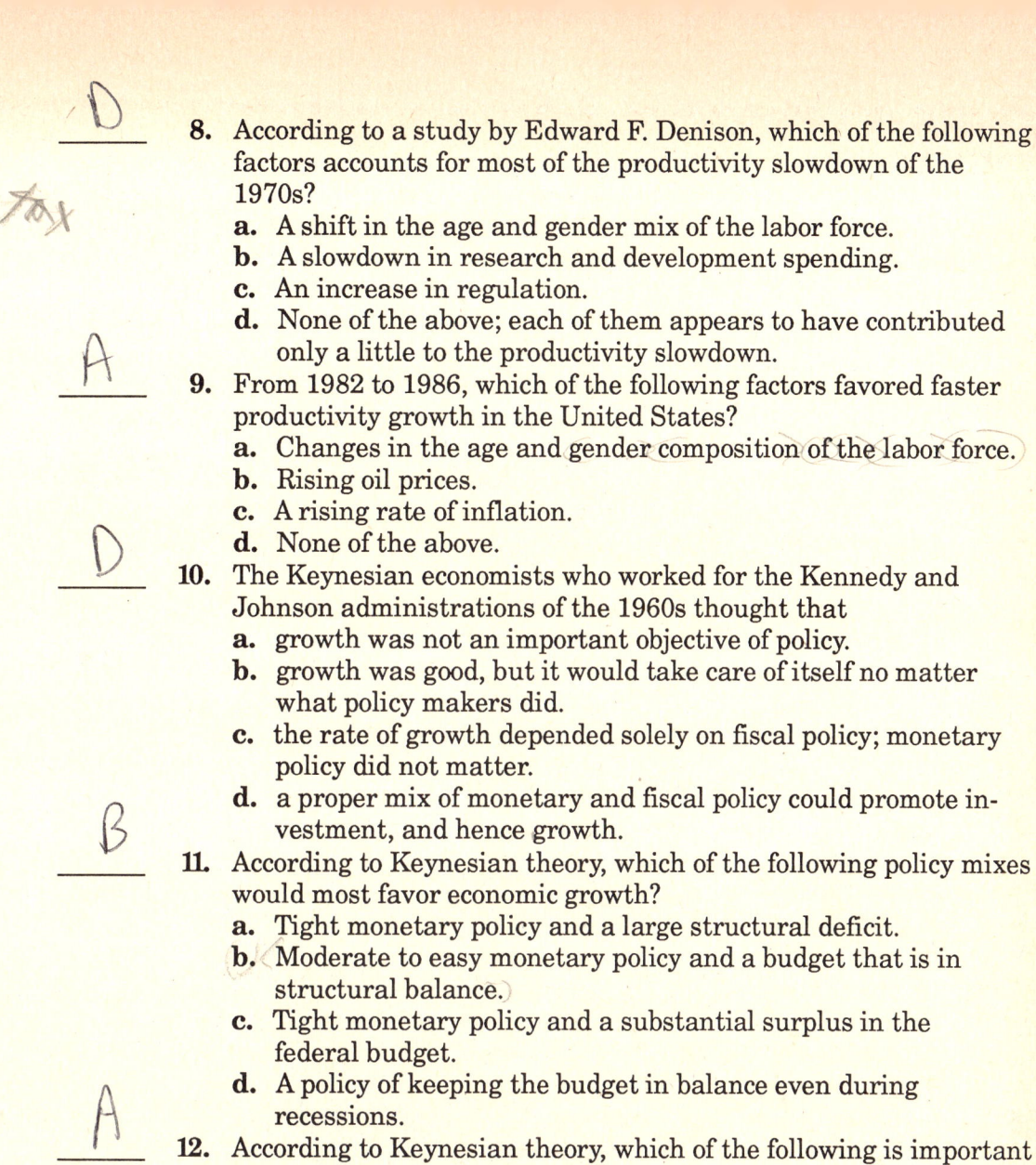

___D___ 8. According to a study by Edward F. Denison, which of the following factors accounts for most of the productivity slowdown of the 1970s?
   a. A shift in the age and gender mix of the labor force.
   b. A slowdown in research and development spending.
   c. An increase in regulation.
   d. None of the above; each of them appears to have contributed only a little to the productivity slowdown.

___A___ 9. From 1982 to 1986, which of the following factors favored faster productivity growth in the United States?
   a. Changes in the age and gender composition of the labor force.
   b. Rising oil prices.
   c. A rising rate of inflation.
   d. None of the above.

___D___ 10. The Keynesian economists who worked for the Kennedy and Johnson administrations of the 1960s thought that
   a. growth was not an important objective of policy.
   b. growth was good, but it would take care of itself no matter what policy makers did.
   c. the rate of growth depended solely on fiscal policy; monetary policy did not matter.
   d. a proper mix of monetary and fiscal policy could promote investment, and hence growth.

___B___ 11. According to Keynesian theory, which of the following policy mixes would most favor economic growth?
   a. Tight monetary policy and a large structural deficit.
   b. Moderate to easy monetary policy and a budget that is in structural balance.
   c. Tight monetary policy and a substantial surplus in the federal budget.
   d. A policy of keeping the budget in balance even during recessions.

___A___ 12. According to Keynesian theory, which of the following is important for encouraging economic growth?
   a. Relatively low real interest rates.
   b. Federal budget deficits equal to at least 4 percent of GNP.
   c. A steadily increasing rate of inflation.
   d. Tight monetary policy.

___A___ 13. Which of the following was the most important component of the supply-side economic policies advanced by some members of the Reagan administration in the early 1980s?
   a. Cuts in marginal tax rates.
   b. Increases in government purchases.
   c. A balanced budget amendment.
   d. All of the above were equally important parts of the supply-side program.

203

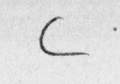

_C_   **14.** Which of the following best expresses the implications of the Laffer curve?
  a. Lower tax rates always mean more tax revenue.
  b. Tax rate reductions reduce the size of the tax base.
  c. If marginal tax rates are high enough to begin with, cutting those rates can increase tax revenue.
  d. The lower the marginal tax rate to begin with, the more likely it is that a cut in the marginal tax rate will increase tax revenue.

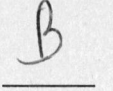

_B_   **15.** Experience with income tax cuts in the United States in the past indicates that
  a. lower tax rates always mean higher total tax revenues.
  b. lower tax rates can increase the share of taxes paid by the richest taxpayers.
  c. lower tax rates shift the tax burden from the rich to the poor.
  d. changes in tax rates have little effect on the way the tax burden is distributed between the rich and the poor.

ANSWERS TO CHAPTER 17

Hands On

Problem 1 (a) The new long-run aggregate supply curve will be a vertical line at a national product of $1,500. See N_2 in the solution graph for Exhibit 17.1. (b) The short-run aggregate supply curve will move to position AS_2 where it intersects the new long-run curve

Exhibit 17.1 (ans.)

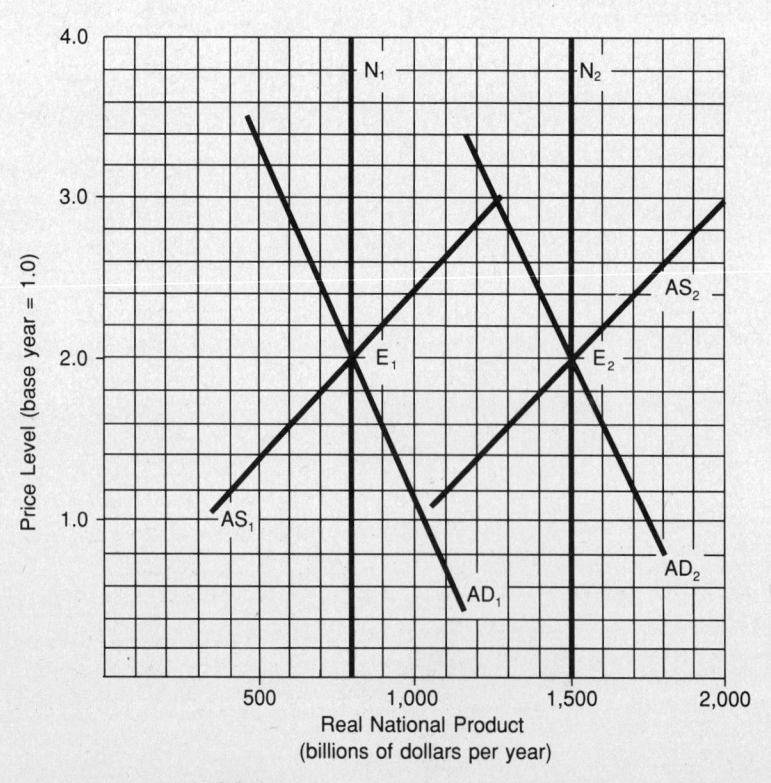

at the same expected price level, 2.0, as before. (c) To maintain price stability, the aggregate demand curve must shift to the right by the same amount as the supply curves. This is shown by the curve AD₂ in the solution graph. The new equilibrium point is E₂.

Problem 2 (a) The long-run aggregate supply curve shifts to the position N₂ shown in the solution graph for Exhibit 17.2. The short-run aggregate supply curve shifts with it, to the position AS₂.
(b) With no change in aggregate demand, the economy will move to a new short-run equilibrium at E₂. As it does so, real output will grow, although by less than natural real output. The price level will fall, and the unemployment rate will rise. This situation would be described as a growth recession.

Exhibit 17.2 (ans.)

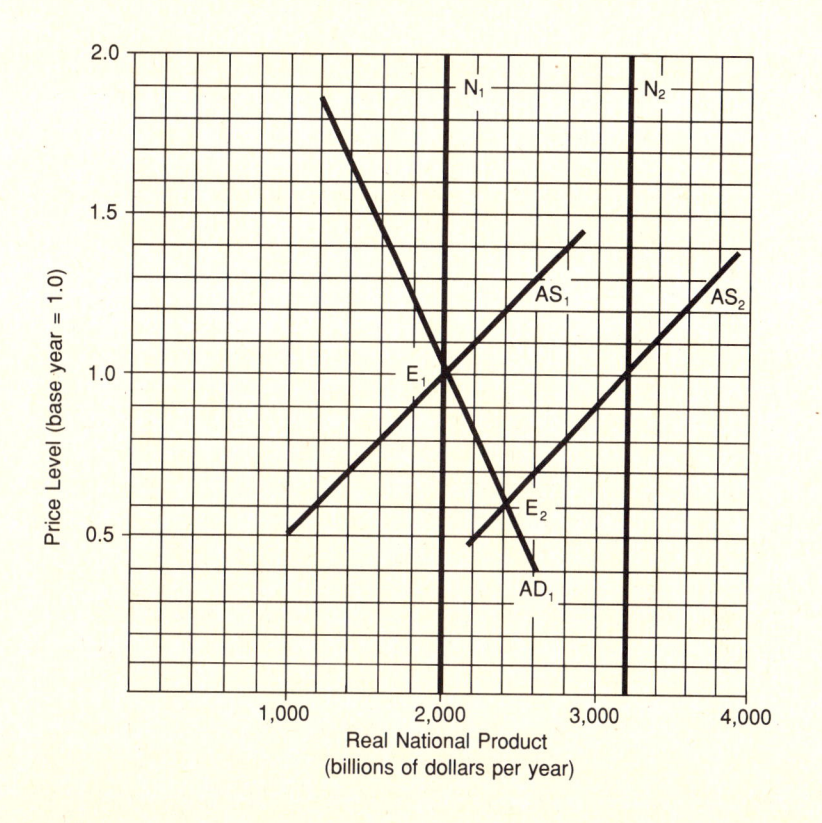

Self Test

1. **d.** In this case, the AS and AD curves shift to the right at the same rate that natural real output grows.
2. **c.** Real output grows, but unemployment increases because the actual level of real output does not keep up with the growth of natural real output.
3. **c.** But **b** would be a slower path to recovery.
4. **b.** The actual level of real output would move above the natural level, at least for a time, but there would be inflation as the economy moved up the short-run aggregate real supply curve.
5. **a.** A steady rate of inflation that was expected would mean that real output would return to its natural level.

6. **b.** The growth of output per worker slowed to about 0.6 from about 2.2 percent per year.
7. **b.** Some economists think this is because inflation disrupts business decision making. But inflation was far from the only factor affecting productivity growth.
8. **d.** Denison and others have not found any single cause that explains more than a small part of the productivity slowdown.
9. **a.** This happened as the adverse changes in age and gender composition during the 1970s were reversed. Falling oil prices and a slower rate of inflation also have favored faster productivity growth.
10. **d.** They favored expansionary monetary policy to keep real interest rates low, and a budget deficit only during recessions.
11. **b.** Choices **a** would keep real interest rates too high, **c** would be too contractionary, and **d** would slow growth by slowing the recovery from recessions.
12. **a.** Low real interest rates are seen as an encouragement to real investment.
13. **a.** These were supposed to encourage saving, investment, and work effort.
14. **c.** Marginal tax rate cuts produce revenue increases only at rates that are high to begin with.
15. **b.** The reason is that the tax base of these taxpayers appears to increase in response to lower marginal tax rates.

Chapter 18

Strategies for Economic Stabilization

WHERE YOU'RE GOING

When you have mastered this chapter, you will understand

1. Why Keynesian economists favor active use of fiscal and monetary policy to stabilize the economy.
2. What are the implications of lags and forecasting errors for the conduct of discretionary policy.
3. Why politics may interfere with the conduct of stabilization policy.
4. What kinds of rules have been proposed for the conduct of monetary policy.
5. What kinds of rules have been proposed for the conduct of fiscal policy.

In addition, you will add the following terms to your economic vocabulary:
Inside lag
Outside lag

WALKING TOUR

After you have read this chapter at least once, you should work step by step through this walking tour. Fill in the blanks and answer the questions as you go along. After you have answered each question, check yourself by uncovering the answer given in the margin. If you do not understand why the answer given is the correct one, refer back to the proper section of the text.

The Debate over Policy Activism

Almost all economists agree that economic policy should aim to moderate the swings in the business cycle, but behind this agreement lies a debate: What kind of policy is right?

On the one hand, there are policy activists, among them, followers of ___Keynes___. On the other hand, there are those who see policy mistakes behind much past economic instability. These include members of the ___monetarists___ and ___new classical___ schools.

Keynes

monetarist, new
   classical

The case for policy activism rests on three propositions. The first is the idea that the private economy is inherently [stable/**unstable**]. The second is confidence in economists' ability to __predict__ the future course of the economy and the effects of policy within a workable margin of error. The third is the idea that policy makers [**will**/will not] heed the technical advice offered by economists.

Monetarists and new classicists doubt the adequacy of economists' tools. Monetarists think that monetary and fiscal policy affect real output and employment only in the [long/**short**] run while new classicists doubt even the short-run effect if policy actions are expected. They also think that even with large-scale computer models, the effects of policy changes [can/**cannot**] be accurately predicted.

Critics of activism are much concerned with the problem of delays, or __lags__ in the policy process. The delay between the time a policy change is needed and the time a decision is made is called the __inside__ lag. The delay between the time a policy decision is made and the time the policy change affects the economy is known as the __outside__ lag.

For monetary policy, the inside lag is thought to be relatively [long/**short**]. The outside lag for monetary policy, by comparison, is [shorter/**longer**]. Changes in the rate of money growth are thought to affect real output with a lag of __3__ to __12__ months. The full effect on the price level takes a [**longer**/shorter] time to be felt.

Fiscal policy lags are [**harder**/easier] to measure accurately. The inside lag for fiscal policy is, in most cases, [shorter/**longer**] than for monetary policy. There is no clear agreement on the length of the outside lag for fiscal policy. It has been estimate to be from several __months__ to several __years__.

In addition to the technical problems of lags and forecasting, critics see political problems with policy activism. One is that the pressure to "do something" about unemployment or inflation comes when it is [**too late**/too early] to take effective action, given the length of policy lags. Another problem is that policy tends to focus on the [**short**/long] run.

New classicists believe that monetary policy makers face a problem of __inconsistency__ between their long- and short-term goals. They have a constant temptation to make a surprise [increase/decrease] in the rate of money growth. If people anticipate that the Fed will give in to this temptation, and adjust their price expectations accordingly, the economy will experience [inflation/price stability].

The Search for Policy Rules

Critics of activist policies propose that it is better to pursue long-term policy rules that are correct on the average rather than follow a flexible policy that is more likely to do harm than good.

The original monetarist proposal was to have the Fed peg the growth of the _money stock_ to a predetermined constant rate. This rate should be as nearly as possible equal to the average rate of growth of _natural real output_. However, such a policy would stabilize the growth of aggregate demand only if _velocity_ remains constant. Velocity [has/has not] in fact been constant over recent decades. Monetarists say, however, that if the Fed had pursued a constant rate of money growth over time, velocity would have varied [more/less] than it has.

To avoid possible problems caused by changes in velocity, others have proposed that nominal national income should be used as the target for monetary policy. However, this rule could cause inflation or deflation if there were changes in the growth of _natural_ real output.

Finally, still other economists have proposed that the price level be used as a target for monetary policy. Aside from problems of lags, which could be serious, a price level target might have undesirable results when the economy was affected by a _supply shock_.

To date, the Fed [has/has not] adopted a specific policy rule.

Rules have also been proposed for fiscal policy. One alternative is to require the federal budget to be balanced each year. However, such a rule might require that taxes be [raised/lowered] or spending be [raised/lowered] during a recession. Such actions, if taken, would tend to make the recession [more/less] severe. To overcome this problem, an alternative would be to require that the budget be balanced on average over the course of the _business cycle_.

209

ECONOMICS IN THE NEWS

WASHINGTON, D.C., OCTOBER 21, 1987—The stock market's Monday collapse has put Federal Reserve Chairman Alan Greenspan on the front line in the fight to prevent a market panic from turning into a general economic slump.

Just a few days ago, Greenspan was under pressure from the financial markets to increase interest rates and prove his willingness to fight inflation. But by yesterday, the focus had changed dramatically. After Monday's unprecedented market crash, traders and analysts were calling on the central bank to ease credit to avoid recession.

Whether Greenspan is up to the task remains to be seen. He tried to calm markets yesterday with a one-sentence statement signaling the Fed's switch from an anti-inflation to an anti-recession policy. It said: "The Federal Reserve, consistent with its responsibilities as the nation's central bank, affirmed today its readiness to serve as a source of liquidity to support the economic and financial system."

The Federal Reserve quickly backed up its statement with action, driving the federal funds rate down to about 6.75 percent late in the day from more than 7.50 percent Monday.

Although an adequate supply of funds in the market and the economy is important, the challenges facing the Fed over the coming weeks are immense. If the Fed doesn't do enough to bolster the economy, the stock-market collapse could quickly drag down other areas of the economy. And if the Fed primes the pump with too much money, it risks a collapse of the dollar and renewed fears of inflation.

Source: Alan Murray, "Stock Market's Frenzy Puts Fed's Greenspan In a Crucial Position," *The Wall Street Journal*, October 21, 1987, p. 1. Reprinted by permission of The Wall Street Journal. © Dow Jones & Company, Inc., 1987. All Rights Reserved.

Questions

1. Other things being equal, what effect would a sharp fall in stock prices have on aggregate demand? On real output, employment, and the price level?
2. The Fed is described in the news item as "allowing the federal funds rate to fall." Just what actions would the Fed have undertaken to bring about a decline in the federal funds rate? Speaking as a policy activist, would you endorse the Fed's statements and actions, as reported in the news item?
3. Now take the position of a monetarist or new classical critic of policy activism. Explain why you think the Fed should maintain a steady growth of the money stock regardless of short-run developments in financial markets or elsewhere.

| | SELF TEST | *These sample test items will help you check how much you have learned. Answers are found at the end of the chapter. Scoring yourself: One or two wrong—on target. Three or four wrong—passing, but you haven't mastered the chapter yet. Five or more wrong—not good enough; start over and restudy the chapter.* |

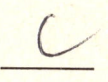

___A___ 1. Policy activists are most frequently found among the ranks of the
   a. Keynesians.
   b. Monetarists.
   c. New classicists.
   d. Friedmanites.

___B___ 2. Which of the following is a proposition that underlies the case for policy activism?
   a. The economy, left to its own devices, tends to be quite stable.
   b. Economists can forecast the future with a reasonable degree of accuracy.
   c. Politicians often tend to ignore the technical advice of economists.
   d. All of the above are part of the case for activism.

___C___ 3. Experience of the 1970s suggests that economic forecasters
   a. can usually forecast major turning points accurately.
   b. never make mistakes.
   c. sometimes miss major turning points in the economy.
   d. always agree with one another even when they are all wrong.

___A___ 4. The delay between the time a policy change is needed and the time a decision is made is known as the
   a. inside lag.
   b. supply-side lag.
   c. demand-side lag.
   d. outside lag.

___B___ 5. Monetarist studies of the post-World War II period indicate that a change in the rate of growth of the money stock tends to affect real output after a lag of
   a. exactly 3 months.
   b. 3 to 12 months.
   c. exactly 12 months.
   d. 2 to 3 years.

___B___ 6. Experience suggests that in the U.S. political system, the inside lag for fiscal policy tends to be
   a. shorter than the lag for monetary policy.
   b. longer than the lag for monetary policy.
   c. about the same as the lag for monetary policy.
   d. shorter than 3 months in most cases.

___C___ 7. Policy activists say
   a. forget about lags and forecasting errors; they don't really exist.
   b. activist fiscal policy is fine, but stay away from activist monetary policy.
   c. lags and forecasting errors are reasons for caution, but cautious activism is still better than doing nothing.
   d. the effects of lags cancels out the effects of forecasting errors.

___C___ 8. The political pressure to "do something" about inflation or unemployment tends to come
   a. before the best time to take action has arrived.
   b. just at the best time to take action.
   c. after the best time to take action has passed.
   d. at no particular time relative to the best time to take action.

___A___ 9. Looking at matters from a political point of view, the short-run consequences of expansionary policy are
   a. more attractive than the long-run consequences.
   b. less attractive than the long-run consequences.
   c. about equally attractive as the long-run consequences.
   d. unattractive in terms of unemployment but attractive in terms of inflation.

___C___ 10. According to new classical economists, once the Fed has established a climate of low inflationary expectations, it will face a temptation to
   a. carry out a surprise slowdown in the rate of money growth.
   b. announce that the rate of money growth will be slowed starting a year hence.
   c. carry out a surprise increase in the rate of money growth.
   d. announce that the rate of money growth will be increased starting a year hence.

___C___ 11. Monetarists and new classicists see which of the following as caused at least in part by policy mistakes?
   a. The Great Depression of the 1930s.
   b. The Great Inflation of the 1970s.
   c. Both a and b.
   d. Neither a nor b.

___A___ 12. The original monetarist proposal for a policy rule focused on which of the following as a target for monetary policy?
   a. The money stock.
   b. Real national income.
   c. Nominal national income.
   d. The price level.

___B___ 13. Which of the following best describes the behavior of M1 velocity in the post-World War II period?
   a. Rose steadily throughout the period.
   b. Rose with some short-term variations until about 1980, then fell with short-term variations in the 1980s.
   c. Remained nearly constant throughout the period except for short-term variations.
   d. Fell steadily throughout the period.

___C___ 14. Which of the following laws attempted to impose rules of a sort for the conduct of fiscal policy?
   a. The Monetary Control Act.
   b. The Sherman Act.
   c. The Gramm-Rudman-Hollings Act.
   d. The Hatch Act.

15. The danger that a balanced budget rule would be destabilizing would be lessened if
    a. tax increases were required during recessions.
    b. the structural deficit were allowed to rise during expansions.
    c. the Fed were also bound by strict policy rules.
    d. a temporary deficit were permitted during recessions.

ANSWERS TO CHAPTER 18

Economics in the News

(1) The collapse of stock prices would represent a reduction of wealth, which would adversely affect consumption. It also might adversely affect the expectations of business managers, thus depressing planned investment. In either case, the aggregate real demand curve would tend to shift to the left. Real output would fall, inflation would slow, and unemployment would rise. (2) The Fed would undertake open market purchases which would both depress the federal funds rate and cause the money stock to expand. A policy activist would endorse these actions. (3) A proponent of policy rules might say that the Fed cannot be sure that the stock market crash will cause a recession, and also cannot be sure that an action taken after the crash will have its effect soon enough to help avoid a recession. Taking a broader view of matters, the advocate of rules might say that adherence to a long-term policy rule would create a more stable climate of expectations in which stock prices might not have been run up to the excessive levels from which they crashed.

Self Test

1. **a.** Choices **b** and **c** tend to favor rules. Choice **d** is slang for **b**.
2. **b.** Activists tend to believe that the reverse of **a** and **c** are true.
3. **c.** They also often disagree among themselves.
4. **a.** The delay between the time the action is taken and the time its effects are felt is the outside lag.
5. **b.** This is very much approximate.
6. **b.** The Fed is able to make decisions quite rapidly; consider the "Economics in the News" item as a case in point.
7. **c.** Today's activists are more cautious than those of the 1960s.
8. **c.** These political pressures make no allowance for lags.
9. **a.** The short-run consequences will include an increase in real output and a reduction in unemployment.
10. **c.** The new classicists also fear that the public will expect the Fed to give in to this temptation.
11. **c.** The Great Depression was caused in part by excessively restrictive monetary policy, and the Great Inflation, in part, by excessively expansionary policy.

12. **a.** Friedman's original proposal was a 3 percent annual growth of M1.
13. **b.** See Exhibit 18.1 in the text book, page 449.
14. **c.** It set forth a schedule of cuts in the budget deficit.
15. **d.** Choices **a** and **b** would tend to be destabilizing.

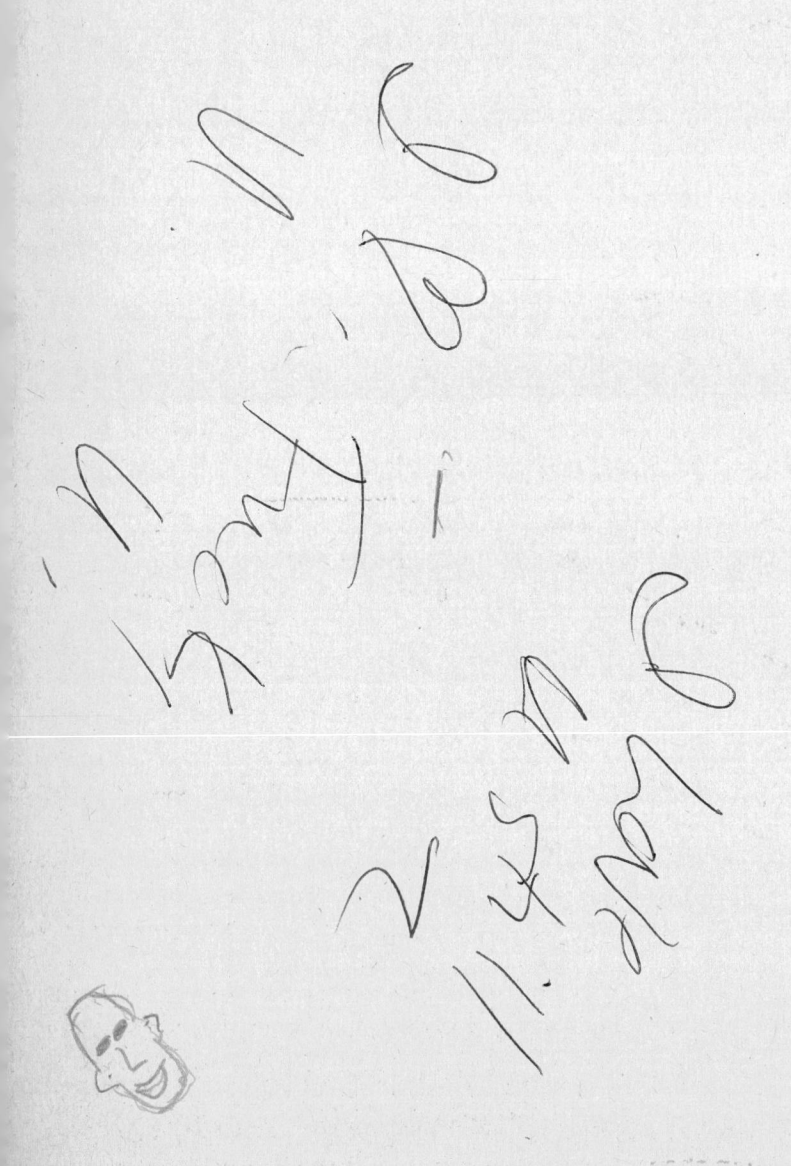

Chapter 19

The Accelerationist Model of Inflation

WHERE YOU'RE GOING

When you have mastered this chapter, you will understand

1. How inflation and unemployment are related.
2. How accelerating inflation affects the economy.
3. How the rates of inflation and unemployment can both rise during an inflationary recession.
4. Why the U.S. economy followed a pattern of alternating inflation and recession from the 1950s to the early 1980s.
5. How the behavior of the U.S. economy in the 1980s differed from that during earlier post-World War II years.

In addition, you will add the following terms to your economic vocabulary:
 Accelerationist model of inflation
 Phillips curve
 Reflation

WALKING TOUR

After you have read this chapter at least once, you should work step by step through this walking tour. Fill in the blanks and answer the questions as you go along. After you have answered each question, check yourself by uncovering the answer given in the margin. If you do not understand why the answer given is the correct one, refer back to the proper section of the text.

The Accelerationist Model of Inflation

accelerationist ✓

The theory according to which changes in the inflation rate affect unemployment and real output is known as the _accelerationist_ model of inflation.

Phillips ✓
negative ✓

decrease ✓

One of the principal foundations of the accelerationist model is a relationship between the inflation rate and the unemployment rate known as the _Phillips_ curve. Graphically, the short-run Phillips curve has a _negative_ slope, indicating that other things being equal, an increase in the rate of inflation will cause a [increase/(decrease)] in the unemployment rate. The long-run Phillips curve is ___vertical___. It intersects the horizontal axis at the ___natural___ rate of unemployment. The short-run and long-run Phillips curves intersect at the ___expected___ rate of inflation. An increase in the expected rate of inflation will cause a [**upward**/downward] [**shift in**/movement along] the short-run Phillips curve.

A second important building block of the accelerationist theory is a relationship between real output and unemployment known as ___Okun's___ law. According to this law, in any year in which actual real output grows at the same rate as natural real output, the unemployment rate will [increase/decrease/**remain unchanged**]. For each three percentage points by which growth of real output exceeds that of natural real output in a given year, the unemployment rate tends to [rise/**fall**] by about ___1___ percentage point(s). For purposes of simplification, the chapter assumes that there is no growth of natural real output. Given this assumption, suppose that the unemployment rate is 7 percent at the beginning of a year, and that during the year, real output grows at a rate of 6 percent. The unemployment rate at the end of the year would then be ___5___ percent.

It is also assumed for the sake of simplification that the government sets a target rate of growth for nominal output each year. The rate of growth of nominal output must equal the sum of the rate of growth of real output and the rate of inflation. For example, if real output grows at 4 percent per year and there is 6 percent inflation, nominal output will grow by ___10___ percent. If the growth of nominal output is 7 percent and the growth of real output is 2 percent, the rate of inflation will be ___5___ percent. And if nominal output grows at 3 percent while the rate of inflation is 5 percent, the rate of growth of real output will be ___-2___ percent.

The Effects of Accelerating Inflation

Suppose that the economy is initially in equilibrium with no actual or expected inflation and with unemployment at the natural rate. The government then undertakes expansionary policy, boosting the rate of growth of nominal output to, say, 9 percent per year. The result will be a [**increase**/decrease] in the rate of inflation and a [increase/decrease] in the unemployment rate. If the same rate of growth of nominal output is maintained in the next year, the rate of inflation will [rise/fall/remain the same]. When the rate of inflation reaches the rate of growth of nominal output, the unemployment rate will stop falling. To keep the unemployment rate from rising will require that the rate of inflation [remain the same/accelerate] each year. The conclusion that the unemployment rate can be kept below the natural rate for a prolonged period only at the cost of constantly accelerating inflation gives the accelerationist model its name.

Inflationary Recession and the Stop-Go Cycle

If the rate of growth of nominal output is slowed after a period of accelerating inflation, the result will be a/an __inflationary recession__. The unemployment rate will __rise__ and the rate of inflation may also __rise__. The inflation rate will not begin to fall until the unemployment rate exceeds the __natural__ rate. Subsequently, for each year that the unemployment rate remains above the natural level, the rate of inflation will [rise/fall].

Suppose that after a period of decelerating inflation, the rate of growth of nominal output is again increased. This would be called a program of __reflation__. The results would be a [increase/decrease] in the unemployment rate, and initially, a [sharp/moderate] increase in the rate of inflation. After the initial episode of reflation, the trade-off between inflation and unemployment would become progressively [more/less] favorable each year that unemployment remains below the natural rate.

If political circumstances are such that episodes of acceleration are longer and stronger than periods of deceleration, a pattern develops that is known as the __stop-go__ cycle. This pattern characterized the economy from the 19__50's__ through the 19__70's__.

The U.S. Experience Since 1980

During the 1980s, the rate of inflation has [risen/fallen] substantially. From 1980 through 1986, the unemployment rate remained [above/below] the natural rate. Compared to estimates made during the 1970s, the cost of the disinflation of the 1980s, measured in

less

credibility
policy regime

falling
rising

terms of unemployment, has been [greater/*less*] than many economists expected.

Economists who want to give maximum credit to Paul Volcker's policy as chairman of the Fed and to the Reagan administration stress the ___credibility___ of the disinflation policy. Some characterize the period as a change of ___policy regime___. However, some skeptics point to special factors that aided the process of disinflation. They point to favorable supply shocks during the first half of the 1980s, especially [rising/*falling*] world oil prices and a [*rising*/falling] international value of the dollar.

HANDS ON

Now that you have reviewed the concepts introduced in this chapter, it is time for some hands-on practice with the analytical tools that have been introduced. Work through each problem in this section carefully, and then check your results against those given at the end of the chapter.

Problem 1

Assume that the growth trend of natural real output is zero and assume a simple adaptive expectations hypothesis under which

Exhibit 19.1a

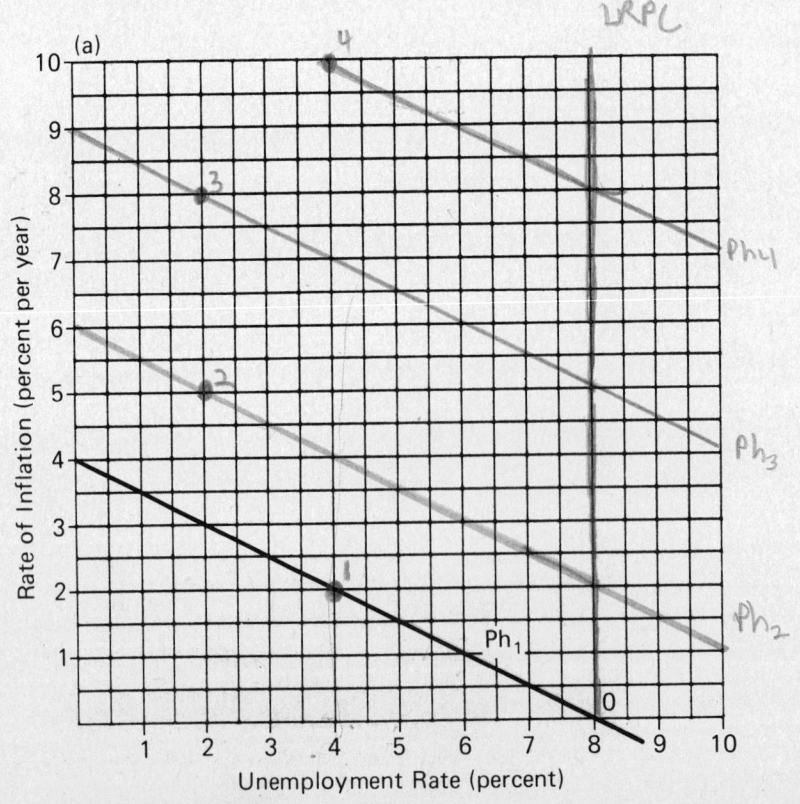

each year's expected rate of inflation is equal to the previous year's actual rate. In working through each part of this problem, draw the appropriate points and curves in Exhibit 19.1a. As you do so, fill in the missing entries in the "scorecard" given in Exhibit 19.1b. When you encounter problems of this type on examinations, you may find that keeping such a scorecard is a useful way to avoid errors.

Exhibit 19.1b

(b)

Year	Growth Rate of Nominal GNP	Unemployment Rate	Growth Rate of Real Output	Actual Rate of Inflation	Expected Rate of Inflation
0	0	8	0	0	0
1	14	4	12	2	0
2	11	2	6	5	2
3	8	2	0	8	5
4	4	4	−6	10	8

Okun's law

$14 = (-3)(\text{change in unemp.}) + \text{infl. rate}$
$11 = (-3)$
$4 = (-3)(-2)$
10

a. Initially, in Year 0, the economy is at a standing start. This position is shown by Point 0 in the graph and line 0 on the scorecard. What is the natural level of unemployment? Sketch in the long-run Phillips curve and label it.
b. In Year 1, the government uses expansionary fiscal policy to induce nominal output to grow at a 14 percent rate. Fill in the missing data in line 1 of the scorecard and label the point reached on the graph with the number 1.
c. In Year 2, the government slows the growth rate of nominal GNP to 11 percent. Fill in the missing items in line 2 of the scorecard. What happens to the short-run Phillips curve? If it shifts, draw the new curve and label it Ph_2. Label the point on the graph reached in this year with the number 2.
d. In Year 3, the government is determined to maintain the unemployment rate at 2 percent. Fill in the missing items in line 3 of the scorecard to show what happens to inflation and real output. Sketch in a new short-run Phillips curve if necessary. Label the point reached with the number 3.
e. In Year 4, the government becomes worried about inflation and decides not to let the rate of price increase rise above 10 percent. Fill in the missing items in line 4 of the scorecard to show what rate of nominal GNP growth is required to keep inflation to

10 percent. What happens to unemployment and real output? Draw in the new Phillips curve if necessary and label the point reached with the number 4. How would you describe the events of Year 4?

Problem 2

Again, assume zero growth of potential real GNP and simple adaptive expectations. Complete Exhibits 19.2a and 19.2b. Note carefully how the vertical axis of the graph is labeled.

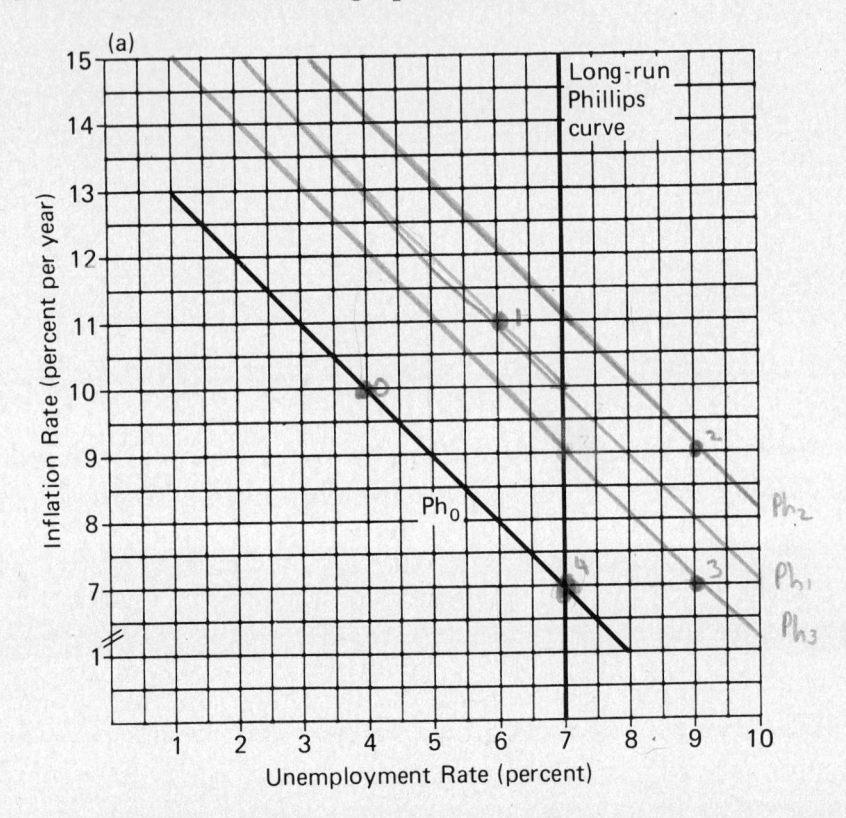

Exhibit 19.2a

a. In Year 0, the economy is well into an episode of accelerating inflation. The short-run Phillips curve has reached the position Ph_0 and the economy is at Point 0, with 10 percent inflation and 4 percent unemployment. The 4 percent unemployment rate is unchanged from the previous year (not shown on the graph or scorecard). Can you fill in the missing items in line 0 of the scorecard?

b. In Year 1, the Fed decides to step on the monetary brakes, slowing the rate of growth of nominal GNP to 5 percent. Fill in the missing items in line 1 of the scorecard. Draw the new Phillips curve and label it Ph_1. Label the point reached with the number 1.

c. The Fed is still not pleased with the progress made against inflation in Year 1. It determines in Year 2 to get the inflation rate below 10 percent at all costs. How much will it have to slow the growth of nominal GNP to reach a 9 percent inflation target? What will happen to real output and unemployment? Complete line 2 of the scorecard. Show the events of Year 2 on the graph.

Exhibit 19.2b

(b)

Year	Growth Rate of Nominal GNP	Unemployment Rate	Growth Rate of Real Output	Actual Rate of Inflation	Expected Rate of Inflation
0	10	4	0	10	7
1	5	6	-6	11	10
2	0	9	-9	9	11
3	7	9	0	7	9
4	13	7	6	7	7

= (-3)(chang in unemp) + inflat.

5 = (-3)

0 = (-3)(3) + 9

) (-3) + 7

(-3)(-2)   7

d. Congress is upset with the rise in unemployment and threatens the Fed with restrictive legislation if unemployment is allowed to rise further in Year 3. Fill in line 3 of the scorecard to find how much progress the Fed can continue to make against inflation without a further rise in unemployment. Show the events of Year 3 in the graph in the usual way.

e. The administration is grateful for the slowdown in inflation, but believes it cannot win the upcoming election unless real output growth is restored at no less than a 6 percent rate. The President replaces the chairman of the Fed with a new person pledged to accomplish the administration goal. Fill in line 4 of the scorecard to find what must be done to nominal output growth to achieve the 6 percent real output growth target. Again, show these events on the graph.

ECONOMICS IN THE NEWS

Inflation Rate Off Sharply to 3.3%, August Data Show

WASHINGTON, D.C., SEPTEMBER 24, 1982—Inflation slowed dramatically last month to 3.3 percent, setting the stage for recovery from recession, Reagan administration officials said yesterday.

But even as Treasury Secretary Donald T. Regan hailed the good news on inflation—the administration's major economic accomplishment—he conceded the economy's other nagging problem—unemployment—is not getting any better.

"Inflation remains low, and the prospects for economic recovery remain high." Regan said yesterday when the consumer price index figures for August were announced by the government.

"I don't think unemployment will go down next month," he acknowledged, admitting that the administration may have to "shade back" its original forecast for economic growth of 4.4 percent next year.

"There is some connection in the short run between inflation and unemployment," the Treasury secretary conceded, saying that the administration never promised to bring both down simultaneously.

August's 3.3 percent annualized increase in consumer prices brought the inflation rate for 1982 to 5.1 percent, well below the 8.9 percent rate in 1981 and 12.4 percent in 1980.

Although inflation has dropped sharply during President Reagan's term in office, that decline has been bought at the cost of a deep recession.

Unemployment has soared to a post-World War II peak. Many analysts fear the jobless rate will rise still further from the 9.8 percent August level and may breach the 10 percent mark when the September figure is released October 8. . . .

"We are now in the recovery phase," Regan said yesterday, telling reporters that, "rehires probably would start very late this year." However, other analysts disagree. One senior administration official said earlier this week that it was not yet clear whether recovery had begun.

Economist Otto Eckstein said yesterday, "Production will surely be falling again in September. . .the economy is still sliding. . .[there is] no recovery."

Martin Feldstein, President Reagan's nominee for chairman of the Council of Economic Advisers, has cautioned that recovery must be slow in order to preserve gains on the rate of inflation. He cited the average private forecast for real growth next year of between 2.9 percent to 3.9 percent. Slower growth would mean a bigger federal deficit, as well as more unemployment. . . .

Source: Caroline Atkinson, "Inflation Rate Off Sharply to 3.3%, August Data Show," *The Washington Post*, September 24, 1982, p. 1. © *The Washington Post*, 1982.

Questions

1. What phase of the stop-go cycle was the economy in during September 1982, when this article was written?
2. According to the article, the reduction in inflation during 1981 and 1982 was purchased only at the cost of a deep recession. Does that finding fit with the accelerationist theory of inflation? Explain.
3. Martin Feldstein is quoted as cautioning that recovery must be slow in order to preserve the gains made against inflation. Does that caution fit with the accelerationist theory of inflation? According to data given in the text book, was inflation in fact kept under control during the recovery, which began soon after this news item appeared?

SELF TEST

These sample test items will help you check how much you have learned. Answers are found at the end of the chapter. Scoring yourself: One or two wrong—on target. Three or four wrong—passing, but you haven't mastered the chapter yet. Five or more wrong—not good enough; start over and restudy the chapter.

C 1. If, beginning from a standing start position, nominal national income were to fall below its previous level, the likely result would be
   a. an inflationary recession.
   b. accelerating inflation and falling unemployment.
   c. a decline in the price level and a rise in unemployment.
   d. a decline in the price level and a drop in unemployment.

B 2. According to the accelerationist theory of inflation, unemployment can be kept below the natural rate for a sustained period under which of the following conditions?
   a. Only at the cost of a constantly high rate of inflation.
   b. Only at the cost of continuously accelerating inflation.
   c. Only at the cost of declining growth of potential GNP.
   d. None of the above; unemployment can fall below the natural rate only temporarily.

B 3. The ability of accelerating inflation to draw the unemployment rate below the natural rate depends, in part, on
   a. an assumption of rational expectations.
   b. an assumption that inflationary expectations do not instantly adjust to the current rate of inflation.
   c. an assumption that the natural rate of unemployment falls at a rate of 3 percent per year.
   d. none of the above.

C 4. The accelerating inflation scenario given in this chapter is best characterized as
   a. an important theoretical possibility, but one not yet experienced in the U.S. economy.
   b. a pattern that prevailed throughout most of the 1950s.
   c. a pattern that prevailed throughout most of the 1960s.
   d. a pattern that prevailed throughout most of the 1980s.

5. Beginning from a standing start position, suppose the rate of growth of nominal GNP accelerates to 4 percent in the next year. Assuming the trend growth rate of natural real output to be zero and the natural rate of unemployment to be 5 percent, which of the following is a possible inflation-unemployment combination for that year?
   a. 4 percent unemployment and 1 percent inflation.
   b. 3 percent unemployment and 1 percent inflation.
   c. 4 percent unemployment and 3 percent inflation.
   d. Insufficient information is given for an answer to be reached.

223

___A___ 6. According to the accelerationist theory of inflation, an inflationary recession is most likely to occur
   a. after a prolonged period of accelerating inflation.
   b. beginning from a standing start.
   c. when fiscal or monetary policy gets too restrictive after a period of deceleration has already begun.
   d. when the rate of growth of nominal GNP is increased while the unemployment rate is already above the natural rate.

___B___ 7. If the expected rate of inflation in each year is equal to the actual rate of inflation in the previous year, can the rate of inflation be the same 2 years in a row?
   a. Only if unemployment is at the natural rate in the first year.
   b. Only if unemployment is at the natural rate in the second year.
   c. Only if unemployment is at the natural rate in both years.
   d. None of the above.

___B___ 8. According to the accelerationist theory of inflation, unemployment higher than the natural rate is associated with
   a. accelerating inflation.
   b. decelerating inflation.
   c. a constant rate of inflation.
   d. a zero rate of inflation.

___D___ 9. If the current rate of inflation is 9 percent, the growth rate of natural real output is zero, last year's unemployment rate was 4 percent, and this year's unemployment rate is 5 percent, this year's rate of growth of nominal GNP must be
   a. 3 percent.
   b. 4 percent.
   c. 5 percent.
   d. 6 percent.

___A___ 10. If, during an inflationary recession, the unemployment rate rises from 4 percent in one year to 6 percent in the next, and if the growth rate of natural real output is assumed to be zero, what will be the growth rate of actual real GNP?
   a. -6 percent.
   b. -3 percent.
   c. 0 percent.
   d. 3 percent.

___D___ 11. During accelerating inflation, the unemployment rate
   a. may be above or below the natural rate, but must be falling.
   b. must be above the natural rate.
   c. must fall each year that the inflation rate increases.
   d. must be below the natural rate.

___B___ 12. The expected rate of inflation must exceed the actual rate during
   a. inflationary recession.
   b. deceleration of inflation.
   c. reflation.
   d. both a and b.

224

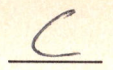

__C__ 13. U.S. macroeconomic experience in the postwar period through 1980 is best characterized as
   a. continuous acceleration of inflation.
   b. a stable stop-go cycle.
   c. a stop-go cycle with an inflationary bias.
   d. prolonged economic stagnation.

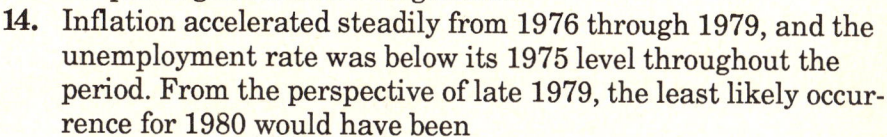

__D__ 14. Inflation accelerated steadily from 1976 through 1979, and the unemployment rate was below its 1975 level throughout the period. From the perspective of late 1979, the least likely occurrence for 1980 would have been
   a. for the unemployment rate to rise and the rate of inflation to fall.
   b. for the unemployment rate to fall and the rate of inflation to rise.
   c. for both the unemployment rate and the rate of inflation to rise.
   d. for both the unemployment rate and the rate of inflation to fall.

__B__ 15. If the rational expectations hypothesis were combined with the accelerationist theory of inflation given in this chapter,
   a. monetary and fiscal policy would have less effect on inflation.
   b. monetary and fiscal policy would have less effect on unemployment.
   c. monetary and fiscal policy would have less effect on nominal GNP.
   d. the short-run Phillips curve would be flatter.

ANSWERS TO CHAPTER 19

Hands On

Problem 1 (a) The natural level of unemployment is 8 percent. Determine this by finding the point on the applicable short-run Phillips curve (Ph_1 in this case) corresponding to the expected rate of inflation (zero percent in this case). The long-run Phillips curve is a vertical line at 8 percent unemployment (see the solution graph for Exhibit 19.1a). (b) First fill in the expected rate of inflation, equal to the previous year's actual rate, in this case, zero. With no change in the expected rate of inflation, the Phillips curve Ph_1 remains applicable in Year 1—no shift. Follow up and to the left along Ph_1 until you get to a point where the real growth rate plus the inflation rate equals the designated nominal growth rate of 14 percent. Remember that, according to Okun's law, you get 3 percent real growth for every 1 percent reduction in unemployment. Thus, at 7 percent unemployment on Ph_1, you would have 3 percent real growth plus 0.5 percent inflation, for a total nominal growth of 3.5 percent; at 6 percent unemployment, 6 percent real growth plus 1 percent inflation, for a total nominal growth of 7 percent; and so on. When you get to 4 percent unemployment (Point 1), you have 12 percent real

Exhibit 19.1a (ans.)

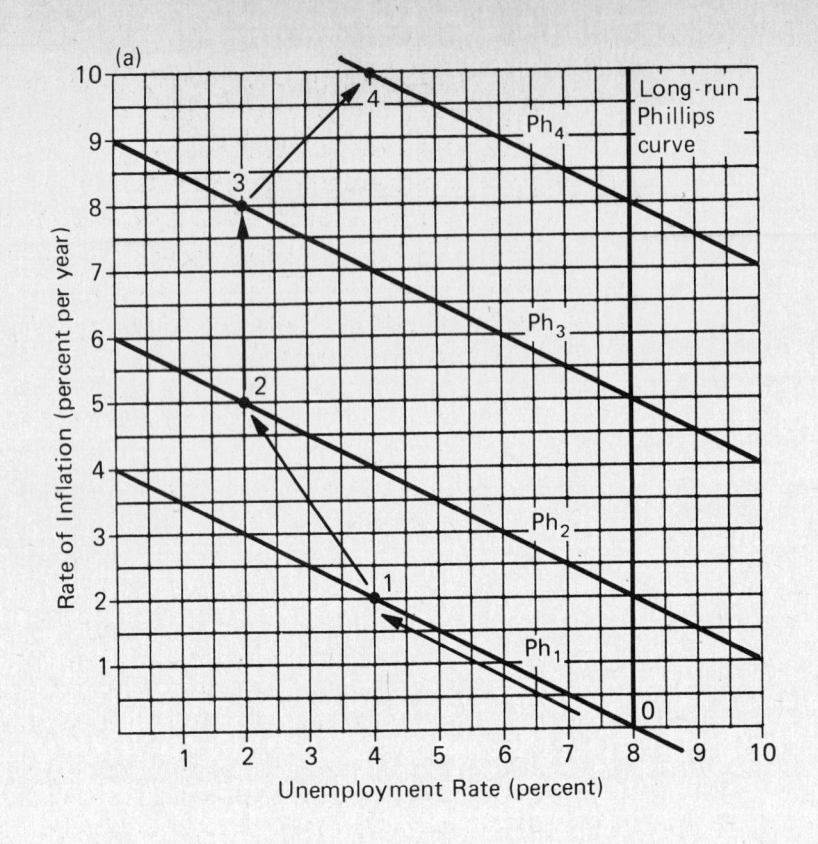

growth (3 times the four percentage point drop in unemployment), plus 2 percent inflation (shown by the height of Ph₁ at Point 1) for a total nominal growth of 14 percent, as required. (c) Again, start by filling in the expected rate of inflation. According to the adaptive expectations hypothesis, this will be 2 percent in Year 2, since 2 percent was the actual inflation rate in Year 1. The short-run Phillips curve thus shifts up to the position Ph₂, where it intersects the long-run Phillips curve at the 2 percent expected inflation rate you have just determined. The real growth rate will again be equal to 3 times the reduction in unemployment—but remember, this time you start from the Year 1 unemployment rate of 4 percent. For example, the point on Ph₂ corresponding to 3 percent unemployment implies 3 percent real growth and 4.5 percent inflation—that is not enough to account for the assumed 11 percent nominal GNP growth. By trial and error, you find that 2 percent unemployment (a two percentage point drop) produces 6 percent real growth, which, when added to the 5 percent inflation shown at Point 2, equals the 11 percent nominal growth rate you are given for Year 2. (d) In Year 3, the expected inflation rate rises to 5 percent (the actual Year 2 rate), so the short-run Phillips curve shifts up to Ph₃. You are told that the unemployment rate is to stay at 2 percent, so you know the economy must go to Point 3 on Ph₃. This corresponds to 8 percent inflation (as you read directly from the graph). There is no change in unemployment, hence, no change in real output. The needed growth rate of nominal GNP is 8 percent. (e) This time all you are given is 10 percent inflation for Year 4. Start by filling in 8 percent for the expected inflation rate and moving the short-run Phillips curve up to Ph₄, which intersects the long-run Phillips curve at the 8 percent expected inflation rate. Point 4 is the only point on Ph₄ where you

226

can get the required 10 percent inflation rate, so that is where you are headed. Going from Point 3 to Point 4 raises the unemployment rate from 2 to 4 percent—a two percentage point increase that produces -6 percent real growth. The sum of 10 percent inflation and -6 percent real growth gives you the required growth rate of nominal GNP—4 percent. Thus the government must set a 4 percent growth target for nominal GNP to achieve its stated policy goals in Year 4. The result would be described as an inflationary recession.

Problem 2 (a) Start by filling in the unemployment rate and actual inflation rate directly from the diagram—4 percent and 10 percent, respectively. Pick up the expected inflation rate by finding the intersection of Ph$_0$ with the long-run Phillips curve—7 percent. Your clue for the real growth rate is the fact that Year 0 unemployment was the same as the previous year. With zero natural real output growth, this means zero actual real output growth. Finally, with zero real output growth and 10 percent inflation, you know nominal output growth must be 10 percent. (b) Take the Year 1 expected inflation rate from the Year 0 actual rate. Move the Phillips curve to Ph$_1$, which intersects the long-run Phillips curve at 10 percent inflation. (See solution graph for Exhibit 19.2a.) By trial and error, find the point on Ph$_1$ where 3 times the change in the unemployment rate plus the inflation rate add to 5 percent. This condition holds only at Point 1. A 2 percent increase in the unemployment rate gives -6 percent real growth, and 11 percent inflation minus 6 percent real growth equals 5 percent nominal growth. (c) In Year 2, all you are given is the 9 percent inflation target. First take the expected inflation rate of 11 percent from the Year 2 actual rate. Shift the short-run Phillips curve to Ph$_2$. Find

Exhibit 19.2a (ans.)

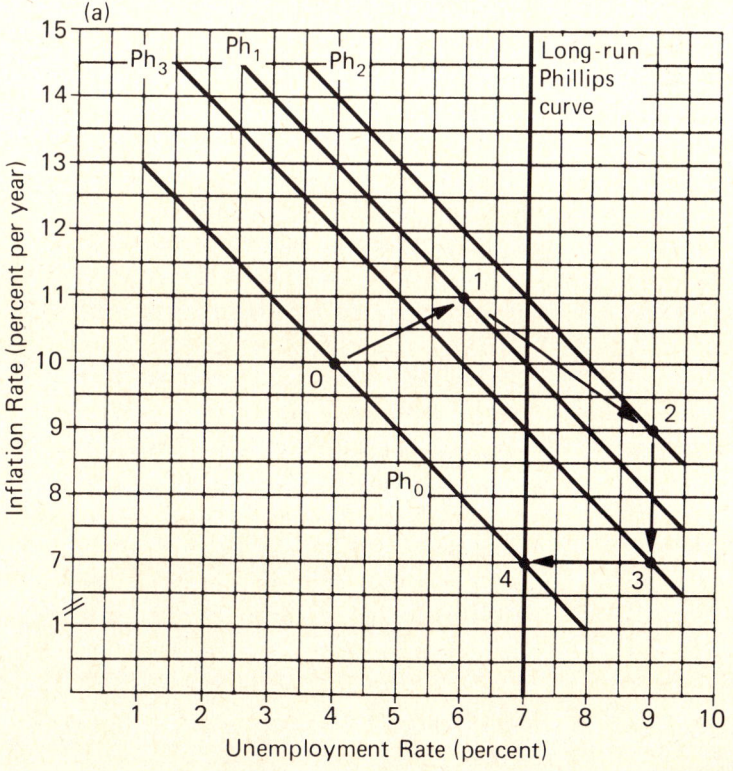

the point on Ph2 corresponding to the 9 percent inflation target—
this is Point 2. Going from Point 1 to Point 2, the economy experiences a three percentage point increase in unemployment (from 6 to 9 percent). By Okun's law, with zero trend growth of natural real output, this means a -9 percent real growth rate. With inflation of +9 percent and real growth of -9 percent, the required nominal output growth rate is zero. (d) Now all you are given is the goal of holding the 9 percent unemployment rate in Year 3. Expected inflation in Year 3 is back down to 9 percent, so shift the short-run Phillips curve to Ph3. The 9 percent unemployment point on Ph3 is Point 3. The actual inflation rate at Point 3, read directly from the graph, is 7 percent. There is no change in unemployment when you go from Point 2 to Point 3 so real growth is zero. With zero real growth, the inflation rate and nominal output growth rate are equal at 7 percent. (e) This time you are given a real growth target. As always, find the expected inflation rate first. In Year 4, it is 7 percent. That puts the short-run Phillips curve back where it started, at Ph0. To get the 6 percent required real growth, you need a two percentage point drop in unemployment. That takes you to Point 4 on Ph0. At Point 4, inflation is unchanged at 7 percent. Finally, to get the required nominal GNP growth rate, add 6 percent real growth and 7 percent inflation. The answer is 13 percent required growth in nominal GNP.

Economics in the News

(1) The economy was in the deceleration phase, with inflation headed down and unemployment above the natural rate. (2) Yes, this fits the theory. According to the accelerationist theory, the inflation rate can be reduced only during a period when unemployment is above its natural rate. (3) This fits too. The accelerationist theory suggests that forcing a rapid recovery that drives unemployment below the natural rate after a period of declining inflation can only temporarily give large gains in output and employment without rekindling inflation. Thus, a cautious recovery would be standard advice. In fact, the recovery, especially during 1984, was stronger than average, but even so unemployment remained above the natural rate and the gains on the inflation front were preserved. This result was helped by favorable developments on the supply side, including oil price decreases and a rise in the international value of the dollar.

Self Test

1. **c.** The economy would move down and to the right along a fixed Phillips curve.
2. **b.** A high rate of inflation is not enough; it must accelerate, hence the name of the theory.
3. **b.** Under rational expectations, unemployment would always remain at the natural rate if inflation were perfectly anticipated, even when the rate of inflation rose or fell.
4. **c.** See "Applying Economic Ideas 19.1" in the text book, page 469.

5. **a.** Apply Okun's law. The sum of inflation plus three times the change in the unemployment rate must equal the rate of nominal GNP growth.
6. **a.** This will produce upward momentum in the short-run Phillips curve.
7. **b.** Because at the natural rate of unemployment, the actual and expected rates of inflation must be equal, and because each year's expected rate is the previous year's actual rate.
8. **b.** This is the deceleration phase, during which the short-run Phillips curve drifts downward.
9. **d.** Apply Okun's law, as in question 5.
10. **a.** According to Okun's law, a two percentage point rise in the unemployment rate will be associated with a 6 percent drop in real output.
11. **d.** It may be falling or steady, or, during an inflationary recession, rising.
12. **b.** This condition must hold whenever the economy is to the right of the long-run Phillips curve.
13. **c.** Because the peak rate of inflation in each cycle was higher than in the one before.
14. **d.** This would require a "left-hand turn," very unusual under the accelerationist theory. Only a strong favorable supply shock could produce this result.
15. **b.** Because the short-run Phillips curve would adjust more quickly to changes in policy.

Chapter 20

Foreign Exchange Markets and International Monetary Policy

WHERE YOU'RE GOING

When you have mastered this chapter, you will understand

1. How supply and demand curves can be used to represent foreign exchange market activity arising from current account transactions.
2. How the supply and demand framework can be extended to incorporate the capital account.
3. How changes in rates of real economic growth affect exchange rates.
4. How changes in real interest rates affect exchange rates.
5. What actions governments take to influence exchange rates.
6. How the international monetary system has evolved since World War II.

In addition, you will add the following terms to your economic vocabulary:
- Depreciation
- Appreciation
- Purchasing power parity
- Capital account net demand curve
- Nominal exchange rate
- Real exchange rate
- J-curve effect
- Exchange controls
- Incovertability

WALKING TOUR

After you have read this chapter at least once, you should work step by step through this walking tour. Fill in the blanks and answer the questions as you go along. After you have answered each question, check yourself by uncovering the answer given in the margin. If you do not understand why the answer given is the correct one, refer back to the proper section of the text.

Foreign Exchange Markets

The set of institutions through which the currency of one country can be exchanged for that of another is known as a _____. [foreign exchange market]

First imagine a world in which the only international transactions that take place are made in payment for imports and exports of goods and services. The foreign exchange market between two countries, say, the United States and France, can be represented by a diagram that has quantity of dollars per day on the horizontal axis and the exchange rate, in francs per dollar, on the vertical axis.

In such a situation, the shape and position of the demand curve for dollars depends on the [U.S./French] demand for [U.S./French] goods. [French, U.S.] The demand curve will have a _____ slope. [negative] The shape and position of the supply curve for dollars depends on the [U.S./French] demand for [U.S./French] goods. [U.S., French] If this demand is elastic, then the supply curve for dollars will have a _____ slope. [positive] If this demand is inelastic, then the supply curve for dollars will have a _____ slope. [negative]

Beginning from equilibrium, if the U.S. demand for French goods increases, the [supply/demand] curve for dollars will shift to [supply] the [right/left] and the dollar will [appreciate/depreciate], that is, [right, depreciate] the exchange rate measured in terms of francs per dollar will [rise/fall]. [fall] If the French demand for U.S. goods increases, the [supply/demand] curve for dollars will shift to the [right/left], [demand; right] and the dollar will [appreciate/depreciate]. [appreciate]

The equilibrium exchange rate tends to move, approximately and in the long run, toward a level where a given sum of money will buy the same market basket when converted from one currency to another at prevailing exchange rates—a situation known as _____. [purchasing power parity]

Now we add capital account transactions to the foreign exchange market. Capital account transactions can be represented

231

negatively, capital account net demand	by a [positively/negatively] sloped curve known as a _____ curve. If capital inflows exceed outflows, the net demand for dollars on capital account is [negative/positive]. If capital outflows exceed capital inflows, the net demand for dollars on capital account is [positive/negative].
positive	
negative	
	The effect of a change in the current exchange rate relative to the expected future rate is represented by a [shift in/movement along] the capital account net demand curve. For example, if the exchange rate rises relative to the value that people expect it to have in the future, the market will move [up/down] along the capital account net demand curve, and there will be a movement toward a net capital [inflow/outflow]. This reflects the fact that other things being equal, people try to [hold/avoid] any currency that they expect to depreciate in the future. They will do so because the higher current value of the dollar relative to its expected future value means [greater/smaller] likelihood of future depreciation in the view of the average market participant. A change in the real interest rate in the United States relative to that in France will cause a [shift in/movement along] the capital account net demand curve. If the U.S. real interest rate increases, the shift will be [upward/downward], and if the U.S. real interest rate decreases, the shift will be [upward/downward].
movement along	
up	
outflow	
avoid	
greater	
shift in	
upward	
downward	

Sources of Changes in Exchange Rates

Exhibit 20.1 shows what happens when the current and capital account demand curves are added together. Initially, the current account demand curve is D_{cur}. When the capital account net demand for dollars is added, the total demand curve is D_1. With D_1

10	and the supply curve S_1, the equilibrium exchange rate is _____ francs per dollar. At this exchange rate, the current account is in [surplus/deficit/balance] and the capital account is in [surplus/deficit/balance].
balance, balance	
	Now suppose the capital account net demand curve shifts upward, moving the total demand curve to D_2. This might be caused by a [rise/fall] in the U.S. real interest rate. The new equilibrium exchange rate would be _____ francs per dollar. At this exchange rate, the current account would be in [surplus/deficit], as indicated by the horizontal gap at the new exchange rate between
rise	
15	
deficit	

Exhibit 20.1

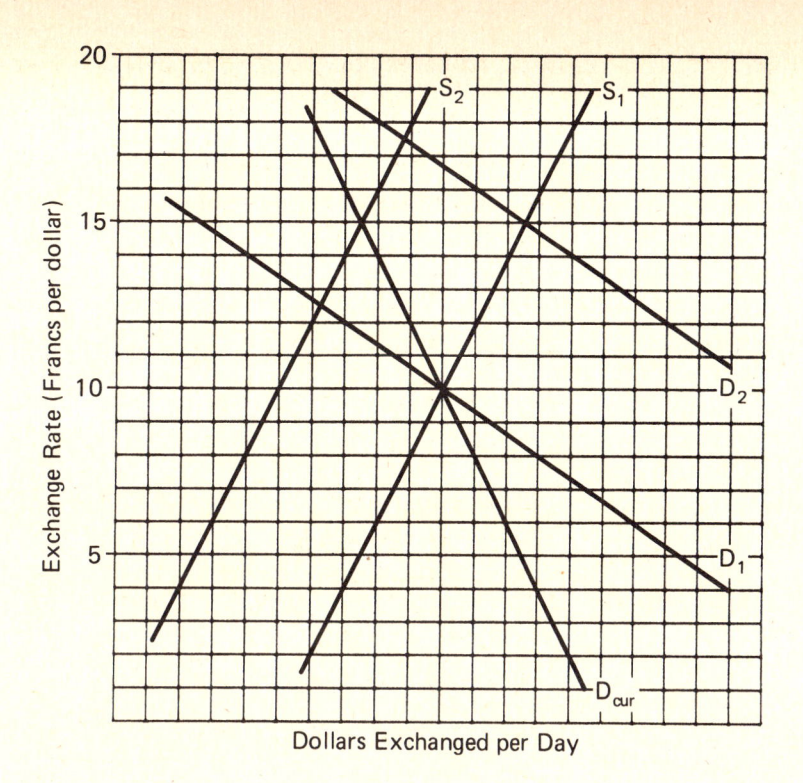

[Graph: Exchange Rate (Francs per dollar) on y-axis from 0 to 20, Dollars Exchanged per Day on x-axis. Curves shown: S₁, S₂, D₁, D₂, D_cur]

supply curve S₁, current account, inflow	the _____ and the _____ demand curve. This would be offset by an equal capital [inflow/outflow].
	Suppose instead that beginning from the initial equilibrium, the total demand curve remains in the position D₁, but the supply curve for dollars shifts to S₂. This could be caused, for example, by a
recession, U.S.	[recession/expansion] in the [U.S./French] economy. Given the demand curve D₁ and the supply curve S₂, the equilibrium exchange
12.5	rate would be _____ francs per dollar. At this exchange
surplus	rate, the current account would be in [surplus/deficit] as indicated by the horizontal distance at the new exchange rate between the
current account outflow	supply curve S₂ and the _____ demand curve. This would be offset by a net capital [inflow/outflow].
	In the examples illustrated by Exhibit 20.1, we note that a depreciation of a country's currency caused by a shift in capital account net demand will move a country's current account balance
surplus	toward [surplus/deficit]. However, this result depends on the assumptions regarding elasticity of supply and demand that underlie the diagram. In the short run, demand for imports and exports
inelastic	tends to be [elastic/inelastic]. This means that the current account
negative	supply curve is likely in the short run to have a [negative/positive] slope. It also means that the current account supply curve may cut

233

below	the current account demand curve from [above/below]. In this case, a depreciation of the currency will, in the short run, move the current account, measured in nominal terms, toward [surplus/deficit].
deficit	
J-curve	This phenomenon is known as the _____ effect. What happens is this: a depreciation of the currency [increases/decreases] the volume of exports, but not by much. At the same time, the real volume of imports [rises/falls], but by a [larger/smaller] percentage than the decrease in the exchange rate. Thus the number of dollars that must be spent to obtain the slightly reduced volume of imports [rises/falls]. The rise in nominal imports swamps the small increase in nominal exports, moving the nominal current account balance initially toward [deficit/surplus].
increases	
falls, smaller	
rises	
deficit	

International Monetary Policy

helped	When the dollar appreciates on foreign exchange markets, U.S. consumers tend to be [helped/hurt]. Firms and workers in U.S. export industries and those that compete with imports tend to be [helped/hurt]. Firms and workers in U.S. industries that depend on imported raw materials tend to be [helped/hurt].
hurt	
helped	
official reserve	To some degree, the government can control the exchange rate via transactions on _____ account. For example, the Fed can cause the dollar to depreciate by [buying/selling] dollars on the foreign exchange market. However, other things being equal, such an action would tend to cause the U.S. domestic money supply to [rise/fall]. To avoid a change in the domestic money supply the Fed could offset its intervention in the foreign exchange market with domestic _____ of securities. Such a practice is known as _____. Economists believe that sterilized exchange rate intervention [is/is not] an effective and practical way to make substantial, long-term changes in exchange rates.
selling	
rise	
open market sales	
sterilization	
is not	
tariffs, quotas	Because sterilized intervention gives only limited control over exchange rates, governments have looked for alternatives. One option is to use restrictions on imports and exports, such as _____ and _____. Another is to impose regulations restricting the access of firms and individuals to foreign exchange markets. These are known as _____. When controls are so extensive that the government maintains a
exchange controls	

	monopoly on access to foreign exchange markets, a currency is said
inconvertible	to be _____.
	After World War II, the world economy operated under the so-
Bretton Woods	called _____ system of exchange rates. This system was
fixed	based on [fixed/floating] exchange rates. Today, the world has
floating	changed to a system of [fixed/floating] exchange rates. Although many economists were critical of the old system of fixed rates, there have been some disappointments with the current floating rate sys-
more	tem. Exchange rates have been [more/less] volatile than was expected. Floating exchange rates may have contributed to world-
inflation	wide _____ in the 1970s. And floating exchange rates
have not	[have/have not] brought an end to protectionism.

HANDS ON

Now that you have reviewed the concepts introduced in this chapter, it is time for some hands-on practice with the analytical tools that have been introduced. Work through each problem in this section carefully, and then check your results against those given at the end of the chapter.

Problem 1

The questions that follow refer to Exhibit 20.2. This exhibit shows the foreign exchange market in which dollars are traded for British pounds. Initially, the current account demand curve for dollars is in position d_1, the total demand curve for dollars is in the position D_1, and the supply curve of dollars is in the position S_1. In shifting curves, assume that each curve retains the slope shown.

a. What is the initial equilibrium point for the foreign exchange market with the curves in the position shown? Mark this as point E_1. In this equilibrium, what is the quantity of dollars demanded on current account? What is the net quantity demanded on capital account? What, approximately, is the U.S. current account surplus or deficit? What is the net capital inflow or outflow, if any? How can you read the net capital inflow or outflow on the figure?

b. Beginning from the initial equilibrium, suppose that the real interest rate in the United States increases, other things remaining equal. If the supply curve is shifted, draw a new supply curve through either S_2 or S_3. If the current account demand curve is shifted, draw a new current account demand curve through either d_2 or d_3. If the total demand curve is shifted, draw a new total demand curve through D_2 or D_3.

Exhibit 20.2

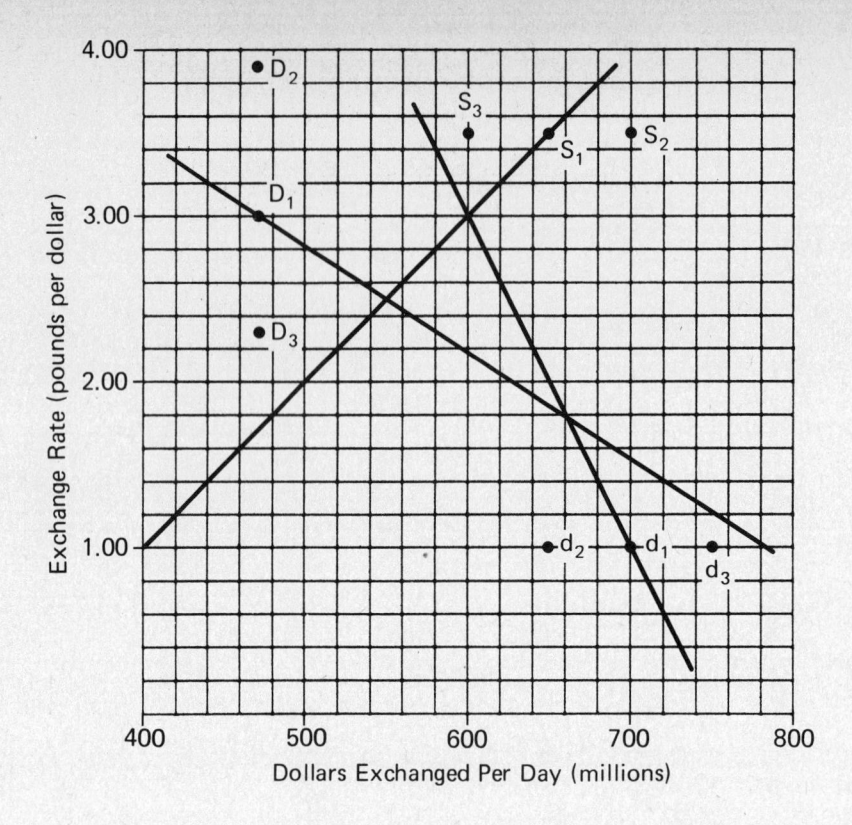

c. Label the new equilibrium point E₂. What is the new equilibrium exchange rate? What is the current account surplus or deficit at E₂? What is the net capital inflow or outflow, if any?

Problem 2

The questions that follow refer to Exhibit 20.3. This exhibit shows the foreign exchange market in which dollars are traded for Italian lire. Initially, the current account demand curve for dollars is in position d₁, the total demand curve for dollars is in the position D₁, and the supply curve of dollars is in the position S₁. In shifting curves, assume that each curve retains the slope shown.

a. What is the initial exchange rate in terms of lire per dollar? Label the equilibrium point E₁. What is the U.S. current account balance? What is the net capital inflow or outflow, if any?

b. Beginning from this equilibrium, assume that there is a recession in Italy. If the supply curve is shifted, draw a new supply curve through either S₂ or S₃. If the current account demand curve is shifted, draw a new current account demand curve through either d₂ or d₃. If the total demand curve is shifted, draw a new total demand curve through D₂ or D₃.

c. Label the new equilibrium point E₂. What is the new exchange rate? What is the new current account surplus or deficit? What is the net capital inflow or outflow, if any? How can you determine the net capital flow from the diagram?

Exhibit 20.3

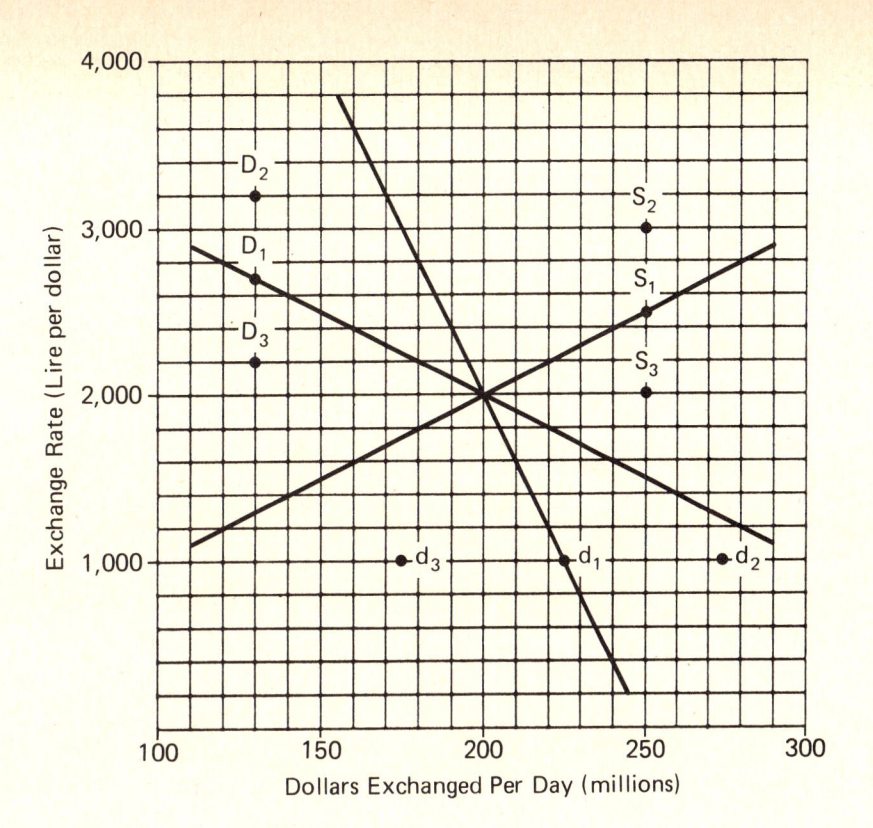

(Graph: Exchange Rate (Lire per dollar) on vertical axis ranging from 1,000 to 4,000; Dollars Exchanged Per Day (millions) on horizontal axis ranging from 100 to 300. Points shown: D₁, D₂, D₃ on the left; S₁, S₂, S₃ on the right; d₁, d₂, d₃ near the bottom.)

SELF TEST

These sample test items will help you check how much you have learned. Answers are found at the end of the chapter. Scoring yourself: One or two wrong—on target. Three or four wrong—passing, but you haven't mastered the chapter yet. Five or more wrong—not good enough; start over and restudy the chapter.

_____ 1. Payments for imports and exports of services are examples of
   a. capital account transactions.
   b. merchandise transactions.
   c. current account transactions.
   d. official reserve account transactions.

_____ 2. The slope and position of the current account demand curve for dollars in the market where dollars are exchanged for Japanese yen (with the exchange rate measured in yen per dollar) is determined by
   a. the U.S. demand for Japanese goods and services.
   b. the U.S. demand for Japanese assets.
   c. the Japanese demand for U.S. goods and services.
   d. the Japanese demand for U.S. assets.

_____ 3. If the U.S. demand for Mexican goods is inelastic, then, in the market where dollars are exchanged for Mexican pesos (with the exchange rate measured in pesos per dollar),
   a. the slope of the current account demand curve is positive.
   b. the slope of the current account supply curve is positive.
   c. the slope of the current account supply curve is negative.
   d. the slope of the capital account net demand curve is positive.

____ 4. If the exchange rate is measured in terms of francs per dollar, then increase in the French demand for U.S. goods, other things being equal,
   a. causes the dollar to appreciate.
   b. causes the franc to depreciate.
   c. both **a** and **b**.
   d. neither **a** nor **b**.

____ 5. Other things being equal, the effects of an increase in the current exchange rate of the dollar relative to its expected future exchange rate are best shown by
   a. an upward shift of the capital account net demand curve.
   b. a downward shift of the capital account net demand curve.
   c. a movement up and to the left along the capital account net demand curve.
   d. a movement down and to the right along the capital account net demand curve.

____ 6. Other things being equal, people try to
   a. invest in assets denominated in a currency they think will appreciate.
   b. take out loans denominated in a currency they think will appreciate.
   c. avoid assets denominated in a currency they think will appreciate.
   d. repay loans if they think the currency in which the loans are denominated will depreciate.

____ 7. Speaking in terms of a diagram where the exchange rate is measured in terms of British pounds per dollar, a recession in Great Britain, other things being equal, will tend to cause
   a. a rightward shift in the current account demand curve for dollars.
   b. a leftward shift in the current account demand curve for dollars.
   c. a rightward shift in the current account supply curve for dollars.
   d. a leftward shift in the current account supply curve for dollars.

____ 8. Beginning from a state in which both the current and capital accounts are in balance, an increase in the U.S. rate of economic growth, assuming no change in the real interest rates in the United States or abroad and no change in the rate of economic growth abroad, is likely to cause
   a. an appreciation of the U.S. dollar.
   b. an increase in the current account deficit.
   c. a net capital outflow.
   d. a leftward shift of the current account dollar supply curve.

_____ 9. Which of the following is one likely cause of the rise in the exchange value of the dollar over the period 1980 to 1985?
   a. Real interest rates became lower in the United States than abroad.
   b. Real interest rates became higher in the United States than abroad.
   c. The federal budget deficit in the United States fell sharply during this period.
   d. Quality of U.S.-made goods and services declined during the period.

_____ 10. Other things being equal, if the U.S. inflation rate increases relative to the rate of inflation in France, we would expect the exchange rate of the U.S. dollar, measured in terms of dollars per French franc, to
   a. appreciate in nominal terms.
   b. depreciate in nominal terms.
   c. appreciate in real terms.
   d. depreciate in real terms.

_____ 11. The J-curve effect refers to a situation in which a depreciation of a country's currency
   a. causes the current account balance to move initially toward deficit in nominal terms.
   b. causes the current account balance to move initially toward deficit in real terms.
   c. causes the current account balance to move initially toward surplus in nominal terms.
   d. fails to have any effect on the current account balance.

_____ 12. If the Federal Reserve wants to push down the exchange rate of the dollar, and to "sterilize" the transaction in order to leave the domestic money supply unchanged, it must
   a. sell dollars in the foreign exchange market.
   b. carry out open market sales of securities in domestic financial markets.
   c. do both **a** and **b**.
   d. do neither **a** nor **b**.

_____ 13. Economists today tend to think that sterilized interventions by central banks in foreign exchange markets
   a. are the cause of most changes in exchange rates.
   b. permit countries to set their exchange rate at any level they wanted.
   c. have only small and short-term effects on exchange rates.
   d. do little good in the short run, but could eliminate exchange rate instability if pursued with vigor over a long period.

_____ 14. Under the Bretton Woods monetary system set up after World War II, the rules of the game called for governments to
   a. stay out of foreign exchange markets.
   b. enter markets in order to promote maximum flexibility of exchange rates.
   c. intervene in markets in order to maintain fixed exchange rates.
   d. use tariffs and quotas to manipulate exchange rates.

15. Experience with floating exchange rates since the mid-1970s proves that
    a. floating exchange rates prevent large variations in exchange rates over time.
    b. floating exchange rates are an effective brake on inflation.
    c. floating exchange rates are an effective way to prevent protectionism.
    d. none of the above.

ANSWERS TO CHAPTER 20

Hands On

Problem 1 (a) The initial equilibrium exchange rate is £2.50, as shown by point E_1 in Exhibit 20.2 (solution). The net quantity of dollars demanded on current account is approximately $625 million per day, as shown by the current account demand curve. There is a net capital outflow of about $75 million per day, as shown by the horizontal gap between the current account surplus of about $75 million matched by a current account demand curve and the total demand curve (see arrow "a" in the solution graph). (b) The real interest rate increase in the United States, other things being equal, will shift the capital account net demand curve, which will cause the total demand curve to shift up to D_2 while the other curves remain in their original positions. (c) The new equilibrium exchange rate is £3.00 per dollar, as shown by E_2 in the solution

Exhibit 20.2 (ans.)

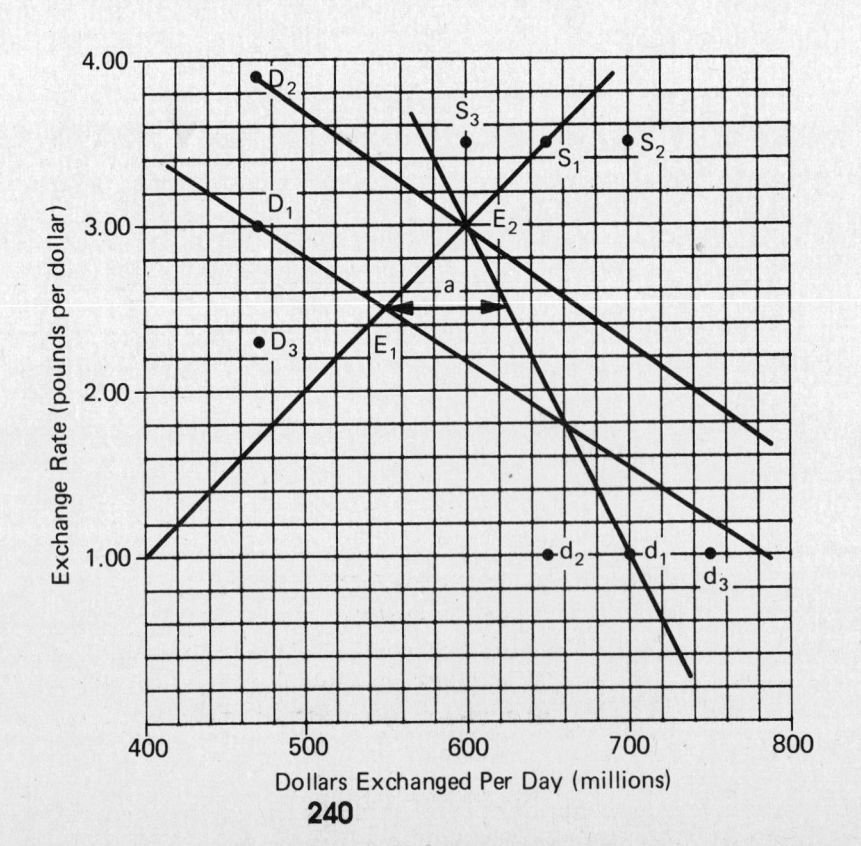

graph. At this point, both the current and capital accounts are in balance. The net capital inflow is zero.

Problem 2 (a) The initial exchange rate is 2,000 lire per dollar, a shown by E_1 in Exhibit 20.3 (solution). Both the current and capital accounts are in balance. (b) A recession in Italy will weaken the Italian demand for U.S. goods, and hence, will shift the current account demand curve for dollars to the left, from d_1 to d_3. The capital account net demand curve itself will not shift, so the total demand curve will be carried leftward the same distance as the current account demand curve moves. That puts the total demand curve in the new position D_3. (c) At E_3, the exchange rate is approximately $1,750 lire per dollar. The current account demand curve lies to the left of the supply curve at this exchange rate, indicating a current account deficit. This is offset by a net capital inflow, shown by the arrow in the solution graph. The net capital inflow is represented by the distance between the total demand curve D_3 and the current account demand curve d_3 at the equilibrium exchange rate.

Exhibit 20.3 (ans.)

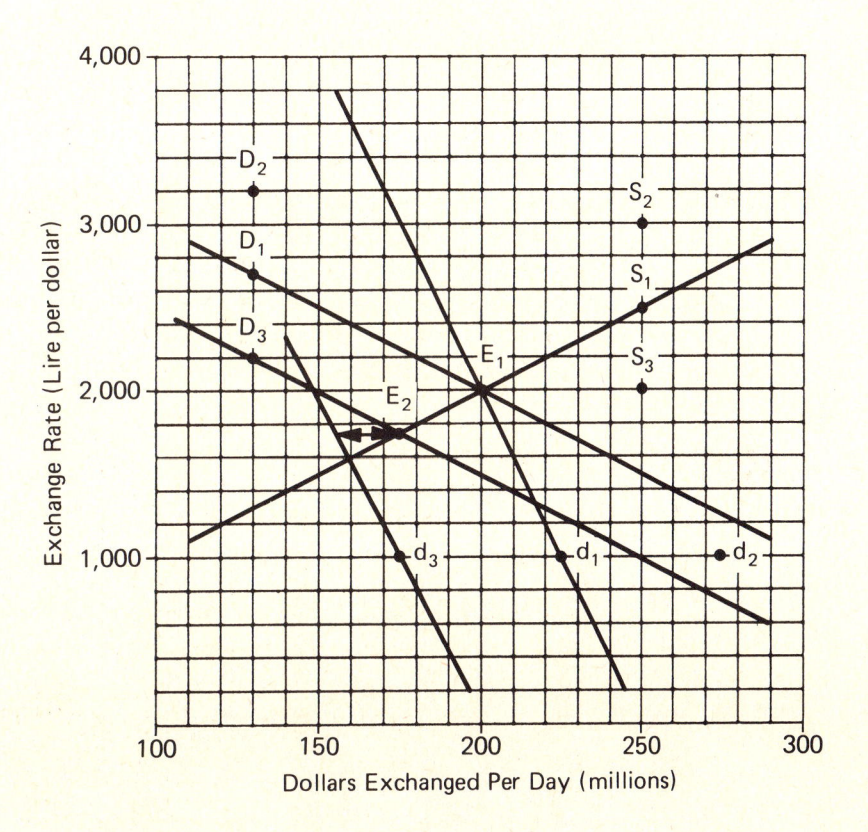

Self Test

1. **c.** The current account also includes merchandise imports and exports, and international transfers.
2. **c.** Because Japanese buyers of U.S. goods and services need to buy U.S. dollars first.
3. **c.** This is likely to be the case in the short run.
4. **c.** An appreciation of the dollar relative to the franc is the same thing as a depreciation of the franc relative to the dollar.

5. **c.** A change in the U.S. real interest rate relative to rates abroad would shift the capital account net demand curve.
6. **a.** The other three choices would result in losses.
7. **b.** Because it will slacken British demand for U.S. goods.
8. **b.** The current account supply curve will shift to the right, the dollar will depreciate, and the current account deficit will be offset by a net capital inflow.
9. **b.** Real interest rates moved relatively higher in the United States, in part because of a large budget deficit.
10. **b.** Nominal exchange rates tend to respond to changes in inflation rates in a way that leaves real exchange rates unchanged.
11. **a.** This happens because, with inelastic demand for imports, depreciation causes nominal imports to rise even though real imports fall.
12. **c.** The foreign exchange market sales of dollars tend to add to reserves of U.S. banks, and the open market sales of securities "sterilize" this by soaking the reserves up again.
13. **c.** The volume of foreign exchange market transactions is so huge than a few billions of sterilized official reserve transactions have little lasting effect.
14. **c.** This was supposed to make it unnecessary to use tariffs and quotas, although things often did not work out that way.
15. **d.** Even supporters of floating rates are disappointed by the results in some respects, but on the other hand, many former supporters of fixed rates agree that floating rates are the only practical system at present.

Chapter 21

Applying Supply and Demand

WHERE YOU'RE GOING

When you have mastered this chapter, you will understand

1. How, in review, markets are represented in terms of the supply and demand model.
2. How the responsiveness of quantity demanded to a price change can be expressed in terms of the notion of elasticity.
3. How the notion of elasticity can be applied to situations other than the responsiveness of quantity demanded to a price change.
4. What determines the distribution of the economic burden of a tax.
5. In what way the notion of elasticity is useful for understanding the problems of the farm sector.

In addition, you will add the following terms to your economic vocabulary:
　　Elasticity
　　Price elasticity of demand
　　Revenue
　　Elastic demand
　　Inelastic demand
　　Unit elastic demand
　　Perfectly inelastic demand
　　Perfectly elastic demand
　　Income elasticity of demand
　　Cross-elasticity of demand
　　Price elasticity of supply
　　Tax incidence
　　Parity-price ratio

	WALKING TOUR — *After you have read this chapter at least once, you should work step by step through this walking tour. Fill in the blanks and answer the questions as you go along. After you have answered each question, check yourself by uncovering the answer given in the margin. If you do not understand why the answer given is the correct one, refer back to the proper section of the text.*

Review of the Basics

Exhibit 21.1 shows hypothetical supply and demand curves for soybeans. As the graph is drawn, the equilibrium price for soybeans is $ __7__ per bushel, and the equilibrium quantity produced is __1600__ million bushels per year.

7
1,600

Exhibit 21.1

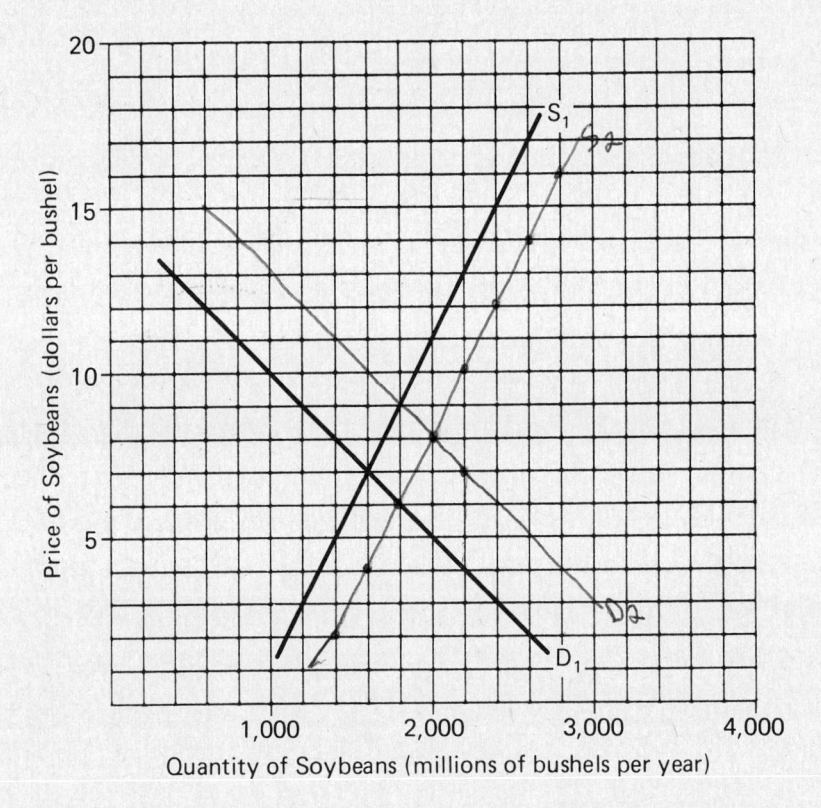

Given demand curve D_1 and supply curve S_1, no other equilibrium price or quantity is possible. For example, if the price were $9 per bushel, there would be an excess quantity [supplied/demanded] of __600__ million bushels per year. Such an excess quantity supplied would result in [accumulation/depletion] of inventories, which in turn would cause [upward/downward] pressure on the price until equilibrium was restored. Similarly, if the price were $3 per bushel, there would be an excess quantity [supplied/demanded] of __1200__ million bushels per year.

supplied
600
accumulation
downward

demanded, 1,200

244

depletion	This situation would cause [accumulation/**depletion**] of inventories
upward	and [**upward**/downward] pressure on price until equilibrium was restored.
	Exhibit 21.1 can also be used to illustrate the effects of changes in economic conditions on the market for soybeans. Suppose, for example, that an improvement in farm technology cut the cost of producing soybeans by $3 per bushel below what it formerly was for
shift in	any given quantity. This change would be represented by a [**shift in**/movement along] the supply curve for soybeans. Sketch in the new supply curve, labeling it S_2. It should be parallel to S_1 and have a
8	height of $_____8_____ at 2,000 bushels per year. The initial effect of this shift in the supply curve would be to create an excess
supply, 300	[**supply**/demand] of _____300_____ million bushels per year,
downward, movement along	causing [upward/**downward**] pressure on price and a [shift in/**movement along**] the demand curve. The new equilibrium price
6	would be $_____6_____ per bushel.
	With the new supply curve S_2 in place, suppose next that a failure of the Brazilian soybean crop caused an increase in demand for U.S. soybeans; at any given price, buyers are now willing to purchase an additional 600 million bushels per year. Sketch in the new demand curve, labeling it D_2. It should be parallel to D_1 and indi-
2,200	cate a purchase of _____2200_____ million bushels at a price of $7 per bushel. The initial effect of this shift in the demand curve
demand, 600	would be an excess [supply/**demand**] of _____600_____ million
upward	bushels per year. This will cause [**upward**/downward] pressure on
movement along	the price, a [shift in/**movement along**] the supply curve, and a new
8	equilibrium with a price of $_____8_____ per bushel and a
2,000	quantity of _____2000_____ million bushels per year.

Elasticity

The price elasticity of demand is the ratio of the percentage change

quantity demanded	in [price/**quantity demanded**] of a good to the percentage change in
price	its [**price**/quantity demanded]. Elasticity is closely related to what happens to total revenue as price changes. If total revenue increases
elastic	as the price decreases, demand is said to be ___elastic___. If total revenue does not change as the price falls, demand is said to
unit elastic	be ___unit elastic___. If total revenue falls as the price falls,

inelastic	demand is said to be __inelastic__. A vertical demand curve
perfectly inelastic	is said to be __perfectly inelastic__ and a horizontal demand curve
perfectly elastic	__perfectly elastic__.

Numerical values for price elasticity of demand can be calculated with the formula given in the textbook. Suppose, for example, that a grocer found that sales of pork chops increased from 100 pounds per day to 200 pounds per day when the price was reduced from $1.20 to 80 cents per pound. This would indicate an elasticity

1.66	of demand of __1.66__.

Applications of Elasticity

The concept of elasticity sheds light on many important economic problems. One is the issue of who bears the economic burden of a

tax incidence	tax, known as the issue of __tax incidence__.

Consider the case of an excise tax on a particular product, say automobile tires. The effect of a $10 tax per tire can be shown by

shift in	means of an upward [**shift in**/movement along] the supply curve for tires. The result of the tax will be a new equilibrium price, including
less than	tax, that is [**less than**/more than/exactly] $10 higher than the original equilibrium price. Sellers' revenue per unit, net of the tax,
less than	will be lowered by [**less than**/more than/exactly] $10. Thus, the economic
partly by both	burden of the tax is borne by [buyers/sellers/**partly by both**].

The exact incidence of the tax depends on the relative elasticities of supply and demand. For a given elasticity of supply, the

smaller	more elastic is demand, the [greater/**smaller**] will be the share of the tax burden borne by buyers. For a given elasticity of demand,
smaller	the more elastic is supply, the [greater/**smaller**] will be the share of the tax burden borne by sellers.

The concept of elasticity also sheds light on certain problems encountered by the farm sector. Demand for many important farm

inelastic	goods is price [elastic/**inelastic**]. This means that a fall in market
lower	price will [raise/**lower**] farm revenues. Also, the less price-elastic is
more	demand, the [**more**/less] the price will fall in response to any given increase in supply.

246

HANDS ON

Now that you have reviewed the concepts introduced in this chapter, it is time for some hands-on practice with the analytical tools that have been introduced. Work through each problem in this section carefully, and then check your results against those given at the end of the chapter.

Problem 1

a. Using the demand curve in Exhibit 21.2a as your source of information, draw a graph in Exhibit 21.2b showing the total revenue associated with each quantity demanded of good X.

Exhibit 21.2a

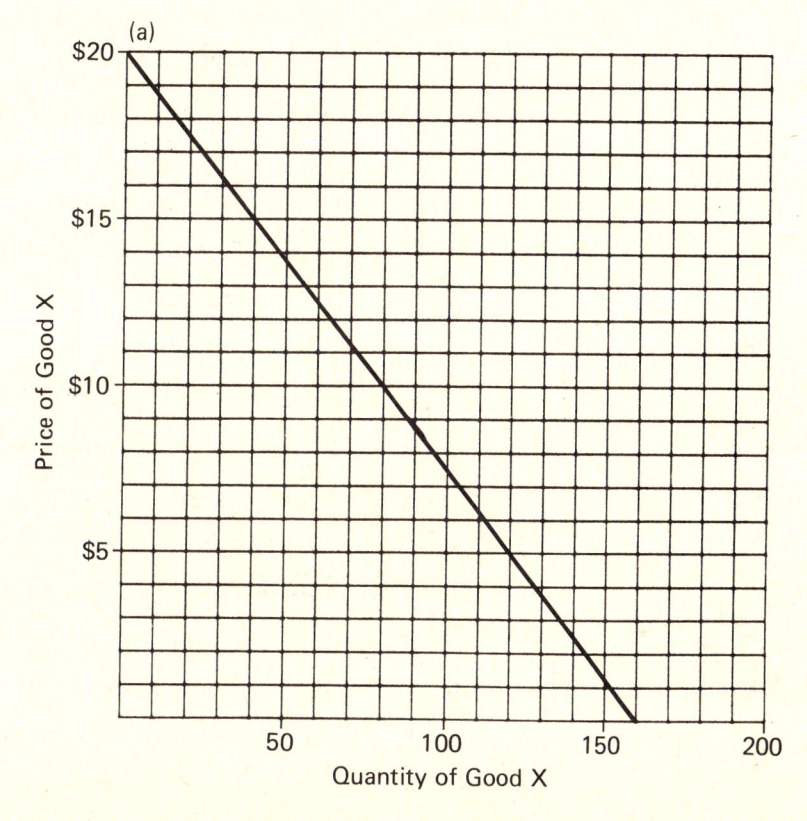

b. Using your total revenue graph as a guide, identify and label elastic, inelastic, and unit elastic points or segments on the demand curve.

Problem 2

The questions that follow are based on Exhibit 21.3.
a. Find the equilibrium price and quantity for the buckwheat market as Exhibit 21.3 is drawn. Label the equilibrium E_1.
b. Suppose an improved seed variety reduces the cost of growing buckwheat, so that farmers are willing to supply any given quantity at a price $6 lower than previously. Indicate any shifts in the supply or demand curves on the diagram. Find the new equilibrium point and label it E_2.
c. In the range between E_1 and E_2, what is the price elasticity of demand for buckwheat?

Exhibit 21.2b

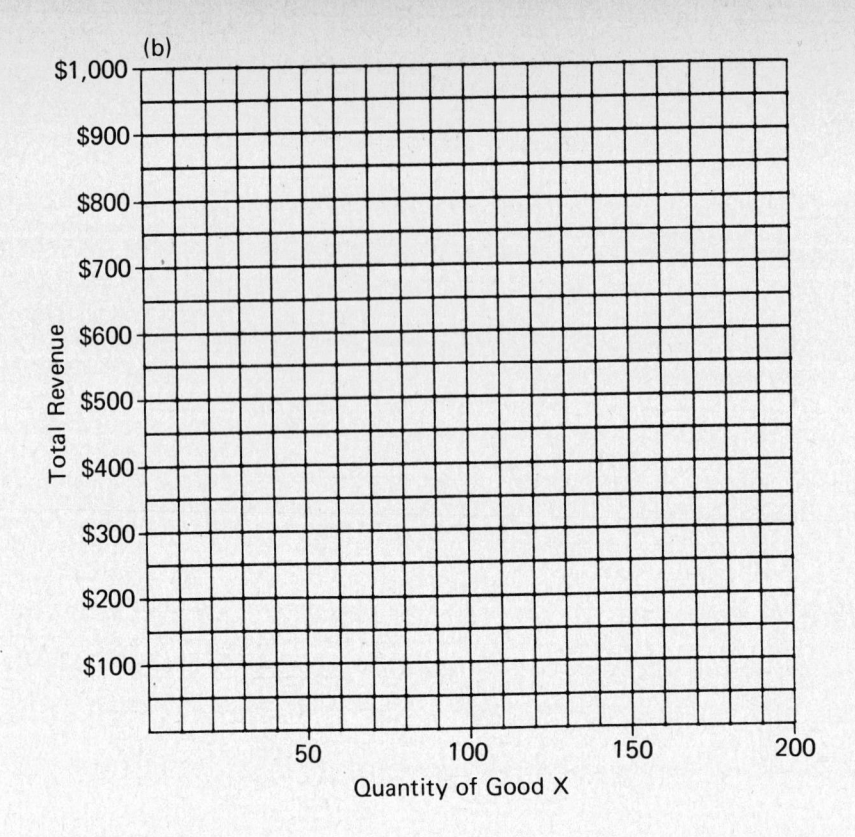

(b)

[Graph: Total Revenue (y-axis, $0 to $1,000) vs. Quantity of Good X (x-axis, 0 to 200). Blank grid.]

d. With the cost reduction still in effect, suppose an increase in the prices of substitute grains increases the amount of buckwheat consumers are willing to buy at any given price by 6 million bushels per year. Indicate any shifts in the supply or demand curves on the diagram. Find the new equilibrium and label it E₃.

e. In the range between E₂ and E₃, what is the price elasticity of supply for buckwheat?

Exhibit 21.3

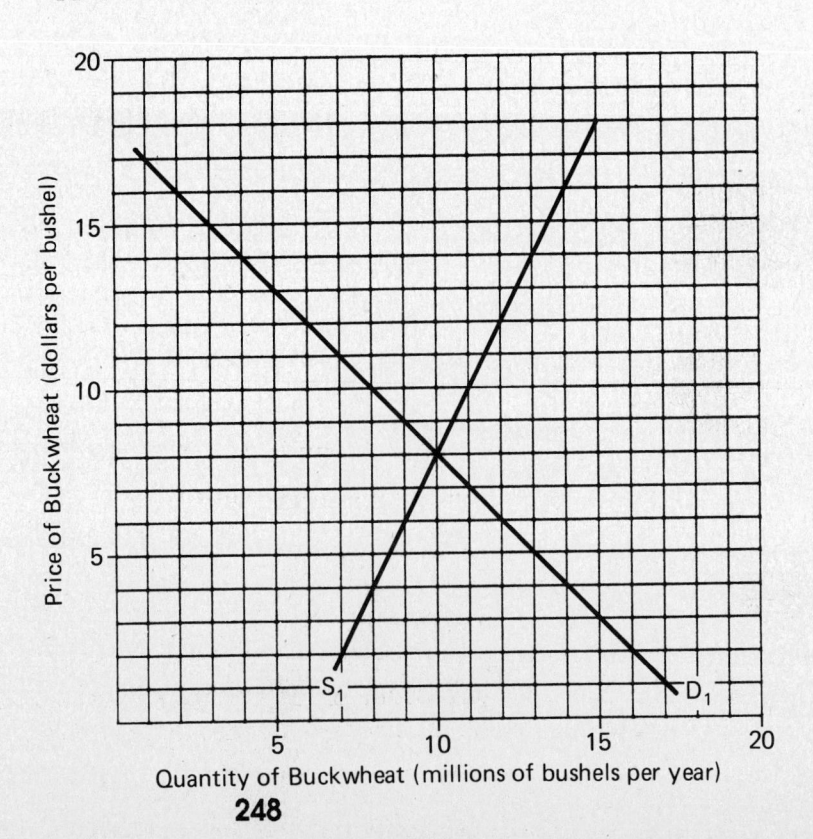

[Graph: Price of Buckwheat (dollars per bushel) on y-axis (0 to 20) vs. Quantity of Buckwheat (millions of bushels per year) on x-axis (0 to 20). Shows supply curve S₁ (upward sloping) and demand curve D₁ (downward sloping) intersecting near (10, 8).]

248

Problem 3

Suppose that the federal government has become concerned about the cost of Coast Guard rescue services provided to yacht owners at the expense of the general taxpayer. It decides to impose a special tax on yacht owners to finance the rescue-service portion of the Coast Guard budget. Two forms of the tax are under consideration. Use Exhibit 21.4 to answer the questions that follow.

Exhibit 21.4

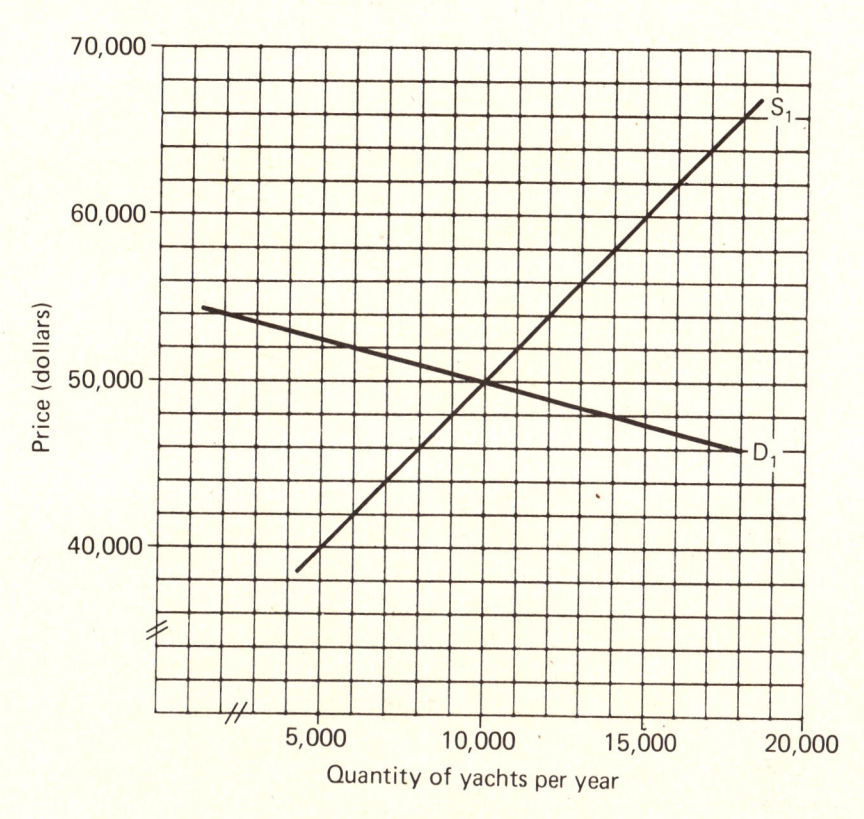

a. Under the first version of the tax, buyers of new yachts will have to pay a one-time registration fee of $5,000 when they first place their new vessel in service. Before the registration fee is imposed, what was the equilibrium price of yachts, and what was the equilibrium quantity sold? How much would the price (not including the fee) have to fall in order for the quantity purchased not to decrease after the fee is in place?
b. From the point of view of yacht builders, the impact of the fee will appear as a shift in the demand curve for yachts. Draw the new demand curve and label it D$_2$. With the tax in place, what is the new equilibrium price (not including the fee)? The new equilibrium quantity? How much revenue will be raised by the fee?
c. In the alternate version, yacht builders will have to purchase a $5,000 permit for each yacht built. If they decide to try to recover the cost of the permit from their customers, they will have to do so by including all or part of it in the price of the yacht when it is sold. From the point of view of yacht buyers, imposition of the permit will appear as a shift in the supply curve. Draw in the new supply curve and label it S$_2$. What will

be the equilibrium price of a yacht with the permit system in place? The equilibrium quantity sold? The revenue raised?
d. Compare the outcome of the two alternative forms of the tax. Which imposes the larger actual economic burden on buyers? On sellers? Which raises greater revenue?
e. How much are yacht owners really hurt by the tax? How much of the burden of the tax rests on yacht builders (together with their employees and suppliers)?

ECONOMICS IN THE NEWS

Metro Fare Rises Averaging 12 Percent Proposed

Fares on most Metro buses and subways will rise by a nickel or more on December 6 if a staff proposal submitted yesterday to the transit system's board is adopted, as appears likely. It would be Metro's third fare increase in 16 months.

Overall, the fare package would raise the cost of an average ride in the area by 12 percent, moving most base fares from 60 to 65 cents. Mileage fees that determine rush-hour rail fares would be raised, as would "crossing charges" for bus rides between jurisdictions.

The new fares would reduce ridership by about 2 percent, according to Metro planner Robert Pickett, accelerating a downward trend in patronage that has emerged in the last year. But revenues would still increase by the $7 million that Metro needs to balance its budget for the fiscal year 1982, Pickett said.

Inflation, dwindling ridership and Reagan administration plans to phase out federal operating subsidies have put Metro in an increasingly tight financial position, proponents of higher fares say.

"I'm not comfortable at this point with raising fares," board chairman Joseph Alexander said. "However, I don't see any alternative."

Bus fares, meanwhile, would rise on the average something over 12 percent. Riders would pay a rush-hour base fare of 65 cents for trips that did not cross jurisdictional lines. The peak-hour District-Maryland Zone 1 charge would rise from $1.10 to $1.25, with the Zone 2 fare rising 10 cents to $1.50.

The District-Virginia Zone G crossing charge would go up from 60 cents to 65 cents, raising the cost of rush-hour trips on Metrobus to and from the inner communities of Northern Virginia from $1.20 to $1.30.

For off-peak hours, bus rides within Virginia and Maryland would cost a flat 65 cents while in the District the rides would continue to cost 60 cents. Off-peak rides between D.C. and Maryland would move from 85 cents to $1 and between D.C. and Virginia $1.20 to $1.30.

Source: John Burgess, from "Metro Fare Rises Averaging 12 Percent Proposed," *The Washington Post*, October 16, 1981, sec A, 1, 8. © *The Washington Post*, 1981.

Questions

1. On the basis of the information given in the article, approximately what is the price elasticity of demand for Metro rides? Explain how you calculate your answer.
2. Why do you think Metro charges more for peak-hour (that is, rush-hour) service than for off-peak (nonrush-hour) service? Does this have anything to do with elasticity of demand?
3. Metro board chairman Joseph Alexander says he is "not comfortable" about raising fares. Why might he not be comfortable, even though his staff assures him the fare increase will give the system a quick $7 million boost in revenue? Explain.

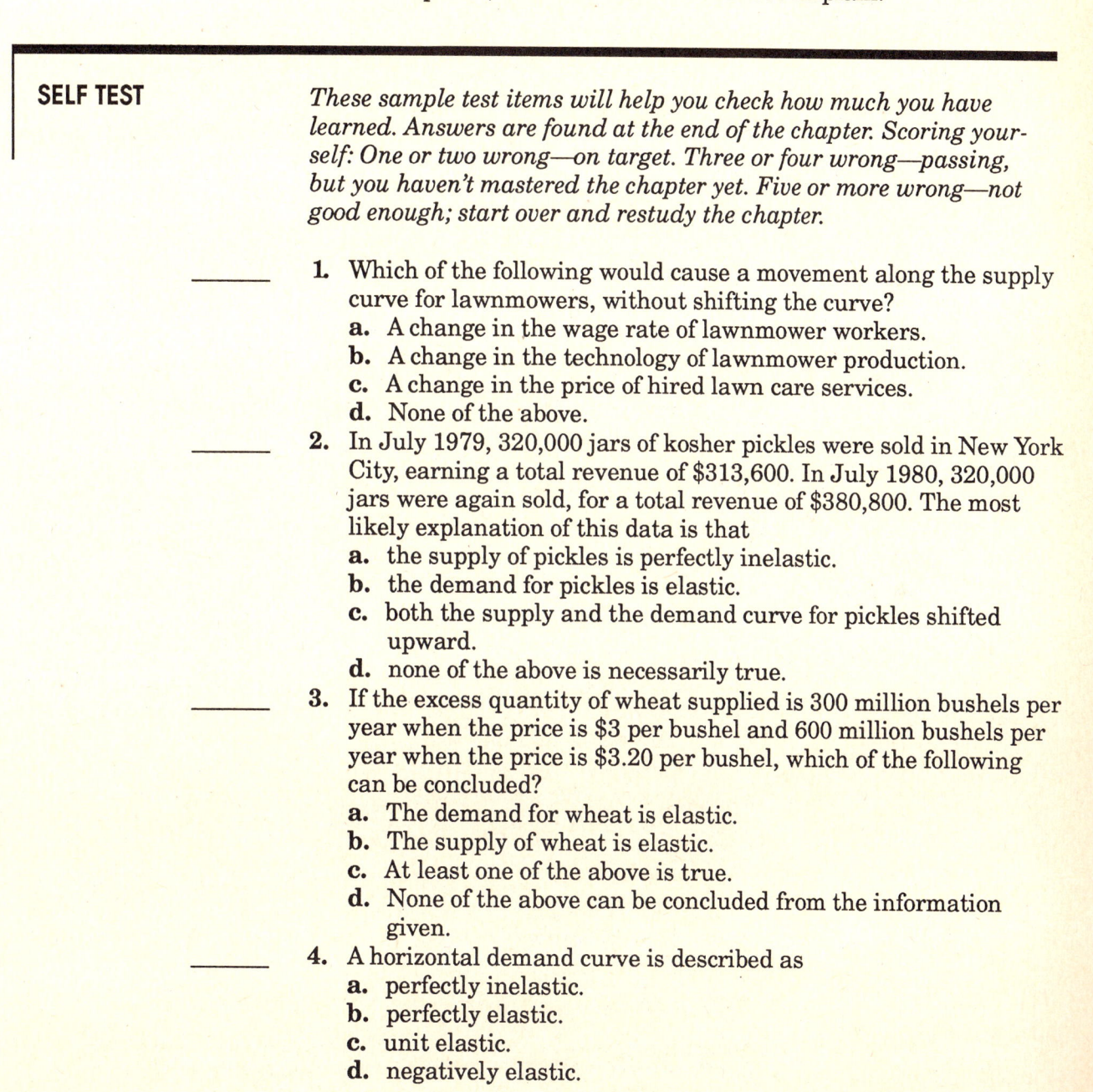

SELF TEST

These sample test items will help you check how much you have learned. Answers are found at the end of the chapter. Scoring yourself: One or two wrong—on target. Three or four wrong—passing, but you haven't mastered the chapter yet. Five or more wrong—not good enough; start over and restudy the chapter.

_____ 1. Which of the following would cause a movement along the supply curve for lawnmowers, without shifting the curve?
   a. A change in the wage rate of lawnmower workers.
   b. A change in the technology of lawnmower production.
   c. A change in the price of hired lawn care services.
   d. None of the above.

_____ 2. In July 1979, 320,000 jars of kosher pickles were sold in New York City, earning a total revenue of $313,600. In July 1980, 320,000 jars were again sold, for a total revenue of $380,800. The most likely explanation of this data is that
   a. the supply of pickles is perfectly inelastic.
   b. the demand for pickles is elastic.
   c. both the supply and the demand curve for pickles shifted upward.
   d. none of the above is necessarily true.

_____ 3. If the excess quantity of wheat supplied is 300 million bushels per year when the price is $3 per bushel and 600 million bushels per year when the price is $3.20 per bushel, which of the following can be concluded?
   a. The demand for wheat is elastic.
   b. The supply of wheat is elastic.
   c. At least one of the above is true.
   d. None of the above can be concluded from the information given.

_____ 4. A horizontal demand curve is described as
   a. perfectly inelastic.
   b. perfectly elastic.
   c. unit elastic.
   d. negatively elastic.

5. If the number of movie tickets sold increases by 10 percent when the price is cut by 20 percent, other things being equal, it can be concluded that
   a. demand is price elastic.
   b. demand is price inelastic.
   c. demand is income elastic.
   d. demand is income inelastic.

6. If deregulation of airline fares, other things being equal, led to lower prices and higher revenues, it could be concluded that
   a. demand was elastic.
   b. demand was inelastic.
   c. supply was elastic.
   d. supply was inelastic.

7. If raising the cigarette tax from 10 cents per pack to 20 cents per pack left cigarette tax revenues unchanged, it could be concluded that the price elasticity of demand for cigarettes was
   a. elastic.
   b. inelastic.
   c. unit elastic.
   d. impossible to calculate from the information given.

8. Which of the following statements can be made about a downward-sloping straight-line demand curve?
   a. It is more elastic at the top than at the bottom.
   b. It is more elastic at the bottom than at the top.
   c. It has a constant elasticity throughout its length.
   d. Insufficient information is given for an answer to be reached.

9. A supply curve that is a straight line passing through the origin
   a. must be unit elastic.
   b. has a constant elasticity, but need not be unit elastic.
   c. is more elastic at the top than at the bottom.
   d. is more elastic at the bottom than at the top.

10. If the quantity of apples sold at a certain fruit stand increases from 20 pounds per day to 30 pounds per day when the price is lowered from 40 cents per pound to 30 cents per pound, the elasticity of demand is closest to which of the following?
    a. 0.2.
    b. 0.7.
    c. 1.4.
    d. 4.1.

11. Other things being equal, we expect that a given change in price will have a greater effect on quantity demanded
    a. in the short run than in the long run.
    b. in the long run than in the short run.
    c. the less income elastic the demand.
    d. the less price elastic the demand.

12. If the income elasticity of demand for intercity bus travel is -0.5, we would expect, other things being equal,
    a. that bus company revenues will rise when incomes fall.
    b. that bus company revenues will fall when incomes fall.
    c. that a is true, but only if demand is also price elastic.
    d. that a is true, but only if demand is also price inelastic.

_____ 13. A $5 per ticket tax is imposed on airline tickets to help pay for improvements in the nation's air traffic control system. Which of the following is most likely to happen to the equilibrium price (including tax)?
   a. The equilibrium price will rise by $5.
   b. The equilibrium price will rise by less than $5.
   c. The equilibrium price will rise by more than $5.
   d. No way to tell without knowing the exact elasticities.

_____ 14. A study shows that demand for cigarettes has a price elasticity of about 0.2, whereas the supply of cigarettes has a price elasticity of 1.3. We can conclude that the economic burden of cigarette taxes falls
   a. more heavily on smokers than on producers.
   b. more heavily on producers than on smokers.
   c. equally on producers and smokers.
   d. no conclusion can be drawn from the information given.

_____ 15. During the Great Depression, demand for goods and services of every type dropped. Also during this period, the prices received by farmers dropped much more, in percentage terms, than the prices farmers paid for manufactured goods. A possible explanation of this pattern is
   a. farm goods are inferior goods in most cases.
   b. demand for farm goods tends to be more price elastic than demand for manufactured goods.
   c. demand for farm goods tends to be less price elastic than demand for manufactured goods.
   d. farm goods have negatively sloped demand curves.

ANSWERS TO CHAPTER 21

Hands On

Problem 1 (a) To construct the total revenue curve, first multiply price times quantity for a representative selection of points along the demand curve, such as points A through E shown in the solution graph for Exhibit 21.2a. Plot these (and more besides if you want) in the lower diagram (see Points a through e in the solution graph for Exhibit 21.2b). Connect the points with a smooth curve. (b) As shown in the solution graph, the elastic range of demand corresponds to the upward-sloping portion of the total revenue curve, and the inelastic range to the downward-sloping portion. The point exactly at maximum revenue is the point of unit elasticity.

Problem 2 (a) The initial equilibrium is at a quantity of 10 million bushels per year and a price of $8 per bushel, shown as E_1 in the solution graph. (b) The cost reduction shifts the supply curve straight down by $6 to the position shown as S_2 in the solution graph for Exhibit 21.3. The new equilibrium is at E_2—12 million bushels at $6 per bushel. (c) Apply the midpoint formula as the

Exhibit 21.2a (ans.)

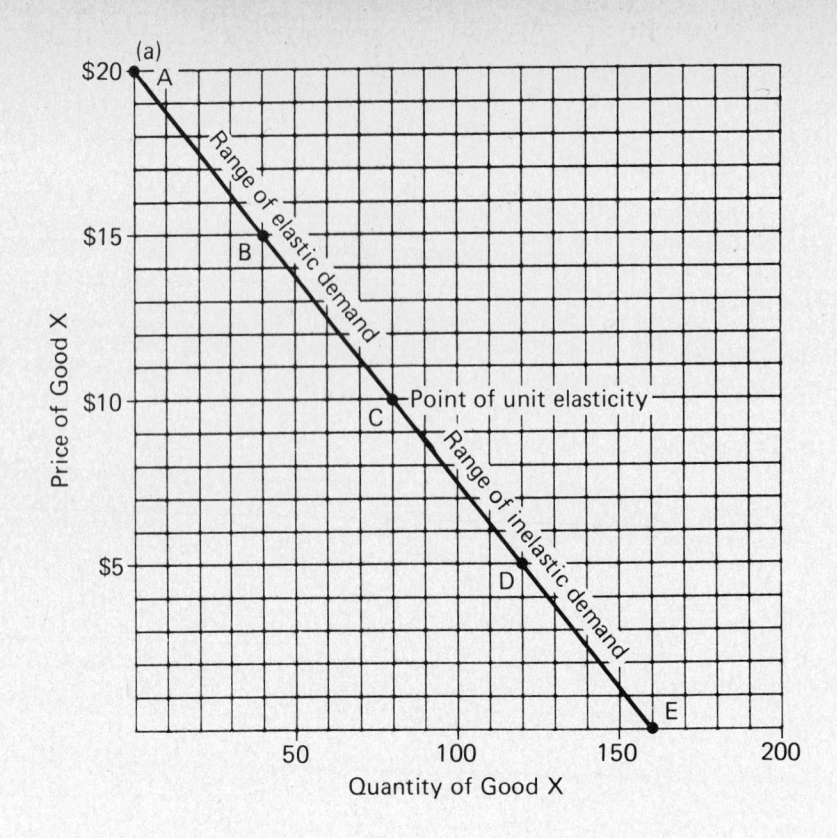

(a)

price falls from $8 to $6 and the quantity increases from 10 million to 12 million. You should get an elasticity of 0.636. (d) The demand curve shifts to the right by 6 million bushels to the position D₂. The new equilibrium will be D₃, 14 million bushels at $10 per bushel. (e) Applying the midpoint formula should give you an elasticity of supply of 0.308.

Exhibit 21.2b (ans.)

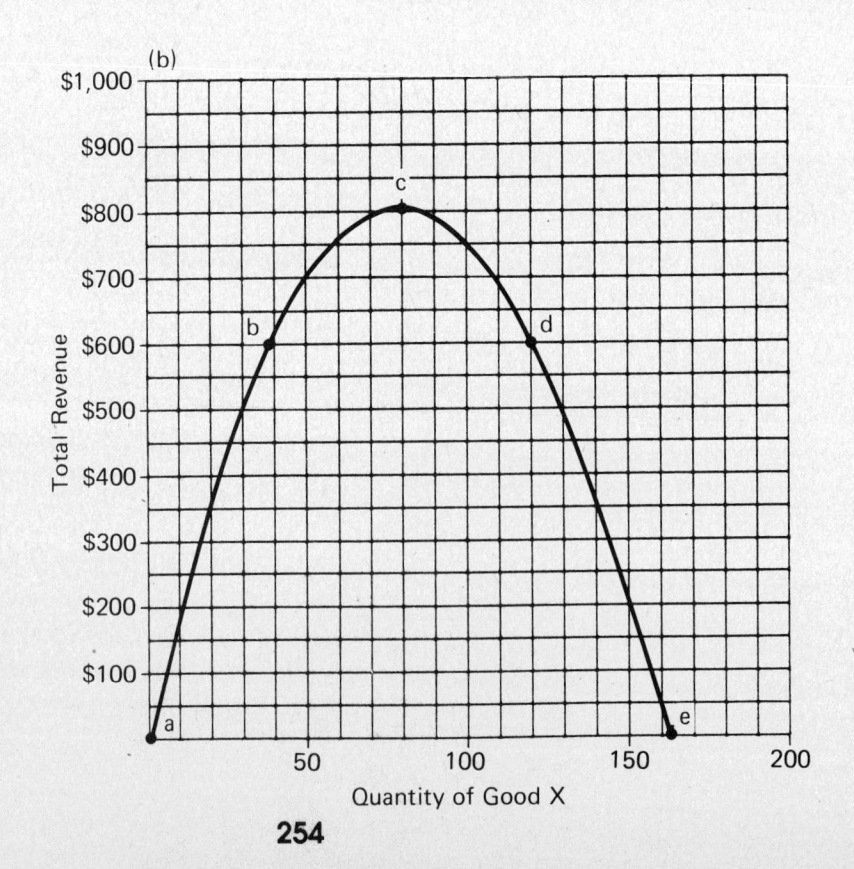

Exhibit 21.3 (ans.)

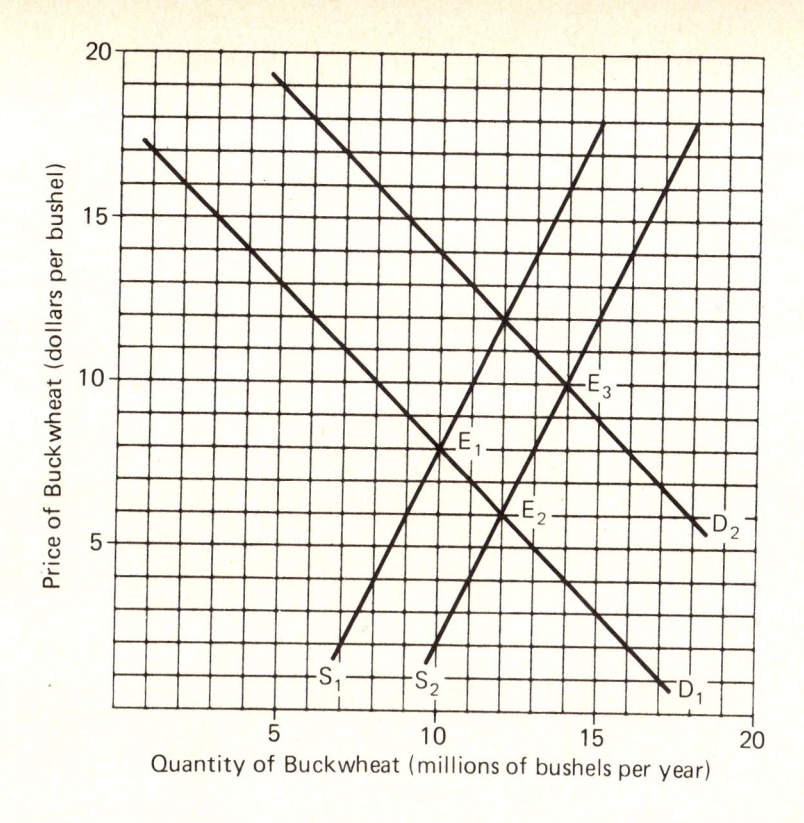

Problem 3 (a) Before the tax, the equilibrium quantity is 10,000 yachts per year and the equilibrium price is $50,000. The price would have to fall by the full amount of the tax to keep the quantity demanded unchanged. (b) Price not including fee becomes $46,000. Quantity will be 8,000. Revenue raised will be $40 million. (c) The price will rise to $51,000 and the quantity will fall to 8,000. Revenue raised will be $40 million. (d) They are identical in all

Exhibit 21.4 (ans.)

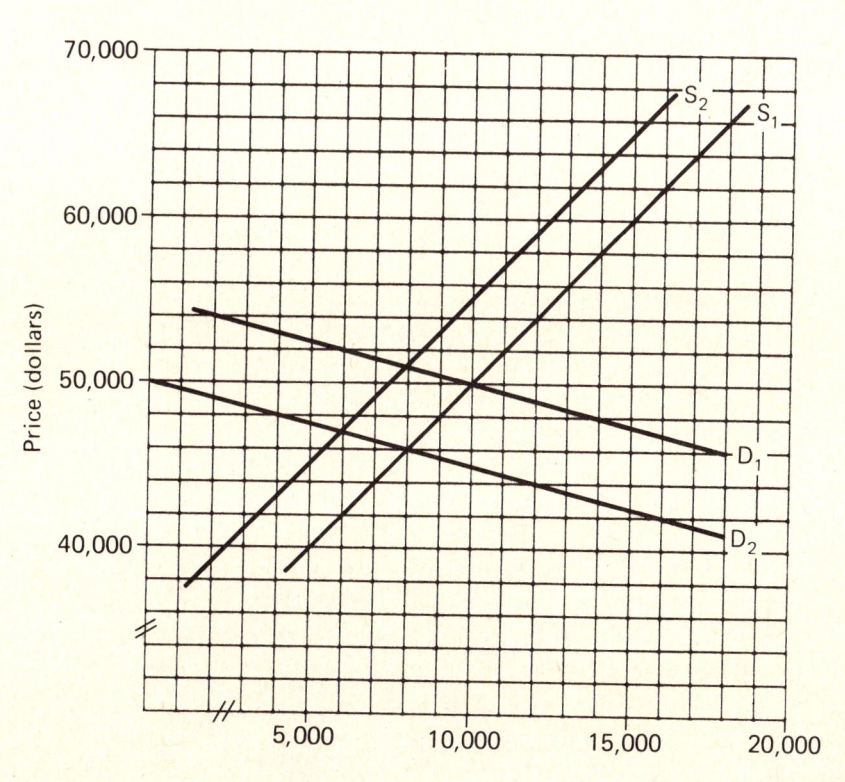

respects. (e) Yacht buyers suffer a $1,000 increase in the price of each yacht, fee included. Some are priced out of the market altogether by this increase. Yacht builders get $4,000 less revenue per unit. Some workers will probably be unemployed. Your completed diagram should look like the solution graph for Exhibit 21.4.

Economics in the News

(1) You don't have enough detailed information to use the midpoint formula. However, you can get the approximate answer by dividing the percentage change in quantity (2 percent) by the percentage change in price (12 percent). The result is a price elasticity of demand of about 0.167. (2) Metro officials probably believe elasticity of demand to be less during peak hours than off-peak hours. In off-peak hours, when traffic on the roads is light, private automobiles are a better substitute for the subway (in terms of travel time) than during peak hours. (3) You have to speculate here, since nothing exact is said, but you can make some good guesses. First, Alexander may be worried that long-term elasticity of demand is higher than short-term elasticity, so that the long-term loss in ridership may be more than 2 percent. Alexander may also be concerned about broader transportation problems than Metro revenue alone. For example, a fare increase that puts more people in private cars carries an opportunity cost in terms of greater traffic congestion. Finally, the Washington, D.C., local government is on record as favoring low fares as an aid to workers from poor households, who rely more heavily on buses and subways to get to work.

Self Test

1. **c.** This is a substitute for lawnmowers, so it would shift the demand curve. Items **a** and **b** would shift the supply curve.
2. **c.** By far the most likely explanation is an upward shift in both the supply and demand curves, each having normal slopes. It is theoretically possible that perfectly inelastic supply (or demand) could produce this result, but in practice, it is not a reasonable possibility.
3. **d.** Elasticity is related to the total quantity demanded, not the excess quantity demanded.
4. **b.** Vertical is perfectly inelastic.
5. **b.** The percentage increase in quantity is less than the percentage decrease in price.
6. **a.** With elastic demand, revenue increases when price decreases. If demand were inelastic, revenue would fall when the price fell.
7. **a.** The fact that revenue is unchanged means that doubling the tax cuts quantity in half, but doubling the tax means less than doubling the price inclusive of tax.
8. **a.** Near the top, a given absolute change in quantity represents a large percentage change and a given price change represents a small percentage change. The reverse is true near the bottom.
9. **a.** The percentage change in price and quantity will always be equal.
10. **c.** Apply the midpoint formula.

11. **b.** Because people will be able to adjust more fully to the change in price.
12. **a.** The demand curve will shift to the right, so both price and quantity will increase regardless of price elasticity.
13. **b.** As a result, the burden of the tax will be split between the two parties. This result will hold as long as neither the supply nor the demand curve is horizontal or vertical.
14. **a.** The incidence of the tax falls more on the party with the less elastic response to price changes.
15. **c.** A uniform decline in demand thus had a proportionately greater impact on farm prices than on the prices of manufactured goods.

Chapter 22

Rational Choice and Consumer Behavior

WHERE YOU'RE GOING

When you have mastered this chapter, you will understand

1. What elements are involved in consumers' rational choices.
2. How consumers balance their selection of goods and services to achieve an equilibrium.
3. What lies behind the effect of a price change on the quantity of a good demanded.
4. Why demand curves have negative slopes.
5. Why consumers and producers both gain from exchange in free markets.
6. Why the burden of a tax exceeds the revenue raised by government.

In addition, you will add the following terms to your economic vocabulary:
   Utility
   Rational choice
   Marginal utility
   Principle of diminishing marginal utility
   Consumer equilibrium
   Substitution effect
   Income effect
   Consumer surplus
   Producer surplus
   Excess burden of a tax

WALKING TOUR

After you have read this chapter at least once, you should work step by step through this walking tour. Fill in the blanks and answer the questions as you go along. After you have answered each question, check yourself by uncovering the answer given in the margin. If you do not understand why the answer given is the correct one, refer back to the proper section of the text.

Utility and the Rational Consumer

Economists refer to the pleasure and satisfaction that people get from the consumption of goods and services as _____.

utility

258

objective   Utility is the _____ of the consumer choice problem. The various ways in which one can get utility—seeing a movie, eating
alternatives   pie, or whatever—are the _____ of the consumer choice problem. The limits on the degree to which the alternatives may be pursued—for example, limits posed by a budget, a diet, or available
constraints   time—are the _____ of the consumer choice problem. Purposeful choice directed systematically toward the achievement of objectives given the alternatives and constraints of the situation
rational   is known as _____ choice.

marginal utility   The utility one gets from the consumption of one additional unit of a good is known as the _____ of that good. The important principle of diminishing marginal utility says that as consumption increases the additional satisfaction received from a one-unit
falls   increase in consumption [rises/falls]. In practice, utility cannot be directly measured, but if there were such a thing as a utility meter, it might give a set of readings like those shown in the following table. Use the data given in the total utility column to fill in the marginal utility column.

Number of Units of Goods Consumed	Total Utility	Marginal Utility
1	100	
2	120	_____
3	135	_____
4	145	_____
5	153	_____

20

15

10

8

marginal   In order to get the greatest utility from a given budget, consumers must choose a selection of goods that makes the [marginal/total] utility per dollar's worth of each good just equal to the marginal utility per dollar's worth of each other good. An equivalent way to express this rule is to say that in consumer equilibrium, the
price   ratio of the marginal utility of each good to its _____ must be the same for all goods consumed.

259

Substitution and Income Effects

The change in quantity demanded of a good whose price has fallen can be divided into two parts. The part of the increase in consumption resulting from substituting more of the relatively cheap good for other goods whose prices have not fallen is known as the _____ effect. The part resulting from the effective increase in real income is known as the _____ effect. The substitution effect taken by itself leads to an increase in quantity demanded when price falls for [normal/inferior/all] goods. The income effect taken by itself leads to an increase in quantity demanded when price falls for [normal/inferior/all] goods and to a decrease in quantity demanded when price falls for [normal/inferior/all] goods. Even for inferior goods, the [income/substitution] effect is normally the stronger of the two, so that in all or virtually all cases, quantity demanded increases when the price [falls/rises].

substitution
income

all

normal
inferior
substitution

falls

Consumer Surplus

A demand curve for a good shows how much consumers will be willing to purchase at a given price, and also how much they would be willing to pay for an additional unit, given the quantity currently consumed. The maximum that would willingly be paid for a given additional unit is shown by the _____ of the demand curve at the corresponding quantity. The amount that will be willingly paid [increases/decreases] as the quantity increases. When many units of a good are purchased at a given market price, the difference between the maximum that a consumer would be willing to pay and the amount that he or she actually pays is called _____.

Similarly, the supply curve can be read to indicate either the quantity of a good that will be supplied at a given price, or the minimum price that must be paid to induce suppliers to offer another unit of the good. This amount can also be considered the _____ of the good. The difference between what producers receive for a good at the market price and the minimum they would willingly accept is known as _____.

In a competitive market, both consumer and producer surplus earned represent the gains from trade. The consumer surplus is shown graphically by a triangle [above/below] market price and

height

decreases

consumer surplus

opportunity cost

producer surplus

above

260

below, demand	[above/below] the [demand/supply] curve. The producer surplus is
below, above	shown by a triangle [above/below] market price and [above/below]
supply	the [demand/supply] curve.
	If the quantity of a good sold is reduced as the result of the imposition of a tax, total revenue collected by the government will
less than	be [greater than/less than/equal to] the total of lost consumer and producer surplus. The difference between total lost consumer and
excess	producer surplus and total government revenue is the _____ burden of the tax.

Appendix: Indifference Curves

An indifference curve is the graphical representation of a set of "baskets" of goods, none of which is preferred by a certain consumer to any other basket in the set. Such curves have certain standard

negative	properties, including the following: They all have [positive/negative] slopes. The absolute value of the slope of an indifference curve at any point is equal to the ratio of the marginal utility of the good on
horizontal	the [horizontal/vertical] axis to the marginal utility of the good on
vertical	the [horizontal/vertical] axis. The slope of an indifference curve
decreases	[increases/decreases] in absolute value as one moves down and to the right along the curve. An indifference curve can be drawn through any point between the axes. Indifference curves do not
transitivity	cross because of the property of _____ preferences.

A line can be drawn on an indifference curve to represent the various combinations of a good that can be purchased at given prices and with a given consumer budget. Such a line is known as a

budget line	_____. Graphically, consumer equilibrium can be repre-
tangency	sented as a point of _____ between an indifference curve and a budget line.

261

HANDS ON

Now that you have reviewed the concepts introduced in this chapter, it is time for some hands-on practice with the analytical tools that have been introduced. Work through each problem in this section carefully, and then check your results against those given at the end of the chapter.

Problem 1

The following questions refer to Exhibit 22.1, which shows supply and demand curves for a certain good sold in a competitive market.

Exhibit 22.1

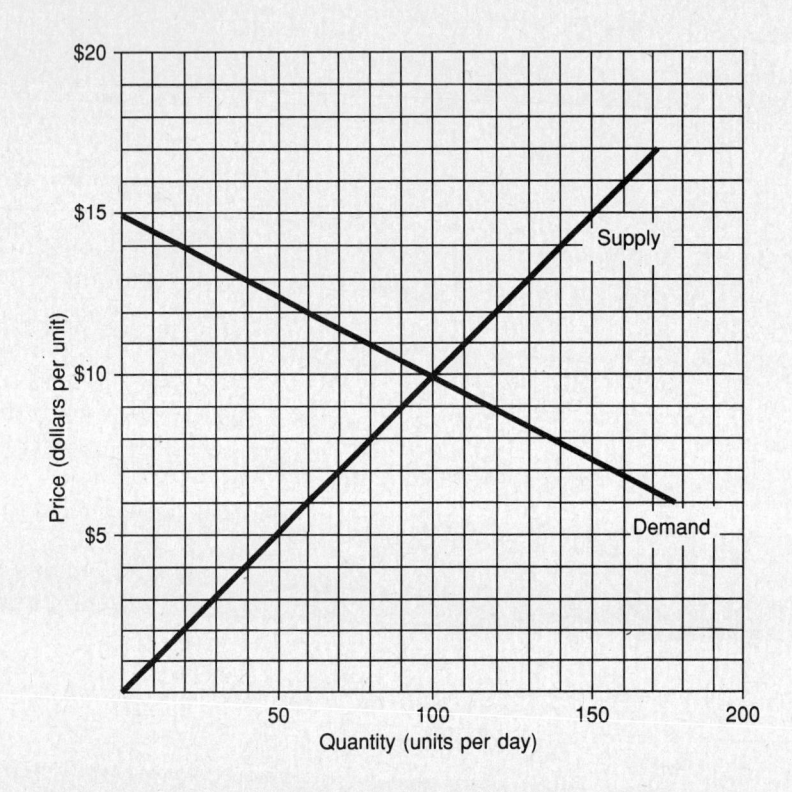

a. Given the supply and demand curves as drawn, what is the equilibrium market price? The equilibrium quantity sold?
b. Assuming that 100 units of the good are consumed per day, approximately how much would consumers be willing to pay for a 101st unit? How much would producers need to receive in order to be willing to supply that unit?
c. What is total consumer surplus at the equilibrium price? Total producer surplus? What are total gains from trade in this market?
d. Suppose that a tax of $7.50 per unit is imposed on this good. What will be the equilibrium price and quantity after the tax is imposed? How much revenue will be collected by government? How much consumer surplus will remain after the tax? How much producer surplus? What will be the excess burden of the tax?

Problem 2

Refer to Exhibit 22.2 in answering the questions that follow. This problem and those that follow are based on the optional appendix to the chapter of the textbook.

Exhibit 22.2

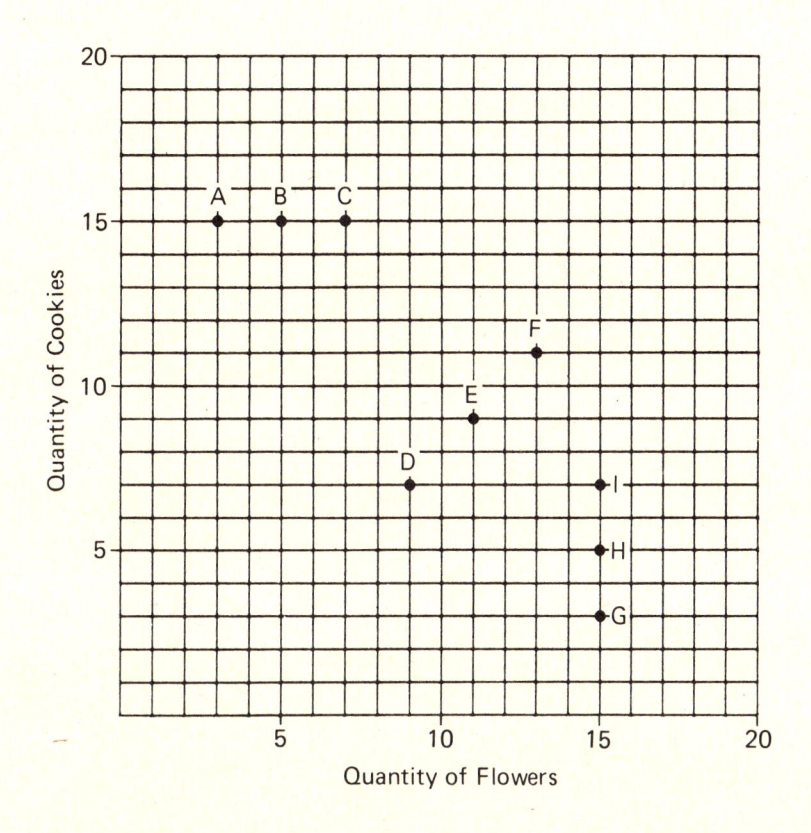

a. Can an indifference curve pass through Points A, D, and H? Through Points A, D, and I? Explain why or why not in each case.
b. Can an indifference curve pass through Points C, F, and I? Through Points B, E, and H? Through Points A, D, and G? Explain why or why not in each case.
c. Can an indifference curve pass through Points A, E, and I? Through Points C, D, and G? If one member of a set of indifference curves passes through C, D, and G, can another member of the same indifference set pass through Points A, E, and I? Explain why or why not.

Problem 3

Suppose that the indifference curves in Exhibit 22.3a represent your preferences regarding two forms of entertainment, books and movies. Assume that a movie ticket costs $3, and that you have a semester's entertainment budget of $60 that you will spend entirely on these two items. Given these assumptions, construct your demand curve for books in Exhibit 22.3b. As an intermediate step,

Exhibit 22.3a

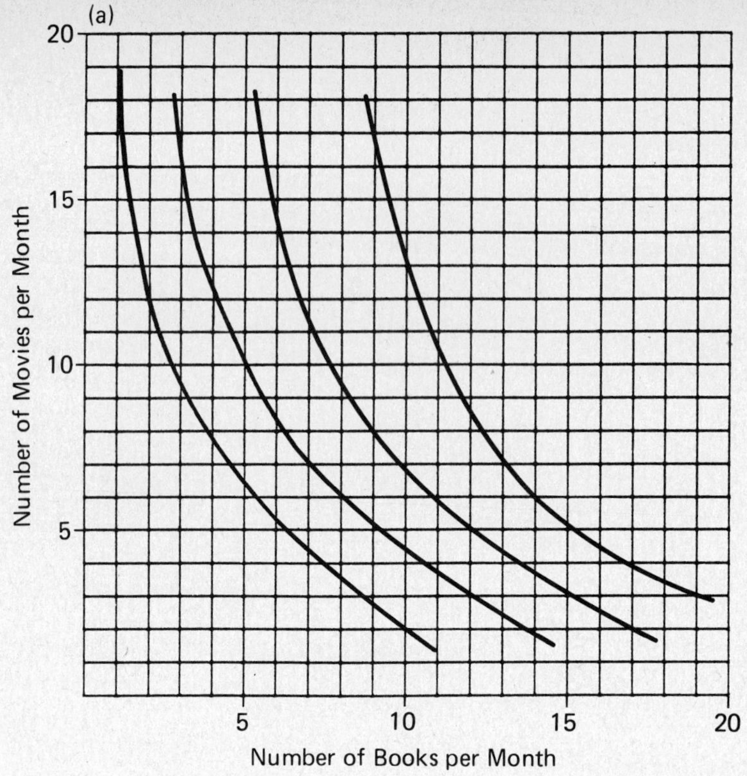
(a)
20
15
10
5
Number of Movies per Month
5
10
15
20
Number of Books per Month

Exhibit 22.3b

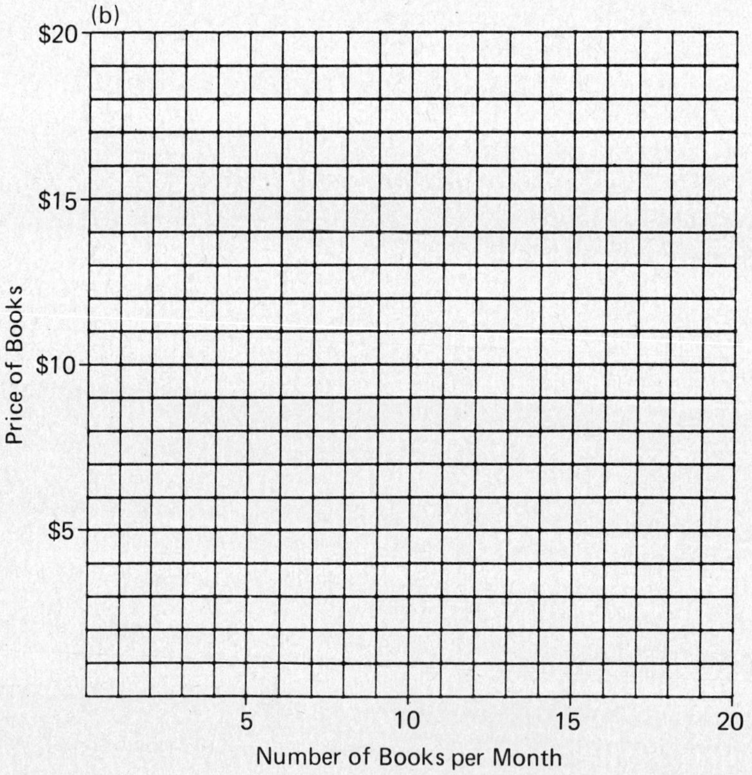
(b)
$20
$15
$10
$5
Price of Books
5
10
15
20
Number of Books per Month

you may want to fill out a table showing the quantity of books demanded at the alternative possible book prices $3, $4, $6, and $12. Bonus question: In the context of the assumptions given, are books and movies substitutes or complements? How can you tell?

Problem 4

The questions that follow are based on Exhibit 22.4

Exhibit 22.4

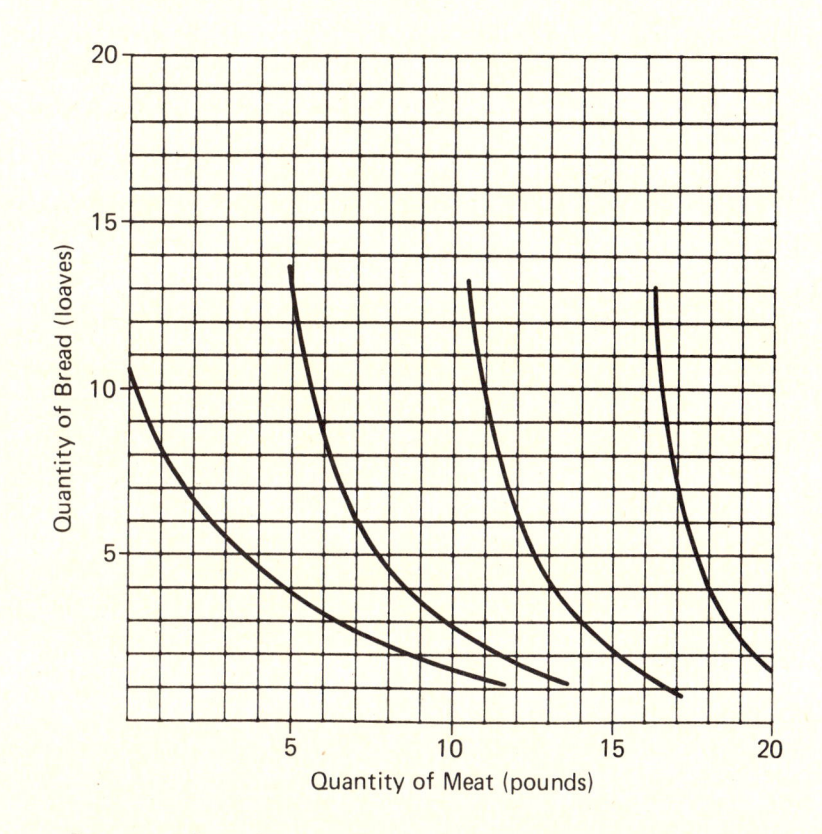

[Graph: Quantity of Bread (loaves) on y-axis (0-20), Quantity of Meat (pounds) on x-axis (0-20), showing four indifference curves]

a. Suppose that the indifference curves shown represent your preferences regarding meat and bread, and that these are the only two foods available to you. Bread costs $1 per loaf and meat costs $2 per pound. Given these, construct budget lines corresponding to food budgets of $10, $20, $30, and $40. Show your consumption equilibrium points for each budget.
b. In the context of the assumptions made here, is meat a normal or an inferior good? Is bread a normal or an inferior good? How can you tell?

Problem 5

"Applying Economic Ideas 22.1" in the text describes an experiment studying the consumption behavior of white rats. The rats are put in cages where root beer and Collins mix are available in response to pushes on different levers. Use the space provided in Exhibit 22.5 to make a graphical analysis of the experiment.

a. Initially, one of the rats is given a "budget" of 300 lever pushes per day, and the "prices" of root beer and Collins mix are set at 20 lever pushes per milliliter for each beverage. Draw the rat's budget line under these circumstances and label it B_1.
b. Under these circumstances, the rat settled down to a regular pattern of drinking about 11 milliliters of root beer per day and about 4 milliliters of Collins mix. Label this Point E_1. What does this suggest to you regarding the shape of the rat's indifference curves? Explain your reasoning.

Exhibit 22.5

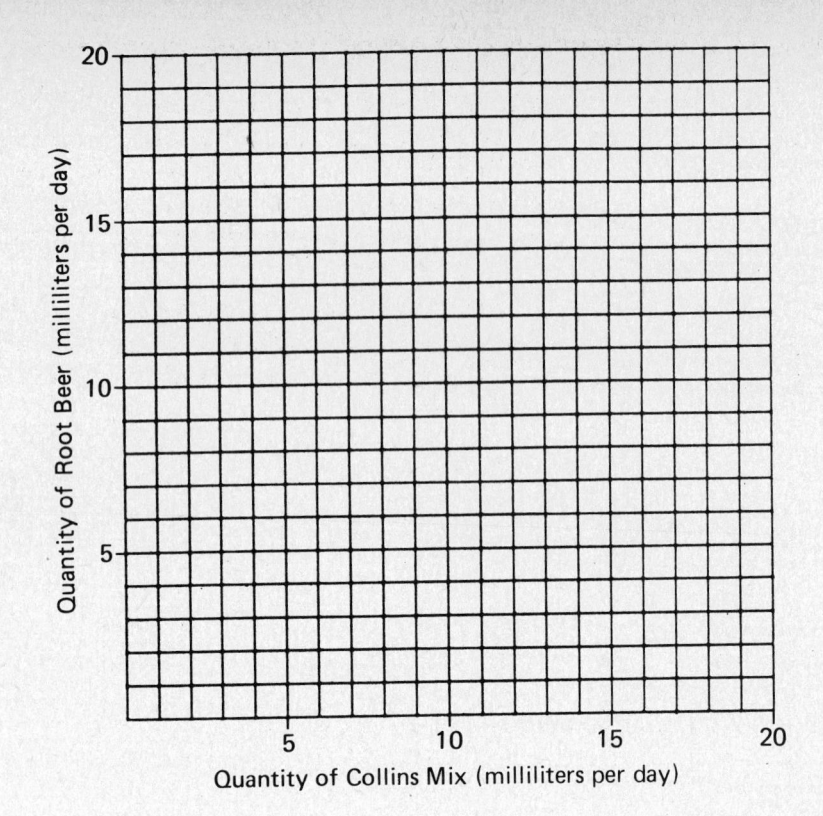

[Graph with x-axis "Quantity of Collins Mix (milliliters per day)" ranging from 0 to 20, and y-axis "Quantity of Root Beer (milliliters per day)" ranging from 0 to 20.]

c. In a second phase of the experiment, the price of root beer was doubled to 40 pushes per milliliter and the price of Collins mix was cut in half to 10 pushes per milliliter. At the same time, the rat's budget of pushes was adjusted to permit it to attain exactly the same consumption pattern as before if it so chose. Draw the new budget line and label it B_2. How many pushes per day must the rat be given to attain this budget line?

d. Given budget line B_2, the rat settled down to a new consumption pattern of about 8 milliliters of root beer and about 16 milliliters of Collins mix per day. Find this point on the diagram and label it E_2.

e. Sketch a possible pair of indifference curves for the rat. You don't have enough information to sketch the whole length of each curve exactly, but make use of all the information you do have.

f. The experimenters concluded that this rat was subject to a substitution effect of the normal type when the relative price of Collins mix was cut. What makes them think the increase in Collins mix consumption was the result of the consumption effect rather than the income effect?

SELF TEST

These sample test items will help you check how much you have learned. Answers are found at the end of the chapter. Scoring yourself: One or two wrong—on target. Three or four wrong—passing, but you haven't mastered the chapter yet. Five or more wrong—not good enough; start over and restudy the chapter.

_____ 1. Joan is Christmas shopping. She has $25 to spend buying gifts for her cousin, her mother, and her father. Which of the following is properly described as the alternatives of her rational choice problem?
   a. The utilities she hopes to provide to her relatives.
   b. Her limited budget, together with the prices of the goods.
   c. The possible gifts—ties, chocolates, calendars, and so on.
   d. All of the above are alternatives.

_____ 2. According to the principle of diminishing marginal utility, if consumption of a third slice of bread with a meal yields 10 utils, consumption of a sixth slice of bread must give
   a. more than 10 utils.
   b. less than 10 utils.
   c. between 5 and 10 utils.
   d. between 0 and 5 utils.

_____ 3. The consumer's budget is best thought of as
   a. a statement of the kinds of goods available to the consumer.
   b. a constraint on the consumer's range of choice.
   c. a representation of the total utility received from various choices.
   d. a representation of the marginal utility received from various choices.

_____ 4. Assume for a moment that utility is measurable. Then if a loaf of bread at 20 cents per loaf gives 10 utils, a quart of milk costing 50 cents must give how many utils in consumer equilibrium?
   a. 5 utils.
   b. 12.5 utils.
   c. 25 utils.
   d. 50 utils.

_____ 5. Let MU_a represent the marginal utility of Good a, MU_b the marginal utility of Good b, P_a the price of Good a, and P_b the price of Good b. Then in consumer equilibrium, which of the following must hold?
   a. $MU_a = MU_b$.
   b. $P_a = P_b$.
   c. $MU_a/MU_b = P_a/P_b$.
   d. $MU_a/MU_b = P_b/P_a$.

_____ 6. In equilibrium, a certain person consumes two units of Good X, which costs 30 cents per unit, and four units of Good Y, which costs 50 cents per unit. It can be concluded that for that person, in equilibrium, the ratio of the marginal utility of Good X to the Marginal utility of Good Y is
   a. 2/4.
   b. 4/2.
   c. 3/5.
   d. 5/3.

_____ 7. The change in consumption of a good that occurs when its price falls is the result of
   a. the substitution effect.
   b. the income effect.
   c. both of the above effects in combination.
   d. the complementarity of normal and inferior goods.

_____ 8. A good with an upward-sloping demand curve would have to
   a. be an inferior good.
   b. be a normal good.
   c. have no substitution effect.
   d. have no income effect.

_____ 9. Martha Smith is observed to consume ten quarts of milk per week at 50 cents per quart. One week the price of milk drops to 40 cents per quart; but in the same week, a thief steals $1 from her purse, reducing her weekly budget by that amount. On the basis of the theory of consumer behavior, which of the following quantities of milk would she be most likely to consume that week?
   a. Less than ten quarts.
   b. Ten quarts.
   c. More than ten quarts.
   d. More than ten quarts, but only if milk is assumed to be a normal good.

_____ 10. In July 1979, Ed Schwartz ate six ice cream cones at a price of 50 cents per cone. In July 1980, he ate seven ice cream cones at a price of 60 cents per cone. Which of the following is the most likely explanation of his behavior?
   a. His demand curve for ice cream cones slopes upward.
   b. Ice cream is an inferior good for him; he prefers cake if he can afford it.
   c. The marginal utility of ice cream increases, rather than decreases, as his consumption goes up, other things being equal.
   d. Both income and the prices of other goods went up from 1979 to 1980 by more, proportionately, than the price of ice cream rose.

Note: The remaining questions are based on the appendix to Chapter 22, in the textbook.

_____ 11. Which of the following baskets of goods cannot be a member of an indifference set to which the other three belong?
   a. Four pounds of meat, four pounds of cheese.
   b. Three pounds of meat, ten pounds of cheese.
   c. Five pounds of meat, three pounds of cheese.
   d. Four pounds of meat, three pounds of cheese.

_____ 12. In 1987, during a series of baseball games, the Reds beat the Astros, the Astros beat the Giants, and the Giants beat the Reds. We conclude that the relationship denoted by the word "beat" is
   a. subject to transitivity.
   b. not subject to transitivity.
   c. inherently meaningless.
   d. none of the above.

_____ 13. A positively sloped indifference curve might be possible in which of the following cases?
   a. If the rule of transitivity were violated.
   b. If the principle of diminishing marginal utility were violated.
   c. If the marginal utility of one of the goods diminished so far that it actually became negative.
   d. None of the above.

_____ 14. If a consumer has a budget of $10 per week, if eggs cost $1 per dozen, and if milk costs 50 cents per quart, then the consumer's budget line will have what slope (assuming eggs to be represented on the vertical axis)?
   a. 1/2.
   b. 1/2.
   c. 2.
   d. -2.

_____ 15. Given an indifference map, a fixed budget, and a fixed price for the good represented on the vertical axis, an increase in the price of the good represented on the horizontal axis is likely to move the consumption point
   a. up and to the right.
   b. up and to the left along the same indifference curve.
   c. to the left, either upward or downward.
   d. to the left and downward so long as the two goods are substitutes.

ANSWERS TO CHAPTER 22

Hands On

Problem 1 (a) The equilibrium market price is $10 per unit and the equilibrium quantity is 100 units per day. (b) Consumers would pay slightly less than $10 per unit for a 101st unit, and producers would not supply the 101st unit unless they received slightly more than $10. (c) Total consumer surplus is $250, equal to the area of the triangle labeled APE in the solution graph for Exhibit 22.1. Total producer surplus is $500, equal to the area of the triangle OPE. Total gains from trade are equal to the sum of the consumer and producer surplus, or $750. (d) The equilibrium price after the tax will rise to $12.50 and the equilibrium quantity will fall to $50. The new equilibrium point is labeled C on the solution graph. Revenue to the government is $375, equal to the area of the rectangle BCFD. Remaining consumer surplus is $62.50, equal to the area of the triangle ABC. Remaining producer surplus is $125, equal to the area of the triangle OFD. The excess burden of the tax is $175, equal to the area of the triangle CEF.

Exhibit 22.1 (ans.)

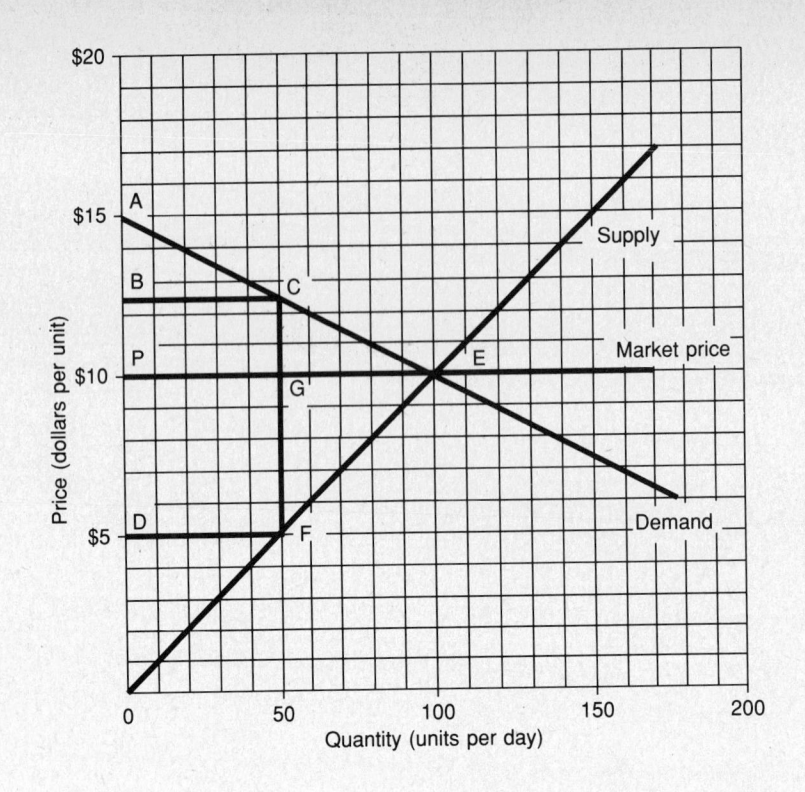

Problem 2 (a) A standard downward-sloping convex indifference curve can be drawn through A, D, and H, but not through A, D, and I. At least part of the section from D to I would have a zero or positive slope. This would contradict the "more is better" assumption on which indifference curves are normally drawn. (b) C, F, and I would give an indifference curve bent the wrong way—the marginal rate of substitution of flowers for cookies would increase rather than diminish. An indifference curve through B, E, and H would be a straight line with constant marginal rate of substitution—also not normally possible. A curve through A, D, and G would be fine, with the normal convex shape and a diminishing marginal rate of substitution. (c) Taken individually, there is nothing the matter with indifference curves through points A, E, and I or C, D, and G. But the two curves would cross, so they can't be part of the same indifference map. If they were, the principle of transitivity would be violated.

Problem 3 Start with a $3 price for books. Your $60 could buy 20 movies, if all spent on movies, or 20 books, if all spent on books. The budget line under these circumstances would be a straight line from 20 on the vertical axis to 20 on the horizontal axis. The equilibrium point would be A, as shown in the solution graph for Exhibit 22.3a. A $4 price for books would give you a new budget line and equilibrium point B (9 books). A $6 price moves you to point C (5 books) and a $12 price to point D (2 books). Using these data, plot the corresponding points a, b, c, and d as shown in the solution graph for Exhibit 22.3b. Sketch a smooth demand curve to pass through them. In the context of this graph, books and movies appear to be substitutes—raising the price of books increases the quantity of movie tickets you buy. If they were complements (for example, if you

Exhibit 22.3a (ans.)

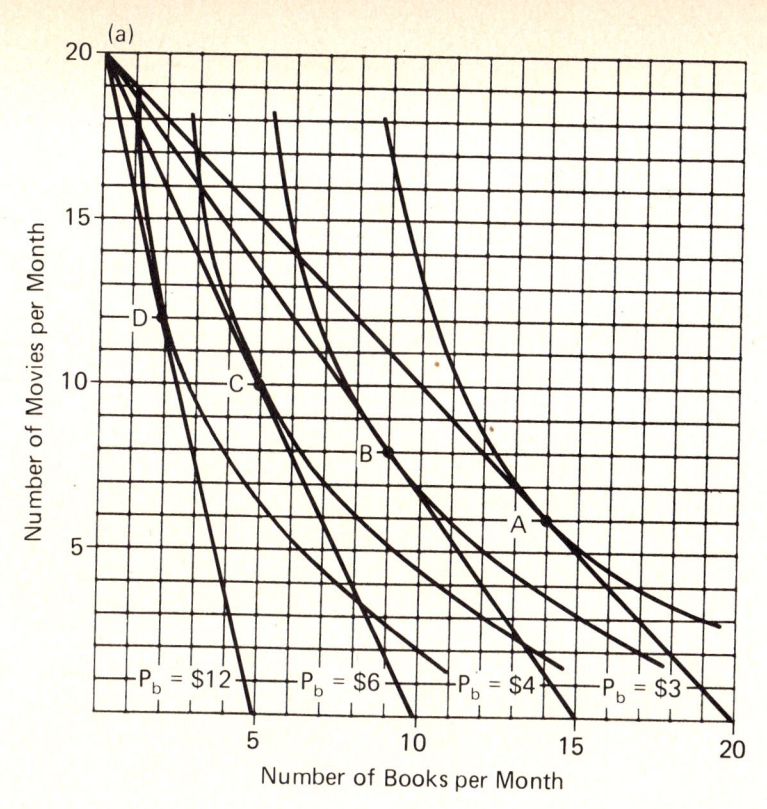

Exhibits 22.3b (ans.)

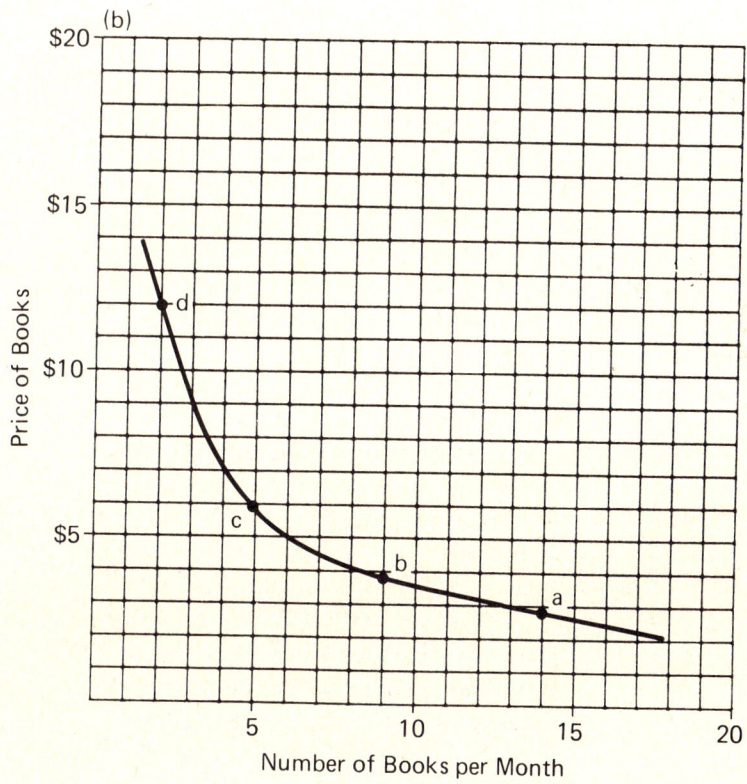

refused to see a movie unless you had already read the book), your indifference curves would be shaped differently, and the number of movies you saw would decrease as the price of books rose. Try sketching this case on a clean piece of graph paper.

Problem 4 (a) The budget lines and equilibrium points are given in the solution graph to Exhibit 22.4. (b) In this context, meat is a normal good, because, with prices unchanged, the quantity consumed increases as income increases. Bread is an inferior good, because the quantity consumed decreases as income increases.

Exhibit 22.4 (ans.)

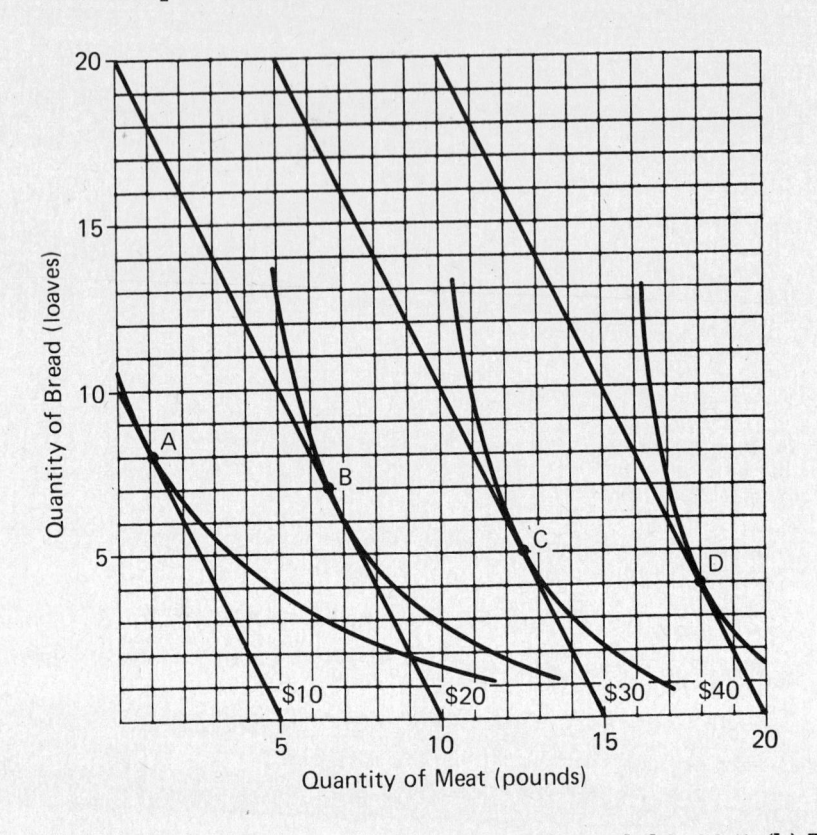

Problem 5 (a) See the solution graph for Exhibit 22.5. (b) This result strongly suggests a downward-sloping, convex indifference curve somewhat like I₂. Other shapes (e.g., concave or straight) would in most cases correspond to a "corner solution," that is, a diet of all one good or all of the other. (c) The slope of the curve is changed to -1/4 by the change in relative prices. At the new prices, the rat would need 440 pushes for the 11 milliliters of root beer plus 40 pushes for the 4 milliliters of Collins mix, or a total of 480 pushes, to reach the same point as before. This gives the budget line B₂ in the solution graph. (d) See solution graph. (e) You do know that I₁ is tangent to B₁ at E₁, and I₂ is tangent to B₂ at E₂. Also, you can assume that the curves are downward-sloping, convex and noncrossing. The curves shown are reasonable choices. (f) The income effect is defined as the part of the consumption change caused by the change in real income when prices change. However, in this case, the budget, in terms of pushes, was adjusted to keep real income the same, that is, to give sufficient purchasing power to buy the original selection. Any change, the reasoning continues, must thus be caused by the substitution effect alone. (Food for thought: Even though the rat's real income has not increased according to the reasoning just given, the rat is better off, that is, on a higher indifference curve after the price change. Compare the rat's

Exhibit 22.5 (ans.)

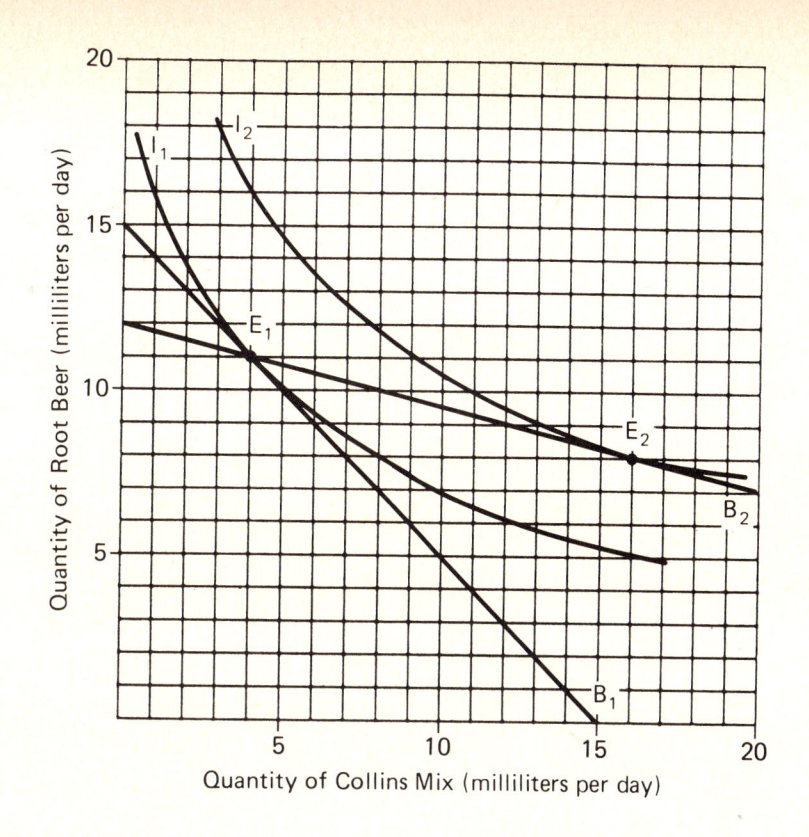

situation to that of a worker whose wages are indexed to the consumer price index. Can you argue that the worker is made better off the more inflation there is, assuming inflation does not affect all goods equally?)

Self Test

1. **c.** Item **a** is the objective and **b** is a constraint.
2. **b.** Diminishing marginal utility means the more you consume, the lower the added utility from an extra unit.
3. **b.** The budget is a constraint because it places a limit on how much of all goods can be consumed.
4. **c.** In equilibrium, the ratio of prices must equal the ratio of marginal utilities.
5. **c.** Same principle as question 4.
6. **c.** Same principle again. The price ratio must equal the ratio of marginal utilities, not the ratio of the quantities.
7. **c.** The income effect can work either way, toward increased consumption if the good is normal or toward decreased consumption if it is inferior.
8. **a.** Not only inferior, but with an income effect stronger than the substitution effect. This is a very unlikely case.
9. **c.** The theft just offsets the income effect of the price cut, which is to say that after both the price change and the theft, she still could buy the same combination of goods as before, but not more of both. But the substitution effect alone is enough to cause her to buy more milk.
10. **d.** The other explanations are very unlikely.
11. **d.** This combination is clearly less attractive than either **a** or **c**, hence it cannot be a member of the same indifference set.

273

12. **b.** This is a common situation in sports, but not in utility theory.
13. **c.** In this case, one of the "goods" would be a "bad."
14. **b.** The slope depends only on the ratio of prices, not the size of the budget.
15. **c.** If substitutes, to the left and up; if complements, to the left and down.

Chapter 23

Cost and Production

WHERE YOU'RE GOING

When you have mastered this chapter, you will understand

1. How economists view the concepts of costs and profits.
2. How short-run and long-run time frames are distinguished.
3. How costs vary in response to changes in the quantity of a variable input.
4. How a firm's cost structure can be represented geometrically.
5. What choices a firm faces in the course of long-run expansion.

In addition, you will add the following terms to your economic vocabulary:

Explicit costs
Implicit costs
Pure economic profit
Accounting profit
Normal profit
Fixed inputs
Variable inputs
Short run
Long run
Total physical product
Marginal physical product
Law of diminishing returns
Marginal cost
Marginal-average rule
Economies of scale
Diseconomies of scale
Constant returns to scale
Minimum efficient scale

	WALKING TOUR *After you have read this chapter at least once, you should work step by step through this walking tour. Fill in the blanks and answer the questions as you go along. After you have answered each question, check yourself by uncovering the answer given in the margin. If you do not understand why the answer given is the correct one, refer back to the proper section of the text.*

The Nature of Costs

All costs arise from the need to choose among alternative uses of scarce resources. This means that all costs are _____ *(opportunity)* costs. The various costs that a firm faces can be divided into categories. Opportunity costs that take the form of payments to outside suppliers, workers, and others who do not share in the firms ownership are called _____ *(explicit)* costs. Opportunity costs of using resources owned by the firm or contributed by its owners are _____ *(implicit)* costs. Classify each of the following as implicit or explicit costs:

1. Wages paid to hourly workers _____ *(explicit)*.
2. Interest paid on a bank loan _____ *(explicit)*.
3. Interest that owners could have earned by placing funds in a bank rather than investing them in their firm _____ *(implicit)*.
4. Salary that a lawyer could have earned by working for a large firm rather than starting her own practice _____ *(implicit)*.

The distinction between implicit and explicit costs is important for understanding the concept of profit. When explicit costs are subtracted from total revenue, the result is _____ *(accounting)* profit. When all types of opportunity costs, including both implicit and explicit costs, are subtracted from total revenue, the result is _____ *(pure economic)* profit. Sometimes the opportunity cost of capital is called _____ *(normal)* profit.

Production and Costs in the Short Run

Inputs that cannot be easily increased or decreased in a short time are called _____ *(fixed)* inputs. Those that can be easily increased or decreased are known as _____ *(variable)* inputs. The distinction between fixed and variable inputs is the basis for distinguishing between the long run and the short run for purposes of model building. The time horizon within which only some inputs

short	can be varied is the [long/short] run. That within which all inputs can be varied, including fixed inputs, is the [long/short] run.
long	
	The added output, expressed in physical units, that is produced by one added unit of a variable input is known as the input's
marginal physical	_____ product. As one such input is increased with all others remaining fixed, a point will be reached beyond which the marginal physical product of the variable input will begin to
decrease	[increase/decrease]. This principle is known as the law of
diminishing returns	_____. In geometric terms, it means that after some point, the slope of the firm's total physical product curve will
decrease	[increase/decrease].
	The increase in cost needed to raise the output of some good or
marginal	service by one unit is called _____ cost. Given a constant input price, the law of diminishing returns implies that a
positive	firm's marginal cost curve will have a [positive/negative] slope, at least beyond some point. Thus, marginal cost curves are commonly
U	drawn with a shape somewhat like the letter [L/U]. The marginal cost will continue to have such a shape even if more than one input
fixed	is varied, so long as there is at least one _____ input.
	A complete set of cost concepts can be developed on the basis of the firm's total fixed and variable costs. Name each of the following types of cost:
total variable	1. Total cost minus total fixed cost: _____ cost.
average total	2. Total cost divided by quantity of output: _____ cost.
average variable	3. Total variable cost divided by quantity of output: _____ cost.
	4. Change in total cost divided by change in quantity of output:
marginal	_____ cost.
average fixed	5. Total fixed cost divided by quantity of output: _____ cost.
	Some basic geometric relationships prevail among the members of the cost-curve family. First, the point of minimum slope on the firm's total cost curve occurs at the same quantity of output as the
minimum	[minimum/maximum] point on the firm's marginal cost curve. This
does	relationship [does/does not] also hold for the total variable cost
height	curve. Thus, the _____ of the marginal cost curve corresponds to the _____ of the total or total variable cost
slope	curve. In addition, according to the marginal-average rule, the marginal cost curve will intersect the average total cost curve at the

average total | point where [marginal/average total] cost is a minimum. The intersection of the marginal cost curve with the average variable cost curve occurs where [marginal/average variable] cost is at a minimum.

average variable

Long-Run Costs and Economies of Scale

all
fixed

In the long run, [all/not all] of the firms inputs are considered variable. The quantity of those inputs that are [fixed/variable] in the short run define the size of a firm's plant. Each plant size can be represented by its own U-shaped short-run average total cost curve. The long-run average cost curve for the firm can be described as the _____ of the set of short-run average total cost curves. The long-run average cost curve [is tangent to/intersects] each short-run average total cost curve. When the long-run average cost curve is U-shaped, the point of tangency occurs at the minimum point on the short-run average total cost curve for [all/only one] of the possible short-run average cost curves.

envelope
is tangent to

only one

economies

When a firm's long-run average cost decreases as output increases, the firm is said to experience _____ of scale. If its long-run average cost increases as output increases, it is said to experience _____ of scale. If the firm experiences neither economies nor diseconomies of scale, then it has _____ to scale. For a firm with a long-run total cost curve that has a negative slope at first, and then becomes flat, the point where economies of scale cease is known as the _____ scale.

diseconomies
constant returns

minimum efficient

HANDS ON

Now that you have reviewed the concepts introduced in this chapter, it is time for some hands-on practice with the analytical tools that have been introduced. Work through each problem in this section carefully, and then check your results against those given at the end of the chapter.

Problem 1

This problem is based on Exhibit 23.1a, which gives some production data for the Bravo Corp. Use the data given there in answering the questions that follow.

Exhibit 23.1a

Labor Hours Input	Total Physical Product	Marginal Physical Product
0	0	
1	1.0	___
2	3.5	___
3	8.5	___
4	15.0	___
5	19.0	___
6	21.0	___
7	22.5	___

a. Use the data in the first two columns of Exhibit 23.1a to fill in the marginal physical product column.
b. Use the data you have entered in the marginal physical product column of the table to plot the firm's marginal physical product curve. Suggestion: plot the points midway between the numbers given on the horizontal axis of the diagram. Thus, your first point will be plotted at 0.5 on the horizontal scale and 1.0 on the vertical scale, the next point at 1.5 on the horizontal scale, and so on. When you have plotted all the points, connect them with a smooth curve.

Exhibit 23.1b

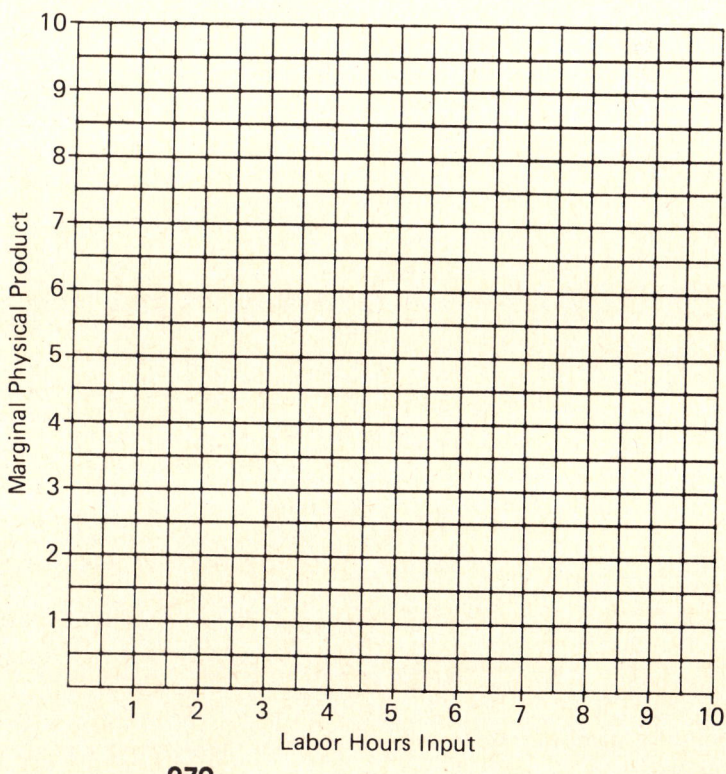

279

c. Does the law of diminishing returns apply to the Bravo Corp? If so, beyond what level of output does the Bravo Corp. encounter diminishing returns?

Problem 2

The questions that follow refer to the total cost curve for a typical firm shown in Exhibit 23.2. In each case, explain how you get your answer.

Exhibit 23.2

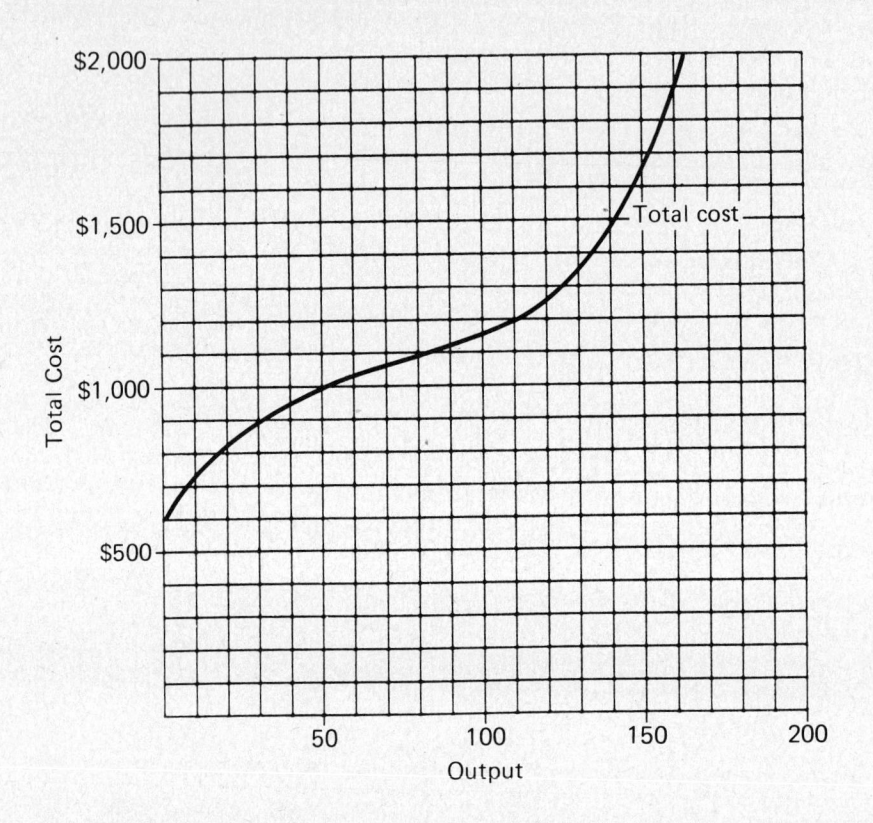

a. What is total fixed cost for this firm?
b. What is average total cost for the firm at 50 units of output? At 150 units? At what level of output does average total cost reach a minimum?
c. What is marginal cost for this firm at 40 units of output? At what level of output is marginal cost at a minimum? At what level of output is marginal cost equal to average total cost?

Problem 3

The questions that follow are based on the average total cost and average variable costs for a typical firm that are shown in Exhibit 23.3. In each case, explain how you get your answer.
a. What is average fixed cost for this firm at 80 units of output? What is total fixed cost for the firm?
b. What is the firm's marginal cost at an output of 70 units? An output of 100 units?
c. Sketch the section of the firm's marginal cost curve lying between about 60 units of output and about 120 units of output.

Exhibit 23.3

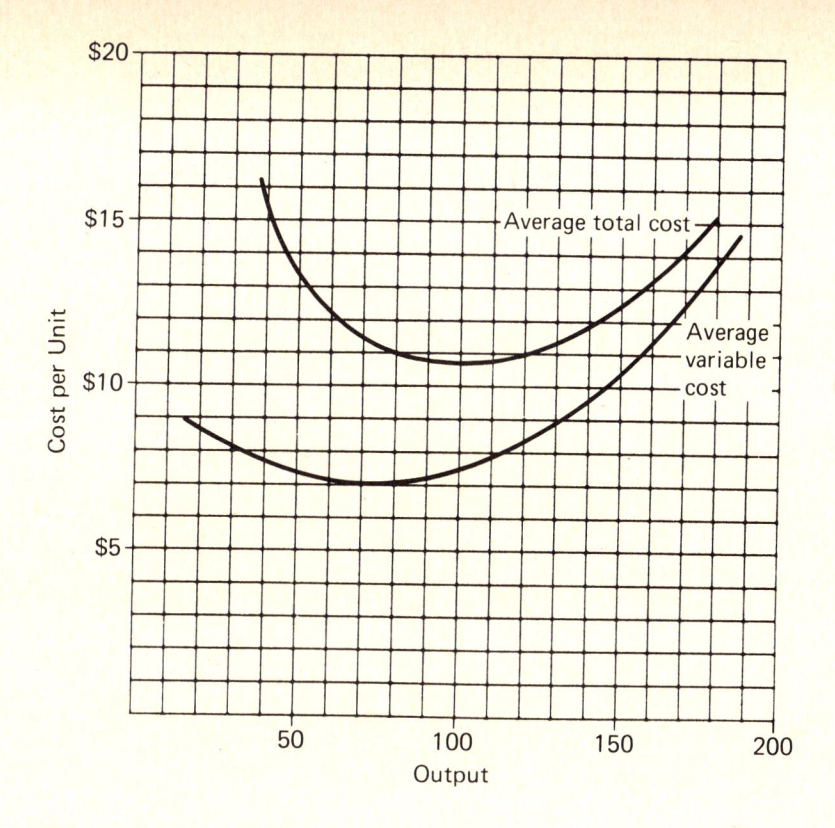

Problem 4

The following questions refer to Exhibit 23.4, which shows a long-run average cost curve and two short-run average total cost curves labeled A and B.

a. If the firm's plant size is such that short-run average total cost curve A applies, what level of output will minimize short-run

Exhibit 23.4

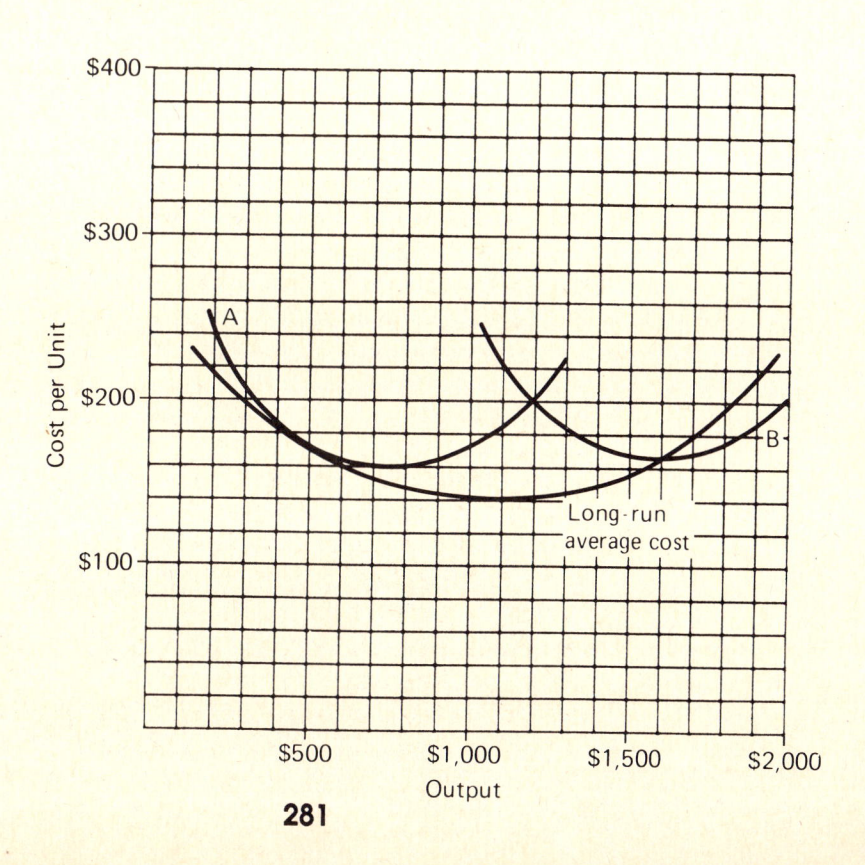

average total cost? For what long-run level of output would a plant of size A be the cost-minimizing plant?
b. One of the two short-run cost curves is not drawn correctly. Which one? What is wrong with it?
c. Over what range of output does this firm experience economies of scale? Diseconomies of scale?

Problem 5

This problem is based on the optional appendix to this chapter of the textbook. The questions refer to the set of isoquants shown in Exhibit 23.5a. The diagram represents a production process in which labor and energy are the only variable inputs.

Exhibit 23.5a

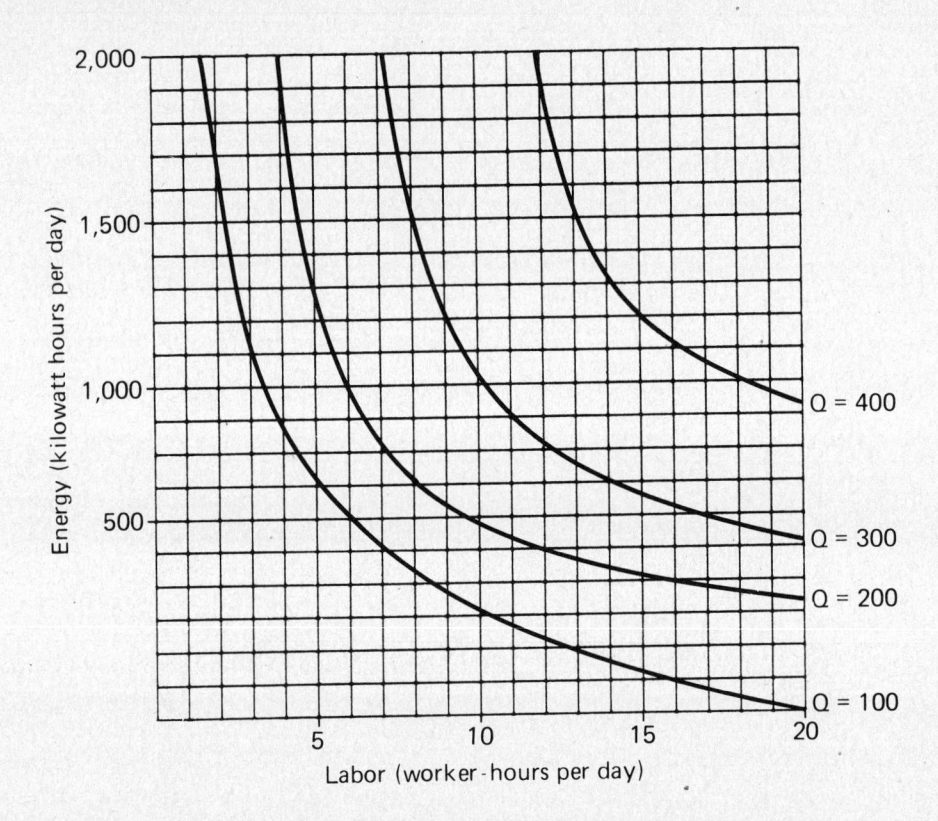

a. Assume that the wage rate is $10 per hour and that energy costs 10 cents per kilowatt hour. Given these input prices, draw a budget line that represents $120 total outlays for variable inputs. Label this budget line L_1. What is the maximum quantity of output that can be produced for a total variable cost of $120?
b. Assuming the same input prices, what is the minimum cost of producing 100 units of output? (The possible production methods are shown by the isoquant labeled Q = 100.) How much labor should be used? How much energy? Label this point A.
c. Still assuming the same input prices, show the least-cost method of producing 200 units of output as point B, the least-cost method for 300 units as point C, and the least-cost method for 400 units as point D. Connect these points and the origin to get the expansion path.

d. Use the information given by the expansion path and the budget lines you have drawn to construct a total variable cost curve in Exhibit 23.5b.
e. Suppose the price of energy rises fourfold to 40 cents per kilowatt hour. What would then be the least-cost method of producing 100 units of output? Show this as point E.

Exhibit 23.5b

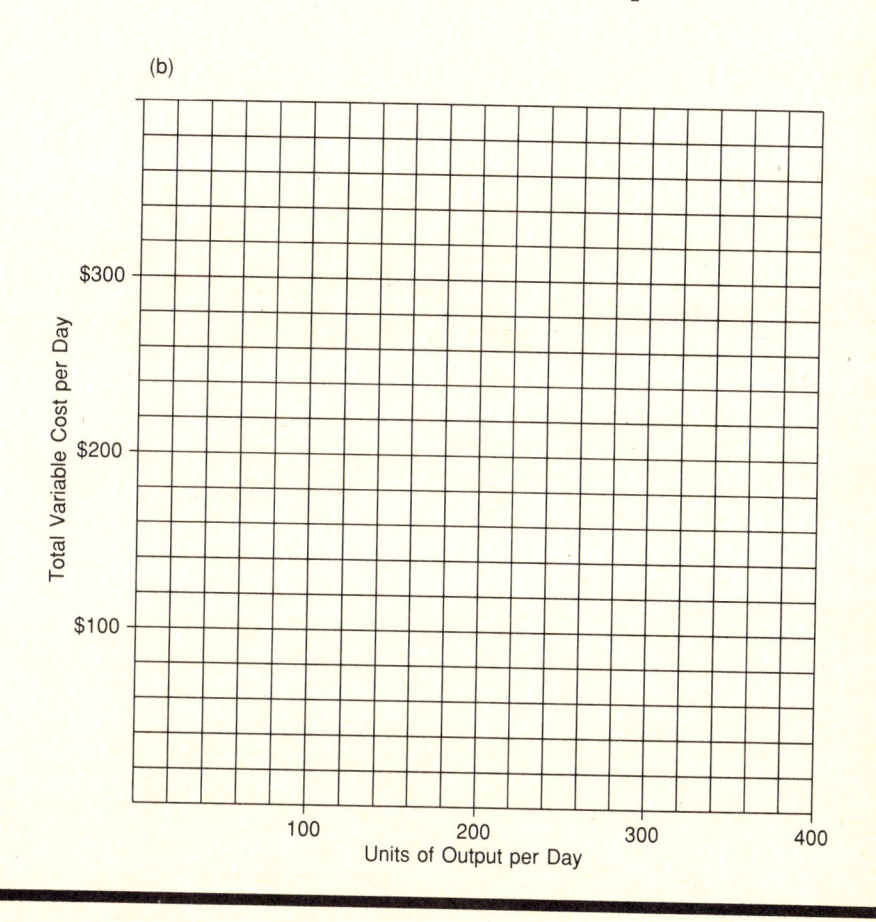

(b)

Total Variable Cost per Day vs *Units of Output per Day*

SELF TEST

These sample test items will help you check how much you have learned. Answers are found at the end of the chapter. Scoring yourself: One or two wrong—on target. Three or four wrong—passing, but you haven't mastered the chapter yet. Five or more wrong—not good enough; start over and restudy the chapter.

_____ 1. If a firm has total revenues of $100 million, explicit costs of $90 million and implicit costs of $20 million, its pure economic profit is
 a. $80 million.
 b. $70 million.
 c. $10 million.
 d. -$10 million.

_____ 2. Let A stand for accounting profit, P for pure economic profit, E for explicit costs, and I for implicit costs. Then
 a. P = A - E.
 b. P = A - I.
 c. A = P - I.
 d. A = P - E.

283

3. A firm has total capital of $500 million. The opportunity cost of capital is 12 percent per year. The firm earns an accounting profit of $65 million and has no other implicit costs. Its pure economic profit is
   a. -$5 million.
   b. $5 million.
   c. $60 million.
   d. $65 million.

4. If a firm decided it could save on total cost by unplugging itself from the local electric utility and buying its own generating equipment, we could assume that
   a. both its fixed and variable costs would fall.
   b. both its fixed and variable costs would rise.
   c. its fixed costs would rise and its variable costs would fall.
   d. its fixed costs would fall and its variable costs would rise.

5. The costs defining the size of a firm's plant are
   a. fixed in the short run and variable in the long run.
   b. fixed in the long run and variable in the short run.
   c. fixed in both the long and the short run.
   d. variable in both the long and the short run.

6. The law of diminishing returns implies that the marginal physical product curve
   a. must be U-shaped.
   b. must be shaped like an upside-down U.
   c. must have a negative slope throughout its length.
   d. must have a negative slope for at least part of its length.

7. If a marginal physical product curve and an average physical product curve were both drawn on a single diagram,
   a. the marginal curve would cut the average curve at the minimum point of the latter.
   b. the marginal curve would cut the average curve at the minimum point of the former.
   c. the marginal curve would cut the average curve at the maximum point of the latter.
   d. the marginal curve would cut the average curve at the maximum point of the former.

8. Where the marginal cost curve is below the average variable cost curve,
   a. the average variable cost curve must have a negative slope.
   b. the marginal cost curve must have a negative slope.
   c. the average variable cost curve must have a positive slope.
   d. the marginal cost curve must have positive slope.

9. The quantity of output where the total variable cost curve stops getting flatter and starts getting steeper must be the quantity corresponding to the minimum of which of the following?
   a. Average total cost.
   b. Average variable cost.
   c. Average fixed cost.
   d. Marginal cost.

_____ 10. Suppose that for a certain firm, average variable cost is $10 per unit at 20 units of output and $11 per unit at 21 units of output. It follows that marginal cost for that range of output must be
   a. about $1.
   b. about $11.
   c. about $31.
   d. impossible to calculate from the information given.

_____ 11. Short-run average total cost curve for a plant of given size is equal to long-run average cost
   a. for all levels of output.
   b. whenever short-run average total cost is at its minimum.
   c. for the level of output for which the plant size is best suited in the long run.
   d. none of the above.

_____ 12. The long-run average cost curve
   a. passes through the minimum points of all short-run average total cost curves.
   b. passes through the minimum points of all short-run average variable cost curves.
   c. is the envelope of all short-run average total cost curves.
   d. is the envelope of all short-run average variable cost curves.

_____ 13. A firm is said to experience economies of scale over the range of output for which long-run average cost
   a. is constant.
   b. is falling.
   c. is rising.
   d. economies of scale are not related to long-run average cost.

_____ 14. The minimum efficient scale for a firm is the level of output at which
   a. economies of scale cease.
   b. diseconomies of scale begin.
   c. short-run average variable cost first exceeds long-run average cost.
   d. none of the above.

_____ 15. A line showing the various combinations of variable inputs that can be used to produce a given amount of output is known as a/an
   a. indifference curve.
   b. isocost curve.
   c. isoquant.
   d. production possibility frontier.

ANSWERS TO CHAPTER 23

Hands On

Problem 1 (a) The entries for the marginal physical product column are: 1.0; 2.5; 5.0; 6.5; 4.0; 2.0; 1.5. (b) See solution graph for Exhibit 23.1b. (c) Diminishing returns begins beyond 3.5 units of output as the graph is drawn, that is, at the point were the slope of the marginal physical product curve becomes negative.

Exhibit 23.1b (ans.)

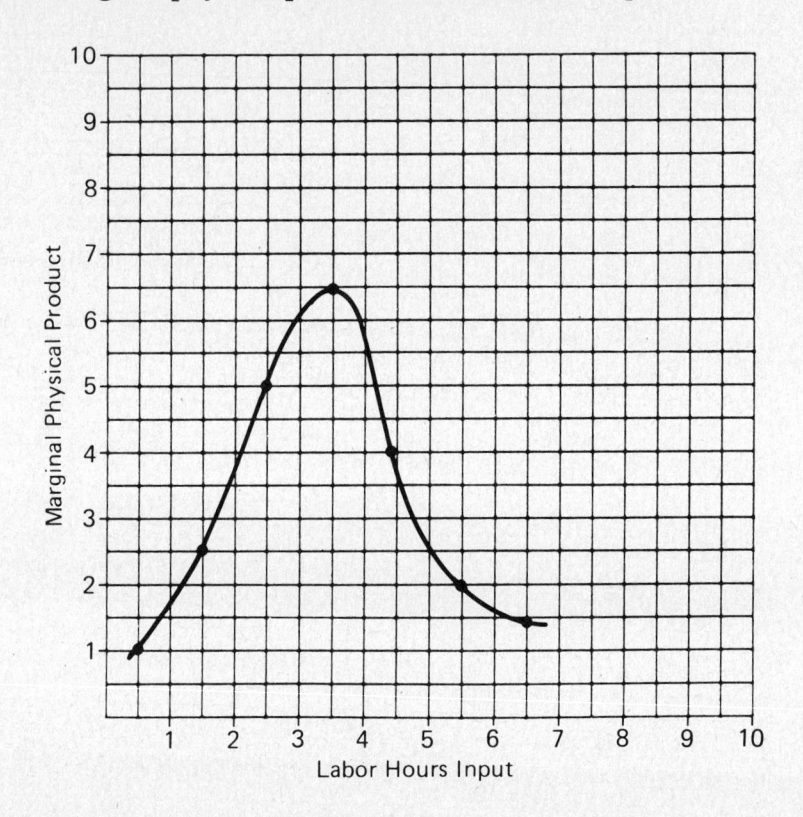

Problem 2 (a) Total fixed cost for this firm is $600. You can determine this by the intersection of the average total cost curve with the vertical axis. When output is zero, the only costs are fixed costs. (b) To find average total cost, divide total cost (the vertical distance) by quantity (the horizontal distance). Thus, average total cost is $20 at 50 units of output and about $11.14 at 150 units of output. Because average total cost is the ratio of the vertical distance to the horizontal distance, it can also be thought of as the slope of a line from the origin to the total cost curve. Place one end of a ruler on the origin and swing the blade up until it just touches the total cost curve (at about 130 units of output). This is the point of minimum average total cost. (c) Marginal cost is equal to the slope of the total cost curve. Draw a tangent to the curve at 40 units of output—the slope is about 0.5, so the marginal cost is about $5. (Be careful to notice that the units on the vertical axis are ten times as large as those on the horizontal axis). Marginal cost is at a minimum at the point where the total cost curve has the least slope, that is, where it

just stops bending down and starts bending up. Find this point (about 80 units of output) by sliding a ruler along the total cost curve, keeping it tangent. Marginal and average total cost are equal at 130 units of output—the point where a line drawn from the origin is just tangent to the total cost curve.

Problem 3 (a) At 80 units of output, average fixed cost is $4. Figure this out by measuring the gap between the average total cost and average variable cost curves. Multiply average fixed cost by quantity to get total fixed cost, which is $320. (b) Marginal cost and average variable cost are equal where average variable cost is at a minimum, which is 70 units of output. Marginal cost at 70 units of output is thus $7. Following the same reasoning, marginal cost is about $10.80 at 100 units of output. (c) As you discovered in answering the previous question, the marginal cost curve must pass through the average cost curves at their respective minimum points. Draw a smooth upward-sloping curve that does this.

Problem 4 (a) The output-minimizing short-run average cost, given plant size A, is about 750 units—the minimum point on A. The level of output for which plant size A produces minimum long-run cost is found where short-run cost curve A is tangent to the long-run curve, or about 500 units. At larger levels of output, some larger plant size with a short-run curve is not shown but tangent to the long-run curve would be better. (b) Short-run cost curve B is drawn wrong. It should not intersect the long-run curve, but instead, should be tangent to it from the inside. As drawn, there is a range of output (1,600 units and up) for which short-run total cost is lower than long-run total cost—an impossibility. (Comment: Although the question asks which of the short-run curves is drawn wrong, one could say instead that if B is a valid short-run curve, the long-run curve is drawn wrong. It should be tangent to B at about 1,800 units of output. Redraw the long-run curve this way. (c) Economies of scale continue to about 1,100 units of output, after which diseconomies of scale begin.

Problem 5 (a) $120 spent on labor would buy 12 labor hours, and $120 spent on energy would buy 1,200 kilowatt hours. Thus, the combinations that can be bought for $120 are shown by the budget line L_1 that runs between 12 on the horizontal axis and 1,200 on the vertical axis, as shown in the solution graph for Exhibit 23.5a. The greatest possible production for this cost is represented by the highest isoquant that the budget line touches—in this case, 100 units of output. (b) The minimum cost of producing 100 units of output corresponds to the lowest budget line that is touched by the isoquant Q = 100. In this case, the isoquant is just tangent to L_1, the $120 budget line, at point A. Any lower cost budget line would miss the isoquant altogether. Point A corresponds to 6 labor hours and 600 kilowatt hours of energy. (c) Construct additional budget lines L_2, L_3, and L_4. Each has the same slope (determined by the input prices) and is drawn just tangent to the isoquants Q = 200, Q = 300, and Q = 400. The expansion path is shown in the solution graph.

Exhibit 23.5a (ans.)

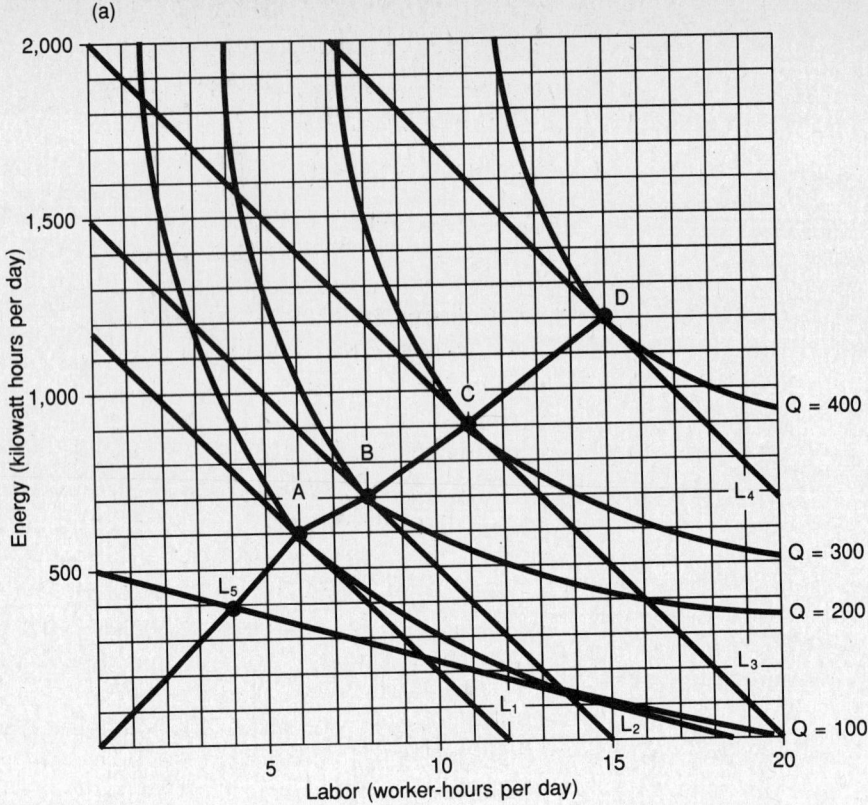

Exhibit 23.5b (ans.)

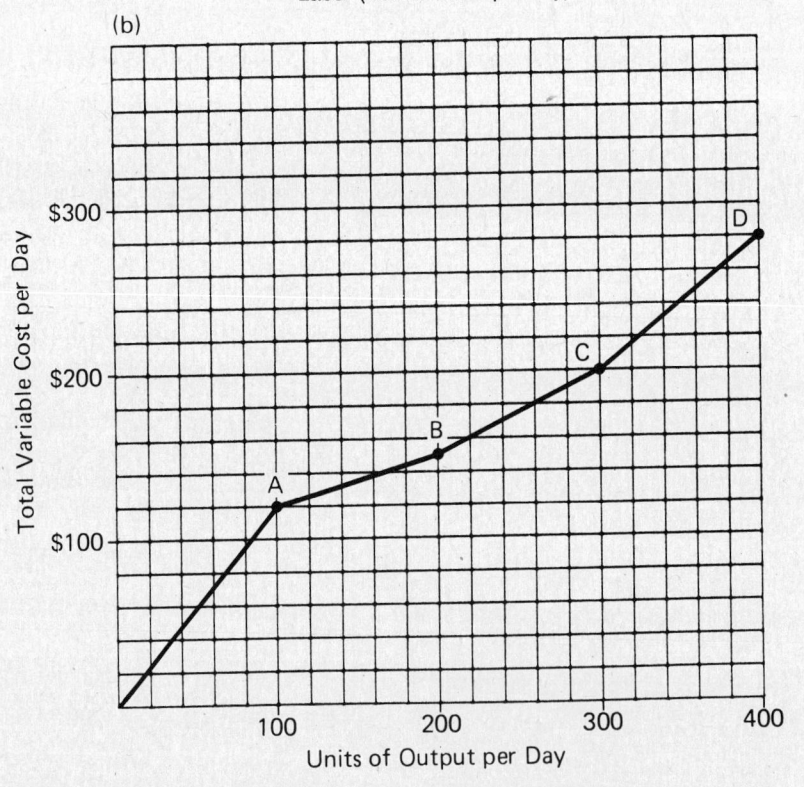

(d) You can tell the total variable cost of each of the points A, B, C, and D by multiplying the quantities of inputs by their prices. Plot these costs and the output to get the curve shown in the solution graph for Exhibit 23.5b. (e) The increase in energy price changes the slope of the budget lines. Budget line L_5, which has a slope of

288

-0.25 and is just tangent to isoquant Q = 100, shows the new least-cost method of producing 100 units of output. This calls for 14 labor hours and 150 kilowatt hours of energy, for a total variable cost of $200 per day.

Self Test

1. **d.** This is a pure economic loss.
2. **b.** Pure economic profit equals accounting profit minus implicit costs. Accounting profit, in turn, means revenue minus explicit costs.
3. **b.** The implicit cost of capital is $60 million ($500 million x 0.12).
4. **c.** The cost of the generating equipment would be a fixed cost, but by assumption, the variable cost of operating the generator would be less than the variable cost of buying electricity.
5. **a.** In the long run the firm can change the size of its plant.
6. **d.** It may have an initial upward-sloping section, but it does not have to.
7. **c.** This is another application of the marginal-average rule.
8. **a.** If marginal cost is less than average cost, each unit of output added will pull the average down. Note that part of the upward-sloping segment of the marginal cost curve lies below the average variable cost curve.
9. **d.** Because the slope of the curve is equal to marginal cost.
10. **c.** Total variable cost at 20 units is $200 (20 units x AVC of $10 per unit), and total variable cost is $231 at 21 units (21 x $11). Marginal cost is the increase in total variable cost.
11. **c.** Answer **b** is true only for the plant size corresponding to the minimum point on the long-run total cost curve.
12. **c.** That is, it is just tangent to them without intersecting any of them.
13. **b.** Answer **a** is constant returns to scale and **c** is diseconomies of scale.
14. **a.** This is the end of the negatively sloped portion of the long-run cost curve.
15. **c.** Isoquant means "equal quantity."

Chapter 24

Supply under Perfect Competition

WHERE YOU'RE GOING

When you have mastered this chapter, you will understand

1. What characteristics define the structure of a market.
2. What determines the profit-maximizing output level in the short run for a perfectly competitive firm.
3. Under what conditions a firm will continue to operate even if it sustains a loss.
4. How a firm's short-run supply curve is related to its cost curves.
5. What are the conditions for long-run equilibrium in a perfectly competitive industry.
6. What determines the shape of the long-run supply curve for a perfectly competitive industry.

In addition, you will add the following terms to your economic vocabulary:
Market structure
Perfect competition
Monopoly
Oligopoly
Monopolistic competition
Price taker
Marginal revenue

WALKING TOUR

After you have read this chapter at least once, you should work step by step through this walking tour. Fill in the blanks and answer the questions as you go along. After you have answered each question, check yourself by uncovering the answer given in the margin. If you do not understand why the answer given is the correct one, refer back to the proper section of the text.

The Concept of Market Structure

Economists refer to the conditions under which competition occurs

market structure   in a market as _____. Market structure is defined in terms of the number and size of firms, the nature of the product, and the ease of entry and exit of firms.

290

A market structure characterized by a large number of small firms, a homogeneous product, and freedom of entry and exit is

perfect competition _____. One in which there is only one firm selling a unique product and protected from the entry of rivals is

monopoly _____. One in which there are a few firms, at least some of which are large in relation to the size of the market, is

oligopoly known as _____. Finally, one in which there are many small firms, a differentiated product, and easy entry and exit is

monopolistic competition known as _____.

are   Oligopoly and monopolistic competition [are/are not] descriptive of many real-world market structures. Perfect competition and

are not monopoly [are/are not] descriptive of many real-world markets.

ideal types They may be called _____. Despite the fact that few markets fit these structures exactly, they are useful because they form the basis for precise models used as a standard of comparison.

    Market structures also differ in terms of how active a role is played by entrepreneurship. Entrepreneurial competition is very

oligopoly important in the market structures of _____ and

monopolistic competition _____. On the other hand, the definitions of the ideal-

perfect competition, type market structures of _____ and _____

  monopoly are such as to leave relatively limited scope for entrepreneurial competition.

Perfect Competition and Supply in the Short Run

Perfectly competitive firms sell their output at prices that are determined by forces beyond their control. For that reason, they are

price takers known as _____. An individual perfectly competitive

horizontal firm thus faces a demand curve that is _____. At all levels of output, marginal revenue for such a firm is equal to

market price _____.

    The profit-maximizing output level for a perfectly competitive firm can be established by comparing marginal revenue (market price) and marginal cost. If, at a given level of output, marginal revenue is greater than marginal cost the firm can increase profit

increasing by [increasing/decreasing] output. If marginal revenue is less than

decreasing marginal cost, profit can be increased by [increasing/decreasing] output. Thus, profit is maximized at the point where marginal cost is

291

equal	_____ to marginal revenue—provided certain other conditions are met.
	In particular, it is necessary to consider average total and variable cost, as well as marginal cost. If market price is above average total cost at the point of profit maximization, the firm will earn a
pure economic profit	_____. If market price is above average variable cost but below average total cost at the point where it equals marginal cost,
loss	the firm will experience a _____. Under these circum-
operate	stances, the firm's best strategy, in the short run, is to [operate/shut down]. If the price is not expected to recover at least to the level of average total cost in the future, then the firm's best long-
shut down	run strategy is to [operate/shut down]. If price is below average variable cost at the point where it equals marginal cost, then the firm's
shut down	best short-run strategy is to [operate/shut down].
	The short-run supply curve for a perfectly competitive firm can
positively	be described as the [positively/negatively] sloped section of its
marginal	_____ cost curve lying above the intersection with the
average variable	_____ cost curve. The short-run supply curve for an
horizontal	industry can be found through [vertical/horizontal] summation of the firms' supply curves, assuming that input prices remain constant as industry output changes in the short run. If input prices in-
steeper	crease, the industry supply curve will be [steeper/flatter] than the sum of the firms' supply curves.

Long-Run Equilibrium under Perfect Competition

In the long run, the free entry and exit property of perfect competition becomes important. The conditions for long-run competitive equilibrium can be characterized in terms of three equalities. In order that each individual firm have no incentive to increase or decrease output, _____ must be equal to _____ for each firm. In order that each firm have no incentive to change the size of the plant in which it operates, _____ cost must equal _____ cost. And in order that firms have no incentive either to enter or to leave the industry, _____ cost for each firm must be equal to _____. Only when these conditions hold for each firm—that is when the marginal cost curve, marginal revenue (price) curve, short-run average total cost

price, marginal cost

SR average total
LR average
LR average
price

curve, and long-run average cost curve all pass through a single point—can the competitive market be in long-run equilibrium.

HANDS ON

Now that you have reviewed the concepts introduced in this chapter, it is time for some hands-on practice with the analytical tools that have been introduced. Work through each problem in this section carefully, and then check your results against those given at the end of the chapter.

Problem 1

The following questions are based on Exhibit 24.1a, which shows total cost and total variable cost curves, together with four alternative total revenue curves, for a typical perfectly competitive firm.
a. Each of the four total revenue curves shown corresponds to a different product price. What is the price for each curve? Explain how you get your answer.
b. Working from the figure, fill in the blanks in Exhibit 24.1b. What happens to the profit-maximizing level of output as the price rises? Does this correspond with your expectations regarding the shape of such a firm's supply curve?
c. Instead of filling in the table, you could find the profit-maximizing level of output for each price directly from the graph. Explain how you would proceed. Do the profit maximization points you get by this method correspond to points where marginal cost and marginal revenue are equal? Explain how you can tell.

Exhibit 24.1a

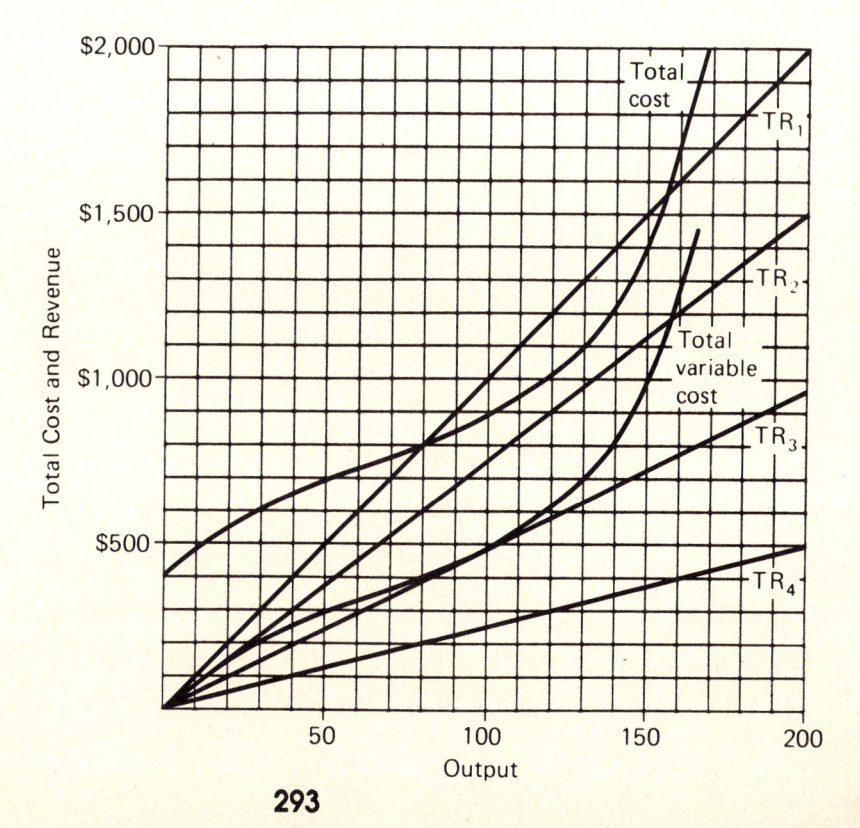

Exhibit 24.1b

Price \ Output	Total Revenue $2.50	Total Revenue $5.00	Total Revenue $7.50	Total Revenue $10.00	Total Cost (same for all prices)	Profit (or Loss) $2.50	Profit (or Loss) $5.00	Profit (or Loss) $7.50	Profit (or Loss) $10.00
0	$___	$___	$___	$___	$___	$___	$___	$___	$___
70	___	___	___	___	___	___	___	___	___
80	___	___	___	___	___	___	___	___	___
90	___	___	___	___	___	___	___	___	___
100	___	___	___	___	___	___	___	___	___
110	___	___	___	___	___	___	___	___	___
120	___	___	___	___	___	___	___	___	___
130	___	___	___	___	___	___	___	___	___
140	___	___	___	___	___	___	___	___	___
150	___	___	___	___	___	___	___	___	___

Problem 2

Working from the cost curves in Exhibit 24.2a, complete the table in Exhibit 24.2b. Then, assuming a price of $1.30, also use the cost curves in 24.2a to complete Exhibit 24.2c. Using a colored pen or pencil, show where this firm's short-run supply curve lies.

Exhibit 24.2a

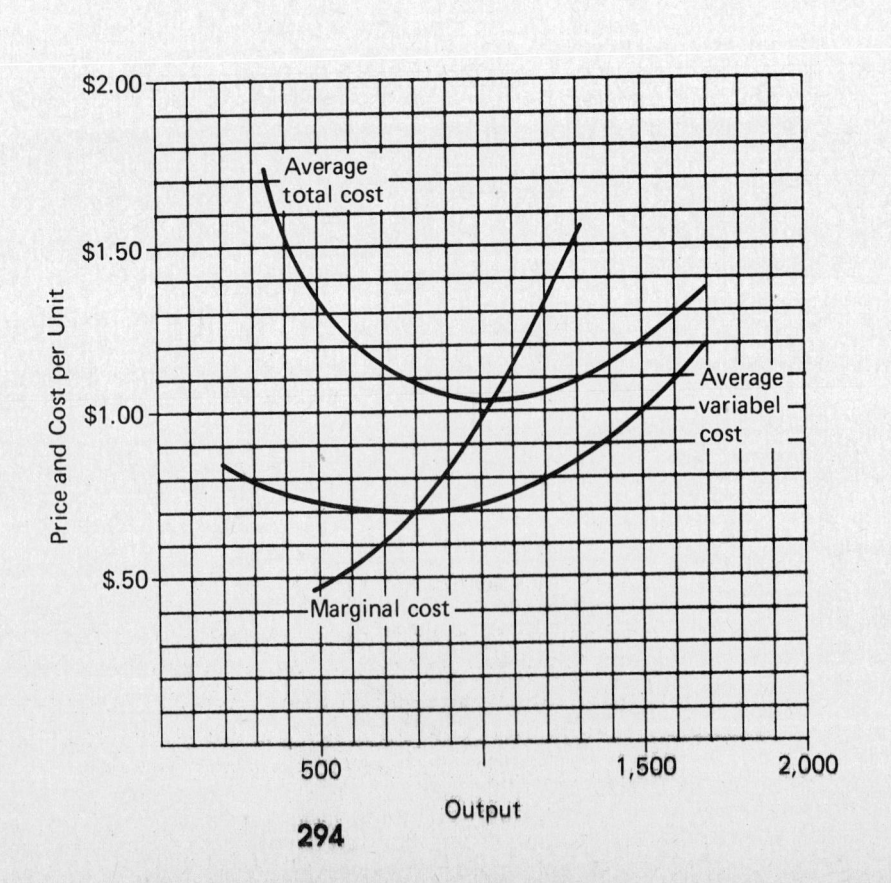

Exhibit 24.2b

Price	Profit-Maximizing Output	Total Revenue	Total Cost	Profit (or Loss)
$ .60	$_____	$_____	$_____	$_____
.70	_____	_____	_____	_____
.80	_____	_____	_____	_____
.90	_____	_____	_____	_____
1.00	_____	_____	_____	_____
1.10	_____	_____	_____	_____
1.20	_____	_____	_____	_____
1.30	_____	_____	_____	_____

Exhibit 24.2c

Output	Total Revenue	Total Cost	Profit (or Loss)
400	$_____	$_____	$_____
600	_____	_____	_____
800	_____	_____	_____
1,000	_____	_____	_____
1,200	_____	_____	_____
1,400	_____	_____	_____
1,600	_____	_____	_____

Problem 3

Exhibit 24.3 shows three alternative short-run supply curves and three alternative short-run demand curves for a typical perfectly competitive industry. In answering the questions that follow, assume that input prices do not change as industry output changes, unless you are told to assume otherwise.

Exhibit 24.3

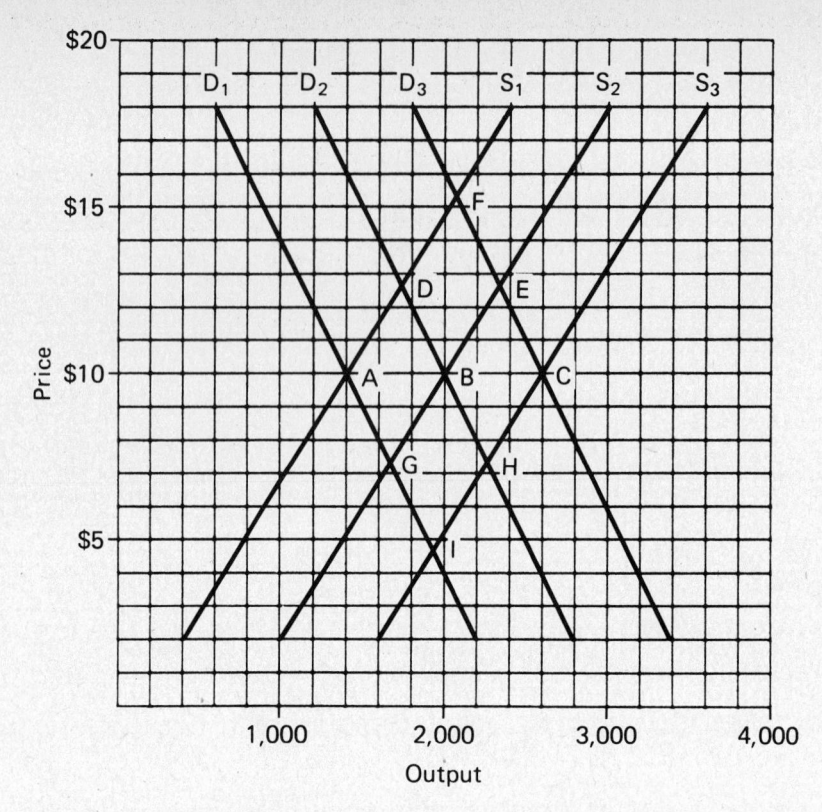

a. Suppose that initially supply curve S_2 and demand curve D_2 apply and that the industry is in long-run equilibrium at point B. Then the price of a good that is a substitute for the product of this industry increases. Of the curves and points shown, which would best represent the path to a new short-run equilibrium to this industry? Which would best represent the path to long-run equilibrium? As the industry moves first to a new short-run and then to a new long-run equilibrium, how would a typical individual firm in the industry react? Would any entry or exit of firms occur?

b. Repeat the analysis required by the previous question for the case in which, beginning from point B, an increase takes place in the price of a good that is a complement to the product of this industry.

c. On the basis of your answers to parts **a** and **b** of this problem, sketch the industry's long-run supply curve. Label it LS_1.

d. Assume now that for this industry, input prices tend to increase as industry output increases. Sketch an alternative long-run industry supply curve, passing through point B, to illustrate this case. Label it LS_2.

e. Suppose finally that the supplier of an important input to this industry experiences strong economies of scale, so that input prices for this industry tend to drop as the industry output increases. Sketch a long-run supply curve LS_3 to illustrate this case.

ECONOMICS IN THE NEWS

Spring Is for Bon Vivants!

It's the season for everything fresh, for the Good Life and something new. . . . Your luncheon will have the inspiration of spring with our Chicken Argentina. It's delicate and unique, light and elegant—it's part of the Good Life. Enjoy it with ripe olives from California.

Chicken Argentina
1 frying chicken (3 lbs.), cut in pieces
1 lime
1 teaspoon salt
1/2 teaspoon pepper
3/4 teaspoon paprika
1-1/2 cups pitted California ripe olives
1 large onion, chopped
1/4 cup oil
1-1/2 cups orange juice
1 medium red pepper sliced
1 medium green pepper sliced

Marinate chicken pieces in juice from the lime (approximately 1/3 cup) for at least 30 minutes. Combine salt, pepper, and paprika; sprinkle over chicken. Brown on all sides in oil. Place chicken in baking pan, add olives, onion, green pepper, red pepper, and orange juice. Cover and bake at 350° for 45 minutes or until chicken is tender. Remove chicken to platter. Serve with pan juices. Serves 4.

For "389 Ways to Use California Ripe Olives" write: California Olive Industry, Dept BA4, P.O.Box 4089, Fresno, California 93744.

Source: Advertisement "Spring Is for Bon Vivants!" from *Bon Appetit*, March 1981, p. 19. Reprinted by permission of the California Olive Industry.

Questions

1. Do you think the California olive industry might be a reasonable approximation of a perfectly competitive industry? What would make you think so, or think not?
2. Why would an advertisement for California olives in a national magazine be sponsored by an industry group, rather than an individual olive grower? Does this type of advertisement fit with what you know about perfect competition?
3. Suppose that this advertising campaign is so successful that the demand curve for California olives is shifted to the right. How will the industry and individual growers react to the demand curve shift in the short run? In the long run?
4. According to the perfectly competitive model, profits return to zero in the long run following a rightward demand curve shift. Does this mean that the industry association that sponsored this advertisement is wasting its members' money? Explain.

SELF TEST

These sample test items will help you check how much you have learned. Answers are found at the end of the chapter. Scoring yourself: One or two wrong—on target. Three or four wrong—passing, but you haven't mastered the chapter yet. Five or more wrong—not good enough; start over and restudy the chapter.

_____ 1. Which of the following is not characteristic of perfect competition?
   a. Many firms, each of which is small.
   b. A homogeneous product.
   c. An intense climate of rivalry among entrepreneurs.
   d. Free entry and exit.

_____ 2. Which of the following markets can contain a number of firms producing differentiated products?
   a. Monopoly.
   b. Monopolistic competition.
   c. Perfect competition.
   d. None of the above.

_____ 3. A perfectly competitive firm sells its output for $50 a unit. At 1,000 units of output, marginal cost is $40 and is increasing, average variable cost is $35, and average total cost is $60. To maximize short-run profit, what should the firm do?
   a. Increase output.
   b. Decrease output but not shut down.
   c. Maintain its current rate of output.
   d. Shut down.

_____ 4. A perfectly competitive firm sells its output for $50 a unit. At 500 units of output its marginal cost is $50 and is decreasing, average variable cost is $55 per unit, and average total cost is $65 per unit. To maximize profit, what should the firm do?
   a. Increase output.
   b. Decrease output or shut down temporarily.
   c. Maintain its current rate of output.
   d. Insufficient information given for an answer to be reached.

_____ 5. A perfectly competitive firm sells its output at $40 per unit. At 100 units of output it has an average total cost of $40. Marginal cost is below average total cost at that point. To maximize profit, what should the firm do?
   a. Increase output.
   b. Decrease output.
   c. Maintain its current rate of output.
   d. Insufficient information given for an answer to be reached.

_____ 6. A perfectly competitive firm's short-run supply curve is best described as
   a. its marginal cost curve.
   b. the upward-sloping portion of its marginal cost curve.
   c. the upward-sloping part of its marginal cost curve lying above average variable cost.
   d. the upward-sloping part of its marginal cost curve lying above average total cost.

7. If a perfectly competitive firm is operating at a point where marginal cost and product price are between average variable cost and average total cost, its accounting profit must be
   a. positive.
   b. zero.
   c. negative.
   d. impossible to determine from the information given.

8. If, in the short run, input prices rise as the output of a perfectly competitive industry expands, then the short-run industry supply curve will
   a. be somewhat steeper than the sum of the individual firms' supply curves.
   b. be somewhat flatter than the sum of the individual firms' supply curves.
   c. be the same as the sum of the individual firms' supply curves.
   d. have a negative slope.

9. Which of the following is not equal to the others for a perfectly competitive firm in long-run equilibrium?
   a. Short-run average variable cost.
   b. Long-run average cost.
   c. Short-run marginal cost.
   d. Marginal revenue.

10. A firm will have no incentive to change the size of its plant in the long run if
    a. price is equal to marginal cost.
    b. short-run average total cost equals long-run average cost.
    c. price is equal to long-run average total cost.
    d. marginal revenue is equal to marginal cost.

11. In long-run equilibrium for a perfectly competitive firm, which of the following is not at its minimum?
    a. Short-run average total cost.
    b. Short-run average variable cost.
    c. Long-run average cost.
    d. All of the above are at their minimum points.

12. If there is an increase in demand for the product of a perfectly competitive industry,
    a. firms already in the industry will for a time earn pure economic profits.
    b. new firms will be attracted to the industry.
    c. price will rise more in the short run than in the long run, assuming the change in demand to be permanent.
    d. all of the above will occur.

13. If there is a permanent increase in demand for the product of a perfectly competitive industry known to have a perfectly elastic long-run supply curve,
    a. each individual firm in the industry will, in the long run, increase its rate of output.
    b. industry output will expand via the entry of new firms.
    c. both of the above will occur.
    d. none of the above will occur.

_____ 14. If input prices for a perfectly competitive industry decline as the output of the industry expands in the long run, the long-run industry supply curve
   a. will have a positive slope.
   b. will have a negative slope.
   c. will be perfectly elastic.
   d. will be vertical.

_____ 15. Which of the following would tend to make the long-run supply curve for a perfectly competitive industry slope upward?
   a. An industry that supplies a major input also has a positively sloped long-run supply curve.
   b. Wages in the industry decline as industry output increases.
   c. Each firm's short-run total cost curve is U-shaped.
   d. The industry has free entry and exit.

ANSWERS TO CHAPTER 24

Hands On

Problem 1 (a) The slope of the total revenue curve tells you the price. Along TR_1, for example, total revenue rises by $10 for each one unit of output, indicating a price of $10 per unit. (Note that the units on the vertical axis are in multiples of 100, whereas those on the horizontal axis are in multiples of 10.) The price of TR_2 is $7.50 per unit; TR_3 $5 per unit; for TR_4 $2.50 per unit. (b) Your completed table should look as shown in the solution to Exhibit 24.1b. As you

Exhibit 24.1b (ans.)

Price / Output	Total Revenue $2.50	$5.00	$7.50	$10.00	Total Cost same for all prices	Profit (or Loss) $2.50	$5.00	$7.50	$10.00
0	$ 0	$ 0	$ 0	$ 0	$ 400	$ (400)	$ (400)	$ (400)	$ (400)
70	175	350	525	700	775	(600)	(425)	(250)	(75)
80	200	400	600	800	810	(610)	(410)	(210)	(10)
90	225	450	675	900	855	(630)	(405)	(180)	45
100	250	500	750	1,000	900	(650)	(400)	(150)	100
110	275	550	825	1,100	960	(685)	(410)	(135)	140
120	300	600	900	1,200	1,025	(725)	(425)	(125)	175
130	325	650	975	1,300	1,120	(795)	(470)	(145)	180
140	350	700	1,050	1,400	1,240	(890)	(540)	(190)	160
150	375	750	1,125	1,500	1,400	(1,025)	(650)	(275)	100

would expect, the quantity supplied—given by the profit-maximizing or loss-minimizing quantity of output at each price—increases as the price increases. (c) Marginal revenue is equal to the slope of the total revenue curve; marginal cost is equal to the slope of the total cost curve. Thus, the point of profit maximization for each price occurs where the appropriate total revenue schedule is parallel to the total cost curve. Since the equality of these slopes means marginal revenue equals marginal cost, the two approaches give the same answer.

Problem 2 To fill in the tables, remember total cost = average cost x quantity, and total revenue = price x quantity. See the solutions to Exhibits 24.2b and 24.2c for details. Answers given are approximate. To show the supply curve, shade the upward-sloping portion of the marginal cost curve that lies above its intersection with average variable cost.

Exhibit 24.2b (ans.)

Price	Profit-Maximizing Output	Total Revenue	Total Cost	Profit (or Loss)
$ .60	$ 0	$ 0	$ 320	$ (320)
.70	800	560	880	(320)
.80	900	720	963	(243)
.90	960	864	1,018	(154)
1.00	1,040	1,040	1,092	(52)
1.10	1,100	1,210	1,166	44
1.20	1,140	1,368	1,208	160
1.30	1,200	1,560	1,284	276

Exhibit 24.2c (ans.)

Output	Total Revenue	Total Cost	Profit (or Loss)
400	$ 520	$ 620	$ (100)
600	780	744	36
800	1,040	880	160
1,000	1,300	1,060	240
1,200	1,560	1,284	276
1,400	1,820	1,610	210
1,600	2,080	2,080	0

Problem 3 (a) In the short run, the demand curve would shift to a position like D$_3$, and the market would move up along S$_2$ from B to E. As it did so, individual firms would be moving up along their marginal cost curves in response to the increase in market price. In the long run, new firms would enter, shifting the supply curve to the right to a position like S$_3$. As the supply curve shifted, the market price would fall, and individual firms that had been in the industry all along would move back down along their short-run marginal cost curves. The entire path to long-run equilibrium would thus be B to E to C. (b) This time the demand curve would shift to the left, toward D$_1$. The market would move toward a short-run equilibrium at G. As it did so, individual firms would move down along their short-run marginal cost curves and would sustain losses. Some firms would be driven out of the market by the losses, shifting the supply curve toward S$_1$ in the long run. As this happened, price would recover and the market would move toward equilibrium at A. (c) With constant input prices, the long-run supply curve would lie along the line ABC. (d) With rising input prices, the long-run curve would be steeper than ABC, but not as steep as GBE. (e) With falling input prices, the long-run supply curve would have a negative slope, but not so steeply negative as DBH.

Economics in the News

(1) Not knowing a lot of specifics about the industry, it would be safe to guess that it is not too bad an example of perfect competition. To really know how good the fit is, you would want to know whether olives are really a homogeneous good (for many crops, uniformity of quality is enhanced by industry grading standards); whether any

one grower has a substantial share of the market (no such information is given here); and whether entry or exit is easy. (Do you need a permit to grow olives? Is the type of land on which olives can be grown already totally planted in olive groves?) (2) If the industry is competitively structured, it would not pay any one firm to advertise. With a homogeneous product and small market share, any new customers the ad generated would probably be served by other growers, not the one that ran the ad. (3) In the short run, growers would move up along their short-run marginal cost curves. Land and trees are fixed factors in the short run, but perhaps output could be increased by using more fertilizer, by hiring more labor to care for the trees, or by other increased use of variable inputs. In the long run, if demand remained strong, more trees would be planted, perhaps by existing olive growers, or perhaps by lemon growers who replaced their lemon trees with olive trees. (4) True, profits will return to zero in the long run. Presumably, though, it takes quite a while to grow an olive tree, so short-run profits for this industry might persist quite a while. Also, owners of specialized factors of production, especially land uniquely suited to olive growing, might find their land values or rental income permanently increased even after pure economic profit returned to zero.

Self Test

1. **c.** There is little open rivalry because no one firm's actions much affect what others do. Also, with a homogeneous product, many avenues of entrepreneurial rivalry are absent.
2. **b.** Monopoly has a single firm, and perfect competition has a homogeneous product.
3. **a.** Because price is above marginal cost, and also above average variable cost.
4. **d.** At the moment, the price is below average variable cost, but because MC is below AVC, AVC is decreasing. Thus, AVC may (or may not) drop below price at some higher level of output. More information is needed.
5. **a.** Price is above marginal cost, and price is also above AVC (because it is equal to ATC).
6. **c.** The rest of the MC curve is not part of the supply curve.
7. **d.** Pure economic profit must be negative, but we don't know about accounting profit, since we have no information on implicit versus explicit costs. With large implicit costs, accounting profit could be positive.
8. **a.** Answer **b** applies if input prices fall.
9. **a.** SR-AVC is below SR-ATC, and hence below price, in equilibrium.
10. **b.** This means that its plant is suited to its current rate of output.
11. **b.** The minimum of AVC occurs at a lower rate of output than the minimum of ATC.
12. **d.** These are all true regardless of what happens to input prices.
13. **b.** Each firm is already operating at the minimum point of its long-run total cost curve, so it has no reason to change size of plant if the price does not change.
14. **b.** It will have a positive slope if input prices increase.
15. **a.** This would cause input prices to rise as output increases.

Chapter 25

The Theory of Monopoly

WHERE YOU'RE GOING

When you have mastered this chapter, you will understand

1. How price and revenue are related for a monopoly.
2. How the profit-maximizing price and output are determined for a monopoly.
3. Why monopolies and other firms sometimes engage in price discrimination.
4. Why monopoly is a source of market failure.
5. Why "natural monopolies" such as electric utilities are regulated and what problems regulation poses.

In addition, you will add the following terms to your economic vocabulary:
  Limit pricing
  Price discrimination
  Deadweight loss
  Natural monopoly
  Rate of return
  Cross-subsidization

WALKING TOUR

After you have read this chapter at least once, you should work step by step through this walking tour. Fill in the blanks and answer the questions as you go along. After you have answered each question, check yourself by uncovering the answer given in the margin. If you do not understand why the answer given is the correct one, refer back to the proper section of the text.

Profit Maximization for the Pure Monopolist

is not
less than

at

halfway

The monopolist [is/is not] a price taker. For such a firm, marginal revenue is always [equal to/less than/greater than] the price at which the product is sold. In the case of a demand curve that is a straight line, the monopolist's marginal revenue curve intersects the vertical axis [above/below/at] the vertical intercept of the demand curve. The marginal revenue curve intersects the horizontal axis at a point _____ from the origin to the

304

horizontal intercept of the demand curve. For that part of the demand curve that is elastic, marginal revenue is [greater than/less than/equal to] zero. For the part of the demand curve that is inelastic, marginal revenue is [greater than/less than/equal to] zero. Marginal revenue is equal to zero when demand is [inelastic/elastic/unit elastic].

greater than

less than
unit elastic

The profit-maximizing quantity of output for a monopolist is found at the point where marginal cost is equal to [price/marginal revenue]. The profit-maximizing price is equal to the height of the [demand/marginal revenue/marginal cost] curve at the profit-maximizing level of output. Thus, for a profit-maximizing monopolist, profit-maximizing price is [greater than/less than/equal to] marginal cost.

marginal revenue

demand

greater than

As in the case of perfect competition, the monopolist's profit-maximizing decision must take average costs into account as well as marginal cost. The monopolist will earn a profit only if price exceeds _____ cost. If the price is below average total cost but above average variable cost, the best short-run strategy for the monopolist is to [operate/shut down]. If the price is below average variable cost, the monopolist's best short-run strategy is to [operate/shut down]. By itself, the fact that a monopolist has no competitors [does/does not] guarantee that a pure economic profit can be earned.

average total

operate
shut down

does not

In practice, even a firm that is alone in its market may face potential rivals. In this case, the firm may charge [less/more] than the short-run profit-maximizing price in order to discourage the entry of rivals. Such a strategy is known as _____.

less

limit pricing

Price Discrimination

The practice of charging different prices for various units of a single product when the price differences are not justified by differences in cost is known as _____. Two things are required for price discrimination to be possible. First, it must be impossible or at least inconvenient to _____ the good or service in question. Second, it must be possible to classify consumers into groups according to _____ of demand. Those with less elastic demand can then be charged relatively [high/low] prices.

price discrimination

resell

elasticity
high

305

is not does not	It [is/is not] necessary to be a monopolist in order to price discriminate. Price discrimination [does/does not] always reduce the efficiency and fairness of markets.
	Monopoly and Market Failure
	A key function of markets is to transmit information in the form of
opportunity	prices about _____ costs. Under perfect competition,
equal to	prices tend to be [equal to/greater than/less than] opportunity costs.
greater than	Under monopoly, on the other hand, prices tend to be [equal to/greater than/less than] opportunity costs.
is	In a competitive market, production [is/is not] carried out to the point where the price consumers are willing to pay is equal to the opportunity cost of an additional unit. Under monopoly, production
stops short of	[is carried past/stops short of] this point. Thus, in monopoly equilibrium, there remain some theoretically possible gains from trade, in
surplus	the form of consumer and producer _____, that are not
deadweight	realized. This lost surplus is called a _____ loss. The deadweight loss is indicative of a market failure.
	Natural Monopoly and Its Regulation
	An industry in which total costs are kept to a minimum by having
natural monopoly	just one producer serve the entire market is known as _____. In an attempt to avoid deadweight losses, such firms are often sub-
regulation	ject to _____. The object of regulation is to move the
opportunity	price to or close to _____ cost.
do not	In practice, regulators [do/do not] have access to full information on a firm's cost and demand curves. Instead, regulators focus on the firms accounting profit expressed as a percentage of its net worth—
rate of return	its _____. Regulators attempt to keep this equal to the
opportunity	_____ cost of capital, or, to use another term, to
normal	_____ profit.
	Regulators do not always succeed in their objective. If they set the regulated firm's rate of return above the opportunity cost of capi-
excessive	tal, the firm will tend to undertake [excessive/insufficient] invest-
A-J	ment. This tendency is known as the _____ effect. On the other hand, if prices are set too low so that the firm's rate of return falls short of the opportunity cost of capital, the firm may
insufficient	undertake [excessive/insufficient] investment. In that case, the

decline

cross-subsidization

quality of service provided by the regulated monopoly will tend to [increase/decline].

Another problem that sometimes occurs in regulated monopoly is a tendency to charge some customers more than the cost of service and others less than the cost of service. This practice is known as _____.

HANDS ON

Now that you have reviewed the concepts introduced in this chapter, it is time for some hands-on practice with the analytical tools that have been introduced. Work through each problem in this section carefully, and then check your results against those given at the end of the chapter.

Problem 1

The following questions are based on Exhibit 25.1, which shows cost curves and two demand curves for a typical monopolist.

Exhibit 25.1

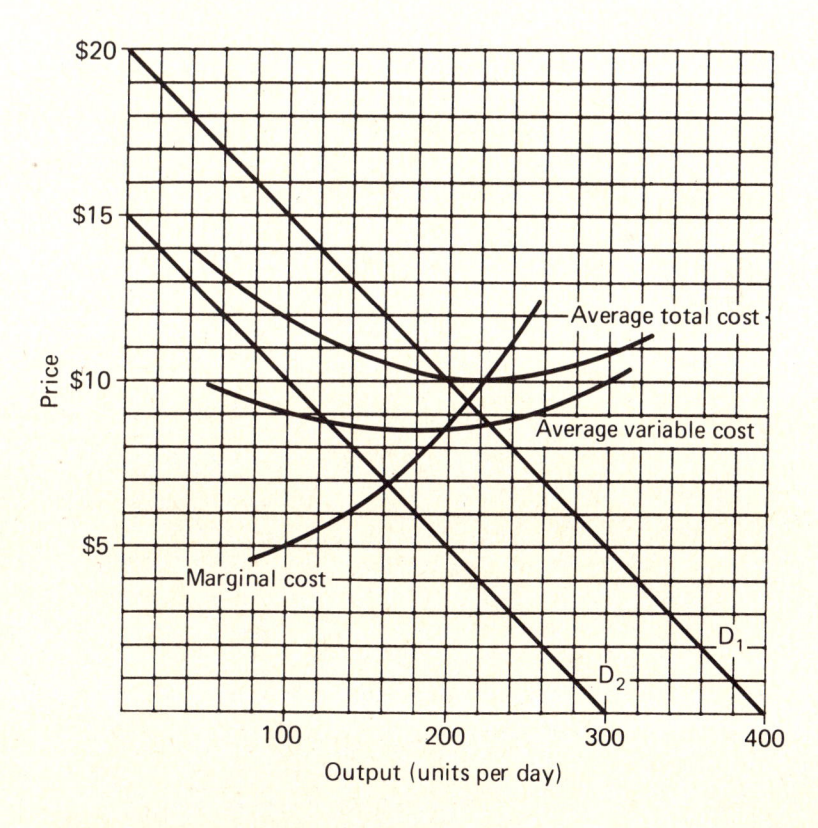

a. Draw the marginal revenue curve corresponding to demand curve D_1. Ignore D_2 for the time being. Label this marginal revenue curve MR_1.

b. Given the demand curve D₁, what will be the monopolist's profit-maximizing output and price? What will be the firm's total profit (or loss)?
c. Suppose that because of a recession in the economy, the demand curve shifts to D₂. Draw the corresponding marginal revenue curve, and label it MR₂. What are the firm's new profit-maximizing price and output?
d. What will be the firm's total profit (or loss) given D₂? What would its profit (or loss) be if the firm shut down? Should it continue to operate in the short run?

Problem 2

This problem is based on Exhibit 25.2. Part a of that figure shows total cost and total revenue curves for a typical pure monopolist.

a. Using the figure in Exhibit 25.2a as your guide, fill in the total revenue, total cost, and total profit columns of the table given in Exhibit 25.2b. What is the profit-maximizing level of output? What price does the monopolist charge to achieve maximum profit?
b. Using the total revenue column as your guide, fill in the marginal revenue column of the table. Notice that the total revenue column moves in steps of 20 units of output. You can get a quick approximation of marginal revenue in the range between each step by dividing the change in total revenue by 20. (Example: From 20 to 40 units of output, total revenue increases by $35, from $45 to $80. $35/20 = $1.75.) Fill in the marginal cost column in the same manner. Now compare the marginal cost and marginal revenue columns to get an approximation of the profit-maximizing level of output. Does this agree with your previous answer?

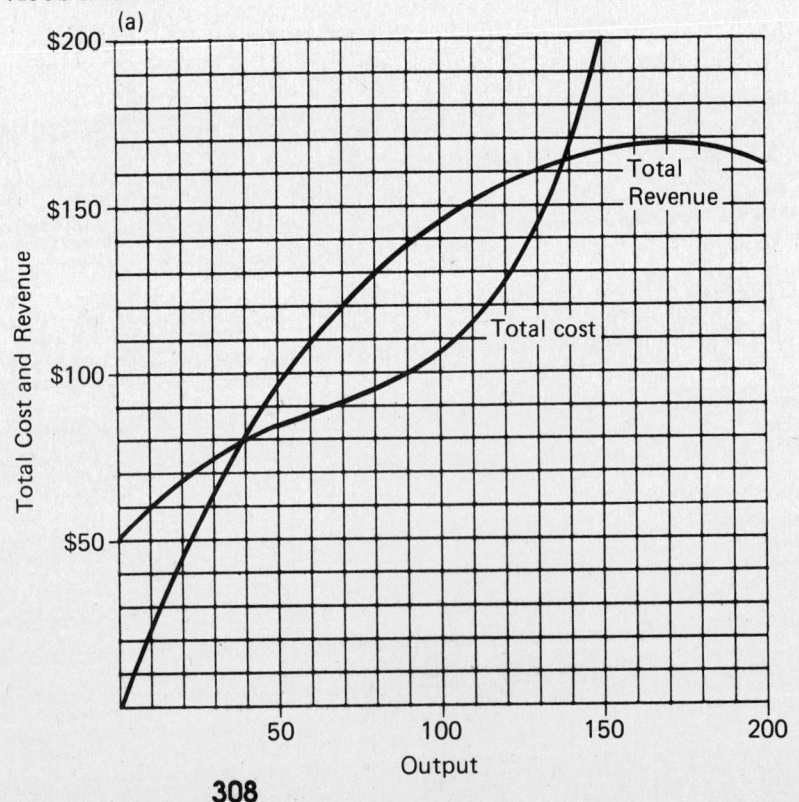

Exhibit 25.2a

Exhibit 25.2b

(b)

Quantity of Output	Total Revenue	Marginal Revenue (approx)	Marginal Cost (approx)	Total Cost	Profit (or Loss)
0	$___	$___	$___	$___	$___
20	___	___	___	___	___
40	___	___	___	___	___
60	___	___	___	___	___
80	___	___	___	___	___
100	___	___	___	___	___
120	___	___	___	___	___
140	___	___	___	___	___
160	___	___	___	220	___

Problem 3

This problem is based on Exhibit 25.3, which shows a demand and a marginal cost curve for a typical pure monopolist.

a. Draw the firm's marginal revenue curve. What is its profit-maximizing price and level of output?

Exhibit 25.3

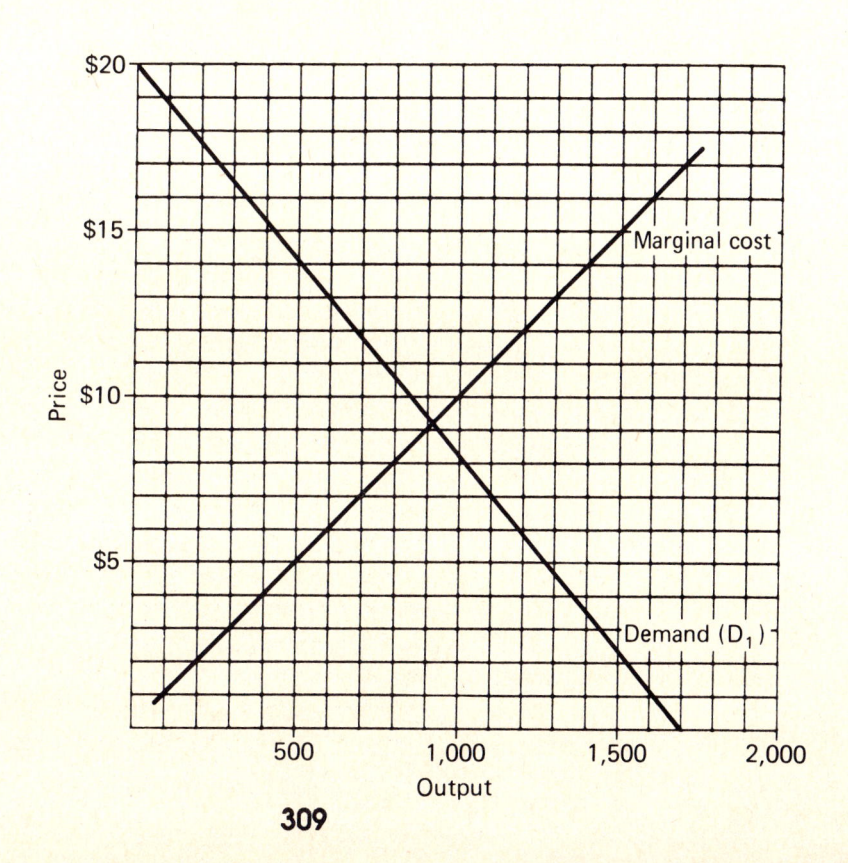

b. If your answer to Part a of this problem was 600 units of output and a price of $6, stop here and read this chapter's "Don't Make This Common Mistake" section before you continue.
c. Suppose now that demand conditions faced by the monopolist change, but that nothing disturbs the marginal cost curve. Specifically, let the demand curve shift to a new position that will keep the monopolist's profit-maximizing quantity at 600 units, as before, but will cause the profit-maximizing price to drop to $10. Draw the new demand curve and its associated marginal revenue curve. Make sure your new marginal revenue curve is consistent with your new demand curve. Label the new curves D_2 and MR_2.
d. Now suppose demand conditions change again, still with the marginal cost curve in its original position. This time, draw demand and marginal cost curves that will give a profit-maximizing output of 1,000 units and a profit-maximizing price of $13. Label these curves D_3 and MR_3.
e. A perfectly competitive firm has a supply curve that gives a one-to-one relationship between quantity and output for the firm. As changing demand conditions cause the price to rise and fall in a competitive market, each firm, and the industry as a whole, follows its supply curve like a train along a track. Each change in price produces a corresponding change in quantity. Does the monopolist shown in this figure also have a supply curve that gives a one-to-one relationship between price and quantity under changing demand conditions?

DON'T MAKE THIS COMMON MISTAKE

Exhibit 25.4 is representative of one of the most common exam questions for this chapter. The figure shows a simple demand curve, a marginal revenue curve (sometimes you are asked to draw this yourself), and a marginal cost curve. Question: What is the profit-maximizing quantity and price for the firm?

There's not much chance you'll miss the part about the quantity. "I'm not dumb," you'll say to yourself. "I know the difference between monopoly and perfect competition. This prof can't fool me into thinking the profit-maximizing quantity is 200 units. I know it is 150 units, because that's where the marginal cost curve intersects the marginal revenue curve."

So far so good. But at this point WATCH OUT for one of the most common and DUMBEST of mistakes—one committed by thousands of economics students all over the country every semester! Just because the intersection of the marginal cost and marginal revenue curves gave you the profit-maximizing quantity, don't think it gives you the profit-maximizing price. The profit-maximizing price for this firm is NOT $4 per unit. To find the correct profit-maximizing price, FOLLOW THE ARROW up from the MC-MR intersection to the DEMAND CURVE. The correct profit-maximizing price, as shown in the figure, is $10 per unit.

What would happen if the managers of this monopolistic firm were as dumb as all those students and put their product on the market at $4 per unit? They would be SWAMPED by customers!

Exhibit 25.4

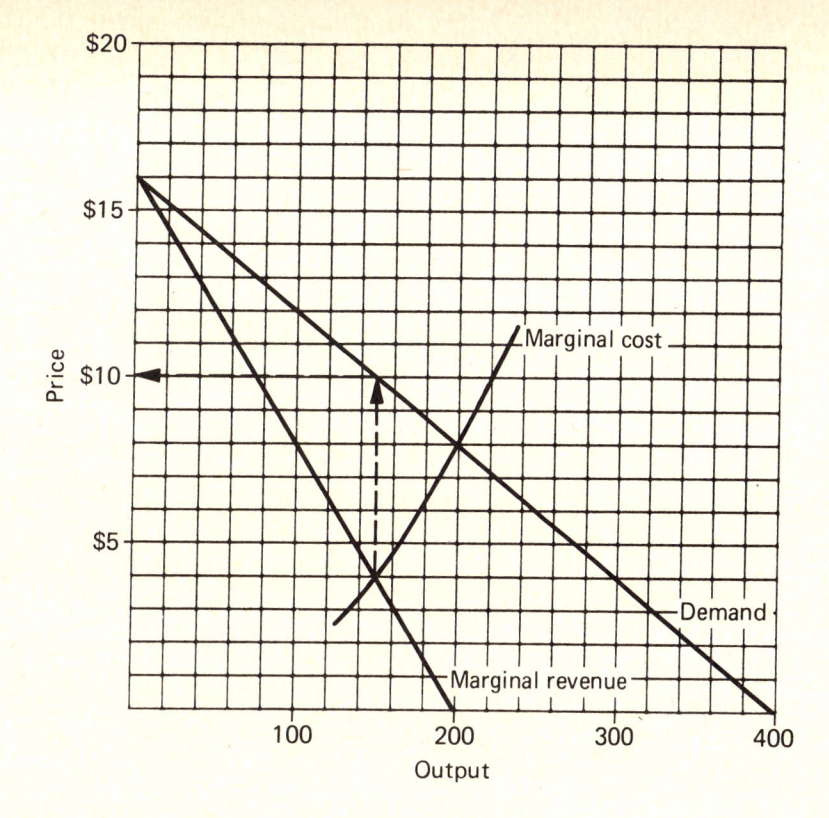

Quantity demanded at $4 is some 300 units. At 300 units of output and a price of $4, the firm would not come close to covering even its marginal costs, let alone its fixed costs. It would make a disastrous loss, not the handsome profit available at a price of $10. So DON'T BE A DUMB MONOPOLIST! Follow the arrow!

SELF TEST

These sample test items will help you check how much you have learned. Answers are found at the end of the chapter. Scoring yourself: One or two wrong—on target. Three or four wrong—passing, but you haven't mastered the chapter yet. Five or more wrong—not good enough; start over and restudy the chapter.

_____ 1. Which of the following is assumed in the ideal-type monopoly model?
    a. The monopolist has no competitors at all—not even small ones.
    b. The product has no close substitutes.
    c. The monopolist is fully protected from the entry of new rivals into its market.
    d. All of the above are assumptions of the ideal-type model.

2. Which of the following is true of a perfect competitor but not of a pure monopolist?
   a. The firm is a price taker.
   b. The firm maximizes profit by setting marginal cost equal to marginal revenue.
   c. The firm may have to shut down in the short run if price does not cover average variable cost.
   d. The firm can earn a pure economic profit in the short run if demand conditions are favorable.

3. If a pure monopolist can sell 100 units of output at $50 per unit and 101 units of output at $49.90 per unit, marginal revenue in that range of output is approximately
   a. -10 cents per unit.
   b. -$10 per unit.
   c. $39.90 per unit.
   d. $49.90 per unit.

4. At the point where the marginal revenue curve intersects the horizontal axis, a monopolist's demand curve must be
   a. elastic.
   b. inelastic.
   c. unit elastic.
   d. perfectly elastic.

5. If a monopolist is operating at a point where its marginal revenue curve intersects its marginal cost curve, and if marginal cost is below average variable cost at that point, then to maximize profit, the firm should do which of the following?
   a. Increase output.
   b. Shut down.
   c. Maintain that rate of output.
   d. Insufficient information given for an answer to be reached.

6. At an output of 100 units, a monopolist's marginal cost is $33, its marginal revenue is $33, its average variable cost is $30, and its average total cost is $38. To maximize profit or minimize loss in the short run, what should the firm do?
   a. Produce more than 100 units of output.
   b. Produce exactly 100 units of output.
   c. Shutdown.
   d. Insufficient information given for an answer to be reached.

7. Pure monopoly resembles perfect competition
   a. in that entry and exit are easy.
   b. in that zero pure economic profit will be earned in the long run.
   c. in that all firms are price takers.
   d. in none of the above respects.

8. Other things being equal, we would expect a price discriminating monopolist to produce which of the following?
   a. More output than a nondiscriminating monopolist.
   b. Less output than a nondiscriminating monopolist.
   c. The same output as a nondiscriminating monopolist.
   d. No reason to expect one rather than another of the above.

_____ 9. Which of the following markets would appear to offer the best opportunity for price discrimination?
   a. Groceries.
   b. Gasoline.
   c. Psychiatric services.
   d. Wheat.

_____ 10. Other things being equal, we would expect a price discriminating monopolist to charge the highest prices to the group with
   a. the least elastic demand.
   b. the most elastic demand.
   c. perfectly elastic demand.
   d. the least per capita income.

_____ 11. In profit-maximizing equilibrium, the price charged by a monopolist tends to be
   a. above the opportunity cost of an additional unit of output.
   b. below the opportunity cost of an additional unit of output.
   c. equal to the opportunity cost of an additional unit of output.
   d. c, but only if the firm is earning zero pure economic profit.

_____ 12. The "deadweight loss" of a monopoly refers to
   a. the difference between total revenue and accounting profit.
   b. a loss of potential gains from trade in the form of producer and consumer surplus.
   c. a lost opportunity to earn a greater pure economic profit by raising price above the level of marginal cost.
   d. none of the above.

_____ 13. A "natural monopoly" is one in which
   a. there are strong diseconomies of scale.
   b. the average total cost curve is positively sloped throughout its length.
   c. average total costs are minimized by having just one firm serve the whole market.
   d. marginal cost is equal to average total cost at the minimum point of average total cost.

_____ 14. A firm's accounting profit expressed as a percentage of its net worth is known as its
   a. normal profit.
   b. rate base.
   c. rate of return.
   d. regulatory base.

_____ 15. If regulators allow a firm to earn a rate of return that exceeds the opportunity cost of capital over an extended period, the firm is likely to
   a. be forced to shut down.
   b. stay in business, but with drastically reduced service quality.
   c. acquire more than the efficient quantity of capital.
   d. charge all of its customers a price that is less than marginal cost.

ANSWERS TO CHAPTER 25

Hands On

Problem 1 (a) Your marginal revenue curve MR_1 should have a vertical intercept of $20 and a horizontal intercept of 200. (b) The profit-maximizing output is found where the marginal cost and marginal revenue curves intersect, which happens at 140 units of output. The profit-maximizing price is determined by the height of the demand curve at this point, $13. Average total cost at $140 units of output is $11, so profit per unit is $2. That makes total profit equal to $280. (c) MR_2 has a vertical intercept of 15 and a horizontal intercept of 150. The new profit-maximizing output is 100 units and the profit-maximizing price is $10. (d) Average total cost at 100 units of output is $12, so the firm now runs a loss of $2 per unit, or a total loss of $200. Note, however, that fixed cost is $3 per unit, shown by the gap between average total cost and average variable cost at this level of output. This means total fixed cost is $300. If the firm shut down, then, it would lose $300, compared with a loss of $200 if it operates. It should stay in operation in the short run. If it thinks demand will not recover to a profitable level in the future, however, the firm should go out of business permanently, thereby shedding its fixed as well as its variable costs.

Problem 2 (a) The profit-maximizing level of output is 100 units. See the solution table for Exhibit 25.2b for details. The profit-maximizing price is $1.45 per unit, as you can see by dividing total

Exhibit 25.2b (ans.)

(b)

Quantity of Output	Total Revenue	Marginal Revenue (approx)	Marginal Cost (approx)	Total Cost	Profit (or Loss)
0	$ 0			$ 50	$ (50)
		$ 2.25	$ .90		
20	45			68	(23)
		1.75	.60		
40	80			80	0
		1.40	.40		
60	108			88	20
		1.10	.35		
80	130			95	35
		.75	.60		
100	145			107	38
		.60	.95		
120	157			126	31
		.35	1.90		
140	164			164	0
		.20	2.80		
160	168			220	(32)

revenue by output at the profit-maximizing quantity. (b) In the range from 80 to 100 units, marginal revenue is still higher, on the average, than marginal cost. By the time the firm reaches the 100 to 120 unit output range, marginal cost, on the average, is above marginal revenue. The two must be equal somewhere between 80 and 120 units, so this approach agrees with the 100 unit estimate from Part a of this problem.

Problem 3 (a) As drawn, the profit-maximizing price is $13 and the profit-maximizing quantity is 600. Note, as explained in the text, that the marginal revenue curve for a straight-line demand curve is a straight line falling halfway between the demand curve and the vertical axis. (See MR_1 in the solution graph for Exhibit 25.3.) (c) This looks tricky, but it really is easy if you work step by step. To draw a straight line, you need just two points. Here is how to get two points each on the demand and marginal revenue curves: First, enter the point corresponding to the given profit-maximizing price and quantity—$10 and 600 units of output in this case. This point is labeled Q in the solution graph. You know that this point must lie on the demand curve. Now you can find your first point on the marginal revenue curve, which you know must pass halfway between Q and the vertical axis. Label the point halfway between Q and the vertical axis R. You also know that the marginal revenue curve must intersect the marginal cost curve at the 600 unit profit-maximizing level of output. Label this Point S. You now have your two points on the marginal revenue curve. Draw MR_2 passing through Points S and R. Label the point where MR_2 hits the vertical axis T. This Point T must also be on the demand curve, since the marginal revenue and demand curves both begin at the same point on the vertical axis. Now you have two points on the demand curve.

Exhibit 25.3 (ans.)

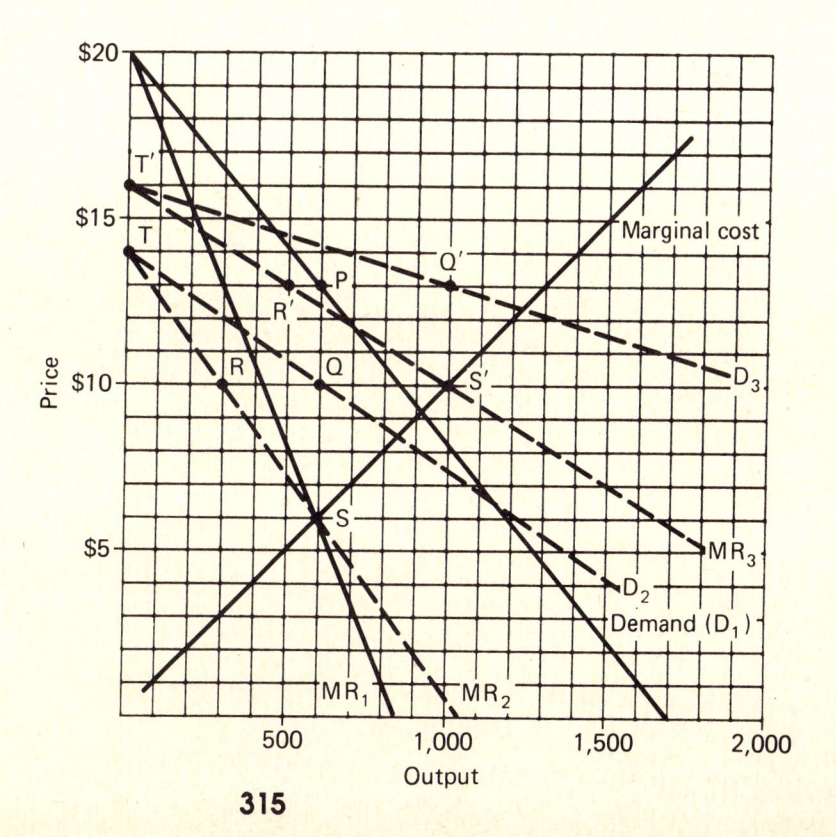

Draw the new demand curve D_2 through Points T and Q, as in the solution figure. (d) Proceed as for Part b, finding Points Q', R', S', and T'. See solution for Exhibit 25.3 for details. (e) A monopolist has no supply curve in the sense that a perfectly competitive firm has one. As you see from this example, there is no 1:1 relationship between price and quantity produced. It is possible for demand to change in such a way that the price changes but not the quantity, or the quantity changes but not the price—or in fact, for the profit-maximizing quantity and price to move anywhere within a wide range of possibilities.

Self Test

1. **d.** However, there are few if any real world markets that meet these conditions.
2. **a.** The monopolist is not a price taker because its output decision affects the maximum price at which it can sell the product.
3. **c.** 100 units times $50 gives $5,000 total revenue; 101 units times $49.90 gives $5,039.90 total revenue. The difference is marginal revenue.
4. **c.** It is elastic where the marginal revenue curve is above the horizontal axis, and inelastic where it is below the axis.
5. **d.** The location of the demand curve must be known to establish price.
6. **b.** The exact location of the demand curve is not given, but it must be above the marginal revenue curve. Hence, price must be greater than average variable cost, so profit is maximized where MC = MR (rather than by shutting down).
7. **d.** Each of these is a point that distinguishes the two market structures.
8. **a.** Because it can sell at least some units (the last ones sold) at a price closer to marginal cost than in the case of nondiscriminating monopoly.
9. **c.** Resale would be impossible, and the therapist would probably have a good idea of the patient's ability to pay.
10. **a.** For example, airlines charge higher prices to business travelers than to tourists.
11. **a.** The opportunity cost of an additional unit of output is given by the marginal cost curve.
12. **b.** Geometrically, the deadweight loss takes the form of a triangle between the marginal cost and demand curves, and between their intersection and the monopolist's profit-maximizing quantity.
13. **c.** Typically this is the case when there are very strong economies of scale.
14. **c.** Regulators try to set a price that will make the rate of return equal to the opportunity cost of capital.
15. **c.** This is the A-J effect. Result **b** will occur if the permitted rate of return is below the opportunity cost of capital.

Chapter 26

Industrial Organization, Monopolistic Competition, and Oligopoly

WHERE YOU'RE GOING	*When you have mastered this chapter, you will understand*

1. The extent to which markets are dominated by a few large firms.
2. How in an oligopoly each firm's decisions depend on those of other firms.
3. How collusion among rival firms may bring increased profits at the expense of consumers.
4. What conditions affect the performance of concentrated markets.
5. What attempts to measure market performance have revealed.
6. How profits are maximized under monopolistic competition.

In addition, you will add the following terms to your economic vocabulary:
    Market concentration
    Concentration ratio
    Barrier to entry
    Oligopolistic interdependence
    Cartel
    Price leadership
    Contestable market

WALKING TOUR

After you have read this chapter at least once, you should work step by step through this walking tour. Fill in the blanks and answer the questions as you go along. After you have answered each question, check yourself by uncovering the answer given in the margin. If you do not understand why the answer given is the correct one, refer back to the proper section of the text.

Market Concentration and Its Determinants

The degree to which a market is dominated by a few large firms is known as _____. market concentration

The most common way of measuring market concentration is through the use of _____. concentration ratios

For example, in an industry where the top four firms had 20, 15, 10, and 5 percent of the market, respectively, the four-firm concentration ratio would be _____. 50 percent

In looking for explanations of the degree of concentration in an industry, your first thought would be of the cost advantages of making a large volume of output—that is, of _____. economies of scale For example, in the auto industry, these would include [plant level/multiplant/both] economies. both You would also want to know if there were any factors that prevented potential new firms from duplicating the performance of firms already in the industry—that is, if there were any _____. barriers to entry, _____ influences might explain much of the remaining extent of concentration. Random

It appears that U.S. markets are becoming [more/less] concentrated over time. less If the impact of growing international competition is taken into account, the degree of competitiveness in U.S. markets may be increasing [more/less] rapidly than concentration ratios indicate. more

The Theory of Oligopoly: Interdependence and Collusion

There is no general model of profit maximization under oligopoly comparable to the models of perfect competition and monopoly. The reason lies in the need of each firm in an oligopoly to pay close attention to the actions of rivals when making price or production decisions, that is, in the problem of _____. oligopolistic interdependence

Oligopolistic interdependence can sometimes lead to intense rivalry, and at other times toward cooperation, or _____. collusion For example, a group of producers may decide to maximize profits by agreeing to fix prices and limit output. Such a group is called a

cartel, raise	_____. The object of a cartel is to [raise/lower] prices by
restricting	[increasing/restricting] output. Like a monopoly, a cartel would maximize profit for the industry as a whole by adjusting the level of output
marginal revenue	to a point where marginal cost was equal to _____ for the industry.
	However, cartels suffer problems of stability. One problem is
entry	that of control over _____. A second serious problem is
output quotas	that of enforcing _____. Here, the problem is that if one firm cheats on its quota while other firms continue to abide by
greater	theirs, the cheater will earn a [greater/smaller] profit than if it too played by the rules. And if a firm thinks other cartel members will
also cheating	cheat, then it will earn a greater profit by [also cheating/playing by the rules]. Experience indicates that successful, long-lived cartels
rare	are [common/rare] in the world economy.
	Even when firms do not form a cartel, they may tacitly coordinate their price and output decisions in a way that will jointly increase their profit compared with open competition. Several conditions are thought to make such tacit coordination more difficult or less difficult. For example, an increase in the number and
more	size of firms in a market is thought to make coordination [more/less] difficult. A homogeneous product is thought to make coordination
less	[more/less] difficult than a heterogeneous product. A rapid rate of
more	innovation is thought to make coordination [more/less] difficult. Finally, barriers to entry and exit are thought to make coordination
less	[more/less] difficult. A market in which there are no barriers either
contestable	to entry or to exit is known as a _____ market.

The Theory of Monopolistic Competition

	Monopolistic competition refers to a market structure in which
many, heterogeneous	there are [few/many] firms, a [homogeneous/heterogeneous]
easy	product, and [easy/difficult] entry and exit. The demand curve faced
negative	by a monopolistically competitive firm has a [positive/negative/zero] slope. The profit-maximizing level of output for the firm is determined by the point where marginal cost is equal to marginal
revenue	_____, and the profit-maximizing price is determined by
demand	the height of the _____ curve at that point. In long-run equilibrium for a monopolistically competitive firm, price is [greater
equal to	than/less than/equal to] average total cost, so that pure economic

zero, greater than

profit is [positive/negative/zero]. The equilibrium price is [equal to/greater than/less than] marginal cost.

HANDS ON

Now that you have reviewed the concepts introduced in this chapter, it is time for some hands-on practice with the analytical tools that have been introduced. Work through each problem in this section carefully, and then check your results against those given at the end of the chapter.

Problem 1

The following questions are based on Exhibit 26.1. Use parts a and b of this exhibit in answering the questions that follow.

a. Exhibit 26.1a shows demand, marginal revenue, and marginal cost curves for an industry composed of 100 identical small firms. Assume that the industry is organized as a cartel. What is the profit-maximizing quantity of output for the industry? The profit-maximizing price? If the 100 members of the cartel agree to share the profit-maximizing quantity of output equally, what is the output quota allowed to each firm?

b. Exhibit 26.1b shows cost curves for one of the 100 identical firms making up the cartel. If the firm holds production to its 100 unit quota, how much profit will it earn? What will the relationship between marginal cost and marginal revenue be for this firm at 100 units of output?

Exhibit 26.1a

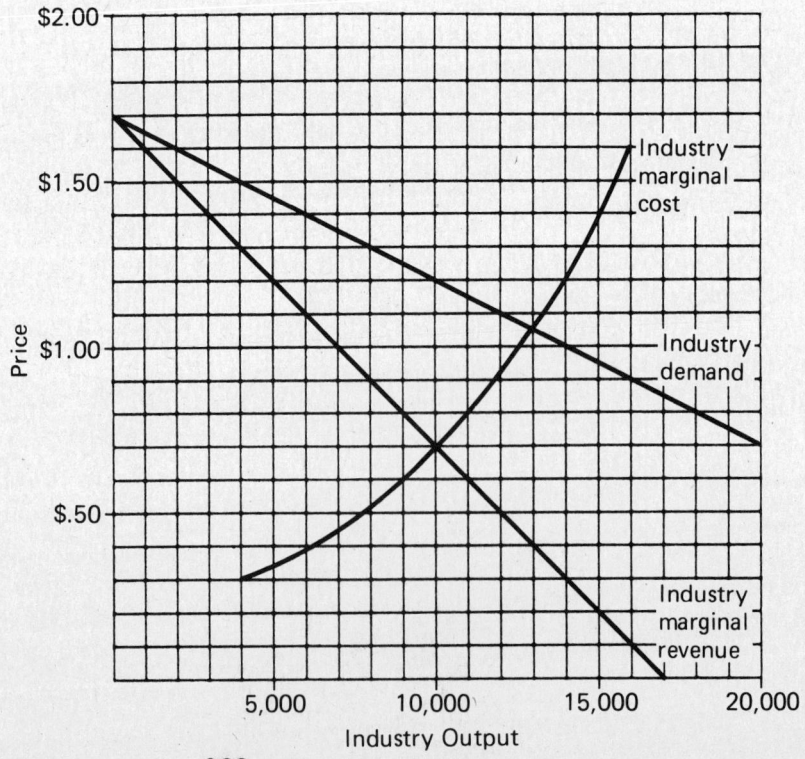

Exhibit 26.1b

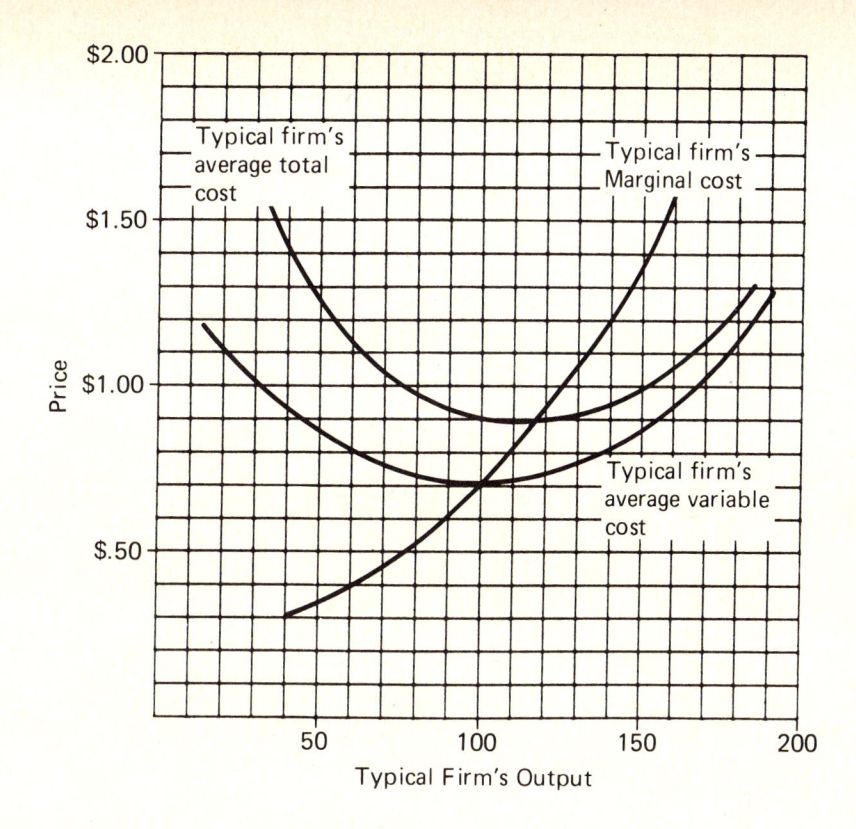

[Graph showing Price vs. Typical Firm's Output, with curves for Typical firm's average total cost, Typical firm's Marginal cost, and Typical firm's average variable cost. Price axis from $0 to $2.00; Output axis from 0 to 200.]

c. Suppose that this firm were to treat the cartel's profit-maximizing price of $1.20 per unit as a given. If it acted like a price taker with a fixed $1.20 per unit price, what would its profit-maximizing level of output be? How much profit would it make?

d. Does this example tell you anything about the temptation of an individual member of a cartel to cheat on the cartel's agreed output quotas? Explain.

Problem 2

The following questions are based on Exhibit 26.2, which shows demand and cost curves for a typical firm in a monopolistically competitive industry.

a. Using the demand curve as a basis, sketch in the firm's marginal revenue curve. What is the firm's short-run profit-maximizing level of output? Its short-run profit-maximizing price?

b. Under conditions of monopolistic competition, can the situation shown prevail in the long run? Why or why not? If not, what will you expect to happen in the long run?

Exhibit 26.2

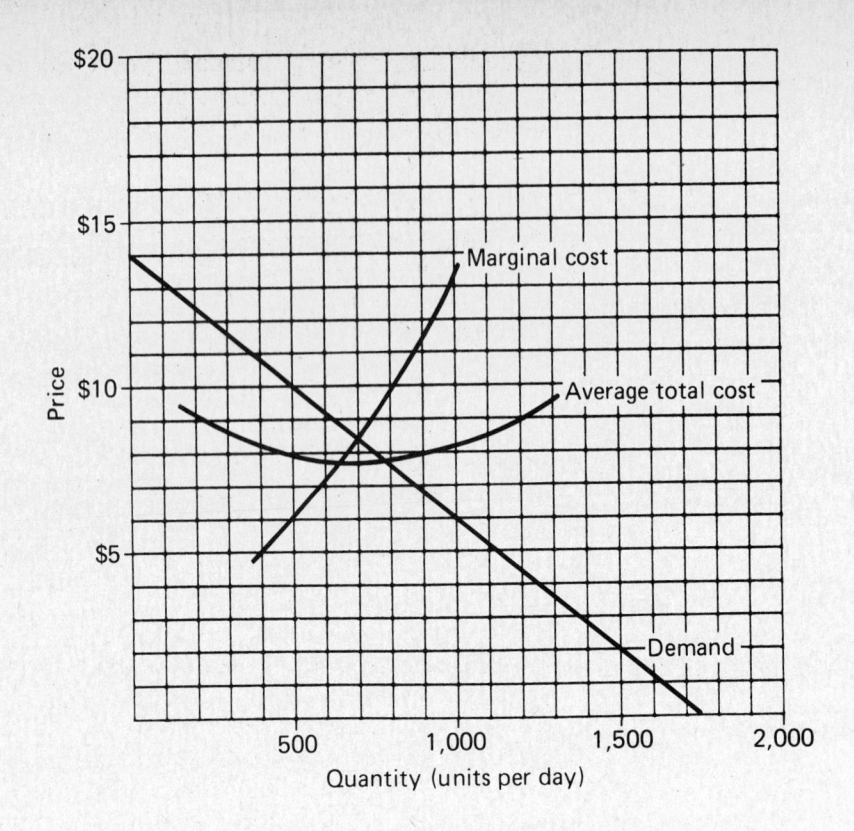

| ECONOMICS IN THE NEWS | **Airlines Step Up Battle for Key Markets**

The big airlines are going to war.
Adding flights and grabbing passengers, Atlanta-based Delta Air Lines is shouldering its way into American Airlines' stronghold at the Dallas-Fort Worth airport. American is counterattacking on Delta's home territory, the Southeast. Both carriers are squeezing United Airlines in Chicago. And all three are feverishly vying for the lucrative Hawaii market.
Currently, United has 19 percent of the domestic market, American 14 percent, and Delta 11 percent, for a combined total of 44 percent.
Forget your effete Harvard Business School strategies; this is crush-the-competition marketing in the John D. Rockefeller style. Unshackled from government regulation and financial hardship, the giant U.S. carriers are muscling each other for every passenger and every scrap of turf. The battle, which could last years and cost billions of dollars, is no game for the meek.
"The only guys who'll survive are those who eat raw meat," a Boeing official says.
United Airlines has announced a series of promotions, including rebates and improved benefits for its frequent-flier program, aimed at recouping traffic lost by the 29-day strike by its pilots. |

American Airlines, United's chief rival, matched some of United's moves, including shortening the time for advance purchase of tickets, and it topped United's offer to frequent fliers.

Source: William M. Carley, "Major Airlines Step Up Battle for Key Markets, Endanger Weak Lines," *The Wall Street Journal*, June 18, 1985, p. 1, and "United Air Offers Passengers Rebates in Post-Strike Move," *The Wall Street Journal*, June 18, 1985, p. 15. Reprinted by permission of The Wall Street Journal. © Dow Jones & Company, Inc., 1985. All Rights Reserved.

Questions

1. What is the structure of the airline industry, judging from the information in this article?
2. What is the maximum possible value for the four-firm concentration ratio in the airline industry, judging from information contained in this article?
3. Is there evidence of oligopolistic interdependence in this article? If so, what evidence?

SELF TEST

These sample test items will help you check how much you have learned. Answers are found at the end of the chapter. Scoring yourself: One or two wrong—on target. Three or four wrong—passing, but you haven't mastered the chapter yet. Five or more wrong—not good enough; start over and restudy the chapter.

1. The steel industry in the United States would best be described as
   a. pure monopoly.
   b. a cartel.
   c. oligopoly.
   d. monopolistic competition.
2. An industry with an eight-firm concentration ratio of 95 percent and a formal agreement on prices and output among the top eight firms would best be described as
   a. pure monopoly.
   b. monopolistic competition.
   c. oligopoly.
   d. a cartel.
3. Markets in which the four-firm concentration ratio is 60 percent or more accounted for about what percent of all output in 1980?
   a. More than 50 percent.
   b. Between 30 and 50 percent.
   c. Between 15 and 30 percent.
   d. Less than 15 percent.

_____ 4. An international comparison study by F. M. Scherer and others indicated that plant level economies of scale
   a. were sufficient to explain the existing degree of concentration in the United States for most industries investigated.
   b. explained most, but not all, of the existing degree of concentration in the United States for most industries investigated.
   c. explained only a small part of the existing degree of concentration in the United States for many industries investigated.
   d. were of no help in explaining concentration for any of the industries investigated.

_____ 5. Which of the following could be considered a barrier to entry into the New York City taxi industry?
   a. The necessity of raising capital to buy cabs.
   b. The necessity of training drivers in knowledge of the city streets.
   c. The fact that the city places a fixed ceiling on the number of "medallions" (permits) without which one cannot operate a cab.
   d. All of the above are barriers to entry.

_____ 6. A cartel maximizes total profits for its membership by setting output at the point where the industry's marginal cost curve intersects
   a. the horizontal axis.
   b. the industry's demand curve.
   c. the industry's marginal revenue curve.
   d. none of the above.

_____ 7. If an individual member of a cartel could be certain of escaping detection, it would be tempted to cheat by
   a. increasing price.
   b. increasing output.
   c. doing both of the above.
   d. doing neither of the above.

_____ 8. Which of the following is likely to make tacit coordination easier in an oligopolistic market?
   a. A small number of firms.
   b. A homogeneous product.
   c. A slow pace of innovation.
   d. All of the above.

_____ 9. Which of the following is likely to make tacit coordination more difficult in an oligopolistic market?
   a. A small number of firms.
   b. Presence of single dominant firm.
   c. Rapid growth and innovation.
   d. All of the above.

_____ 10. Economists who have made empirical studies of the relationship between concentration and market performance have generally looked at the data relating to
   a. marginal cost.
   b. marginal revenue.
   c. producer surplus.
   d. rates of return and the opportunity cost of capital.

_____ 11. An early study by Joe Bain concluded
   a. that profits were always higher in more concentrated than in less concentrated industries.
   b. that there was a moderate but persistent tendency for firms in concentrated industries to earn relatively high profits.
   c. that there was no difference in terms of profits between more concentrated and less concentrated industries.
   d. that concentrated industries had satisfactory market performance.

_____ 12. Which of the following might cause firms in more concentrated than industries to earn higher rates of return, on the average, than firms in less concentrated industries?
   a. Oligopolies operate much like formal cartels.
   b. Concentrated industries happen, on the average, to grow faster than less concentrated industries.
   c. Data on rates of return are distorted by failure to account properly for advertising expenditures.
   d. Any of the above might cause such a relationship.

_____ 13. It is universally agreed among economists that
   a. rivalry among a few firms is just as good as perfect competition.
   b. oligopolies perform less well than perfectly competitive markets.
   c. oligopolies closely resemble formal cartels in terms of price and output decisions.
   d. all of the above conclusions are still being actively debated.

_____ 14. Which of the following aspects of decision making under oligopoly can easily be explained by formal economic models?
   a. Determining an optimal advertising strategy.
   b. Determining how to react to a rival's price changes.
   c. Determining how and when to enter a new market.
   d. None of the above.

_____ 15. Which of the following is true in long-run equilibrium for both perfect competition and monopolistic competition?
   a. Average total cost equals price.
   b. Marginal cost equals price.
   c. Average total cost is at its minimum.
   d. All of the above.

ANSWERS TO CHAPTER 26

Hands On

Problem 1 (a) The profit-maximizing quantity is 10,000 units and the profit-maximizing price is $1.20. If each firm produces an equal share of the total, the quota will be 100 units of output per firm. (b) At 100 units of output, this firm's average total cost is 90 cents per unit. It would thus make $30 profit if it sold 100 units for $1.20 per unit, according to the cartel's plan. Under these circumstances, marginal revenue will exceed marginal cost at 100 units of output by 30 cents. (c) If the firm acted as a price taker with a price of $1.20, it would increase output to the point where marginal cost rose to $1.20. That would occur at 140 units of output. Average total cost at 140 units is about 95 cents, so the firm would earn a $35 profit. (d) In this, and every other cartel situation, each individual firm would be able to increase its profit by producing more than its quota, provided all other firms stuck to their quotas, thus keeping the market price high. Of course, if all firms cheated, the price would fall to the competitive level, and no one would earn monopoly profits.

Problem 2 (a) The vertical intercept of the marginal revenue curve is $14 and the horizontal intercept is 875. The profit-maximizing output is 500 units per day, which corresponds to the intersection of the marginal cost and marginal revenue curves. The profit-maximizing price is $10, which corresponds to the height of the demand curve at 500 units of output. (b) This situation cannot prevail in the long run. At 500 units of output, as the figure is drawn, price exceeds average total cost by $2 per unit. The firm thus earns a pure economic profit of $1,000 per day. If other firms in the industry are earning similar profits, new entrants will be attracted. As new firms enter, the demand curve will shift to the left. Entry will stop when pure economic profits disappear.

Economics in the News

(1) The industry is clearly an oligopoly. This is shown by the degree of concentration, and also by the fact that firms perceive one another as rivals in battles for key markets. (2) The three top firms account for 44 percent of the market. The smallest, Delta, has 11 percent, so the fourth largest must have 11 percent or less of the market. Thus, the four-firm concentration ratio can be no greater than 55 percent. (3) Oligopolistic interdependence is shown by the fact that each firm reacts to marketing initiatives of its rivals. American's reactions to United's post-strike discount and bonus program is a clear example of this type of behavior.

Self Test

1. **c.** It has relatively few firms, some of which are quite large, and has no system of formal collusion.
2. **d.** It is the formal agreement that makes it a cartel. The concentration wouldn't have to be so high.
3. **c.** According to Shepherd, the figure was 18 percent for 1980, down from 36 percent in 1958.
4. **c.** The rest is presumably explained by other factors, such as economies of scale above the plant level, barriers to entry, and random influences.
5. **c.** The first two items are available to newcomers on the same terms as to existing firms, but existing firms control all the medallions that the city is willing to issue. They are thus a true barrier to entry.
6. **c.** The condition is the same as that for a monopolist.
7. **b.** Alternative **a** would reduce the firm's profit if customers went elsewhere.
8. **d.** For these and other reasons, the degree of tacit coordination is likely to vary greatly from one industry to another.
9. **c.** Items **a** and **b** are thought to make it easier.
10. **d.** Information on items **a**, **b**, and **c** is not generally available.
11. **b.** Studies since then have found sometimes **a**, sometimes **b**, and sometimes **c**. The issue is still controversial.
12. **d.** Differing interpretations of the data on rates of return are one source of controversy in this area.
13. **d.** Some economists can be found to defend each position.
14. **d.** They all depend on judgment, psychology, and other hard-to-analyze factors.
15. **a.** In long-run equilibrium under monopolistic competition, price exceeds marginal cost and average total cost is declining.

Chapter 27

Entrepreneurship and the Market Process

WHERE YOU'RE GOING

When you have mastered this chapter, you will understand

1. The role that entrepreneurship plays in the market process even when markets are not in equilibrium.
2. How economists view the area of business activity known as marketing.
3. How advertising affects market performance.
4. How market structure affects efficiency in both a static and a dynamic sense.

In addition, you will add the following terms to your economic vocabulary:
   Arbitrage
   Marketing
   Static efficiency
   Dynamic efficiency

WALKING TOUR

After you have read this chapter at least once, you should work step by step through this walking tour. Fill in the blanks and answer the questions as you go along. After you have answered each question, check yourself by uncovering the answer given in the margin. If you do not understand why the answer given is the correct one, refer back to the proper section of the text.

Entrepreneurship and the Market Process

Models of equilibrium under various market structures are products

neoclassical   of the _____ school of economics. These models treat technology, product characteristics, consumer tastes, and many other aspects of reality as givens. Economists who study entrepreneurship are concerned with the way that these "givens" change over time. One school of thought that has made entrepreneurship a

Austrian   focal point is the _____ school.
like   Austrian economists, [like/unlike] neoclassical economists, see
spontaneous   the market economy as a system of _____ order in

328

not through unintended	which an orderly structure is established [through/not through] the plan of any person or group, but as the _____ outcome of individual choices made with narrower ends in mind. However, rather than focusing on equilibrium states, they focus on the
market process entrepreneur	_____ that maintains order in periods of disequilibrium. A key player in the market process is the _____.
	Recognizing and taking advantage of opportunities is one aspect of entrepreneurship. The activity of buying something at a low price in one market and selling it at a higher price in another market is
arbitrage disequilibrium	known as _____. Arbitrage can exist only when markets are in [equilibrium/disequilibrium].
innovation	Arbitrage is concerned with the way entrepreneurs take advantage of changes that arise from forces beyond their control. Another important aspect of entrepreneurship is making change happen—the process of _____.
selection	In addition to arbitrage and innovation, a third element of the market process is _____ through profit and loss. Selection ensures that entrepreneurs who make correct decisions will prosper and expand their field of influence, where those who make incorrect decisions will find their field of influence diminished.

Marketing as a Form of Entrepreneurship

One of the most fruitful places to look for examples of entrepreneurship in action is in the process of finding out what customers want and channeling a flow of goods and services to meet those wants—

marketing	the activity known as _____. The activity of marketing is traditionally considered to comprise four aspects:
product	1. _____,
distribution (place)	2. _____,
promotion	3. _____, and
price	4. _____.
less	These activities are [more/less] visible in perfectly competitive markets than in markets having the structure of oligopoly or monopolistic competition.
3	Of the various aspects of marketing, perhaps the most controversial is advertising. Advertising accounts for about _____ percent of the cost of all consumer goods purchased. Many economists have criticized advertising, in both oligopolistic and

monopolistically competitive industries, as being harmful to market performance. For example, economists W. S. Comanor and T. A. Wilson concluded that advertising was a _____, on the basis of a study that seemed to show that firms that advertised heavily has [higher/lower] profits than others. However, other economists, such as Yale Brozen, have argued that advertising is [more/less] important as a weapon for breaking into new markets than as a means of keeping firms out. They claim that results like Comanor and Wilson's are the result of _____ practices that do not reflect the categories of economic theory.

barrier to entry

higher

more

accounting

Entrepreneurship and Market Dynamics

A distinction can be made between a type of economic efficiency that consists in getting the most out of available resources, called _____ efficiency, and a type that consists in successfully expanding output through growth and innovation, called _____ efficiency. In earlier chapters, it was noted that many economists think perfect competition to be superior to monopoly, oligopoly, and monopolistic competition in terms of _____ efficiency. However, according to the Schumpeter hypothesis, perfect competition may not necessarily be superior in terms of _____ efficiency. Attempts have been made to test this hypothesis empirically; these tests have for the most part been [conclusive/inconclusive], largely because of the difficulty of measuring the rate of _____ in an industry.

static

dynamic

static

dynamic

inconclusive

innovation

ECONOMICS IN THE NEWS

New Firm Backed by Family, Friends

Asmeret Seile arrived in Philadelphia in 1980 on a tourist visa, but she said her real goal was to further her education. In Ethiopia, she had completed high school and business school, receiving a degree in bookkeeping, and she planned to study accounting here.

She had a brother-in-law here, but she knew few people. She was a frightened and lonely 19-year-old, she recalled. "I cried all the time," said Seile, who has large dark eyes and a shy smile.

Even when her tourist visa ran out, she was determined to stay, viewing the United States as "the land of opportunity." She finally was granted political asylum by the government.

Later, moving to the Washington, D.C. area with a sister, she took a part time job as a waitress and enrolled in an accounting program at the University of the District of Columbia. All her tips went into savings; her paycheck to food and tuition.

It was her experience as a waitress—watching other Ethiopians managing their own businesses—that convinced her that she wanted her own restaurant. She would rather have the headache of working for herself than the headache of working for others, she said.

With little in savings, she and her sister were turned down when they applied for a bank loan. However, she was able to raise $85,000 with the help of two cousins who had sold a taxicab business in Boston. An Ethiopian friend told them of a boutique soon to be vacated on Columbia Road. They rented it for $4,350 a month.

For help in mastering the licensing requirements and in finding suppliers, they went up the street, to the proprietor of the Asmara restaurant, a friend of Seile's.

Seile said she saw nothing remarkable in seeking help from a competitor, particularly because he is a longtime friend. Neither did the owner of the Asmara, Tesfmichael Gebre. "There is nothing to lose to be a nice person," he said.

During the start-up period, Seile said, she called upon a unique Ethiopian tradition to help her meet personal expenses: The *ekub*, a kind of mutual assistance savings plan to which members contribute a set amount of money each week. The pot is given to a different member on a rotating basis. Those in need can be bumped to the front of the line.

After much discussion, the four decided to name the restaurant Selam, an Ethiopian greeting that means peace.

The future of Selam is uncertain. The restaurant has six waitresses, who, incidentally, have now formed their own *ekub*. It is jammed on weekends but slow during the week. The rents are rising the neighborhood. And there are 12 other Ethiopian restaurants nearby.

But it is off the ground, another immigrant business born in Washington.

Source: Sandra Sugawara and Elizabeth Tucker, "New Firms Backed by Family, Friends," *The Washington Post*, December 16, 1987, sec. A, 1. ©*The Washington Post*, 1987. Used by permission.

Questions

1. How would you characterize the market structure of the restaurant industry, based on information given in this article?
2. What aspects of entrepreneurship are illustrated by Seile's restaurant? Are any aspects of entrepreneurship not illustrated?
3. What elements of the market process—arbitrage, innovation, selection—are illustrated by this story?

SELF TEST

These sample test items will help you check how much you have learned. Answers are found at the end of the chapter. Scoring yourself: One or two wrong—on target. Three or four wrong—passing, but you haven't mastered the chapter yet. Five or more wrong—not good enough; start over and restudy the chapter.

1. Which of the following distinguishes the Austrian school of economics from the neoclassical school?
   a. The Austrian school puts more emphasis on states of equilibrium.
   b. Unlike the neoclassical school, the Austrian school views the market economy as a system of spontaneous order.
   c. The Austrian school puts more emphasis on entrepreneurship.
   d. All of the above statements are valid.

2. The activity of earning a profit by buying something at a low price in one market and reselling it at a higher price in another is known as
   a. arbitration.
   b. arbitrage.
   c. market articulation.
   d. disequilibration.

3. Austrian economists consider it important that useful and productive innovations survive, while less beneficial attempts at innovation wither. Which of the following mechanisms do they see as best for accomplishing this end?
   a. Government regulation via patents and trademarks.
   b. Government regulation via health and safety standards.
   c. Legal regulation via antitrust laws.
   d. Market selection via profit and loss.

4. The process of finding out what customers want and channeling a flow of goods and services to meet those wants is called
   a. production.
   b. entrepreneurship.
   c. marketing.
   d. promotion.

5. Which of the following aspects of marketing is considered an important area for competition in oligopolistic and monopolistically competitive markets?
   a. Promotion.
   b. Distribution.
   c. Price.
   d. All of the above.

6. On the basis of studies discussed in this chapter, advertising is least likely to be able to do which of the following?
   a. Cause consumers to perceive an advertised brand of food as tasting better than a physically identical unadvertised brand.
   b. Cause consumers to try a new, previously unknown brand.
   c. Induce repeat purchases of a product that consumers have tried and found to be inferior to an unadvertised brand.
   d. Strengthen existing brand loyalties.

7. Which of the following pieces of evidence would not tend to confirm the hypothesis that advertising is a barrier to entry?
   a. Firms in industries that advertise heavily earn higher than average profits.
   b. Firms in concentrated industries advertise more than firms in less concentrated industries.
   c. Brand loyalty is highest in markets where advertising expenditures are highest.
   d. New brands tend to be advertised more heavily than old brands.

8. To say that advertising is a barrier to entry implies, among other things,
   a. that advertising is not available to newly entering firms on the same terms as it is available to existing firms.
   b. that advertising represents a large share of total costs.
   c. that advertising conveys little useful information to consumers.
   d. all of the above.

9. Which of the following best characterizes the effect of introducing advertising into the legal profession?
   a. Lower prices and an increased variety of services.
   b. Lower prices and a decreased variety of services.
   c. Higher prices and an increased variety of services.
   d. Higher prices and a decreased variety of services.

10. A study showing that, other things being equal, eyeglasses cost less in states where advertising is permitted than in states where it is prohibited would be evidence that
    a. advertising is an important barrier to entry.
    b. eyeglasses production is not monopolistically competitive.
    c. advertising is not detrimental to good market performance.
    d. the eyeglasses market is perfectly competitive where no legal restrictions on advertising exist.

11. Which of the following corresponds to good static efficiency?
    a. The economy is operating on its production possibility frontier.
    b. The economy is operating inside its production possibility frontier.
    c. The production possibility frontier is shifting outward rapidly.
    d. The production possibility frontier is becoming less curved.

12. Which of the following best characterizes the Schumpeter hypothesis?
    a. Dynamic efficiency is possible only under perfect competition.
    b. Only monopolistic firms can safely undertake research and development spending.
    c. The traditional categories of market structure are largely irrelevant to dynamic efficiency.
    d. Oligopoly is inferior to monopolistic competition and monopoly as a source of innovation.

_____ 13. The Schumpeter hypothesis implies that which of the following policies would do the most, in the long run, to improve consumer welfare?
   a. Break up large firms into small ones.
   b. Permit firms introducing major innovations to earn temporary monopoly profits.
   c. Reward firms making major innovations by giving them long-term protection from foreign competition.
   d. Increase government subsidies to research and development.

_____ 14. Attempts to subject the Schumpeter hypothesis to empirical tests appear to indicate which of the following?
   a. Large firms provide a more than proportional share of innovations in all industries.
   b. Small firms provide a more than proportional share of innovations in all industries.
   c. Supergiant firms are more innovative in proportion to their size than merely giant firms.
   d. Firms of all sizes manage to make important contributions to innovation.

_____ 15. Policies designed to break up large firms into small ones would tend to be supported by which of the following?
   a. A finding that the existing degree of concentration in most markets is the result of artificial barriers to entry.
   b. Confirmation of the Schumpeter hypothesis.
   c. A finding that larger firms spend a higher portion of their revenues on research and development than smaller firms.
   d. A finding that monopolistic competition is just as efficient as perfect competition.

ANSWERS TO CHAPTER 27

Economics in the News

(1) The restaurant industry is characterized by many small firms, product differentiation, and fairly easy entry. It is a typical monopolistically competitive industry. (2) Seile's restaurant does not appear to be especially innovative in terms of its product or its methods of operation. However, the case illustrates two other important aspects of entrepreneurship. First, alertness to opportunities: Seile recognized that there was an opportunity for a restaurant; her cousins also recognized this as an opportunity to invest the proceeds of the sale of their cab business; and Seile used her contacts in the Ethiopian community to find a suitable location for the restaurant. Second, overcoming barriers: as a recent arrival with little by way of savings, Seile did not have access to mainstream financial intermediarios like banks. Instead, she made use of family contacts and the Ethiopian mutual-help institution of the *ekub*. (3) The first person to open an Ethiopian restaurant in Washington, D.C. was certainly an innovator, however, Seile's brand of entrepreneurship is

more like that of an arbitrageur, in that it consists in spotting an opportunity that exists and taking advantage of it. The story also illustrates the process of selection through profit and loss: Seile's restaurant may or may not be successful. Theoretical considerations would lead us to expect a late entry into an already well-populated monopolistically competitive industry to operate close to zero pure economic profits unless it represented some decisive innovations.

Self Test

1. **c.** The Austrians put less emphasis on equilibrium; both they and the neoclassics see the market economy as a system of spontaneous order.
2. **a.** This, together with innovation, is an important element of entrepreneurship.
3. **d.** The Austrians think that the market achieves spontaneous order without the need for government intervention.
4. **c.** Answers **a** and **d** are particular aspects of marketing. In many ways, marketing is a manifestation of entrepreneurship.
5. **d.** Creating a product to serve customer needs is a fourth aspect of marketing.
6. **c.** Advertising might, for a time, cause consumers to overlook a product's drawbacks, but once they have decided they don't like the product, it is hard for advertising to win them back.
7. **d.** The others have all been cited as evidence that advertising is a barrier to entry in one or more studies. Answer **d** implies that advertising is a means of entry.
8. **a.** Cost alone (answer **b**) does not make something a barrier to entry if the cost is the same for new and old firms.
9. **a.** Thus, advertising appears to have improved market performance.
10. **c.** If the market were perfectly competitive, no advertising would take place.
11. **a.** Answer **c** would correspond to good dynamic efficiency.
12. **c.** Oligopolistic industries were viewed by Schumpeter as major innovators.
13. **b.** Temporary profits are an inducement to innovations, but long-term protection might prevent the next generations of innovations from entering the market. Foreign competition is often a spur to innovation.
14. **d.** There are some industries in which each of the first three answers may be true, but none of them is true in all industries.
15. **a.** Answers **b** and **c** would argue for keeping the firms big.

Chapter 28

Pricing in Factor Markets

WHERE YOU'RE GOING

When you have mastered this chapter, you will understand

1. The role that factor markets play in determining how and for whom goods are produced.
2. What determines demand for a factor of production.
3. What determines the supply curve for labor.
4. What are the characteristics of equilibrium in a competitive labor market.
5. What are the characteristics of labor market equilibrium with only one or a few employers.
6. Why wages are not the same for all labor markets and all individuals within a labor market.

In addition, you will add the following terms to your economic vocabulary:
   Factor markets
   Marginal revenue product
   Value of marginal product
   Marginal factor cost
   Marginal productivity theory of distribution
   Monopsony
   Human capital
   Efficiency wage theory

WALKING TOUR

After you have read this chapter at least once, you should work step by step through this walking tour. Fill in the blanks and answer the questions as you go along. After you have answered each question, check yourself by uncovering the answer given in the margin. If you do not understand why the answer given is the correct one, refer back to the proper section of the text.

The Demand for Factors of Production

firms
households

Factor markets differ from product markets in that _____ are the buyers and _____ are the sellers. Thus, the theory of factor market demand is based on the way that firms maximize their _____.

profit

According to the law of diminishing returns, as the amount of a variable factor used is increased, a point is reached beyond which the ____product____ of that factor declines. This means that the marginal physical product curve for a factor of production will have a [positive/~~negative~~] slope.

In addition to the marginal physical product of a factor, a firm must also take into account the ____revenue____ that can be earned by selling the added output. The change in revenue that results from the sale of the added output produced by one additional unit of factor input is called the ____MR____ product of that factor. In the case of a firm that is a perfect competitor in the market where it sells its output, marginal revenue product is equal to marginal physical product times ____price____, or ____VMP____. In the case of a firm that faces a negatively sloped demand curve for its product, marginal revenue product is [greater than/~~less than~~/equal to] value of marginal product.

(MRP = MPP)

The amount by which a firm's total factor cost must increase in order for the firm to obtain an additional unit of that factor of production is called ____MFC____. For a firm that is a price taker in the market where it buys factors, marginal factor cost is equal to the ____price____ of the factor.

For all firms, whether price takers or not, profit is maximized by hiring each factor of production up to the point where ____MFC____ equals ____MRP____.

A consequence of this rule is that for firms that are price takers in factor markets, the demand curve for a factor is equal to its ____MRP____ curve. An increase in demand for the output that a factor produces will shift the factor demand curve to the [~~right~~/left]. A decrease in the price of another factor that is a substitute for the given factor will cause the demand curve for the given factor to shift to the [right/~~left~~]. A decrease in the price of another factor that is a complement to the given factor will cause the demand curve for the given factor to shift to the [~~right~~/left]. Finally, any change in technology that increases the marginal physical product of a factor will cause the demand curve to shift to the [~~right~~/left].

Margin notes: marginal physical product; negative; revenue; marginal revenue; price; value of marginal product; less than; marginal factor cost; price; marginal factor cost; marginal revenue product; marginal revenue product; right; left; right; right

Supply and Demand in the Labor Market

Individuals' decisions regarding how much labor to supply are part of the general problem of ___consumer choice___. This choice can be approached in terms of the trade-off between income and ___leisure___. The "price," or more exactly, the ___OP___ of leisure is represented by the ___WR___. As the wage rate increases, the substitution effect causes the quantity of labor supplied to [**increase**/decrease]. At the same time, assuming leisure to be a normal good, the income effect causes the quantity of labor supplied to [increase/**decrease**]. The result is that the labor supply curve for an individual worker is likely to have a [**positive**/negative] slope at low wages and a [positive/**negative**] slope at higher wage rates. However, the labor supply curve for a particular kind of labor in a labor market—say the labor of accountants or truck drivers—will have a [**positive**/negative] slope throughout.

In competitive labor markets, the wage rate is determined by the intersection of the ___supply___ and ___demand___ curves. In such a case, each factor of production will receive a payment equal to its ___MR___ product. This conclusion is known as the ___M Products___ theory of distribution.

Markets in which there is only a single buyer of labor are called ___Monopsonies___. The supply curve of labor faced by a monopsonist has a [**positive**/negative/zero] slope. The marginal factor cost curve for a monopsonist lies [**above**/below] the supply curve. For a monopsonist, the profit-maximizing quantity of labor is determined by the intersection of the marginal revenue product curve with the ___MFC___ curve. The profit-maximizing wage rate is determined by the height of the ___labor supply___ curve at that point. Thus, in monopsony equilibrium, the wage rate is [above/**below**/equal to] the marginal revenue product of labor.

Why Wage Rates Differ

If employers are unwilling to hire members of one group of workers at the same wage rate paid to equally productive members of another group, they are said to _____. If there are no legal barriers to discrimination, the equilibrium wage rate of the disfavored group of workers will be [higher than/**lower than**/equal to] that of favored workers. If there is an equal pay law, but if

338

will	employers still discriminate, the disfavored group [will/will not] be harmed by the discrimination. This is because the discriminating
fewer	employers will hire [more/fewer] workers from the disfavored group than they would if there were no equal pay law. In a competitive labor market where some employers discriminate and others do not,
lower	those that discriminate will tend to earn [higher/lower] profits, other things being equal. In this sense, competition tends to
erode	[reinforce/erode] discrimination. If discrimination originates with customers or workers rather than with employers, competition is
less	[more/less] likely to erode discrimination.
nonwage	In addition to discrimination, _____ characteristics of jobs also cause wages to differ. Innate abilities are another source of wage variation. However, more important that innate abilities are learned abilities acquired through formal training or on-the-job
human capital	experience. These abilities are known as _____.
	Some economists think that wages higher than the minimum needed to attract the required numbers of qualified workers can raise productivity and increase profit. This proposition is called
efficiency	_____ wage theory.

HANDS ON

Now that you have reviewed the concepts introduced in this chapter, it is time for some hands-on practice with the analytical tools that have been introduced. Work through each problem in this section carefully, and then check your results against those given at the end of the chapter.

Problem 1

This problem is based on Exhibit 28.1, which shows marginal revenue product and supply curves for a monopsonistic employer.

a. If the supply and marginal revenue product curves in Exhibit 28.1a applied to a perfectly competitive labor market, what would be the equilibrium wage rate and the equilibrium quantity of labor employed?

b. Instead, we assume that the employer is a monopsonist. On this assumption, fill in the blanks in Exhibit 28.1b. Using the completed table as your guide, draw in the monopsonist's marginal labor cost curve. What is the equilibrium quantity of labor employed by the monopsonist? The equilibrium wage rate?

Exhibit 28.1a

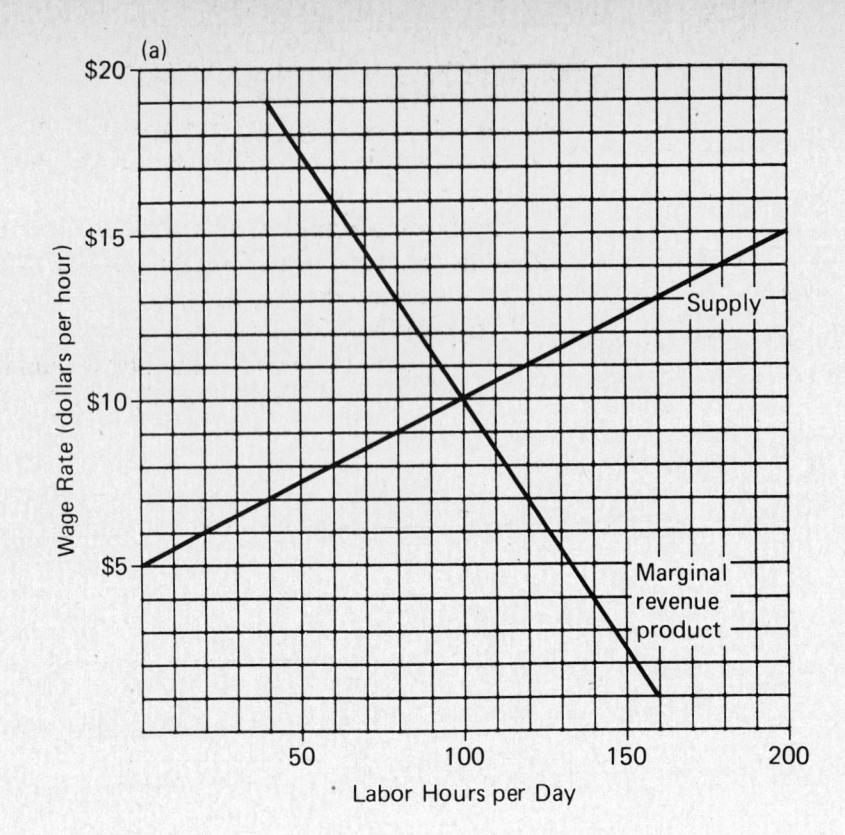

(a)

[Graph showing Wage Rate (dollars per hour) on y-axis from $0 to $20, and Labor Hours per Day on x-axis from 0 to 200. A downward-sloping "Marginal revenue product" line from about $19 at 0 hours to near $0 at 160 hours, and an upward-sloping "Supply" line from $5 at 0 hours to $15 at 200 hours. The curves intersect at approximately 100 hours, $10.]

Exhibit 28.1b

Labor Hours Per Day	Wage Rate	Total Labor Cost	Marginal Labor Cost
49	$____	$____	
			$____
50	____	____	
51	____	____	
⋮			
99	____	____	
			____
100	____	____	
			____
101	____	____	

c. Does the position of the marginal labor cost curve in Exhibit 28.1a suggest to you a shortcut method of drawing such a curve when the supply curve is a straight line? Can you prove that the shortcut method works?

Problem 2

This problem relies on indifference curve analysis, introduced in the optional appendix to Chapter 22. If you did not cover that appendix, skip this problem.

a. The horizontal axis of Exhibit 28.2a shows hours of leisure per day for one individual worker. The vertical axis shows dollars of income earned per day. At any given wage rate, the worker faces a budget line, indicating that earning more income requires giving up some leisure hours. Draw budget lines corresponding to wage rates of $2.50, $5, $7.50, $10, $12.50, and $15 per hour.

Exhibit 28.2a

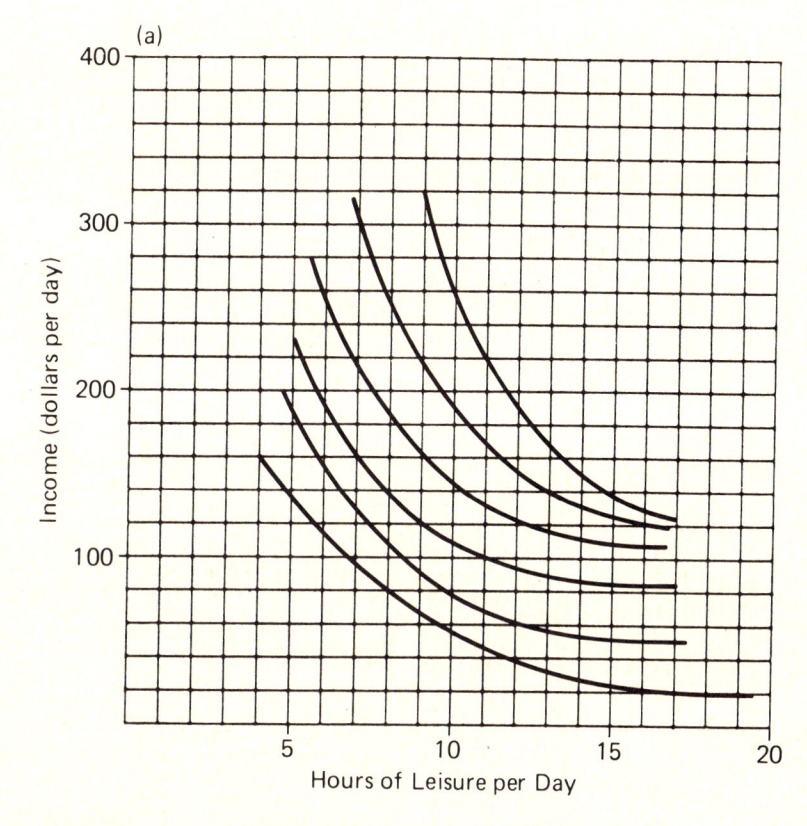

b. Using the budget lines you have just drawn, locate the equilibrium points for each wage rate. Label these points A through F, beginning with the lowest wage rate.
c. The budget lines and equilibrium points you have drawn provide you with the information you need to construct this worker's individual labor supply curve. First locate points a through f in Exhibit 28.2b corresponding to points A through F in Exhibit 28.2a. Then connect the points with a smooth free hand curve.
d. Is leisure time a normal or an inferior good for this worker? How can you tell? At about what wage rate does the income effect of a wage increase begin to outweigh the substitution effect?

Exhibit 28.2b

(blank graph: Wage Rate (dollars per hour) vs. Hours of Work per Day, both axes 0 to 20)

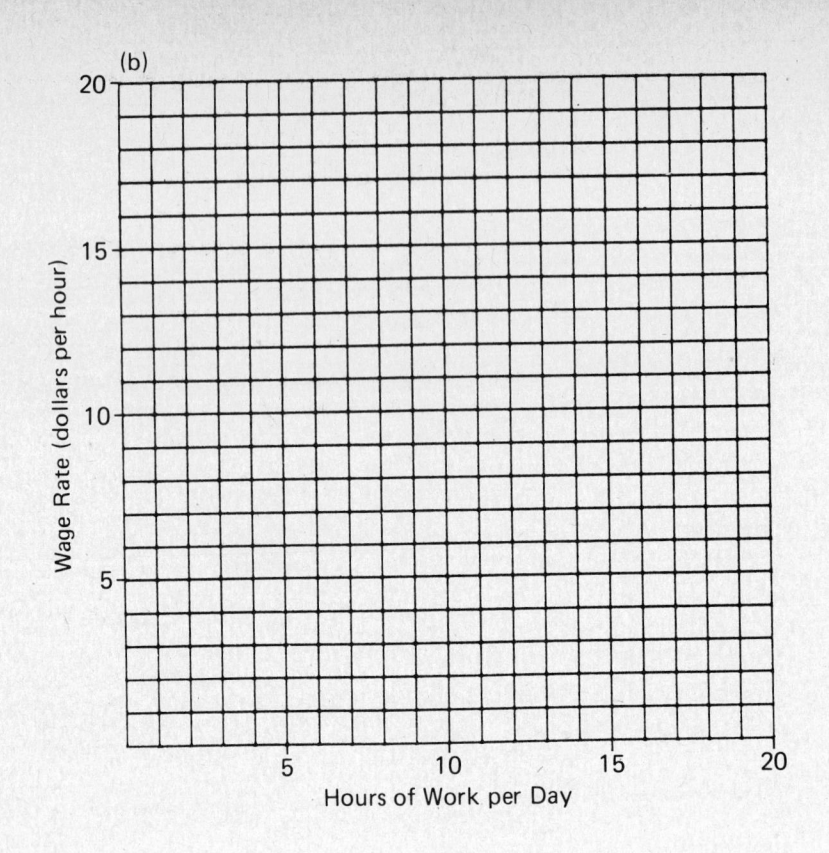

DON'T MAKE THIS COMMON MISTAKE

When you used Exhibit 28.1 to determine the equilibrium quantity of labor employed under monopsony, you went straight to the intersection of the marginal revenue product curve and marginal factor cost curve. Your correct answer: 80 labor hours per day hired by the monopsonist. If you then put down $13 per hour as the equilibrium wage rate under monopsony, you made the MOST COMMON MISTAKE for the material covered in this chapter.

If you look at the supply curve for this labor market, you will see that at a wage rate of $13 per hour, not 80, but 160 labor hours per day would be offered. TWICE AS MANY WORKERS AS NEEDED would apply for the available jobs. Instead, to maximize profit, the monopsonist will offer a wage rate just high enough to attract the quantity of labor needed. Given this supply curve, only $9 per hour need be offered to get 80 labor hours per day.

In short, AFTER you find the equilibrium quantity at the intersection of the marginal revenue product and marginal factor cost curves, LOOK STRAIGHT DOWN to the SUPPLY CURVE to get the equilibrium wage. Don't let a long line of disappointed workers pile up at your factory gate!

ECONOMICS IN THE NEWS

NURSES—Part time on call
$84 per shift (nights)

For 1150 15th St, NW Location:
  MONDAY-SATURDAY 8am-4pm; 4pm-midnight;
    midnight-8am
  SUNDAY 4pm-midnight; midnight-8am

For 2nd and Virginia Ave., SE Location:
  WEDNESDAY-SUNDAY 9pm-5am

For Springfield, Va. Location:
  MONDAY-FRIDAY 7am-3pm
  MONDAY-SUNDAY 9pm-5am

REQUIREMENTS:
  —Depending on location, VA or DC RN license
  —Ability to work independently
  —Occupational or public health experience preferred

If you are available to work on-call for any of these shifts, please send your resume to

THE WASHINGTON POST
BOX 12732
1150 15th St., NW
Washington, D.C. 20071

Source: Advertisement "Nurses—Part time on call", *The Washington Post*, October 7, 1981, sec. C, 17. © *The Washington Post*, 1981.

Questions

1. Do you think the market for nurses in Washington, D.C. is competitive? What makes you think so?
2. Would a monopsonistic employer ever run an ad in the paper asking for workers at some stated wage rate? Or would only an employer that is a price taker in the labor market do so?
3. If the wage paid to nurses in the Washington, D.C. area increased, would you expect the number of people applying for jobs as nurses also to increase? Why or why not?
4. Suppose a study of jobs at a big Washington, D.C. hospital showed (a) that 95 percent of nurses were women, and (b) that when factors such as responsibility, training, and job hazards were taken into account, nurses' pay was 25 percent less than maintenance workers, 85 percent of whom were men. A committee of nurses charges discrimination, and asks that their wage be raised to a level comparable to maintenance workers. The hospital administration replies, "We don't discriminate. But when we run an ad for maintenance workers at $105 per shift, hardly any women apply." Can you think of any reason other than discrimination for the difference in wages? Do you think nurses should be paid the same as maintenance workers even if discrimination is not the reason for their low pay?

SELF TEST

These sample test items will help you check how much you have learned. Answers are found at the end of the chapter. Scoring yourself: One or two wrong—on target. Three or four wrong—passing, but you haven't mastered the chapter yet. Five or more wrong—not good enough; start over and restudy the chapter.

_____ 1. Factor markets help determine
   a. how output is produced.
   b. for whom output is produced.
   c. both **a** and **b**.
   d. neither **a** nor **b**.

_____ 2. The increase in quantity of output resulting from a one unit increase in a variable factor, with the quantities of fixed factors held constant, is known as
   a. the marginal physical product of that factor.
   b. the marginal revenue product of that factor.
   c. the marginal factor cost of that factor.
   d. the increasing marginal product of that factor.

_____ 3. If by a one-unit increase in the quantity of labor employed, other things being equal, a monopolist can increase its total revenue by $50, then the marginal revenue product of labor for the firm is
   a. $50.
   b. less than $50.
   c. greater than $50.
   d. impossible to determine from the information given.

_____ 4. In a competitive factor market, the equilibrium wage rate for each factor will be equal to the value of marginal product if the firm is
   a. a monopolist in its output market.
   b. a perfect competitor in its output market.
   c. both **a** and **b**.
   d. neither **a** nor **b**.

_____ 5. Which of the following would cause the demand curve for a factor of production to shift to the left?
   a. An increase in demand for the product.
   b. A decrease in the price of a good that is a substitute for the product.
   c. An improvement in technology that increases the marginal physical product of the factor.
   d. A decrease in the price of a factor that is a complement for the factor in question.

_____ 6. Which of the following is represented graphically by a movement along a given labor demand curve?
   a. The effects of a change in the wage rate.
   b. The effects of a change in raw materials prices.
   c. The effects of a change in output prices.
   d. None of the above.

7. The substitution effect of a wage increase, considered in isolation, causes the number of labor hours supplied by a worker per time period
   a. to increase as the wage increases.
   b. to decrease as the wage increases.
   c. first to increase, then to decrease as the wage goes higher still.
   d. first to decrease, then to increase as the wage goes higher still.

8. The market supply curve for economics professors most likely has which of the following shapes?
   a. First slopes up, then bends back as the salary level rises.
   b. First has a negative slope, then a positive slope at high salary levels.
   c. A positive slope throughout.
   d. A negative slope throughout.

9. In equilibrium in a perfectly competitive labor market, the wage rate is equal to
   a. marginal revenue product.
   b. marginal factor cost.
   c. the height of the supply curve.
   d. all of the above.

10. If a firm must raise its wage rate from $20 per hour to $20.05 per hour in order to increase the quantity of labor it hires from 1,000 labor hours to 1,001 labor hours, its marginal labor cost is closest to which of the following values?
    a. $20.
    b. $50.
    c. $70.
    d. $140.

11. In equilibrium, a firm that is an imperfect competitor in its output market and a monopsonist in its labor market will pay a wage rate
    a. equal to marginal revenue product.
    b. less than marginal revenue product.
    c. greater than marginal revenue product.
    d. impossible to determine from the information given.

12. Given the same marginal revenue product and supply curves, the wage rate in a monopsonistic labor market will be
    a. higher than that in a competitive labor market.
    b. equal to that in a competitive labor market.
    c. lower than that in a competitive labor market.
    d. impossible to determine from the information given.

13. If there is no equal pay law, discrimination is likely to have which effect on the disfavored group?
    a. Lower the wage rate.
    b. Lower the number of jobs available.
    c. Both a and b.
    d. Neither a nor b.

____ 14. Which of the following is believed to contribute to the wage gap between men and women in the U.S. labor market?
   a. Discrimination.
   b. Differences in human capital between men and women.
   c. Differences in nonwage characteristics of jobs.
   d. All of the above probably play a role.

____ 15. According to efficiency wage theory, a profit-maximizing employer may pay a wage rate that is
   a. less than the marginal revenue product of labor.
   b. equal to the monopsony wage rate, even if the employer is a price taker.
   c. greater than the wage needed to attract the required number of qualified workers.
   d. less than the wage rate needed to attract the required number of qualified workers.

ANSWERS TO CHAPTER 28

Hands On

Problem 1 (a) Under perfect competition, the equilibrium wage rate would be $10 per hour and the equilibrium quantity of labor employed would be 100 labor hours per day. (b) See the solution to Exhibit 28.1. The equilibrium quantity under monopsony is 80 labor hours per day. The equilibrium wage rate is $9 per hour. (Not $13 per hour! See "Don't Make This Common Mistake") (c) The shortcut

Exhibit 28.1a (ans.)

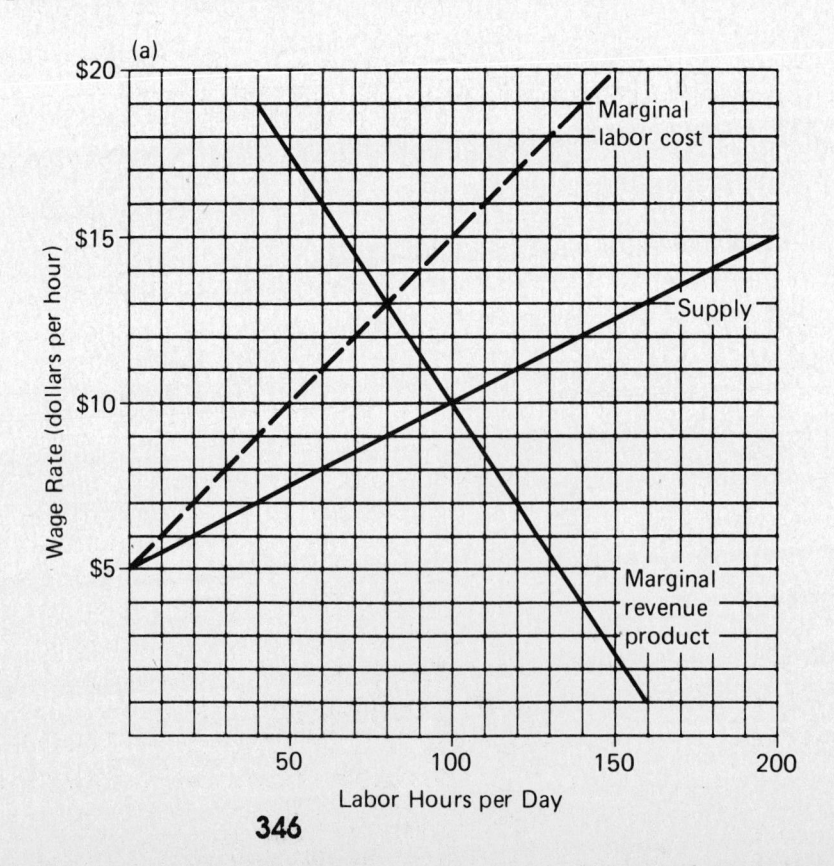

Exhibit 28.1b (ans.)

Labor Hours Per Day	Wage Rate	Total Labor Cost	Marginal Labor Cost
49	$ 7.45	$ 365.05	
			$ 9.95
50	7.50	375.00	
			10.05
51	7.55	385.05	
⋮			
99	9.95	985.05	
			14.95
100	10.00	1,000.00	
			15.05
101	10.05	1,015.05	

relies on the fact that the marginal labor cost curve passes halfway between the supply curve and the vertical axis at all wage levels. If you know elementary calculus, here is a simple proof. (If you don't know calculus, don't worry about it—just take the shortcut method on faith.) Let the supply curve be represented by the equation $W = a + bL$, where W is the wage rate, L is the quantity of labor supplied, and a and b are constants. Total labor cost equals the wage rate times the quantity of labor at any point on the supply curve. To get a total labor cost function, multiply the supply curve equation by L, getting the equation $T = aL + bL^2$. The marginal labor cost curve is the first derivative of this total labor cost equation. Thus, using T' to represent marginal labor cost, we get $T' = a + 2bL$. Comparing the equations for the supply curve and marginal labor cost curve reveals that both have the same vertical intercept, but the slope of the marginal labor cost curve is twice that of the supply curve.

Problem 2 (a) Begin with the budget curve for a wage of $2.50 per hour. If the worker takes 24 hours per day of leisure, money income will be zero. Thus, the point (24,0) on the horizontal axis is one end of the budget line. If the worker were to work 24 hours per day, leisure time would be zero and total money income would be $60. Thus, the point (0,60) on the vertical axis is the other end of this budget line. Construct other budget lines in the same manner, as shown in the solution graph for Exhibit 28.2a and b. (b) At $2.50 per hour, the worker would maximize utility by taking 14 hours of leisure per day, that is, by working 10 hours per day. This is shown as the tangency of the $2.50 budget line to an indifference curve at Point A. The remaining points are shown in the solution graph.
(c) At $2.50 per hour, quantity supplied is 10 hours per day (Point a in part b of the solution graph). Fill in the other points and connect them as shown. (d) Leisure is a normal good. An increase in the wage rate is also an increase in the price (that is, the opportunity

Exhibit 28.2a (ans.)

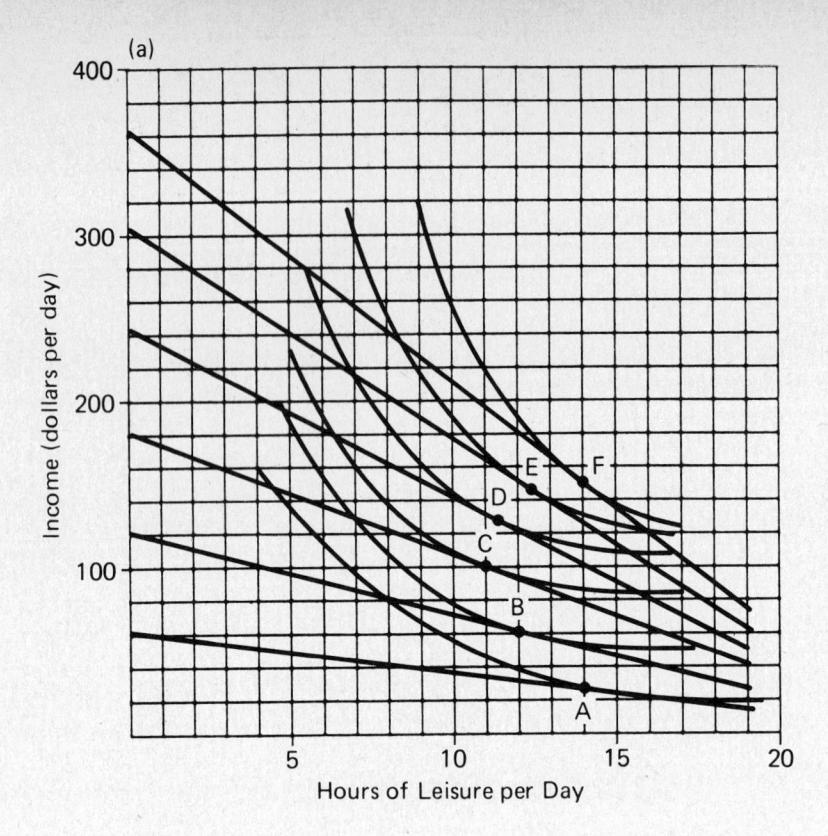

Exhibit 28.2b (ans.)

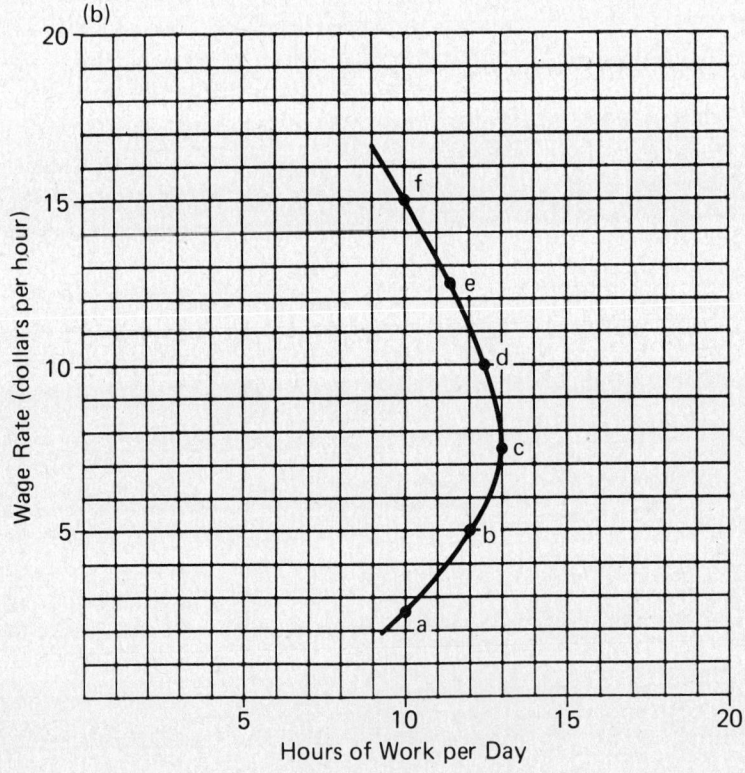

cost) of leisure, and also increases the worker's real income. The substitution effect of an increase in the price of leisure will always be in the direction of reducing leisure. If leisure were an inferior good, the income effect of an increase in the wage rate would also cause a reduction in leisure. Thus, if leisure were an inferior good, both effects would work in the same direction, and the supply curve would never bend backward. The fact that this supply curve does bend backward at wages above $7.50 per hour indicates that leisure is a normal good, and that the income effect begins to outweigh the substitution effect at wages higher than $7.50 per hour.

Economics in the News

(1) The market for nurses in a big city is fairly close to perfect competition in structure. Many employers require nurses. The number of people with such training is large. Uniform licensing requirements for registered nurses help maintain at least a moderate degree of homogeneity of skill level among applicants. (2) Although the employer that ran this ad is probably a price taker in the nurse market and simply believes $84 to be about the current prevailing wage rate, the fact that the wage rate is stated in the ad does not itself prove that the employer is a price taker. Consider a monopsonistic situation, e.g., one huge hospital in a relatively isolated community. Such an employer might run an ad at a set rate, such as $84 per shift and wait to see if enough people applied. If they did not, the offer could be raised in next month's ad, and so on, until by trial and error, the lowest wage was discovered at which all the jobs could be filled. (3) The supply curve of nurses in the Washington, D.C. area presumably does slope upward. At wage rates too low, some people with RN training would take other jobs or might withdraw from the labor market altogether. At high enough wage rates, Washington would get a reputation as a good place for nursing jobs and applications would be drawn from a wide geographic area. This would be the case whether each individual nurse's supply curve had a positive or negative slope at the prevailing wage rate. (4) The difference in pay could be caused by differences in the supply of workers to the two occupations. Perhaps women typically don't like the nonwage characteristics of maintenance jobs, or perhaps the pool of women trained for them is small. Opinions differ as to whether the proper policy is to eliminate discrimination and then let the market determine wages; to let the market determine wages but to make more active efforts to recruit women for higher paid occupations; or to pay comparable wages regardless of supply and demand considerations.

Self Test

1. **c.** How, because relative factor prices determine production methods, and for whom, because they determine household incomes.
2. **a.** Answer **b** is the increase measured in dollar terms.
3. **a.** This is the definition of marginal revenue product.
4. **b.** For a monopolist, marginal revenue product is below value of marginal product, so the equilibrium wage rate is also below the value of marginal product.
5. **b.** The others would cause the curve to shift to the right.
6. **a.** Items **b** and **c** produce a shift in the labor demand curve.

7. **a.** An increase in the wage rate raises the opportunity cost of leisure, and causes the worker to substitute goods (income) for leisure.
8. **c.** Because new professors will be attracted to the profession as the salary rises.
9. **d.** The supply curve and marginal factor cost curve are the same in perfect competition.
10. **c.** $20.05 for the added worker, and $50 at 5 cents each to the 1,000 workers already on the job.
11. **b.** Because the supply curve is below the marginal factor cost curve, and in equilibrium, marginal factor cost is equal to marginal revenue product.
12. **c.** Because the wage rate will in each case correspond to a point on the supply curve, and because for the monopsonist, the quantity hired will be less.
13. **c.** Only **b** if there is an equal pay law.
14. **d.** Item **a** operates on the demand side, while **b** and **c** operate on the supply side.
15. **c.** The theory holds that a higher wage rate induces increased productivity.

Chapter 29

Labor Unions and Collective Bargaining

WHERE YOU'RE GOING

When you have mastered this chapter, you will understand

1. How labor unions have developed over time in the United States.
2. The main provisions of U.S. labor law.
3. How wage rates are determined in unionized markets.
4. What unions do in addition to bargaining over wages and benefits.

In addition, you will add the following terms to your economic vocabulary:
    Craft unionism
    Industrial unionism
    Bilateral monopoly

WALKING TOUR

After you have read this chapter at least once, you should work step by step through this walking tour. Fill in the blanks and answer the questions as you go along. After you have answered each question, check yourself by uncovering the answer given in the margin. If you do not understand why the answer given is the correct one, refer back to the proper section of the text.

History of Unionism in the United States

The earliest unions in the United States were formed from local groups of workers all practicing the same trade. Such unions are

craft   known as _____ unions. The first national labor organi-
Knights of Labor   zation was the _____ formed in the post-Civil War
did not   period. This union [did/did not] limit itself to craft union activities.
700,000   Its membership reached a peak of about _____ in 1886,
AFL   but declined rapidly thereafter to be replaced by the _____.
craft   This organization once again emphasized _____
unionism and avoided political activity not closely related to bread-and-butter issues.

351

industrial	Unions made up of all workers in an industry, regardless of trade, are known as _____ unions. The most successful
United Mine Workers	early industrial union was the _____, founded in
1890	_____. However, industrial unions did not become
1930s, CIO	strong until the _____. The _____ was formed at that time, and by the end of World War II, union member-
35	ship reached an all-time peak of about _____ percent of the nonagricultural labor force. Since that time, union membership
18	has stagnated, and now only about _____ percent of the nonagricultural labor force is unionized.

Public Policy Toward Unions

with hostility	In the early days, unions were treated [protectively/with hostility] by the courts. A favorite weapon of employers were court orders, or
injunctions	_____, barring unions from striking, picketing, and other activities. In 1932, these injunctions were made illegal by the
Norris-LaGuardia	_____ Act. This was followed in 1935 by legislation more
Wagner	favorable still to unions—the _____ Act. This act set up
National Labor Relations, employers	the _____ Board to oversee labor policy, and listed certain unfair labor practices of [unions/employers/both]. Under the
increased	Wagner Act, labor union membership [increased/stagnated/decreased].
	After World War II public fear of damaging strikes and a changed political climate led to passage of legislation that some-
Taft-Hartley	what limited union powers. This was the _____ Act of
union	1947. This act added a list of unfair [union/employer] labor prac-
secondary	tices, outlawed _____ boycotts, and limited the
closed	_____ shop, under which union membership is a condition of employment. In 1959, Congress passed further legislation aimed at fostering internal union democracy and fighting union cor-
Landrum-Griffin	ruption. This was the _____ Act.

Collective Bargaining and Wage Rates

	One approach to unions is to treat them as maximizing organizations. In a competitive labor market, a union strike threat [can/
can	cannot] result in an increased wage rate. If successful in raising
a decrease	wages, a strike will result in [an increase/a decrease/no change] in the number of jobs.

Some economists have suggested that unions aim to maximize employment, which would call for setting the wage where the

supply, demand _____ and_____ curves intersect. Others have suggested that unions aim to maximize the wage bill, which

unit would mean setting wages at the point of _____ elasticity of demand. Still others have suggested that unions maximize the difference between the wage bill and worker opportunity costs,

rents that is, worker _____. In order to maximize worker rents, the wage should be set to give a quantity of employment corresponding to the point where the curve representing the marginal

supply curve gain in total wage income crosses the _____. In theory, unions can increase both the quantity of labor employed and the

monopsonist wage rate if they bargain with an employer who is a _____.

Other economists doubt that unions behave as maximizers. The

do not reason is that workers [do/do not] share a single wage that would maximize utility for all. Thus, more senior workers might benefit from a higher wage rate that would cause more junior workers to lose their jobs. Under these circumstances, the behavior of unions depends on political considerations. One model suggests that the wage the union aims for will be governed by the interests of the

median _____ union member.

What Else Do Unions Do?

do not Unions [do/do not] limit their activities to bargaining over wages. Another major function is to give workers a voice in how the workplace is run. For example, unions often bargain with employers

health and safety over _____ conditions. They also play a role in settling

grievances the _____ of individual union members.

Some researchers have suggested that unions raise productivity.

higher productivity However, many top nonunion companies contend that [higher productivity/a lower wage] is the main benefit of operating in a nonunion environment. The discovery that well-managed nonunion companies pay wages that are as high or higher than unionized

efficiency companies is consistent with _____ wage theory.

353

HANDS ON

Now that you have reviewed the concepts introduced in this chapter, it is time for some hands-on practice with the analytical tools that have been introduced. Work through this section carefully, and then check your results against those given at the end of the chapter.

The questions that follow are based on Exhibit 29.1, which shows demand and supply curves for a typical labor market in which employers are perfectly competitive.

Exhibit 29.1

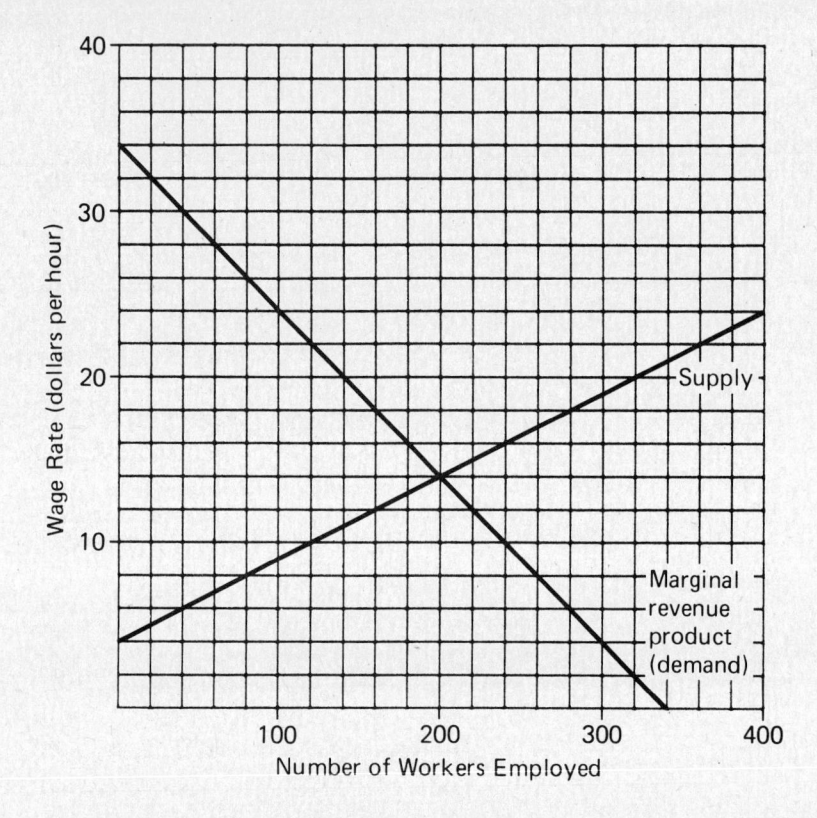

a. If workers behave competitively and are nonunionized, what will be the equilibrium wage rate and number of workers employed?
b. What wage rate would a union bargain for if its objective were to maximize the number of jobs in this labor market?
c. What wage rate would a union bargain for if its objective were to maximize the total sum of wages paid to all workers in this labor market?
d. What is the opportunity cost of taking a job in this labor market to the 100th worker to take a job there? To the 120th? To the 140th? At what wage rate is total worker rent maximized?
e. Suppose the union has 199 members who decide by majority vote what wage the union should bargain for. If workers were interested only in getting jobs for themselves at the highest possible wage, what wage would the median voter model predict?

354

ECONOMICS IN THE NEWS

Ingersoll-Rand Fights the Unions

Five years ago, union workers at Ingersoll-Rand Co. made bearings in South Bend, Indiana, hand tools in South Deerfield, Massachusetts, and pneumatic tools in Athens, Pennsylvania.

Today, the bearings plant is closed, the work shifted to a nonunion factory. The hand-tool plant has been sold. And although Ingersoll-Rand still makes tools in Athens, the workers have voted to disband their union.

In the past few years, Intersoll-Rand has moved production from union plants in the North to nonunion plants in the South. It has withdrawn from businesses, including some that were heavily unionized. And where it has had the chance, it has encouraged workers to reject their unions. The result: 30 percent of Ingersoll-Rand's U.S. production workers are now represented by unions, down from 60 percent at the end of 1981. Similar strategies are being employed successfully by other big industrial companies that once were union strongholds.

"Some of the problems confronting labor can be laid at the feet of the government and anti-union companies, but some of the blame must be shared by the labor movement itself," says James Medoff, a Harvard labor economists and adviser to the AFL-CIO."

Source: Daved Wessel, "Fighting Off Unions, Ingersoll-Rand Uses Wide Range of Tactics," *The Wall Street Journal*, June 13, 1985, p. 1. Reprinted by permission of The Wall Street Journal. © Dow Jones & Company, Inc., 1985. All Rights Reserved.

Questions

1. What can unions offer workers that would persuade them not to vote to disband their unions? Can unions offer anything that is potentially attractive to both firms and workers?
2. What benefits do you think Ingersoll-Rand hopes to get by reducing unionization?
3. If Ingersoll-Rand wants to operate as a nonunion firm, what sorts of policies might it want to pursue to maintain a loyal, productive labor force?

SELF TEST

These sample test items will help you check how much you have learned. Answers are found at the end of the chapter. Scoring yourself: One or two wrong—on target. Three or four wrong—passing, but you haven't mastered the chapter yet. Five or more wrong—not good enough; start over and restudy the chapter.

1. Approximately what percentage of the nonagricultural labor force belonged to unions in the United States as of the mid 1980s?
   a. Less than 10 percent.
   b. Less than 20 percent.
   c. About 30 percent.
   d. More than 50 percent.

_____ 2. Which of the following labor organizations was founded at the earliest date?
   a. American Federation of Labor.
   b. Congress of Industrial Organizations.
   c. Knights of Labor.
   d. Industrial Workers of the World.

_____ 3. Which of the following did not characterize the American Federation of Labor in its early years?
   a. Craft unionism.
   b. Business unionism.
   c. Lobbying in support of labor.
   d. Support of a national labor party.

_____ 4. Which of the following industries was the first to be organized on industrial union principles?
   a. Coal.
   b. Steel.
   c. Tires.
   d. Automobiles.

_____ 5. Which of the following union organizations was most radical in its political activities?
   a. American Federation of Labor.
   b. Congress of Industrial Organizations.
   c. Knights of Labor.
   d. International Workers of the World.

_____ 6. Which of the following labor laws was passed at the earliest date?
   a. The Norris-LaGuardia Act.
   b. The Wagner Act.
   c. The Taft-Hartley Act.
   d. The Landrum-Griffin Act.

_____ 7. Which of the following pieces of labor legislation established the National Labor Relations Board?
   a. The Norris-LaGuardia Act.
   b. The Wagner Act.
   c. The Taft-Hartley Act.
   d. The Landrum-Griffin Act.

_____ 8. Which of the following labor laws established a list of unfair union labor practices?
   a. The Norris-LaGuardia Act.
   b. The Wagner Act.
   c. The Taft-Hartley Act.
   d. The Landrum-Griffin Act.

_____ 9. Which of the following labor laws is concerned with the rights of rank-and-file union members in internal union affairs?
   a. The Norris-LaGuardia Act.
   b. The Wagner Act.
   c. The Taft-Hartley Act.
   d. The Landrum-Griffin Act.

_____ 10. A union formed in a previously competitive labor market, in which the competitive equilibrium lies on an elastic portion of the labor demand curve, can reasonably hope to be able to increase which of the following in the market where it operates?
   a. The wage rate.
   b. The total wage bill.
   c. Total employment.
   d. All of the above.

_____ 11. A union facing a straight-line labor demand curve maximizes the total income of its members by setting the wage at
   a. the highest possible level.
   b. the point of unit demand elasticity.
   c. the competitive equilibrium wage.
   d. b or c, whichever is the higher wage.

_____ 12. A union formed in a monopsonistic labor market can, at least within limits, reasonably hope to raise which of the following for its members?
   a. Wages.
   b. Total employment.
   c. Both a and b.
   d. Neither a nor b.

_____ 13. A union formed in a previously monopsonistic labor market has already raised the wage of its members up to the equivalent of the competitive equilibrium wage. Which of the following will happen if it raises the wage further?
   a. Employment will increase and total labor income will decrease.
   b. Employment will decrease and total labor income will increase.
   c. Employment and total labor income will both decrease.
   d. Insufficient information is given for an answer to be reached.

_____ 14. In a situation of bilateral monopoly in a labor market, the equilibrium wage rate will be?
   a. Equal to the competitive equilibrium wage.
   b. Above the competitive equilibrium wage.
   c. Below the competitive equilibrium wage.
   d. Impossible to determine from the information given.

_____ 15. A study by Freeman and Medoff of the effects of unions on wage rates indicate that
   a. unions significantly raise the wage rates of their members.
   b. unions have no effect on wage rates in most industries.
   c. unions do not affect average wage levels, but they do increase the inequality of wages within an industry.
   d. wages are higher in nonunion industries.

ANSWERS TO CHAPTER 29

Hands On

(a) The competitive equilibrium would be $14 per hour and 200 workers employed. (b) The job-maximizing equilibrium is the same as the competitive equilibrium. (c) The wage rate that maximizes the total wage bill is $17 per hour. At that wage, 170 workers would be employed. Find this by drawing a marginal revenue curve corresponding to the demand curve shown. (A straight line from $34 on the vertical axis to 170 workers on the horizontal.) (d) The supply curve measures the opportunity cost to the marginal worker of taking the job. For example, the reason you can't get more than 100 workers in this market if you pay $9 an hour is that all but 100 workers have something else to do that is worth more than $9 to them. For some workers, the best alternative activity on which the opportunity cost calculation is based may be another job. For others, the most favorable alternative opportunity may be that of searching for a still better job. For still other workers, the best alternative may be staying out of the labor force in order to engage in leisure, child care, or "underground" economic activities. The opportunity cost to the 120th worker is $10 per hour. To the 140th worker, it is $11 per hour. Beyond 120 workers (a wage of $22 per hour measured by the demand curve), the increase in total labor income (measured by the height of the marginal revenue curve) is less than the opportunity cost to the added worker of taking the job. That is thus the wage rate that maximizes worker rents. (e) According to the median voter model, a majority coalition of the 100 most senior workers would bargain for a wage of $24 per hour. That is as high as they could go and all keep their jobs, as the figure is drawn.

Economics in the News

(1) First, unions must convince firms and workers that they will not demand wages so high as to make the firm uncompetitive. Second, they must convince both firms and workers that they are not enemies of productivity. Third, they should accent positive services they perform, such as giving workers a voice in settling grievances, making sure employers observe fair play, and increasing the quality of work life. (2) Ingersoll-Rand undoubtedly would like lower wage rates, but surveys of managers of nonunion firms find that they productivity is considered a bigger advantage than low wages in many industries. (3) A study by Fred K. Foulkes found that in top nonunion firms, managers work hard to maintain a sense of equality; try to avoid layoffs; promote from within; offer wages and fringe benefits that are competitive with unionized firms (at least in many industries); and are careful to be fair in handling grievances.

Self Test

1. **b.** About 18 percent of the nonfarm workforce in 1984.
2. **c.** It was founded in 1869.
3. **d.** In this, it was unlike European labor movements of the period.
4. **a.** The United Mine Workers was founded in 1890; the others were not organized until the 1930s.
5. **d.** Opposition to World War I made it very unpopular.
6. **a.** It was passed in 1932.
7. **b.** This act was viewed as more prolabor than the preceding Norris-LaGuardia Act.
8. **c.** The Wagner Act established unfair employer labor practices.
9. **d.** It was passed in response to charges of widespread union corruption.
10. **a.** As the union moves up and to the right along the elastic portion of the demand curve, both employment and the total wage bill will fall.
11. **d.** The answer is **b** only if the original equilibrium is on the inelastic portion of the demand curve.
12. **c.** Provided it does not raise the wage too far above the competitive level.
13. **d.** Impossible to say without knowing the elasticity of demand at the point of competitive equilibrium.
14. **d.** No simple determination of the wage can be made for this market structure; it depends on relative bargaining power.
15. **a.** By 20 percent on average, and by as much as 30 percent in some cases, according to these economists.

Chapter 30

Rent, Interest, and Profit

WHERE YOU'RE GOING

When you have mastered this chapter, you will understand

1. What role interest plays in credit markets and markets for capital.
2. How payments made at different points in time can properly be compared.
3. How the theory of rent can be applied to land as a factor of production.
4. Where profits come from in the views of various economists.

In addition, you will add the following terms to your economic vocabulary:
   Present value
   Discounting
   Pure economic rent
   Capitalized value of a rent

WALKING TOUR

After you have read this chapter at least once, you should work step by step through this walking tour. Fill in the blanks and answer the questions as you go along. After you have answered each question, check yourself by uncovering the answer given in the margin. If you do not understand why the answer given is the correct one, refer back to the proper section of the text.

Interest and Capital

Interest can be earned both on loans made for consumption purposes and on those made for productive investment. Investors are willing to pay interest on production loans because of the superior

roundabout   productivity of __roundabout__ methods of production. By this is

present   meant methods of production are those that use __present__ resources to produce capital equipment that, in turn, will increase

future   the rate of __future__ output.

    In the short run, the supply of capital equipment is fixed and

vertical   can be represented by a [vertical/horizontal] supply curve. The intersection of this supply curve with the demand curve for the services of capital equipment determines the current lease price of the

360

capital equipment. If the lease price of the equipment, capitalized at the prevailing rate of interest, is [higher/lower] than the replacement cost of the equipment, it will be profitable to invest in more of such equipment. As the capital stock increases, the short-run supply curve shifts to the [left/right] and the lease price [rises/falls]. Eventually, if the demand curve remained stationary, an equilibrium would be reached in which no further investment would be profitable.

Investment decisions require that firms be able to compare payments made at different points in time. In a world where funds can be loaned out at compound interest, it is always worthwhile to receive a sum as [early/late] as possible. The interest that could have been earned by receiving a sum earlier rather than later represents the ___opp___ cost of a deferred payment. Thus, a sum to be received in the future has a present value that is [more/less] than an equal sum to be received in the present.

To be specific, let V_p be the sum that if invested today at r percent interest will grow to the sum V_t after t years. V_p is known as the ___pv___ of the sum V_t. The procedure for calculating present value is known as ___discounting___. The discount formula is _____.

The Markets for Land and Natural Resources

Pure economic rent is the income earned by a factor of production that is in perfectly ___inelastic___ supply. The supply curve of such a factor is a ___vertical___ line. The rental value of the factor is determined in a competitive market by the intersection of the vertical supply curve with the marginal ___RP___ curve of the factor.

If a rent-earning factor of production, such as a parcel of land, is sold outright, its rental value becomes *capitalized* into the purchase price. In the simplest case, where a resource is expected to earn a constant annual rent in perpetuity, the capitalized value of the resource can be calculated by dividing the ___lease R___ by the ___i rate___. For example, given a 5 percent rate of interest, a property producing an annual rental income of $2,000 would have a capitalized value of $___40___.

Profit and Entrepreneurship

According to one theory, profit is a reward that entrepreneurs earn for bearing risk. This theory assumes that most people [like/dislike] risk, other things being equal, and hence are willing to pay to avoid it. For example, an entrepreneur starting a new business contracts to pay workers and suppliers even if the firm fails and is thus able to buy their labor and resources at a [higher/lower] price than would be the case if they share more of the risk. Other economists have considered entrepreneurship to be a _____, and have counted profit as its reward. According to the Austrian theory, profits are earned by buying [high/low] and selling [high/low], that is, through _____, and also through _____.

Margin answers: dislike; lower; factor of production; low, high; arbitrage, innovation

HANDS ON

Now that you have reviewed the concepts introduced in this chapter, it is time for some hands-on practice with the analytical tools that have been introduced. Work through this section carefully, and then check your results against those given at the end of the chapter.

GFM Corp. is considering the purchase of a stamping machine to make certain small metal parts it has previously bought from a subcontractor at a cost of $40,000 per year. Two firms submit bids to supply the machine. Supplier A offers its machine for $100,000. The machine will cost $15,000 per year to operate and will last 5 years. At the end of the fifth year it will have a salvage value of $5,000. Supplier B offers its machine for $95,000. This machine will also last 5 years and have a salvage value of $5,000, but it will cost $20,000 per year to operate. In an effort to offset the disadvantage of higher operating costs, Supplier B offers to pay the entire $20,000 operating cost during the first year. Which machine is a better buy, if the two proposals are evaluated at a 10 percent discount rate? Complete the tables in Exhibit 30.1 to determine which proposal offers the greater discounted net cash flow.

Exhibit 30.1

Year (1)	Net Cash Flow (2)	Discount Factor (10 percent discount rate) (3)	Discounted Net Cash Flow (4)
Supplier A			
0	-$100,000	_____	$_____
1	25,000	_____	_____
2	25,000	_____	_____
3	25,000	_____	_____
4	25,000	_____	_____
5	30,000	_____	_____
	Total discounted net cash flow		$_____
Supplier B			
0	-$95,000	_____	$_____
1	40,000	_____	_____
2	20,000	_____	_____
3	20,000	_____	_____
4	20,000	_____	_____
5	25,000	_____	_____
	Total discounted net cash flow		$_____

SELF TEST

These sample test items will help you check how much you have learned. Answers are found at the end of the chapter. Scoring yourself: One or two wrong—on target. Three or four wrong—passing, but you haven't mastered the chapter yet. Five or more wrong—not good enough; start over and restudy the chapter.

_____ 1. The term "interest" can be used to mean
  a. the income earned from consumption loans.
  b. the income earned from production loans.
  c. the return to capital as a factor of production.
  d. any of the above.

_____ 2. Other things being equal, an increased preference by households for present rather than future consumption would mean
  a. a rightward shift in the demand curve for loanable funds.
  b. a leftward shift in the demand curve for loanable funds.
  c. a movement down along the loanable funds demand curve.
  d. a movement up along the loanable funds demand curve.

_____ 3. Other things being equal, which of the following would cause a decline in the rate of interest?
   a. An improvement in the productivity of roundabout production methods.
   b. A rightward shift in the marginal revenue product curve of capital equipment.
   c. An increase in the average life expectancy, causing households to postpone some present consumption.
   d. None of the above.

_____ 4. If household saving were the only source of loanable funds and if the only reason to save were to build up a "nest egg" of fixed nominal size for retirement, we would expect the supply curve of loanable funds to be
   a. positively sloped.
   b. negatively sloped.
   c. vertical.
   d. horizontal.

_____ 5. If an office word processor expected to last seven years (with no scrap value) has a rental value of $1,000 per year to a firm and a cost of $10,000, it will not pay for the firm to acquire such a machine unless the rate of interest is which of the following?
   a. At least 10 percent.
   b. Exactly 10 percent.
   c. Less than 10 percent.
   d. It will not pay no matter what the rate of interest.

_____ 6. The best explanation of why we have not reached a "steady state" in which no further capital investment of any kind is worthwhile is that
   a. the demand curve for capital is perfectly elastic.
   b. the supply curve of capital is perfectly elastic.
   c. technological progress constantly shifts the supply curve to the right.
   d. technological progress constantly shifts the demand curve to the right.

_____ 7. The present value of a sum of $80, payable 4 years in the future, discounted at a rate of 12 percent per year, is closest to which of the following?
   a. $80.
   b. $64.
   c. $51.
   d. $35.

_____ 8. Which of the following might be said to earn a pure economic rent?
   a. A parcel of farmland.
   b. An operatic tenor with a voice of rare quality.
   c. A cab owner in a city where the supply of cab licenses is perfectly inelastic.
   d. All of the above.

_____ 9. A parcel of land having a perpetual rental value of $400 per year would have what capitalized value, assuming a 4 percent rate of interest?
   a. $1,000.
   b. $10,000.
   c. $1,600.
   d. $16,000.

_____ 10. Assuming a 5 percent rate of interest, what would be the capitalized value of an apartment building that produced a rental income of $100,000 per year and was expected to become worthless at the end of twenty years?
   a. $2 million.
   b. Less than $2 million.
   c. More than $2 million.
   d. Insufficient information is given for an answer to be reached.

_____ 11. Pure economic profit means total revenue minus
   a. implicit costs.
   b. explicit costs.
   c. both **a** and **b**.
   d. neither **a** nor **b**.

_____ 12. The theory of profit as a reward for risk bearing implies that most people, given a choice between a $100 bill and a lottery ticket having one chance in a thousand of winning $100,000, would show which preference?
   a. They would prefer the lottery ticket.
   b. They would prefer the $100 bill.
   c. They would be indifferent between the two.
   d. None of the above is implied by the theory.

_____ 13. A person who, on a certain date, bought 100 ounces of gold in the London gold market at $402 per ounce and simultaneously sold 100 ounces of gold in the Zurich market at $403.50 per ounce would be said to earn an income primarily through
   a. risk bearing.
   b. arbitrage.
   c. innovation.
   d. rent seeking.

_____ 14. The writings of Joseph Schumpeter placed particular emphasis on which of the following sources of profit?
   a. Arbitrage.
   b. Risk bearing.
   c. Innovation.
   d. Factor services.

_____ 15. Entrepreneurship differs from the factors of production labor, capital, and natural resources, in that
   a. it is not necessary for production.
   b. it produces no income for the person who supplies it.
   c. it is not scarce.
   d. it is not measurable.

ANSWERS TO CHAPTER 30

Hands On

The completed table is shown in the solution for Exhibit 30.1. Supplier A's proposal produces a negative discounted net cash flow; it would not be worth purchasing even if it were the only option. Supplier B's proposal produces a positive net cash flow. It should be accepted.

Exhibit 30.1 (ans.)

Year (1)	Net Cash Flow (2)	Discount Factor (10 percent discount rate) (3)	Discounted Net Cash Flow (4)
Supplier A			
0	-$100,000	1.00	-$100,000
1	25,000	0.91	23,750
2	25,000	0.83	20,750
3	25,000	0.75	18,750
4	25,000	0.68	17,000
5	30,000	0.62	18,600
	Total discounted net cash flow		-$ 2,150
Supplier B			
0	-$95,000	1.00	-$95,000
1	40,000	0.91	36,400
2	20,000	0.83	16,600
3	20,000	0.75	15,000
4	20,000	0.68	13,600
5	25,000	0.62	15,500
	Total discounted net cash flow		$ 2,100

Self Test

1. **d.** All of these, expressed as a percentage rate of return, must be equal when all markets are in equilibrium, leaving aside considerations of risk and maturity.
2. **a.** Because the demand for consumption loans would increase.
3. **c.** This would cut the demand for consumption loans, whereas **a** and **b** would increase the demand for production loans.

4. **b.** In this case, a higher rate of interest would mean that less would have to be put into the retirement fund each year in order to achieve the desired nest egg at retirement age.
5. **d.** The machine never pays for its replacement cost, let alone having anything left over to cover interest.
6. **d.** Technological progress improves the productivity of capital, making new projects worthwhile.
7. **c.** Apply the present value formula.
8. **d.** Any resource that is in perfectly inelastic supply is said to earn a pure economic rent.
9. **b.** The capitalized rental value is equal to the annual rent divided by the rate of interest in the case of a perpetual rent.
10. **b.** The building would have a capitalized value of exactly $2 million if it had an infinite life; because its life is limited, the present value of the future rental payments are less than that.
11. **c.** Revenue minus explicit costs is accounting profit.
12. **b.** However, this theory does not provide a good explanation of gambling.
13. **b.** This is one explanation of profit.
14. **c.** He called the process of innovation "creative destruction."
15. **d.** Also, entrepreneurs earn profits only under disequilibrium conditions.

Chapter 31

The Problem of Poverty

| **WHERE YOU'RE GOING** | *When you have mastered this chapter, you will understand*

1. The importance factor markets have for income distribution and the problem of poverty.
2. What poverty is and how it can be measured.
3. What trends in poverty have been experienced in the United States in recent decades.
4. How social insurance differs from public assistance.
5. Why poor households are often subject to higher net tax rates at the margin than nonpoor households.
6. Which poverty programs emphasize factor markets.

In addition, you will add the following terms to your economic vocabulary:
    Lorenz curve
    In-kind transfers
    Social insurance
    Public assistance
    Benefit reduction rate
    Net marginal tax rate
    Negative income tax

| **WALKING TOUR** | *After you have read this chapter at least once, you should work step by step through this walking tour. Fill in the blanks and answer the questions as you go along. After you have answered each question, check yourself by uncovering the answer given in the margin. If you do not understand why the answer given is the correct one, refer back to the proper section of the text.*

The Nature of Poverty

The distribution of income depends partly on the operation of

factor   _____factor_____ markets and partly on the operation of government

taxes, transfer   _____taxes_____ and _____transfer_____ programs. The extent of

inequality can be shown in terms of a diagram known as a

Lorenz   _____Lorenz_____ curve. If income were distributed perfectly

369

straight line	equally, this curve would be a ___5___. As it is, the line is
curved	distinctly ___curved___.
	The official government definition is based on the view that
income	poverty is primarily a matter of inadequate ___income___. It
food	begins with a minimum cost budget for ___food___, which is
3	then multiplied by ___3___ to get an official low-income
	level. An alternative view understands poverty as characterized not
behavioral dependency	only by low income but also by _____. Particular concern is expressed with self-destructive behavior in the areas of
education	1. _____,
family	2. _____,
work	3. _____, and
crime	4. _____.
	Part of the reason for the government's income-based definition of poverty is to be able to measure progress toward eliminating poverty. The percentage of the population officially classified as poor
19, 12	fell from about ___19___ percent in 1964 to about ___12___
did not	percent in 1969. During the 1970s, this official percentage [did/*did not*] fall much further. However, various unofficial attempts to
in-kind	adjust incomes for the value of ___in-kind___ transfers shows that the incidence of poverty relative to the official low-income level
did	[*did*/did not] fall further during the 1970s. Then, from 1979 to 1983,
rose	the poverty rate [*rose*/fell/stayed the same] when measured both by the official data and when adjusted for in-kind transfers, before falling again in the mid-1980s.
	The rise in poverty rates from 1979 to 1983 coincided with
rising	[*rising*/falling] levels of total means-tested transfer payments. This fact has caused some observers to wonder whether antipoverty programs might be part of the problem. Other observers point out that poverty rates within specific population groups, such as
fallen	households headed by women, have [risen/*fallen*], but that the size
increased	of such high-poverty groups has [*increased*/decreased].

Transfer Strategies

Transfer strategies for helping the poor fall into two groups. Those that are available to all citizens regardless of need upon retirement,

social insurance   disability, or some other occurrence are known as _____.

public assistance

social security

payroll

regressive

Those available only to people who can demonstrate that they are poor are known as _____.

The biggest single social insurance program is _____. Much of the criticism of the social security system is focused on the _____ tax used to finance it. This [regressive/progressive] tax is believed to have serious disincentive effects. The social security program has also been criticized as unfair to women and members of minority groups.

Public assistance programs include AFDC, Medicaid, food-stamps, and some others. Such programs are subject to gradual reductions of benefits as income rises, and the benefit reduction rates of various programs are additive. For example, if each dollar of income results in a 30 cent reduction in AFDC benefits and a 20 cent reduction in food stamp benefits, the net marginal tax rate on a household benefiting from both programs is _____ percent.

50

replace

gradually

Some economists have suggested that all income-conditioned transfers should be combined into a single negative income tax program. Such a program would [supplement/replace] existing programs. It would provide a minimum benefit that would be reduced [abruptly/gradually] as income rose. Above a break-even point, the normal income tax would take over.

Helping the Poor: Job Market Strategies

Job market strategies for aiding the poor are based on the notion that poverty is in part a result of labor market failure. These strategies are seen as especially important by those who view poverty in terms of [income replacement/behavioral dependency]. Job market strategies include

behavioral dependency

antidiscrimination laws
public employment
minimum-wage laws
work and education
  programs

1. _____,
2. _____,
3. _____, and
4. _____.

Of these, minimum wage laws are among the most controversial. Many economists criticize them because such laws tend to [increase/decrease] the quantity of low-skill labor demanded, and thus to reduce the number of low-skill workers hired. In addition, many workers receiving the minimum wage (_____

decrease

over half

according to one study) come from households in the upper half of the income distribution.

ECONOMICS IN THE NEWS

NEW YORK, DECEMBER 1987—Add the Salvation Army to the list of those hurt by the stock-market crash.

Not because the crash created so many more of the destitute people the Army helps—thought it probably created a few. But because the Army, like most charities, depends heavily on year-end generosity, and the October 19 crash seems to have lowered the generosity level considerably.

During October and November 1986, for example, contributors gave the Army's New York division about $200,000 in securities. The figure this year for the same two months and December: about $7,000.

But the division—which covers the city, Long Island and seven counties north of the city—marches on. It has a job on its hands, and the job is getting bigger.

Four years ago, a dozen people typically turned up for Sunday-morning services in the Army's religious citadel on 52nd Street in Manhattan. Today the services attract ten times as many people. For them, Christmas is a season far removed from the abundance celebrated in the store windows of nearby Fifth Avenue. Many of the worshippers are families living in welfare hotels and single men and women who sleep in streets or public buildings.

Captain John Rondon, who directs the organization's activities in Fort Green and downtown sections of Brooklyn, characterizes the Army's strategy as "Soup, soap, and salvation."

Every afternoon, the captain and his crew set up tables in the temple's basement gymnasium, where they feed over 250 people. In the evening, the tables are cleared away and about 15 cots are set up for men seeking a night's shelter. But despite his concern for the homeless, the captain mixes his compassion with firmness. "Sometimes we overindulge them," he says. "We provide all kinds of services, and that can destroy character. We need to provide programs where there is more structure and consistency."

The men who stay in Capt. Rondon's gymnasium are expected to work for their night's lodging by sweeping the building, helping to serve the next day's meal or now during the holiday season, manning the Christmas kettles. Walter, a wizened elf of a man, bounced around from the shelters to the streets and back again after his cancerous larynx was removed three years ago. Last month, he landed at the temple, where the odd jobs he is assigned have given him a new sense of purpose. "I found a home," he whispers, painfully forcing air through his trachea. "Everybody loves me and I love them. I'm home."

Isaiah Williams, 30, had been a cabinetmaker and a happily married father of two until he began using crack. When Williams spent the rent money to support his drug habit, his wife put him out. For three weeks he slept on subway trains or in Central Park.

He came in from the cold after attending Sunday supper at the citadel and hearing about the high-school program.

Williams appreciates the rules and credits them with getting his life back on track. He has started visiting his children and is hoping to go on to college, where he will "probably major in business."

Source: Janice C. Simpson, "Salvation Army's Job Is Growing Tougher As Cries for Help Rise," *The Wall Street Journal*, December 21, 1987, p. 1. Reprinted by permission of The Wall Street Journal. © Dow Jones & Company, Inc., 1987. All Rights Reserved.

Questions

1. Characterize the problems of "Walter" and Isaiah Williams in terms of income inadequacy and behavioral dependence. How does the Salvation Army address the needs of each?
2. In a country where the government spends more than $60 billion a year on means-tested transfer payments, why is there still a need for private antipoverty efforts like that of the Salvation Army? Do you think more generous funding for government transfer payment programs would end the need for organizations like the Salvation Army? Or do you think such private organizations should play a continuing or even expanded role in the antipoverty effort?

SELF TEST

These sample test items will help you check how much you have learned. Answers are found at the end of the chapter. Scoring yourself: One or two wrong—on target. Three or four wrong—passing, but you haven't mastered the chapter yet. Five or more wrong—not good enough; start over and restudy the chapter.

1. In a society with perfect equality of income distribution, the Lorenz curve would be
   a. horizontal.
   b. vertical.
   c. a straight line with a slope of 1.
   d. curved, with the slope increasing as the level of income rises.
2. Which of the following views of poverty is the basis of official U.S. government poverty statistics?
   a. Poverty as a matter of lifestyle.
   b. Poverty as a matter of behavior.
   c. Poverty as a matter of relative income.
   d. Poverty as an objectively defined minimum income standard.

3. Those who take the "behavioral dependency" view of poverty often stress that
   a. a high school education by itself is little help in avoiding poverty.
   b. getting and holding a job is not much help in avoiding poverty because so many jobs pay only the minimum wage.
   c. fathering a child without marrying the mother or contributing to the child's support increases the likelihood that the child will be poor.
   d. wealthy people are more likely than the poor to be victims of crime.
4. The official measurements of poverty fail to take which of the following into account?
   a. Food stamp benefits received.
   b. Public housing benefits received.
   c. Medicaid benefits received.
   d. The official measurements do not take any of the above into account.
5. Which of the following grew most rapidly during the 1970s?
   a. Cash transfer programs.
   b. In-kind transfer programs.
   c. The number of people officially counted as poor.
   d. The number of people counted as poor after adjustment for in-kind transfers.
6. Approximately what percentage of the U.S. population was officially classified as poor as of the 1986?
   a. 6.
   b. 10.
   c. 14.
   d. 33.
7. Social security is considered
   a. a social insurance program.
   b. a public assistance program.
   c. an in-kind transfer program.
   d. a supply-side transfer program.
8. The social security system is subject to criticism because
   a. it is financed by a regressive tax.
   b. it displaces private saving.
   c. blacks tend to collect fewer benefits that whites who make equal contributions.
   d. all of the above.
9. Which of the following is a public assistance program?
   a. Aid to Families with Dependent Children.
   b. Food stamps.
   c. Medicaid.
   d. All of the above.
10. The benefit reduction rate for the AFDC program is typically
    a. 10 percent.
    b. 22 percent.
    c. 33 percent.
    d. 50 percent.

___ 11. If a certain family benefits from Program A, which has a benefit reduction rate of 40 percent, and also from Program B, which has a benefit reduction rate of 15 percent, the effective marginal tax rate on the family (taking no other tax or transfer programs into account) is
   a. 15 percent.
   b. 25 percent.
   c. 40 percent.
   d. 55 percent.

___ 12. A family with an earned income of $5,000 receives a total income of $6,000 after all taxes and transfers are taken into account. A similar family earning $10,000 receives no transfer payments and pays $2,000 in income and payroll taxes. The effective net marginal tax rate in the $5,000 to $10,000 range is thus
   a. 20 percent.
   b. 40 percent.
   c. 60 percent.
   d. 100 percent.

___ 13. If the benefit reduction rate for a negative income tax program is reduced while the basic benefit remains the same, which of the following groups will probably work less than previously?
   a. Those with zero earned income.
   b. Those with earned incomes greater than zero but less than the basic benefit.
   c. Those made eligible for payments for the first time by the change in the benefit reduction rate.
   d. All of the above.

___ 14. A study by Johnson and Browning found that
   a. most people working at minimum wage jobs came from poor households.
   b. minimum wage jobs were the major source of income for a majority of low-income households.
   c. an increase in the minimum wage would do little or nothing to raise the incomes of households living in poverty.
   d. an increase in the minimum wage would reduce unemployment among black teenagers.

___ 15. Which of the following is not considered a labor market strategy for helping the poor?
   a. AFDC.
   b. Job training.
   c. Antidiscrimination measures.
   d. Public employment.

ANSWERS TO CHAPTER 31

Economics in the News

(1) Walter's lack of income appears at least in part to be a function of forces beyond his control—old age and illness. Isaiah's are more arguably of his own making—his drug habit and his consequent separation from an apparently otherwise stable family and work situation. Note, however, that the Salvation Army does not deal with either simply through income replacement. Recognizing the difference in circumstances, both men are expected to change their behavior in return for assistance rendered. In Walter's case, this means undertaking odd jobs. In Isaiah's, it means staying off drugs and pursuing a high-school equivalency program. (2) Part of the problem with government programs is that they do not reach all the poor. Also, the Salvation Army's approach, which emphasizes responsibility and behavioral change may be more suitable for some of the poor than simple income replacement. Opinion will differ as to the balance between private and public antipoverty efforts. Government efforts certainly have an advantage when it comes to fundraising, but not all government programs are well tailored to the actual needs of their beneficiaries. It is doubtful that any degree of funding for government programs would altogether obviate the need for private efforts.

Self Test

1. **c.** With inequality, the shape is as in answer **d**.
2. **d.** The standard attempts to define an income level that would permit adequate nutrition while also allowing for other needs.
3. **c.** Answers **a**, **b**, and **d** are the opposite of the truth
4. **d.** The official definition does not take any in-kind benefits into account.
5. **b.** The growth rate of these programs tapered off in the 1980s.
6. **c.** This is up from a low of 11.1 percent in 1973.
7. **a.** Because it is paid to people regardless of their income if they otherwise qualify.
8. **d.** All of these are frequent criticisms.
9. **d.** Answer **a** is a cash public assistance program, whereas **b** and **c** are in-kind public assistance programs.
10. **c.** The total benefit reduction rate is even greater for most poor families when other programs are considered together with AFDC.
11. **d.** The benefit reduction rates are additive.
12. **c.** After-tax income with an earned income of $10,000 is $8,000, so the $5,000 of earned income adds only $2,000 to net income after taxes and transfers.
13. **c.** Group a would probably not be affected at all, and group b would probably work more.

14. c. The study found that a majority of minimum wage workers came from households in the upper half of the income distribution, and that minimum-wage jobs accounted for only 14 percent of total income of poor households.

15. a. AFDC is a public assistance program.

Chapter 32

Antitrust and Regulation

WHERE YOU'RE GOING

When you have mastered this chapter, you will understand

1. The economic and social goals of antitrust laws.
2. Which business practices are illegal under the antitrust laws.
3. How antitrust policy has changed over time.
4. Why some industries are regulated despite their inherently competitive structure.
5. The effects of regulatory reform.
6. Current trends in health and safety regulation.

In addition, you will add the following terms to your economic vocabulary:
  Antitrust laws
  Price fixing
  Horizontal merger
  Vertical merger
  Conglomerate merger
  Herfindahl index

WALKING TOUR

After you have read this chapter at least once, you should work step by step through this walking tour. Fill in the blanks and answer the questions as you go along. After you have answered each question, check yourself by uncovering the answer given in the margin. If you do not understand why the answer given is the correct one, refer back to the proper section of the text.

Antitrust Laws and Policies

The first federal antitrust act in the United States was the

Sherman Act, 1890   _____ of _____. This act outlaws conspiracies to restrict commerce and attempts to monopolize. The act was

felony   strengthened in 1974, when violation was made a _____.

jail sentences   A practical result of that has been more frequent _____ for violators.

378

Clayton	In 1914, two more antitrust acts were passed. One lists specific anticompetitive practices and is known as the _____ Act. The other established an independent agency to initiate antitrust cases, the _____. The antitrust laws were further strengthened by the Robinson-Patman Act of 1936, which deals with _____, and the Celler-Kefauver Act of 1950, which deals with _____.
FTC	
price discrimination	
mergers	
price fixing	The antitrust laws, as currently enforced, prevent the formation of cartels by outlawing _____ and related practices such as _____ and _____. Attempts to form single-firm monopolies through _____ mergers are also effectively prohibited. In addition, the government has at times opposed mergers among firms in a seller-customer relationship (_____ mergers) and mergers among firms in unrelated lines of business (_____ mergers). Many kinds of agreements among suppliers and customers, known as _____, have also at times been found in violation of the antitrust laws. Sometimes, but not as often now as formerly, the government has prosecuted _____ under the Robinson-Patman Act.
output restrictions, market division, horizontal	
vertical	
conglomerate	
vertical restraints	
price discrimination	
consumer welfare	Many economists are critical of antitrust laws. The laws, they say, pay too little attention to _____ and too much attention to ill-defined social concerns. In the 1980s, the scope of antitrust prosecution has been [broadened/narrowed]. Price fixing is [still/no longer] a focus of vigorous enforcement. However, [stricter/more permissive] guidelines have been adopted regarding horizontal mergers and antitrust authorities are placing [more/less] emphasis on vertical and conglomerate mergers in their enforcement activities.
narrowed	
still, more permissive	
less	

Regulation of Competitive Behavior

Antitrust is not the only activity whose object is the control of competition. The first major industry to come under regulation was the

railroad	_____ industry. The big surge in regulation came during the _____.
1930s	
trucking	The ICC, which was given responsibility to regulate _____ in the 1930s and the CAB, which regulated _____ are typical of agencies established in the period. Their policies [encouraged/restricted] entry and [enforced/prohibited]
airlines	
restricted, enforced	

379

	establishment of minimum prices. In these regards, the arrangements they fostered resembled _____. The regulated trucking and airline firms did not always earn high profits, however. Some of the benefits went to _____ and _____ as well. These results of regulation are consistent with the theory of _____.
cartels	
customers	
unions	
rent seeking	

Since the late 1970s, regulatory reform has been undertaken in several industries. The following results have occurred in most industries affected by regulatory reform: A [higher/lower] average level of prices, a [greater/smaller] variety of services, and many [new entrants/business failures/both].

lower
greater
both

Health and Safety Regulation

While the traditional forms of regulation have been on the retreat in transportation, communications, and finance, health and safety regulation has [contracted/expanded]. One set of issues faced by health and safety regulation is whether an economic value can be put on health an safety, and if so, whose values should govern the process. These are an examples of [positive/normative] issues in regulation. Another set of issues concern how to attain goals, once they are chosen, at least cost. These are issues of [positive/normative] economics.

expanded

normative

positive

ECONOMICS IN THE NEWS

A. New York Juries Indict 17 in Plot to Fix Milk Prices

Grand juries in Brooklyn and Queens indicted 17 of New York City's major milk distributors for conspiring to fix prices and allocate customers, state Attorney General Robert Abrams announced.

The defendants, including Dellwood Foods Inc., Yonkers, N.Y., the state's second largest milk distributor, pleaded innocent to the alleged criminal felony violations of the state's antitrust law.

One of the counts in the indictments charged that the companies used harassment, intimidation, coercion and threats to reduce, or cut off, milk deliveries in order to raise wholesale milk prices to stores that didn't maintain suggested retail prices.

The indictments also charged that the companies established a system of sanctions and reprisals for taking each other's retail customers.

Eight milk dealers, including Dellwood, were indicted on similar charges in the Bronx last April. In all, 24 companies that sell more than 50 percent of the milk sold in downstate New York have been indicted on such charges, a spokesman for Abrams said.

Nineteen officials and salesmen of the indicted companies were released with bail. A trial date hasn't been set. The 17 companies face maximum fines of $1 million each if convicted on the conspiracy charges.

The indictments said the conspiracy began in 1971 in Brooklyn and in 1972 in Queens and continued until this year.

Abrams said it was impossible to estimate accurately the added costs to consumers as a result of the alleged price-fixing, but he noted that each penny per quart overcharge would boost prices to consumers by a total of $6.1 million a year. . . .

Source: "New York Juries Indict 17 Distributors of Milk For Plot to Fix Prices," *The Wall Street Journal*, November 11, 1981, p. 7. Reprinted by permission of The Wall Street Journal. © Dow Jones & Company, Inc., 1981. All Rights Reserved.

Questions

1. Did the firms discussed in this article engage in horizontal price fixing? What indication of such activity does the article give?
2. Were vertical restraints also imposed? How did they work?
3. The legal actions discussed in this article were brought under New York State antitrust laws. Would they also violate federal antitrust law? What law or laws in particular?

B. Bowen Used Illegal Drugs To Comfort Dying Wife

With his term as Indiana's governor ending and his wife, Beth, dying of bone cancer, Otis Bowen took the law into his own hands. Moved by his wife's suffering, the physician-politician used illegal drugs to ease her pain.

Bowen rubbed away her pain with an industrial solvent used to treat arthritis in animals, soothed the nausea caused by chemotherapy with an extract of marijuana and tried to cure her with a bone-mending drug illegally imported from France.

Mrs. Bowen died January 1 as Bowen prepared to step down from the governorship he had held for two terms, the maximum allowed by law.

In the final months of her illness, Mrs. Bowen had been in agony, slowly dying of multiple myeloma, a type of bone cancer.

Bowen—now on the faculty of the Indiana University Medical School at Indianapolis [and later to become Secretary of Health and Human Services under President Reagan]—said he turned to illegal drugs to help her, and himself, live with the pain.

He turned to dimethyl sulfoxide, an industrial solvent known as DMSO and widely used to treat arthritis in animals. The FDA forbids use of the drug on humans. But Bowen obtained the ointment from a veterinarian friend and, he said, it relieved his wife's pain "in minutes."

"Why can't dying persons, with severe pain, have easy prescription access to it?" he asked in a speech at an American Medical Association leadership conference.

"The only excuse I could find was that, after prolonged use and heavy dosage, it caused an occasional cataract in dogs only. The container said 'For horses only'.

"We laughed together about it but it really wasn't funny."

The chemotherapy intended to lengthen Mrs. Bowen's life added nausea to her sufferings. Bowen turned to tetrahydrocannabinol or THC, the active ingredient of marijuana, to alleviate that problem.

"I'll not tell you where I got the capsules but it worked and it was not then available for prescription use," Bowen told the conference.

THC use in humans was considered experimental and restricted, though clinical tests had proven it effective in treating side effects of chemotherapy. The drug is legal in some states but has not won full FDA approval.

Bowen also illegally obtained an unnamed cancer drug from France in a futile effort to strengthen his wife's cancer-ravaged bones.

"I understand our government had not okayed its manufacture and use even though it had been in use safely in France for a long time," he said.

Source: "Bowen Used Illegal Drugs to Comfort Dying Wife," in *The Washington Post*, February 15, 1981, sec. A, 4. Used by permission of United Press International.

Questions

1. This article raises a major issue of positive economics regarding the costs and benefits of regulation of new drugs by the Food and Drug Administration (FDA). What are the benefits of FDA regulation of new drugs? What are the costs? What would be the optimum degree of regulation?
2. The article raises major issues in normative economics as well. In particular, it raises the issue of whether informed consumers (in consultation with their physicians when necessary) should be allowed to assume the risks of using incompletely tested drugs, or drugs with known side effects. Discuss this issue in the light of the article.

SELF TEST

These sample test items will help you check how much you have learned. Answers are found at the end of the chapter. Scoring yourself: One or two wrong—on target. Three or four wrong—passing, but you haven't mastered the chapter yet. Five or more wrong—not good enough; start over and restudy the chapter.

_____ 1. In the nineteenth century, people were hostile to the "trusts" primarily because
   a. they were economically inefficient.
   b. they were dominated by foreign stockholders.
   c. they were big and powerful.
   d. they were blamed for the Civil War.

_____ 2. The original antimerger section of the Clayton Act was aimed specifically at which of the following types of mergers?
   a. Vertical mergers.
   b. Conglomerate mergers.
   c. Mergers via acquisition of stocks.
   d. Mergers via acquisition of assets.

_____ 3. Except where special antitrust exemptions exist, it is not possible for firms in the United States to form cartels, because it is illegal to
   a. fix prices.
   b. divide markets.
   c. restrict output.
   d. do any of the above.

_____ 4. Which of the following practices would be subject to challenge under U.S. antitrust law?
   a. A contract requiring buyers of Kodak cameras to use only Kodak film.
   b. An agreement that Kodak dealers would not sell the cameras below the manufacturer's suggested retail price.
   c. An agreement that Kodak dealers would not sell Polaroid cameras.
   d. All of the above would probably be subject to challenge under the antitrust laws.

_____ 5. An industry with four equal-sized firms would have a Herfindahl index of
   a. 400.
   b. 625.
   c. 2,500.
   d. 4,000.

_____ 6. In the *Utah Pie* case, the defendants were convicted, in part,
   a. because they cut prices.
   b. because they competed vigorously against a dominant local firm.
   c. because they refused to bow out of the market when a new competitor entered.
   d. because of all of the above.

_____ 7. Vertical restrictions
   a. are an example of a trade practice that even antitrust critics condemn.
   b. are decreasing in importance as a target of antitrust enforcement.
   c. are not illegal under antitrust laws.
   d. are none of the above.

_____ 8. Which of the following factors would make it less likely that the Justice Department would oppose a merger between two large firms?
   a. The product is homogeneous.
   b. The product has no close substitutes.
   c. Technological change is rapid.
   d. There has been collusion among the firms in the past.

_____ 9. Current trends in antitrust law tend to emphasize vigorous enforcement action in cases where
   a. consumers are clearly harmed.
   b. small dealers may be forced to change traditional practices or go out of business.
   c. firms have grown large as a result of cost advantages over their rivals.
   d. vertical restraints or vertical mergers are involved.

_____ 10. A major rationale for introducing regulation of airlines and trucking during the 1930s was
   a. the fear of excessive competition.
   b. the fear that many firms would fail, leaving a monopoly.
   c. the fear that without regulation, the firms would form private cartels.
   d. the desire to lower excessive rates of return in the industries.

_____ 11. A major argument in favor of ending regulation of airlines and trucking was
   a. such regulation did not benefit workers in the industries.
   b. such regulation failed to restrain competition and keep prices high as it had been intended to do.
   c. such regulation was harmful to consumers.
   d. the strong support regulated firms themselves gave to deregulation.

_____ 12. Which of the following has occurred in most newly deregulated industries in the 1980s?
   a. Lower prices for all customers.
   b. A narrowing of variety of available services.
   c. Many new entrants, but also many mergers and business failures.
   d. All of the above.

_____ 13. Which of the following regulatory agencies grew most rapidly during the 1970s?
   a. The CAB.
   b. OSHA.
   c. The ICC.
   d. None of the above grew during the 1970s.

_____ 14. Economists who think that regulatory agencies should take into account trade-offs between health and safety, on the one hand, and dollar costs, on the other, do so in part because
   a. they think people make such trade-offs every day in the normal course of living.
   b. they are confident that modern empirical methods can measure the dollar value of health and safety accurately.
   c. they think that normative considerations should play no role in policy formation.
   d. they think health and safety unimportant relative to economic efficiency.

_____ 15. To deal with the hazards of cigarette smoking by using warning labels and publicity campaigns rather than by outlawing tobacco implies that trade-offs between health and other consumer goals should be made according to the values of
   a. the consumers themselves.
   b. government-appointed experts.
   c. econometricians.
   d. the tobacco industry.

ANSWERS TO CHAPTER 32

Economics in the News

A. (1) The system of sanctions and reprisals for taking one another's customers would be considered horizontal price fixing, since it involves a conspiracy among firms on the same level of the distribution chain. (2) The use of harassment, intimidation, and coercion to force retailers to maintain retail prices would be considered a vertical restraint. (3) Price fixing of the type described here would be a violation of the Sherman Act.

B. (1) The costs of regulation take the form of unnecessary death and suffering by those who do not have access to the drugs during the lengthy testing period required by the FDA. The benefits come when drugs with side effects that outweigh their benefits are kept off the market. From the standpoint of positive economics, regulators should aim to make the testing process just restrictive enough that the suffering of one group of victims about balances the suffering of the other at the margin. Compared with regulatory agencies in other countries, the FDA in the United States leans toward reduction of the risk of premature approval, thus delaying benefits of drugs that do eventually prove safe and effective. The fact that Bowen used a bone mending drug already approved in France, but not in the United States, is one example. Critics say the FDA is overcautious, and that the costs of its restrictions outweigh the benefits. (2) There is no simple right answer here. The article seems to make a case for access to new drugs by informed users.

Self Test

1. **c.** The fact that they were efficient only made them bigger and more powerful still.
2. **c.** The others were not effectively brought under the antitrust laws until the Celler-Kefauver Act.
3. **d.** Any aspect of cartel-like behavior is proscribed by the antitrust laws.
4. **d.** At one time or another, vertical restraints similar to each of these have been challenged.
5. **c.** The formula is $SA^2 + SB^2 + SC^2 + SD^2$, where the S's are the market shares in percent of the various firms.
6. **d.** All of these were considered "unfair" even though they would appear to have benefited consumers.
7. **b.** They are now rarely the target of government suits but private suits may still be brought.
8. **c.** The others would make opposition more likely.
9. **a.** The government is increasingly unlikely to bring cases in the other instances, even though it often did so in the past.
10. **a.** It was thought that excessive competition was one cause of the Great Depression.
11. **c.** Often workers benefitted, and the regulated firms in many cases favored continuation of regulation.
12. **c.** Prices have been lower on average, but not lower for all customers, and the variety of available services has increased.
13. **b.** The CAB was abolished altogether, and the ICC decreased in size after rail and trucking deregulation.
14. **a.** Deciding how fast to drive or where to cross the street are examples of such decisions.
15. **a.** A lively issue is whether the value of "passive smokers" should also be taken into account.

Chapter 33

Externalities and Environmental Policy

WHERE YOU'RE GOING	*When you have mastered this chapter, you will understand*
	
	 1. How the problem of pollution can be understood in terms of the concepts of externalities and market failure.
	 2. How the optimal quantity of pollution can be determined.
	 3. How a production possibility frontier can be used to examine the problem of pollution.
	 4. How supply and demand analysis can be applied to pollution control policy.
	 5. What problems have been encountered by pollution control policy in the case of acid rain.
	
	 In addition, you will add the following terms to your economic vocabulary:
	     Marginal social cost of pollution
	     Marginal cost of pollution abatement

WALKING TOUR	*After you have read this chapter at least once, you should work step by step through this walking tour. Fill in the blanks and answer the questions as you go along. After you have answered each question, check yourself by uncovering the answer given in the margin. If you do not understand why the answer given is the correct one, refer back to the proper section of the text.*

How Much Pollution, How Much Cleanup?

production possibility
  frontier

B

A
opportunity cost

Exhibit 33.1 uses a _____ to illustrate the tradeoff between environmental quality and the quantity of material goods. On this diagram, an uninhabited wilderness in which nothing is produced by humans is represented by point _____. A situation in which all efforts are focused on producing material goods with no effort made to maintain environmental quality is represented by point _____. The slope of the curve connecting these points represents the _____ of environmental quality in terms of material goods. Starting from a point like C,

Exhibit 33.1

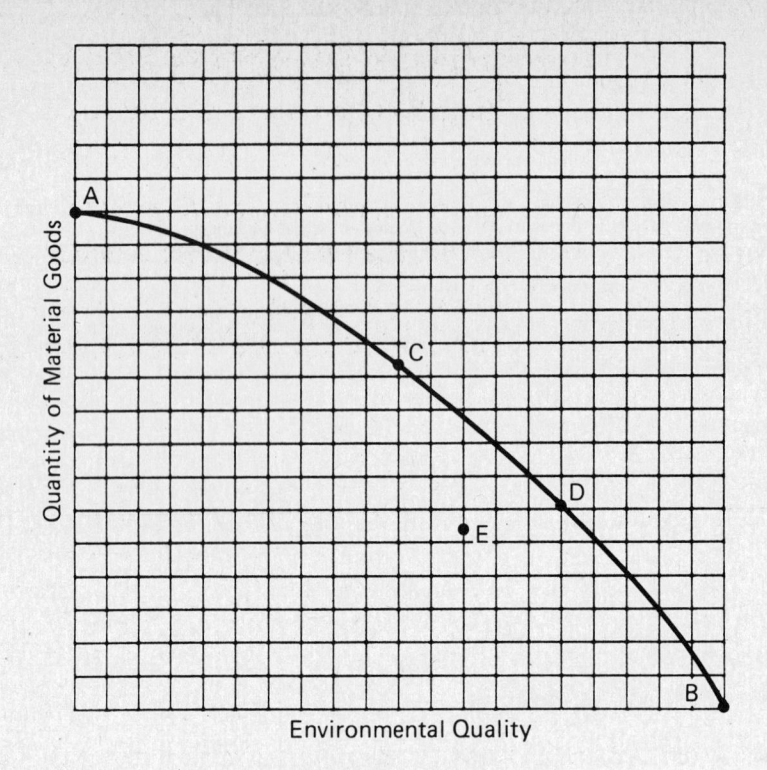

[Figure: Production possibilities frontier with axes "Quantity of Material Goods" (vertical) and "Environmental Quality" (horizontal), showing points A, C, D, E, B along/near a concave curve.]

sacrificing some material goods to achieve a cleaner environment would mean moving toward [A/B]. If the policies used to achieve the improvement in environmental quality were efficient, the economy could move to a point like _____. If inefficient policies were used, the economy would end up at some point like _____.

Movements along the frontier can also be thought of in terms of balancing two kinds of costs. One is the cost to society of another unit of pollution, known as the _____. The other is the cost of reducing pollution by one unit, known as the _____. As the quantity of pollution increases, the marginal social cost of pollution tends to [increase/decrease], and the marginal cost of pollution abatement tends to [increase/decrease]. The point where the two types of cost are equal is considered to be the _____ quantity of pollution. Because of problems of _____ and problems of _____, it [is/is not] easy to achieve agreement in practice about just where the optimal quantity of pollution lies.

B

D

E

marginal social cost of pollution, marginal cost of pollution abatement, increase

decrease

optimal

measurement

rights, is not

388

Economic Strategies for Pollution Control

Exhibit 33.2 allows comparison of alternative strategies of pollution control. It contains a positively sloped marginal social cost of pollution curve, and a negatively sloped marginal cost of pollution abatement curve. Of these two, the [social cost/abatement cost] curve can also serve as a demand curve for pollution opportunities. Add that label to the diagram. As the curves are drawn, the optimal quantity of pollution is _____ units.

abatement cost

100

Exhibit 33.2

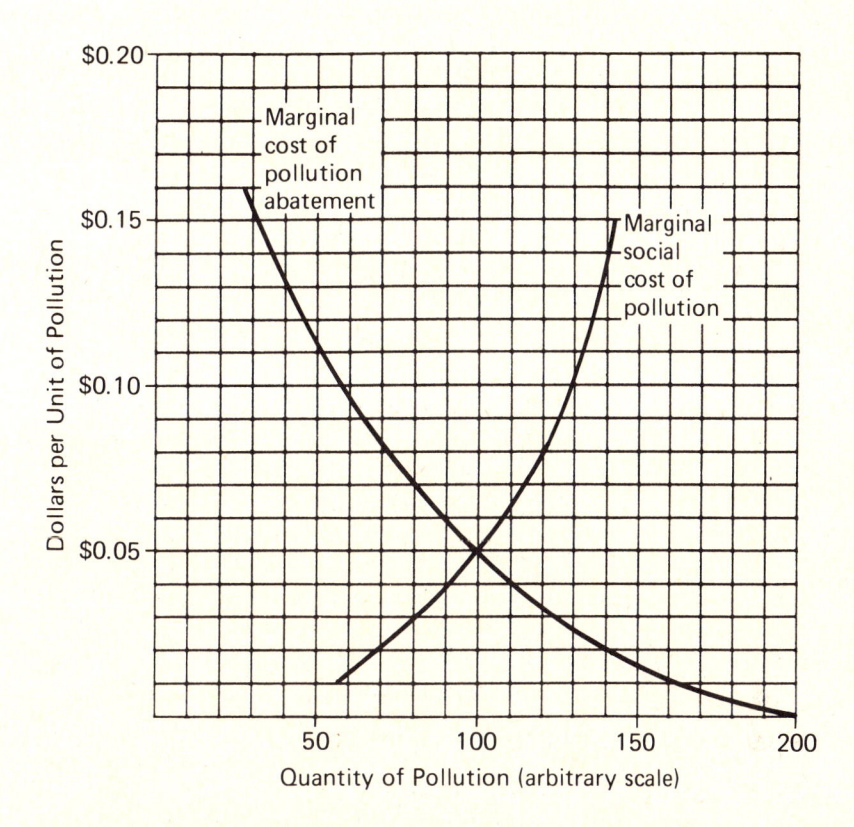

[Graph: Dollars per Unit of Pollution (y-axis, $0.05 to $0.20) vs. Quantity of Pollution (arbitrary scale, x-axis, 50 to 200). Downward-sloping curve labeled "Marginal cost of pollution abatement" and upward-sloping curve labeled "Marginal social cost of pollution" intersecting near (100, $0.05).]

Begin by considering the situation in which no pollution control measures are taken. If it costs nothing for firms and households to dispose of wastes by discharging them into the environment, the supply curve of pollution opportunities will be a _____ line at a height of _____. With such a supply curve, the equilibrium quantity of pollution will be _____ units.

horizontal

zero

200

Next consider the marketable permit approach. Under this approach, a target level of pollution is chosen that, in principle, coincides with the optimal quantity of pollution. If they have a permit, firms can pollute without charge; without a permit, pollution is (in principle) strictly prohibited. The supply curve of pollution opportunities under such a program can thus be represented by a

389

vertical	_____ line drawn at the target level, which in this case we assume to be 100 units.
	The third pollution control strategy to be considered is a pollution charge. A constant pollution charge per unit of pollution makes
horizontal	the supply curve of pollution opportunities a _____ line at a height equal to the charge per unit. In this case, in order to achieve the optimal degree of pollution abatement, the charge
5 cents	should be set at _____ per unit.
	Finally, consider a rights-based strategy. Under this approach, each source of pollution is legally liable for all damage done by pollution that it emits. If the legal system functioned without transactions costs to impose exactly the proper burden on each pollution source, the supply curve of pollution opportunities would coincide
social cost of pollution	with the marginal _____ curve. If imperfections in the legal system raised the burdens on polluters above this level, for example, by adding court costs to damages paid, there might be too
abatement	much [pollution/abatement]. If imperfections in the system prevented victims of pollution from imposing on polluters the full
pollution	cost of damages suffered, there would be too much [pollution/abatement].

The Problem of Acid Rain: A Case Study

Acid rain is believed to result, at least in substantial part, from emissions of sulfur dioxide, especially from electric power plants. Various technologies for reducing emissions have been studied, of

cheapest	which fuel switching is often the [most costly/cheapest] and "scrub-
most costly	bing" is usually the [most costly/cheapest]. The benefits of reducing
less	emissions are [more/less] easily estimated than the costs. The fact
does not mean	that the benefits cannot be accurately estimated [means/does not mean] that the benefits of reducing such emissions are small.
do not	In practice, current regulations [do/do not] require use of the least costly means of abatement. The current regulations are better
rent seeking	explained in terms of _____ than in terms of efficiency.

ECONOMICS IN THE NEWS

Exhibit 33.3 shows an ad that appeared in *The Wall Street Journal*. Use the ad as a basis for answering the following questions:

Exhibit 33.3

> **Pennsylvania Industrial**
>
> # EMISSION CREDITS FOR SALE
>
> 750 tons of hydrocarbon emissions per year which can be used as offset credits for a new or modified source within 40-mile radius of CONSHOHOCKEN, PENNSYLVANIA in southeast Pa. Air Basin. Write or call:
>
> **GOODYEAR
> REAL ESTATE DEPARTMENT**
>
> 1144 E. Market St,
> Akron, Ohio 44315
> Tel: 216-796-2238—
> J.A. Armstrong

1. What kind of pollution control strategy is represented in this ad?
2. What possible advantages and disadvantages does this pollution control strategy have by comparison with others?
3. Does this strategy guarantee an optimal quantity of pollution? Why or why not?

SELF TEST

These sample test items will help you check how much you have learned. Answers are found at the end of the chapter. Scoring yourself: One or two wrong—on target. Three or four wrong—passing, but you haven't mastered the chapter yet. Five or more wrong—not good enough; start over and restudy the chapter.

_____ 1. Pollution is an example of which of the following?
   a. A monopoly.
   b. A rent control.
   c. An externality.
   d. A vertical restriction.

2. The marginal social cost of pollution means
   a. the total damage done to all people by all pollution.
   b. the damage done to one person by one more unit of pollution.
   c. the total damage done to all people by one more unit of pollution.
   d. the total damage done to one person by all pollution.
3. Which of the following is best represented by a positively sloped curve?
   a. The marginal social cost of pollution.
   b. The marginal cost of pollution abatement.
   c. The command and control curve of pollution limitation.
   d. The trade-off between environmental quality and material goods.
4. If a production possibility frontier is drawn to represent the trade-off between environmental quality (horizontal axis) and material goods (vertical axis), then an efficient pollution control strategy would
   a. move the economy down and to the right along the frontier.
   b. move the economy up and to the left along the frontier.
   c. move the economy outside the frontier.
   d. move the economy to a point inside the frontier.
5. The optimal quantity of pollution is found at the point where the marginal cost of pollution abatement curve crosses
   a. the horizontal axis.
   b. the vertical axis.
   c. the marginal social cost of pollution curve.
   d. the production possibility frontier.
6. Which of the following pollution control strategies was emphasized by several major pollution control laws passed in the 1970s?
   a. Command and control.
   b. Rights-based strategies.
   c. Marketable permits.
   d. Pollution charges.
7. Which of the following is a major advantage claimed for pollution charges, compared to the command and control approach?
   a. It guarantees that the optimal quantity of pollution will be achieved.
   b. It eliminates measurement problems that prevent command and control from achieving and optimum.
   c. It ensures that pollution will be cut back the most at the sources where abatement costs are lowest.
   d. It guarantees a zero level of pollution.
8. A pollution control strategy under which all emissions from a given plant are treated as a single group, with trade-offs permitted within the group, is known as a/an
   a. bubble.
   b. offset.
   c. residual charge.
   d. bank.

_____ 9. Under which type of policy would the supply curve of pollution opportunities tend to coincide with the marginal social cost of pollution curve, if the policy were well implemented?
   a. Command and control.
   b. Pollution charges.
   c. Marketable permits.
   d. A rights-based strategy.

_____ 10. Under a marketable permit approach to pollution control, the supply curve of pollution opportunities is best represented by
   a. a horizontal line above the horizontal axis.
   b. a horizontal line coincident with the horizontal axis.
   c. a vertical line.
   d. a line coincident with the marginal social cost of pollution curve.

_____ 11. Which of the following is believed to be a chief cause of acid rain?
   a. Emissions of sulfur dioxide.
   b. Emissions of carbon dioxide.
   c. Emissions of alkaline substances.
   d. All of the above.

_____ 12. Given present technology, the cheapest way of reducing sulfur emissions from electric power plants is
   a. switching to low-sulfur coal.
   b. cleaning the coal before it is burned.
   c. using better combustion methods.
   d. using scrubbers.

_____ 13. Which of the following is most easily measured in dollar terms?
   a. Health benefits of reducing acid rain.
   b. Benefits to forests of reducing acid rain.
   c. Benefits to recreation of reducing acid rain.
   d. Costs of reducing sulfur dioxide emissions that are believed to cause acid rain.

_____ 14. The current measures used to control acid rain in the United States are an example of which pollution control strategy?
   a. Command and control.
   b. Marketable permits.
   c. Pollution taxes.
   d. Rights-based approaches.

_____ 15. Which of the following groups supported the approach to controlling acid rain that is embodied in the Clean Air Act and its amendments?
   a. Environmentalists.
   b. Coal mining interests.
   c. Politicians of older industrial states.
   d. All of the above formed a coalition.

ANSWERS TO CHAPTER 33

Economics in the News

(1) This ad appears to be for credits that Goodyear has deposited in a pollution "bank"—an example of the marketable permit approach. Presumably, Goodyear "earned" these credits by cleaning up one of its plants by more than the degree required by law. The extra credits can be used by some other firm wanting to build a new plant in the area. The total pollution from the old and new plant together will still meet the required standard. (2) The advantage of the "banking" approach is to encourage firms that can clean up pollution at relatively low cost to do so, while still allowing for growth and flexibility. Under the command-and-control approach, Goodyear would have no incentive to do more than the minimum amount of pollution control, while some other company might find it impossible to build a productive (and perhaps clean) new plant in the area. (3) This strategy does not guarantee the optimal amount of pollution. The EPA must still make a guess as to how much total pollution should be allowed. Given measurement problems and political pressures, it might guess too high or too low. However, pollution banks and other devices are intended to make it possible to meet a given pollution target in a least-cost manner, even if the target itself may not be exactly optimal.

Self Test

1. **c.** Its effects are felt by third parties, the victims of pollution, but its costs are not borne by polluters or their customers.
2. **c.** This must be balanced against the cost of reducing pollution by one unit.
3. **a.** Assuming that the damage from each added unit is more serious than the damage from the previous unit.
4. **a.** Answer **b** would move toward more pollution; **d** would be inefficient; and **c** would be impossible with given technology and resources.
5. **c.** At this point the benefits of more abatement just balance the costs at the margin.
6. **a.** The others are now used to at least a limited extent.
7. **c.** The result may still not be optimal if the charge is set at the wrong level.
8. **a.** The idea is that the plant is covered by an imaginary "bubble" that catches pollution of all types from within that plant.
9. **d.** People would relinquish their rights to a clean environment only if they were compensated.
10. **c.** The line is drawn at a quantity of pollution corresponding to the total number of permits issued.
11. **a.** Oxides of nitrogen are a second, somewhat less important cause Alkaline substances help neutralize acid rain before it falls.

12. **a.** At least this is the case in much of the industrial Midwest.
13. **d.** The acid rain problem is typical, in that the costs of cleanup are more easily measured than the benefits. However, this does not mean they are smaller.
14. **a.** Stack scrubbers must be used whether they are the most cost-effective method at a given site or not.
15. **d.** Environmentalists appear to have felt that even flawed measures to control pollution were better than none at all. Coal miners hoped to save jobs, and the politicians hoped to block the movement of firms to western states where low-sulfur coal is cheap.

Chapter 34

The Theory of Public Choice

WHERE YOU'RE GOING

When you have mastered this chapter, you will understand

1. How economic theory can be applied to government.
2. What role self interest plays in the theory of public choice.
3. How public expenditures are determined under direct democracy.
4. How representative democracy differs from direct democracy.

In addition, you will add the following terms to your economic vocabulary:
　　Public choice theory
　　Logrolling

WALKING TOUR

After you have read this chapter at least once, you should work step by step through this walking tour. Fill in the blanks and answer the questions as you go along. After you have answered each question, check yourself by uncovering the answer given in the margin. If you do not understand why the answer given is the correct one, refer back to the proper section of the text.

The Self-Interest Assumption of Public Choice Theory

According to the market failure theory, government plays a limited role, stepping in only when the market produces results that are unsatisfactory in terms of efficiency or fairness. Examples of market failures said to justify government intervention are

externalities
public goods
insufficient competition
unfair income
　distribution, not all

1. _____,
2. _____,
3. _____, and
4. _____.

In practice, [all/not all] government programs fit one of these categories of market failure. Some programs appear to promote neither efficiency nor fairness. Such programs can often be

rent seeking

explained in terms of _____. The branch of economics

396

public choice theory	that studies how people use the institutions of government in pursuit of private ends is called _____ theory.
act	A basic principle of public choice theory is that people [act/do not act] in the same way in public and private roles. Thus, public choice theory assumes that legislators, bureaucrats, and other government officials are guided by _____.
self-interest	

Public Choice in Direct Democracy

direct	A political system in which people affected by policies have a right to vote in person on each policy is called a _____ democracy. Efficiency requires that in any political system, each project should be funded to the point where the total added benefit to all citizens of another unit of expenditure equals the added
cost	_____ of the additional unit. In a direct democracy, the
in proportion	efficient spending will be achieved if costs are shared _____ to benefits received. If the costs are distributed equally but the benefits are disproportionately concentrated on a few citizens, the
less	direct democracy will tend to spend [more/less] than the efficient amount. And if the benefits are shared equally while the costs are borne disproportionately by a minority, the direct democracy will
more	tend to spend [more/less] than the efficient amount.

Public Choice and Rent Seeking in a Direct Democracy

	In a direct democracy, programs that benefit a small minority of citizens while the costs are shared equally among all would be
rare	[common/rare]. Also, tax loopholes that excuse a small group of citizens from bearing their share of the costs of programs that
rare	benefit everyone would be [common/rare]. In a representative
common	democracy, however, programs of both types are [common/rare]. The difference stems from features of representative democracy that are not found in direct democracy.
	Some of the differences stem from the costs of information and political expression. Small, well organized groups with strong com-
more	mon interests tend to be [more/less] effective in terms of political expression than their numbers would suggest.
	Another feature of representative democracy is vote trading, or
logrolling	_____. This practice makes it possible for representatives to trade away votes on issues which are not important to

rents — them in exchange for votes on a few issues that strongly affect their own constituents. This practice makes it possible to obtain majorities for programs that generate _____ for a few people while dispersing costs widely. In a system where representatives are elected on a geographical basis, logrolling tends to

local, national — promote [local/national] interests at the expense of [local/national] interests.

A final difference between direct and representative democracy

self-interest — lies in the _____ of representatives. Because of their interest in reelection, representatives do not act as perfect

agents, principals — _____ of their _____, the voters.

ECONOMICS IN THE NEWS

Trade Bill Loaded With Provisions Aiding Local Interests

Senator Max Baucus worries that congressional passage of protectionist trade legislation "could cause uncertainty in the market.... We want fair trade, but we must make sure we're not too restrictive."

Except when it comes to lamb imports. Then the Montana Democrat isn't at all sheepish about favoring restriction. He is pushing a provision for the pending trade bill that would protect the U.S. lamb industry from a surge in imports. He acknowledges that it could restrict trade, but he says "It's good for my state."

Baucus's amendment would set a floating ceiling on lamb imports to prevent a surge form Australia and New Zealand. It would put lamb on the same footing as beef, veal, and mutton under the Meat Import Act, which controls imports in relation to domestic production and consumption. When the Finance Committee considered the amendment, even GOP Senator Malcolm Wallop of Wyoming, an avid free-trader, went along in the interest of his sheep-producing state.

Baucus didn't tell his Senate colleagues that he owns stock in a family ranch that has more than 6,000 sheep in Helena, Montana.

Other provisions in the pending trade legislation benefit interests in other states. For example, in years past, U.S. sugar refiners have paid tariffs on imported sugar they refine and then re-export. Currently, they can claim refunds for duties paid during the 5 years immediately preceding the date of export. But a provision being pushed primarily by Louisiana Democratic Senators John Breaux and J. Bennett Johnston would extend the refunds to duties paid more than a decade ago—even though U.S. Customs records that far back have been destroyed and can't be used to verify the refund claims, technically called "drawbacks."

If the new provision stays in the law, the Treasury will have to write refund checks to a few large sugar refiners. Just how much is in some dispute: The Congressional Budget Office sees the 1988 to 1992 cost ranging from $260 million to as much as $600 million, while the administration says refunds could reach $800 million.

No one, though, disputes that a few large refiners would profit handsomely. The principal beneficiaries would be Amstar Corp. of New York, which would get at least $135 million; Savannah Foods and Industries Inc. of Savannah, Georgia, at least $91 million; and Imperial Sugar Co. of Sugar Land, Texas, at least $38 million.

Supporters say the provision is needed to keep U.S. sugar refiners competitive and to save thousands of American jobs. Sugar refining is an important business in Louisiana; Johnston notes that Amstar's refinery in his state employs 500 workers.

At one point, some opponents noted that the provision would help only cane-sugar interests, and they wondered aloud whether sugar-beet growers were opposed. Senator Breaux sprang into action. His office quickly called the Sugarbeet Growers Association, he recalls, "and had them dictate letters stating their positions"—which were that they "did not oppose" the provision. Senator Johnston then introduced the letter on the Senate floor, ensuring that senators from sugar-beet states wouldn't vote against it.

Source: Monica Langley, "Trade Bill Is Loaded With Import Curbs Aiding Local Interests," *The Wall Street Journal*, November 12, 1987, p. 1. Reprinted by permission of The Wall Street Journal. © Dow Jones & Company, Inc., 1987. All Rights Reserved.

Questions

1. Who would benefit from the import restrictions on lamb and the "drawbacks" on sugar exports? Who is harmed by these restrictions? Why are the beneficiaries effective lobbyists despite their relatively small numbers?
2. What features of representative democracy facilitate the passage of special interest legislation like that discussed here?

SELF TEST

These sample test items will help you check how much you have learned. Answers are found at the end of the chapter. Scoring yourself: One or two wrong—on target. Three or four wrong—passing, but you haven't mastered the chapter yet. Five or more wrong—not good enough; start over and restudy the chapter.

1. Which of the following is thought to justify government intervention in the economy, according to the market failure theory?
    a. Externalities.
    b. Public goods.
    c. Insufficient competition.
    d. All of the above.

_____ 2. As a working hypothesis, public choice theorists assume that government officials act in accordance with self-interest
   a. in their private lives.
   b. in their public roles.
   c. both **a** and **b**.
   d. neither **a** nor **b**.

_____ 3. A method of determining the efficient amount that should be spent on any given category of public good is
   a. direct voting.
   b. representative voting.
   c. benefit-cost analysis.
   d. logrolling.

_____ 4. Under which of the following circumstances is the amount spent on a public good most likely to be efficient in a direct democracy?
   a. costs shared in proportion to benefits.
   b. benefits shared equally, costs concentrated on a few.
   c. costs shared equally, benefits concentrated on a few.
   d. benefits shared equally, a few exempt from sharing the costs.

_____ 5. Suppose that everyone in a community will benefit equally from flood control expenditures, and that a minority of wealthy taxpayers will bear almost all of the cost. In a direct democracy, we would expect
   a. exactly the efficient amount of expenditure on flood control.
   b. too much expenditure on flood control.
   c. not enough expenditure on flood control.
   d. no reason to think one rather than another of the above.

_____ 6. Suppose that a few sheep farmers will benefit from restrictions on wool imports, while all consumers of woolen clothing will be harmed. In a direct democracy, we would expect
   a. tight restrictions on wool imports.
   b. moderate restrictions that balance benefits and costs.
   c. no restrictions.
   d. a complete ban on wool imports.

_____ 7. Tax loopholes that allow a few to escape from paying the cost of programs that benefit all citizens would be most likely under
   a. direct democracy.
   b. representative democracy.
   c. equally likely under direct or representative democracy.
   d. impossible under either direct or representative democracy.

_____ 8. In what way does the "political marketplace" differ from the economic marketplace?
   a. In the political marketplace, voters have more frequent opportunities to express their opinions.
   b. In the economic marketplace, consumers have no opportunity to express their opinion.
   c. In the economic marketplace, consumers can choose a selection of goods to suit their individual preferences.
   d. In the political marketplace, voters are not able to select "package deals."

9. The activity of communicating with elected officials in order to advocate some policy is called
   a. pork barreling.
   b. logrolling.
   c. lobbying.
   d. marketing.

10. Which of the following groups would tend to be most effective, in proportion to their numbers, in terms of lobbying and political expression?
    a. People who pay income taxes.
    b. People who are consumers of food products.
    c. Owners of Mississippi River barges.
    d. People who use postal services.

11. The practice of trading votes among members of a legislative body is known as
    a. logrolling.
    b. protectionism.
    c. lobbying.
    d. expressionism.

12. A bill consisting largely of a series of small, local projects funded by general revenues is called a
    a. logjam.
    b. lobby.
    c. line-item veto.
    d. pork barrel.

13. Senators are to voters as
    a. consumers are to manufacturers.
    b. borrowers are to lenders.
    c. corporate managers are to stockholders.
    d. corporate managers are to employees.

14. The practice of logrolling makes which of the following more likely in a representative democracy than would be the case in a direct democracy?
    a. Trade restrictions that benefit a few producers at the expense of the majority of consumers.
    b. Civil rights laws that protect the freedoms of racial and religious minorities.
    c. Both a and b.
    d. Neither a nor b.

15. A conclusion of public choice theory is that
    a. Whenever there is a chance of market failure, the government should take action.
    b. The government should never attempt to correct a market failure.
    c. The possibility of government failure should be weighed against the possibility of market failure in making economic policy decisions.
    d. None of the above.

ANSWERS TO CHAPTER 34

Economics in the News

(1) The restrictions on lamb would benefit sheep ranchers at the expense of consumers. The sugar drawbacks would benefit the producers and possibly their employees at the cost of taxpayers, who would have to make up the revenue shortfall resulting from increased drawbacks. In each case, the beneficiaries are a small, well-organized group while those who bear the costs are a large, poorly organized group. (2) Several features of representative democracy are at work here. One is the fact that representatives are elected on a geographical basis, which favors local interests like those of the refiners and sheep ranchers. A second is the self-interest of representatives, who can count on the votes of sheep ranchers and the political contributions of sugar refiners. A third is logrolling. This is suggested by the support of sugar beet growers for the benefits to cane sugar refiners. It is implicit that the cane refiners will support the beet producers when some issue arises that is of interest to them.

Self Test

1. **d.** All of these are potential sources of market failure.
2. **c.** Public officials are considered to be the same people, 24 hours a day, in both their public and private roles.
3. **c.** The others are ways of determining how much will actually be spent.
4. **a.** Some programs, such as financing highways with gasoline taxes or parks with entrance fees try to approximate this situation.
5. **b.** In this case, the median voter's share of the benefits is greater than his or her share of the costs.
6. **c.** But in a representative democracy, restrictions would be entirely possible.
7. **b.** They would be rare under direct democracy.
8. **c.** In the political marketplace, voters must choose package deals, and can express their preferences only at wide intervals.
9. **c.** This is a broad use of the term.
10. **c.** They are a small group, geographically localized, and having a strong enough common interest to make it worth their while to communicate with one another and make expenditures on political expression. The others are large, unorganized, and geographically dispersed groups.
11. **a.** Logrolling facilitates the expression of minority interests.
12. **d.** Pork barrel legislation is facilitated by the geographical basis of representation.
13. **c.** Legislators are agents of their principals, the voters, just as corporate managers are agents of their principals, the stockholders who own the firm.

14. c. Minority interests of all kinds are protected by logrolling.
15. c. Public choice theory acknowledges the possibility of both market and government failure.

Chapter 35

International Trade and Trade Policy

WHERE YOU'RE GOING

When you have mastered this chapter, you will understand

1. How the principle of comparative advantage can be applied to international trade.
2. How the notion of "competitiveness" is related to that of comparative advantage.
3. The trend of trade policy during the post-World War II period.
4. How international trade affects income distribution within each country.
5. How protectionist policies can be explained in terms of public choice theory and rent seeking.

In addition, you will add the following terms to your economic vocabulary:
   Absolute advantage
   Protectionism
   Tariff
   Import quota

WALKING TOUR

After you have read this chapter at least once, you should work step by step through this walking tour. Fill in the blanks and answer the questions as you go along. After you have answered each question, check yourself by uncovering the answer given in the margin. If you do not understand why the answer given is the correct one, refer back to the proper section of the text.

Comparative Advantage and International Trade

Imagine two countries called, for the sake of example, England and Portugal. These are the only two countries in the world, and they produce only two products, wool and cheese. The only factor of production is labor. In England it takes 6 labor hours to produce a pound of wool and 3 labor hours to produce a pound of cheese; in Portugal 3 labor hours will produce a pound of wool and just 1 labor

404

wool	hour a pound of cheese. Under these conditions, England is said to have a comparative advantage in _____ and Portugal
cheese	to have a comparative advantage in _____. Note,
absolute	incidentally, that Portugal has a/an _____ advantage in both products.
	Suppose that each country has 1,200 labor hours available to it and that each divides these labor hours equally between the two products. That would give England a production of _____
100	pounds of wool and _____ pounds of cheese and Portugal
200	a production of _____ pounds of wool and _____
200, 600	pounds of cheese. Total world production of wool would be
300	_____ pounds, and total world production of cheese,
800	_____ pounds.
	In England, the opportunity cost of a pound of wool is
2	_____ pounds of cheese, and in Portugal, the opportunity cost of a pound of wool is _____ pounds of cheese.
3	This difference in opportunity costs is what creates a possibility of mutually advantageous trade between the two countries. England will export a pound of wool if it can get anything more than
2	_____ pounds of cheese in return, whereas Portugal will
3	export up to _____ pounds of cheese if it can get a pound of wool in return. Any trading ratio between 2 for 1 and 3 for 1, then, will potentially benefit both parties.
	To demonstrate this possibility of mutual advantage, suppose a trading ratio of 2.5 pounds of cheese per pound of wool is decided on. England decides to make an initial export shipment of, say, 6 pounds of wool. To produce the 6 pounds of wool for export, it must
36	withdraw _____ labor hours from the production of
12	cheese, which means foregoing production of _____ pounds of cheese. When it sends the 6 pounds of wool to Portugal,
15	however, it receives _____ pounds of cheese in exchange, more than compensating for the loss in domestic production. To produce the 15 pounds of cheese for export to England, Portugal
15	must shift _____ hours of labor from producing wool to
5	producing cheese. This means foregoing production of _____ pounds of wool. However, in return for the 15 pounds of cheese it
6	exports, it receives _____ pounds of wool from England, more than making up the loss in domestic production. Both

405

wool, cheese	countries are thus better off than before trade; England has just as much _____ and more _____ than before,
cheese	whereas Portugal has just as much _____ and more
wool	_____. Note also that total world production of both products has increased: total world output of wool is now
301	_____ pounds and total world production of cheese is
803	now _____ pounds. Further trade at the same ratio would bring still further gains in production and consumption.
	When trade takes the form of barter, as in the previous example, imports and exports of goods and services balance. In the real
is not	world, this [is/is not] always the case. For example, a country can import more goods and services than it exports if its trading
real or financial assets	partners use part of their earnings to purchase _____ rather than goods or services.
	A further complication is the fact that real world international
money	transactions are, for the most part, conducted using _____ as a means of payment. This means that before one can buy goods or services from another country, one must first visit the
foreign exchange	_____ markets. The rates at which any two currencies
supply	are exchanged are determined by _____ and
demand, affect	_____. Exchange rates [affect/do not affect] the ability of a country's exporters to compete in world markets. For example, when the value of the dollar goes up relative to the value of some
more difficult	foreign currency like the French franc, it becomes [easier/more
easier	difficult] for U.S. firms to sell exports in France, and [easier/more difficult] for French firms to sell their goods in the United States. Thus, when a country experiences a balance of trade deficit, the
does not	lack of "competitiveness" [does/does not] necessarily reflect a lapse of management skills, technological leadership, or marketing ability.

Trade Policy and Protectionism

	The post-World War II period as a whole has seen a movement
freer	toward [freer/less free] trade. Examples of international organizations set up to facilitate free trade include
GATT	1. _____,
IMF	2. _____, and
Common Market	3. _____.

However, trade has not become completely free, and new protectionist devices have sprung up to supplement traditional tariffs and quotas. In understanding the reasons for protectionism, it is helpful to understand the effects of trade when there are multiple factors of production.

Suppose we modify the previous example to allow for more than one factor of production, say land as well as labor. Suppose that production of wool uses land relatively intensively and production of cheese uses labor relatively intensively. Now, when England begins to export wool to Portugal in exchange for cheese, the shift in production patterns within each country will increase demand for _____ relative to _____ in England and will increase demand for _____ relative to _____ in Portugal. As a result of this shift in demand, relative factor prices will change. In England, land rents will [rise/fall] and wages will [rise/fall] while in Portugal, land rents will [rise/fall] while wages [rise/fall]. Trade will thus definitely make English [workers/landowners] and Portuguese [workers/landowners] better off. Whether English workers and Portuguese landowners end up better off or worse off in real terms is uncertain. Trade raises total real incomes in both countries but leaves English workers and Portuguese landowners with a smaller relative share of the larger total. They might gain in absolute terms, or they might lose; the outcome would depend on such things as the degree of difference in factor intensity between the two production processes, the mobility of the factors from one industry to another, and the elasticity of demand for the factors from each type of producer.

Although there are always some who benefit from protectionism, the total gains to the winners tend to be [greater/smaller] than the total cost to the losers. The political success of protectionism can be explained in terms of _____ theory, and the notion of _____.

land, labor
labor, land

rise
fall, fall
rise, landowners
workers

greater

public choice
rent seeking

HANDS ON

Now that you have reviewed the concepts introduced in this chapter, it is time for some hands-on practice with the analytical tools that have been introduced. Work through this section carefully, and then check your results against those given at the end of the chapter.

In this problem, assume that the two countries and two goods are the only ones in existence, that labor is the only factor of production, and that costs per unit are constant.

a. In the United States, a tractor can be produced with 100 labor hours and shoes require 2 labor hours per pair. In China, 500 labor hours are required to build a tractor and 2.5 labor hours to make a pair of shoes. Which country has a comparative advantage in shoes? In tractors? Which country has an absolute advantage in shoes? In tractors?

b. Assume that the United States has 1 billion labor hours available for production of the two goods and that China has 5 billion labor hours. In the three panels of Exhibit 35.1, draw production possibility frontiers for the United States, China, and the world as a whole.

c. Assume that initially, the United States and China each split their available labor hours evenly between tractor and shoe production. What quantities of the two goods will each country produce? Label the initial production point for the United States P_u; that for China P_c; and that for the world P_w.

d. Would trade of any kind between the two countries be mutually advantageous? If so, which country should export which product? What is the range of relative prices within which trade would be mutually advantageous?

Exhibit 35.1a

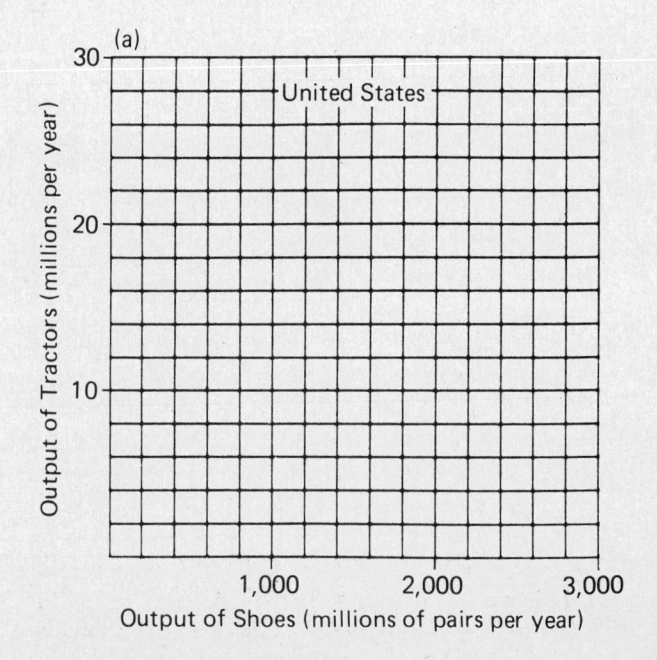

(a) United States

Output of Tractors (millions per year) vs. Output of Shoes (millions of pairs per year)

Exhibit 35.1b

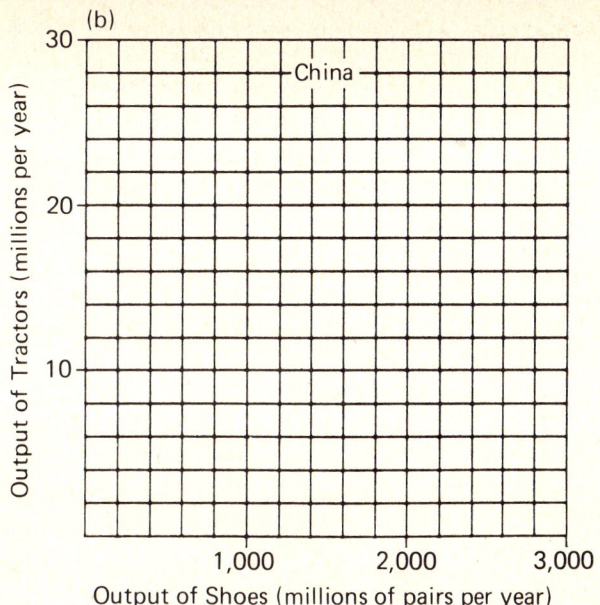

(b)

China

Output of Tractors (millions per year)

Output of Shoes (millions of pairs per year)

Exhibit 35.1c

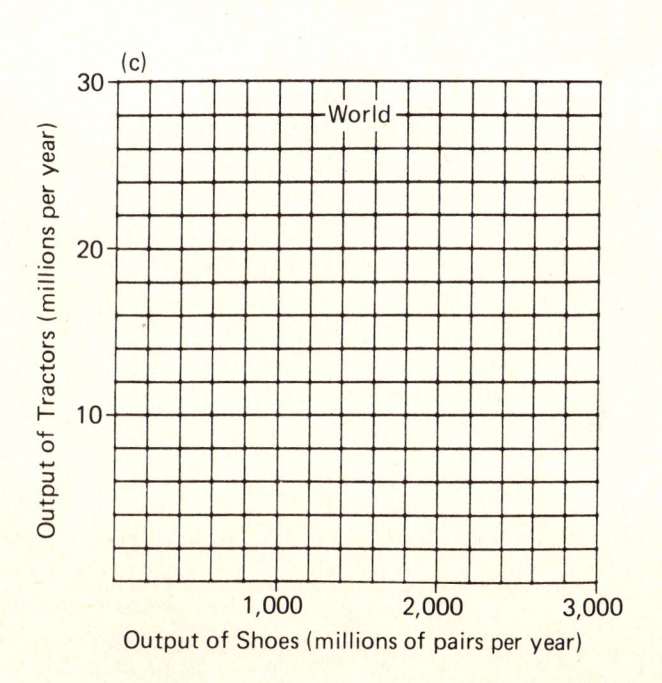

(c)

World

Output of Tractors (millions per year)

Output of Shoes (millions of pairs per year)

e. Assume that a trading ratio of 1 tractor for 100 pairs of shoes is established. The United States completely specializes in tractors, produces no shoes of its own, and exports 40 tractors in exchange for 400 pairs of shoes. China diverts just enough labor from tractor production to produce the necessary shoe exports. What quantities of each good does each country now produce? Label the new production points Q_u, Q_c, and Q_w, respectively.

How much does each country now consume? Label the new post-trade consumption points R_u, R_c, and R_w, respectively.

f. Is either country better off? Are both? How can you tell? Is world production organized more efficiently than before? How can you tell?

ECONOMICS IN THE NEWS

A Parable of Advantage

In a time past, one George the lawyer hired unto himself a splendid young typist named Minnie.

His friends leered and sniggered, because they knew that George was an excellent typist in his own right. In fact, they said, the lawyer could type far faster than this young woman, and he could easily do his own typing and save money.

George ignored them, because his motives were pure. And very practical.

Of course, George could practice law at the going rate of $50 an hour. Given a 40-hour week, he could spend 30 hours on law to earn a whacking $1,500, and then knock off all his typing in the other 10 hours.

Instead, George chose to practice law all 40 hours of the week, to take in $2,000. He paid slow-typing Minnie the going $5 an hour, or $200 for her 40-hour week, leaving himself with a decidedly improved net income of $1,800.

Regardless of George's superior typing skills, it paid him to spend his time doing that which maximized his gains—that is, in the argot of the trade, "exporting" legal services and "importing" typing services.

Thus, lawyer George gave mankind the Law of Comparative Advantage. In short, always export the goods you have the *relative* advantage in, and import the rest.

His friends gathered around George in awe—all except one who stood back, frowning.

But what if Minnie should join a powerful wage-fixing cartel? the puzzler asked.

Or what if hard times came, and George could "export" only 20 hours a week of legal services? Clearly, his wisest course then would be to eliminate the "imports" and do his own typing.

The lawyer thought for a moment. And then he replied with a chuckle:

"Silly boy! Whoever heard of such one-sided interventions? And won't there always be full employment? Why let such thoughts muck up a perfectly good theory?"

All exited, laughing.

Source: "A parable of advantage," *The Financial Post*, June 28, 1980, p. 17. Reprinted by permission.

Questions

1. Who has a comparative advantage in providing law services? In typing? How much faster does George type than Minnie types? How do you know? Is there some crucial assumption left unsaid in this example? If so, what?
2. What is George's opportunity cost of typing if he types himself? If he hires Minnie?
3. "What if Minnie should join a powerful wage-fixing cartel?" a friend asks. You answer. Can you think of any real-world parallel to this situation?
4. "What if hard times came, and George could 'export' only 20 hours of legal services?" Should he then do his own typing? Why or why not? Can you think of any real world parallel here?

SELF TEST

These sample test items will help you check how much you have learned. Answers are found at the end of the chapter. Scoring yourself: One or two wrong—on target. Three or four wrong—passing, but you haven't mastered the chapter yet. Five or more wrong—not good enough; start over and restudy the chapter.

1. Suppose John can sew four shirts per day or knit six caps per day, whereas Jane can sew three shirts per day or knit four caps per day. It can then be said that
   a. John has a comparative advantage in sewing shirts.
   b. John has a comparative advantage in knitting caps.
   c. both of the above are true.
   d. neither of the above is true.

2. According to international trade theory, a country should
   a. export goods in which it has a comparative advantage.
   b. never export goods in which it has an absolute advantage.
   c. never import goods in which it has an absolute advantage.
   d. import goods in which it has a comparative advantage.

3. It takes 5 labor hours to produce a ton of steel in Japan and 3 labor hours in the United States, and it requires 20 labor hours to produce a car in Japan and only 15 labor hours in the United States. If Japan and the United States were the only two countries involved in trade, we would expect
   a. Japan to import cars and export steel.
   b. Japan to export cars and import steel.
   c. Japan to export both cars and steel.
   d. Japan to import both cars and steel.

4. Trade in meat and wheat between two countries is least likely to be profitable if
   a. one country has an absolute advantage in both goods.
   b. one country has a comparative advantage in both goods.
   c. the opportunity cost of meat, in terms of wheat, is the same in both countries.
   d. each country has an absolute advantage in one of the goods.

5. In a two-good, two-country world, international trade can increase
   a. consumer welfare in both countries, but not total output of both goods.
   b. total output of both goods, but not consumer welfare in both countries.
   c. consumer welfare only if output of both goods is increased.
   d. output of both goods and consumer welfare in both countries.

6. In Norway, it takes 5 labor hours to produce a ton of wheat and 5 to produce a ton of fish; in Greece it takes 3 labor hours to produce a ton of wheat and 3 to produce a ton of fish. If these are the only two goods and the only two trading countries, we would expect
   a. Norway to export both products.
   b. Norway to import both products.
   c. Norway to export wheat and import fish.
   d. no trade.

7. England and Germany both produce wheat and oatmeal. Oatmeal is an inferior good, and England has a comparative advantage in producing it. If the two countries begin to trade, we would expect
   a. consumer welfare in England to decline.
   b. the English to eat less oatmeal than before.
   c. world output of wheat to decline.
   d. none of the above—mutually advantageous trade would be impossible.

8. If the value of the dollar in foreign exchange markets increases from 2 German marks to 3 German marks, which of the following is most likely to benefit?
   a. U.S. firms that export goods to Germany.
   b. U.S. firms that compete with goods imported from Germany.
   c. U.S. consumers of goods imported from Germany.
   d. All of the above will benefit.

9. In the absence of trade, world production will tend to be
   a. outside the world production possibility frontier.
   b. inside the world production possibility frontier.
   c. on the world production possibility frontier, but too far down along it.
   d. on the world production possibility frontier, but too far up along it.

10. If a country exports products of land-intensive industries and imports products of labor-intensive industries, we would expect that the country's
    a. landowners will gain at the expense of workers.
    b. workers will gain at the expense of landowners.
    c. landowners will gain for sure, workers may gain.
    d. workers will gain for sure, landowners may gain.

11. It is more likely that at least some groups in a country will be hurt by trade
    a. the higher the country's initial standard of living.
    b. the lower the country's initial standard of living.
    c. the less mobile the country's factors of production.
    d. the more mobile the country's factors of production.

_____ 12. If a country exports fish and imports wheat, an interruption of trade will be likely to decrease
   a. the welfare of wheat eaters in that country.
   b. the welfare of fishery workers in that country.
   c. total world output of both products.
   d. all of the above.

_____ 13. Either a tariff or a quota can be used to cut imports of Japanese television sets by an equal amount; comparing the two policies, it is likely that
   a. the tariff will hurt consumers more than the quota.
   b. the quota will hurt domestic producers but the tariff will help them.
   c. the quota will hurt Japanese producers less, and may actually help them.
   d. the quota will raise the domestic price by less than the tariff.

_____ 14. According to economic studies of the effects of quotas on the imports of Japanese autos,
   a. wage gains to U.S. workers were greater than costs to U.S. consumers.
   b. profits of Japanese auto firms fell substantially.
   c. the effect on prices of cars made in the United States was slight.
   d. the effects of the quotas resembled those of an international automobile cartel.

_____ 15. Proponents of protectionism commonly base their case on
   a. the pure theory of comparative advantage.
   b. the need to "level the playing field" of international trade.
   c. positive economic studies of costs and benefits of protectionism.
   d. none of the above.

ANSWERS TO CHAPTER 35

Hands On

(a) In the United States, the opportunity cost of a tractor is 50 pairs of shoes. In China, the opportunity cost of a tractor is 200 pairs of shoes. The United States thus has a comparative advantage in tractors, and China in shoes. The United States has an absolute advantage in both products. (b) See solution graph for Exhibit 35.1. (c) Initially, the United States produces 5 million tractors and 250 million pairs of shoes. China produces 5 million tractors and 1,000 pairs of shoes. These points are marked "P" on the solution graphs. (d) The United States should export tractors and import shoes. Any trading ratio between 1 tractor for 200 pairs of shoes (the opportunity cost ratio in China) and 1 tractor for 50 pairs of shoes (the opportunity cost ratio in the United States) would be mutually advantageous. (e) Under these assumptions, the United States would produce 10 million tractors and no shoes. China would

Exhibit 35.1a (ans.)

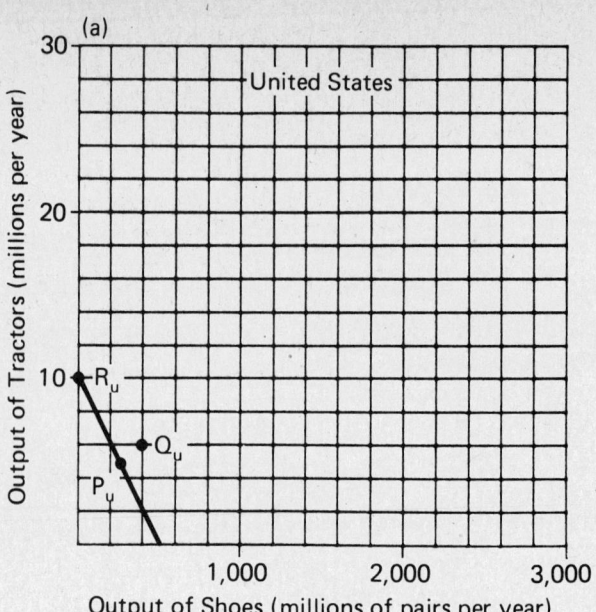

(a) United States

Output of Tractors (millions per year) vs Output of Shoes (millions of pairs per year)

Points marked: R_u at ~10 tractors, Q_u, P_u

Exhibit 35.1b (ans.)

(b) China

Output of Tractors (millions per year) vs Output of Shoes (millions of pairs per year)

Points marked: Q_c, P_c, R_c

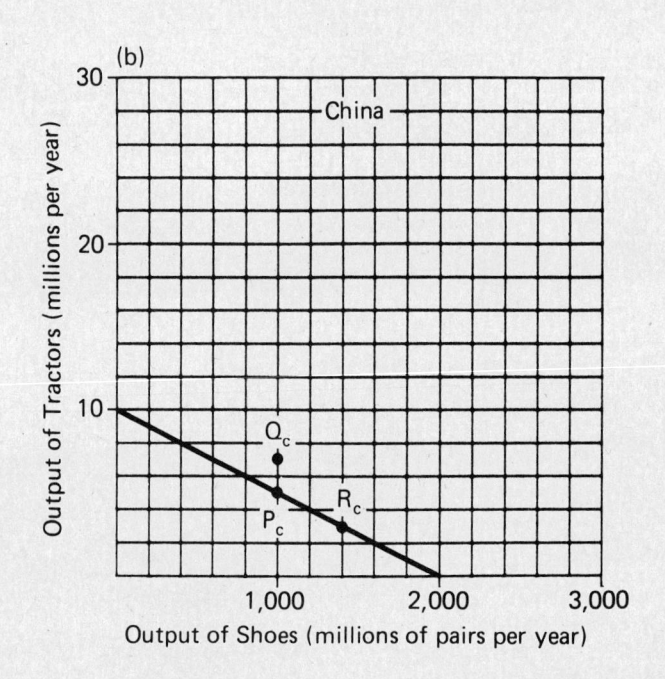

shift 1 billion labor hours from tractors to shoes, lowering tractor production to 3 million and raising shoe production to 1,400 million. These points are marked R in the solution exhibit. Consumption points are 6 million tractors and 400 million pairs of shoes in the United States; 7 million tractors and 1,000 million pairs of shoes in China. These are marked Q in the exhibit. (f) Both countries are better off; the United States now consumes more of both products;

Exhibit 35.1c (ans.)

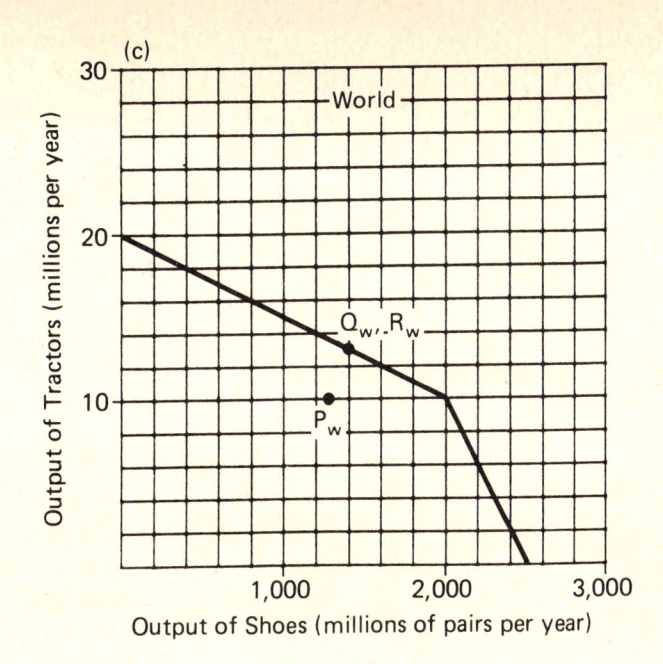

China consumes more tractors and no fewer shoes. World production has gone up from 10 million to 13 million tractors, and from 1,250 million to 1,400 pairs of shoes. Each individual country has moved outside its domestic production possibility frontier. The world as a whole has moved from an inefficient point inside its frontier to an efficient point on the frontier.

Economics in the News

(1) The article asserts that George has a comparative advantage in legal service and Minnie in typing—but it doesn't quite give all the information you need to really be sure. We do know that it takes George 20 minutes to type up the results of each hour of his legal research, whereas it takes Minnie a full hour to type up the results of 1 hour of George's research. What we are not really told, however, is how good Minnie's legal research skills are. She is only one-third as good a typist, so if she is to have a comparative advantage in typing, it must be that she is less than one-third as good as a lawyer. But what if Minnie, although lacking a law degree, has some paralegal training? What if she, in 20 hours, could research and draft a will that George could knock off in 10 hours? Who then should do the typing and who the research? The surprising answer is that under these assumptions, Minnie should do the legal work and George the typing! (2) George's opportunity cost of typing for himself is 20 minutes of legal work (worth $16.67) to do the quantity of typing generated by an hour's legal work. If he hires Minnie, his opportunity cost is only one-tenth of an hour of legal work ($5) for the same amount of typing. (3) The answer here is simple: If the wage-fixing cartel sets a price below $16.67 for the amount of typing George can do in 20 minutes, it will still pay George to hire Minnie.

415

If the cartel wage goes above $16.67 for that amount of work, George should quit practice as a lawyer, and instead, join the cartel to seek employment as a typist. United States policy toward OPEC provides a real world parallel. Suppose OPEC were to raise the price of oil from $20 per barrel to $40. Should the United States then seek energy independence by producing synthetic oil from coal? Only if coal oil costs less than $40 to produce. For the United States to subsidize production of $100 synthetic oil in order to avoid importing $40 OPEC oil would be as foolish as for George to do his own typing in retaliation for an increase in typists' wages to $10 per hour. (Of course, the United States might rationally threaten to produce synthetic oil, and George to his own typing, as bargaining tactics in the hope of breaking up their respective cartels.) (4) This one is tricky, but true-blue free traders have an answer. The answer is that George should meet the drop in demand for lawyer's service not solely by cutting back his output, but at least in part by cutting back his hourly rate for legal services. In fact, if the legal market were competitive, the "hard times" would manifest themselves to George not in the form of a shortage of work, but instead in the form of a fall in the going lawyering rate. Unless lawyers' fees dropped below $15 per hour, George still shouldn't do his own typing. More than that: If the "hard times" depressed the demand for lawyers' labor only, and not for typists', George should not do his own typing when the lawyering rate dropped below $15 per hour—he should instead quit lawyering altogether and seek full time employment as a typist! If instead the "hard times" were general, the typists' wages would drop too, and George could keep lawyering away. Real world examples abound. How should the United States react to hard times for its domestic auto industry? By keeping out imports and producing all its own cars? No! It should instead do one of two other things. First, it should allow auto workers' wages to fall enough to keep the domestic factories running, or second, it should shift auto workers out of that industry into other industries, such as chemicals or construction equipment, where the United States still has a comparative advantage. Moral of the story: Free traders always have an answer.

Self Test

1. **b.** For John, the opportunity cost of knitting a cap is two-thirds of a shirt; for Jane it is three-quarters of a shirt.
2. **a.** It may either import or export those in which it has an absolute advantage, depending on circumstances.
3. **b.** Japan has a comparative advantage in cars, and the United States a comparative advantage in steel.
4. **c.** Gains from trade depend on differences in opportunity costs.
5. **d.** But even if output did not increase, simply redistributing existing goods to better serve consumer preferences would increase welfare.
6. **d.** There is no difference in opportunity costs on which trade could be based.
7. **b.** For two reasons. The increase in real income in England will reduce the consumption of oatmeal, an inferior good. Also, as

England specializes in oatmeal, its relative price will rise, reducing consumption via the substitution effect.
8. **c.** The firms in **a** and **b** will be hurt.
9. **b.** Even if each country is on its local production possibility frontier.
10. **c.** Both will gain as consumers, but workers will earn relatively lower wages.
11. **c.** Mobility helps adjustment to changes in patterns of production.
12. **d.** Wheat producers and fish eaters in that country might gain.
13. **c.** Both policies will raise domestic prices. With a tariff the increased price per unit goes to the Treasury, whereas with quotas, it goes to Japanese producers. If demand is inelastic, Japan's total revenue will rise.
14. **d.** Answers **a**, **b**, and **c** are the opposite of the truth.
15. **b.** Positive economics and economic theory usually favor the free traders.

Chapter 36

The Soviet Economy: Central Planning and Reform

WHERE YOU'RE GOING

When you have mastered this chapter, you will understand

1. The historical and ideological origins of the Soviet economic system.
2. The key features of the Soviet economy's formal and informal structure.
3. The chief accomplishments and failures of Soviet economic performance.
4. Prospects for reform of the Soviet economy.

In addition, you will add the following terms to your economic vocabulary:
Extensive growth
Intensive growth

WALKING TOUR

After you have read this chapter at least once, you should work step by step through this walking tour. Fill in the blanks and answer the questions as you go along. After you have answered each question, check yourself by uncovering the answer given in the margin. If you do not understand why the answer given is the correct one, refer back to the proper section of the text.

Origins of the Soviet Economic System

centralized

Karl Marx

V.I. Lenin

The origins of the _____ socialist economic system of the Soviet Union can be traced to the writings of _____ and the revolutionary practice of _____. For both men, the postrevolutionary economy was supposed to replace the "anarchy of the market" with the "planning principle," that is, to replace

market, managerial

_____ coordination with _____ coordination at the national level.

did

After the revolution, Lenin [did/did not] attempt to implement many features of a centralized system. Coming during a period of civil war, these radical measures led to chaos. They were followed by a period of increased reliance on the market known as the _____ (*new economic policy*). Central planning was once again instituted at the end of the 1920s, together with a policy of _____ (*collectivization*) of agriculture. At that time, the structure of the Soviet economy took on most of the important features it retains to this day.

Structure of the Soviet Economic System

Under current practice, the activities of each firm are guided by a technical-industrial-financial plan that determines [inputs/outputs/*both*] for the firm. These plans, in turn, are based on a set of _____ (*material balances*) for 200 or 300 of the most important goods which are supposed to ensure the balance of supply and demand. These material balances are refined at lower levels of the planning hierarchy, and individual firms are given a chance to negotiate with central authorities about details of the plan at that time. In practice, a major objective of enterprise managers at this stage is to develop a _____ (*safety factor*) that will make it possible to fulfill the plan even if everything does not go smoothly during the year.

Performance of the Soviet Economy

During the 1930s, immediately after the introduction of comprehensive central planning, official Soviet data show growth rates of 15 percent per year or more for national output. Western observers believe that these high growth rates are somewhat exaggerated by the use of a very [*early*/late] base year for constructing growth indexes. Nonetheless, growth rates were clearly high at that time. The type of growth that took place is best described as [*extensive*/intensive] growth, because it was based largely on mobilization of new factor inputs. Since World War II, the growth rate of the Soviet economy has gradually slowed. This apparently indicates difficulties in achieving [extensive/*intensive*] growth through the more efficient utilization of available factor supplies. The declining growth rate [has/*has not yet*] led to comprehensive reforms of the centralized planning system. As it has throughout the past 50 years, the _____ (*agricultural*) sector continues to lag behind the _____ (*industrial*) sector.

Reforming the Soviet Economy

In the classical Soviet system, enterprise managers depend on central authorities for every detail of operations. Thus, one of the most needed elements of reform is _____. According to a 1987 law, planning will be [ended/limited]. Enterprises will finance their operations from _____. And workers will be given rights to elect leaders and managers.

Under the classical Soviet system, prices are far from _____ costs. Thus, another element of reform is reform of the _____. However, there are difficulties to be faced. It hard to grant enterprise independence without price reform, but also hard to have price reform without enterprise independence. Also, there is the problem that prices of many key consumer goods, such as meat, bread, and housing, are currently [above/below] opportunity cost. However, bringing these prices in line with opportunity costs would possibly provoke political opposition.

A third element of reform is to be the liberation of _____ enterprises and cooperatives. This has been a notable feature of economic reform in _____.

Margin notes: enterprise independence, limited revenues; opportunity; price system; below; small-scale; China

---

ECONOMICS IN THE NEWS

A Soviet Economist Discusses Price Reform

The following passages are excerpted from the verbatim transcript of an interview with Tatiana Zaslavskaya, one of the Soviet Unions foremost "new economists."

Q: What reaction will there be—that is, in the economy, among the people of the Soviet Union, if food prices suddenly rise?

ZASLAVSKAYA: . . . [T]he current system can in no way be justified. Meat, as is well known, is one of the scarcest goods in the USSR, there is not enough of it, and at the same time it sells at a price which is actually, at the most, 35 to 40 percent of its real value. It is the same as giving a privilege to every man, a reward, which buys him an extra kilogram of meat. That means, through this he gains about 3 rubles a kilogram. . . .

[O]bviously, it must be worthwhile for the enterprises that produce the meat, it must be profitable for them. To bring in a profit and keep a low, what is already a very low, understated level of established retail prices, is of course a very considerable obstacle. The cost of the subsidy is well known; in fact the state subsidizes the wholesale price of meat, which it pays the collective and state farms at a level higher than the cost price—otherwise they simply would not produce—and it then sells the meat at a lower price. There is a great discrepancy between the two. This discrepancy is paid for out of the budget and is valued at approximately 70 billion rubles. . . .

[If] measures are laid down directed at raising retail prices, there will at the same time be compensation through wage increases. . . . If legislation to raise retail prices is discussed, it is all the same fairly remote from the population, it has not been discussed with the people, not explained on the television, and on the radio; there should be dozens of training programs to tell every man why this is extremely necessary, and what makes these scarce goods almost free. There would have to be appearances of leading officials—that is, Party officials who would explain, with chalk in hand, on the blackboard, that everyone will be compensated; then it can be talked about.

Q: But can things go forward without this?

ZASLAVSKAYA: They can, they can. This, of course, is such a serious factor, but public opinion must support it; in my opinion, the preparation for this step is extremely serious. Because otherwise it inevitably would be perceived by the population simply as the next attempt to lower the standard of living, for the state to take more and give the people less—this is very dangerous.

Source: *Radio Liberty Research Bulletin*, No. 37 (RL 365/87), September 16, 1987, pp. 2-4.

Questions

1. Explain why price reform is a necessary complement to greater independence of enterprises, including collective and state farms.
2. Discuss the political obstacles of price reform in the light of Zaslavskaya's comments.

SELF TEST

These sample test items will help you check how much you have learned. Answers are found at the end of the chapter. Scoring yourself: One or two wrong—on target. Three or four wrong—passing, but you haven't mastered the chapter yet. Five or more wrong—not good enough; start over and restudy the chapter.

_____ 1. During which of the following periods did the Soviet economy rely least on central planning?
   a. War communism.
   b. The NEP.
   c. Collectivization.
   d. The post-World War II period.

_____ 2. Which of the following measures was not instituted by Stalin in 1928?
   a. A five-year plan for industry.
   b. Collectivization of agriculture.
   c. Abolition of the use of money.
   d. All of the above were instituted.

3. In which of the following respects can the collectivization drive of the 1930s be considered a success, given the goals of the Soviet leadership?
   a. Increased grain output.
   b. Increased livestock output.
   c. Increased flow of agricultural products to the cities.
   d. All of the above.

4. Which of the following aspects of the operation of individual Soviet enterprises is detailed in the central plan?
   a. Assortment of products.
   b. Quantity of output.
   c. Timing of output deliveries.
   d. All of the above.

5. Under the classical Soviet planning system,
   a. plans are drawn up in final form at the center and handed down to enterprises in finished form.
   b. each enterprise draws up its own plan, which the central authorities then combine into one big plan.
   c. the planning process begins at the center, and suggestions for modifications are made by enterprises.
   d. **c** until the advent of computers; now **a**.

6. Which of the following sectors of the Soviet economy relies most on market mechanisms to move resources to their desired uses?
   a. Industry.
   b. Labor.
   c. Transportation.
   d. Energy.

7. Which of the following would be considered a "horizontal" communication channel in the Soviet economy?
   a. The plan is transmitted from Gosplan to the enterprise.
   b. A manager bargains with Gosplan for easier plan targets.
   c. A manager barters scarce inputs with the manager of another enterprise.
   d. Central authorities use the Communist Party as a check on the performance of planning system bureaucrats.

8. A "safety factor" for a Soviet manager might take the form of
   a. an easy plan.
   b. large inventories of inputs.
   c. concealed productive capacity.
   d. any of the above.

9. Which of the following best characterizes the attitude of Soviet authorities toward the informal, and sometimes illegal, actions managers take to meet plan targets?
   a. They are often tolerated if successful.
   b. They are severely punished when discovered.
   c. They are studied for a while; then, if they work, they are incorporated into the formal structure of the system.
   d. Soviet central authorities are apparently unaware of most of what goes on in this respect.

_____ 10. Which of the following, although it is not supposed to be a major concern of enterprise managers in the Soviet Union, is a major concern in practice?
   a. Meeting plan targets for assortment.
   b. Procuring inputs.
   c. Improving labor productivity.
   d. Earning bonuses.

_____ 11. Which of the following might be a likely reaction to a plan that specifies a target in tons of equipment for an agricultural equipment manufacturer in the Soviet economy?
   a. Equipment would be made so light and brittle that it would quickly break down.
   b. Managers of such firms would compete vigorously on the black market for supplies of aluminum to replace steel in such machines.
   c. Tractors would be made so heavy they would sink deep into the mud.
   d. Only small garden tractors would be produced.

_____ 12. Which of the following best characterizes the economic advances of the past 50 years in the Soviet economy?
   a. Transformation of an essentially underdeveloped country into a modern superpower with moderate living standards.
   b. Reduction of living standards once as high as those of Italy to a level lower than those of Brazil today.
   c. Achievement of true parity with the United States in terms of living standards.
   d. Transformation of a country once as poor as Nepal into one now comparable to Mexico in living standards.

_____ 13. The Soviet Economy is believed to be as efficient as the U.S. economy
   a. in static, but not in dynamic terms.
   b. in dynamic, but not in static terms.
   c. in both static and dynamic terms.
   d. in neither static nor dynamic terms.

_____ 14. Which of the following will be a necessary element of Soviet economic reform?
   a. Greater dependence of enterprises on central planning.
   b. Bringing prices more closely into line with opportunity costs.
   c. Elimination of the "second economy" and other forms of small-scale enterprise.
   d. All of the above.

_____ 15. Which of the following has been a problem with Chinese economic reform?
   a. Small-scale farming has not yet benefitted from reform.
   b. The problem of price reform has not yet been solved.
   c. During the reform period, GNP and living standards have fallen.
   d. All of the above.

ANSWERS TO CHAPTER 36

Economics in the News

(1) Independence of enterprises requires two things. First, they must bring in enough from sale to cover their costs. Otherwise they cannot survive as independent entities. Second, they must have an incentive to increase the output of goods that are best suited to meeting customers' needs. Both of these require prices that reflect opportunity cost. Thus, enterprise independence is impossible without price reform. However, it is not possible to know the "correct" prices except by supply and demand, and for supply and demand to find their expression, enterprises must be independent. Thus, the two parts of reform are complementary; neither can succeed without the other. (2) For years the government has appeased consumers by keeping the prices on basic goods low, even though this gives rise, in many cases, to shortages and rationing. Price increases tend to be strongly resisted by consumers. Thus, although price reform is logically required as a part of economic reform as a whole, any increases in prices run the danger of undercutting the political support for reform. Raising wages at the same time prices are raised is a possible way out of this situation, but it risks setting off an inflationary spiral.

Self Test

1. **b.** The New Economic Policy occupied the mid-1920s.
2. **c.** Abolition of money was attempted and failed during the civil war that followed the 1917 revolution.
3. **c.** Both grain and livestock output fell, but a larger proportion of total output was sent to the cities.
4. **d.** Plus many additional details.
5. **c.** Computers have not made much difference. Answer **b** has been suggested as a possible part of reform of the system.
6. **b.** The matter of who does what job is determined by the market to a substantial degree.
7. **c.** The others are vertical communication channels.
8. **d.** Each of these would protect the manager against supply interruptions or other forces beyond local control that made the plan difficult to meet.
9. **a.** Some observers think the system could not operate without these actions.
10. **b.** In theory, the plan is supposed to take care of supplies of all inputs.
11. **c.** In some cases, this has actually happened in the Soviet Union.
12. **a.** Growth was rapid during the 1930s and the 1950s, but has slowed by the 1980s.
13. **d.** Static efficiency at a minimum means getting on the production possibility frontier, and dynamic efficiency means moving the frontier outward rapidly.

14. **b.** The others are enterprise independence and encouragement of small-scale industry.
15. **b.** Small-scale agriculture has largely powered a considerable increase in living standards.